D0947282

THE DOMESDAY GEOGRAPHY OF
EASTERN ENGLAND

In Basingborne ten̅ isd̅ eps̅ .i. hiđ .7 ii. uirg̅ 7 dim̅ .
tra̅ e̅ .iii. car̅. In d̅nio .i. hiđ 7 ibi e̅ .i. car̅. Ibi un̅
uitt̅s 7 iiii. bord̅ cū .i. car̅. 7 altera pot̅ fieri. Ibi
ii. molini de .xx. sot̅. p̅ti .i. car̅. Val̅ .lx. sot̅. X do
recep̅. xl. sot̅. T.R.E. lx. sot̅. b̅ t̅ra iacuit 7 iacet
in eccta s̅ p̅tri Winton̅. 7 ibi fuit .i. sochs̅ ho̅. S.
archi̅epi. dimiđ uirg̅ tenuit. 7 dare 7 uende pot̅uit.

Ⅲ. ¶TERRA EP̅I LINCOLIENSIS. ~~In Witelesford ho̅~~
Ep̅s Lincoliensis̅ ten̅ in histretone .ii. hiđ.
7 Robt̅ de eo. Tra̅ e̅ .ii. car̅. Una e̅ ibi. 7 alia pot̅
fieri. Ibi ii. uitti̅ 7 ii. bord̅. p̅ti .ii. car̅. 7 i. mot̅
de .viii. sot̅. Val̅ .xl. sot̅. X do p̅cep̅ xx. sot̅. T.R.E.
iiii. lib̅. hanc t̅ra tenuit Siuuard̅ de b̅raldo.
7 pot̅uit dare cui uoluit. ~~In floreston ho̅~~
In Madinglei. ten̅ picot̅ de ep̅o. R. i. uirg̅ t̅re
7 dim̅. Val̅ 7 ualuit .v. sot̅. T.R.E. x. sot̅. hanc t̅ra
tenuit Blacuin ho regis̅. E. 7 recede pot̅uit. f̅ soca
Wluuio ep̅o remansit. ~~In cestretone ho̅~~
ⓜ DISTONE. p̅ xx. vi. hiđ 7 dim̅ se defđ. hoc m̅ est
unū de duodeci m̅aneriis d̅nicis ep̅iscopat̅ lin
coliensis̅. Ibi ten̅ .R. eps̅ .x. vii. hiđ ii. t̅rg̅ min.
Tra̅ e̅ .xii. car̅. In d̅nio .vii. hiđe. 7 ibi sun̅. ii. car̅.
7 iii. pot̅ fieri. Ibi x. viii. uitti̅ 7 xxiiii. bord̅ cū .x. car̅.

By courtesy of the Public Record Office.

Lower portion of right-hand column of folio 190 of the Domesday Book
(same size as original). For extension and translation, see p. 380.

THE
DOMESDAY GEOGRAPHY
OF
EASTERN ENGLAND

BY

H. C. DARBY

Professor of Geography in the
University of Cambridge

CAMBRIDGE
AT THE UNIVERSITY PRESS
1971

WITHDRAWN

LIBRARY OF MOUNT ST. MARY'S COLLEGE EMMITSBURG, MARYLAND

Published by the Syndics of the Cambridge University Press

Bentley House, 200 Euston Road, London N.W.1
American Branch: 32 East 57th Street, New York, N.Y.10022

This edition © Cambridge University Press 1971

Library of Congress Catalogue Card Number: 70-108106

International Standard Book Number: 0 521 08022 3

First Edition 1952
Second Edition 1957
Third Edition 1971

First printed in Great Britain at the University Press, Cambridge
Reprinted in Great Britain by John Dickens & Co. Ltd, Northampton

MUGHAM

CHAPTER I

THE DOMESDAY BOOK

Anyone who works upon the Domesday Book very soon has two views about it. On the one hand, he can have nothing but admiration for what is probably the most remarkable statistical document in the history of Europe. The continent has no document to compare with this detailed description covering so great a stretch of territory. And the geographer, as he turns over the folios, with their details of population and plough-teams, of woodland, meadow and the like, cannot but be excited at the vast amount of information that passes before his eyes. There are other valuable documents that provide evidence of past geographical conditions in many areas; but, more often than not, they are fragmentary and incomplete. If they are detailed, they usually cover only a small area. If they cover a larger area, they are far from detailed. But the Inquest of 1086 was carried out with a fairly high degree of uniformity over almost the whole of England, and the results give us today a unique opportunity of reconstructing some of the main features of the landscape of the eleventh century.

But there is another point of view. When this great wealth of data is examined more closely, perplexities and difficulties arise. The Domesday Book is far from being a straightforward document. It bristles with difficulties. Many of them have been resolved as the result of the activity of a long line of editors and commentators, working, more particularly, since the middle of the nineteenth century. The publication of J. H. Round's *Feudal England*, in 1895, was a great landmark in the history of Domesday scholarship. But many problems still remain, some for ever insoluble. Moreover, the Domesday clerks themselves, as we shall see time and time again, were but human; they were frequently inaccurate or forgetful or confused. 'No one', wrote Round, 'who has not analysed and collated such texts for himself can realise the extreme difficulty of avoiding occasional error. The abbreviations and the *formulæ* employed in these surveys are so many pitfalls for the transcriber, and the use of Roman numerals is almost fatal to accuracy.'[1] Anyone who attempts an arithmetical exercise in Roman numerals will soon see something of the

[1] J. H. Round, *Feudal England* (London, 1895), p. 20.

difficulty that faced the clerks. Their work, for example, sometimes convicts itself of inaccurate addition.

A casual reading of the text confronts us with obscurities, but once we start to examine it more closely, other and more complicated problems appear. The account of each shire presents its own difficulties. In the light of all the uncertainties, it would be more correct to speak not of 'the Domesday Geography of England', but of 'the Geography of the Domesday Book'. The two may not have been quite the same thing, and how near the record was to the reality of the time we can never know. The gaps can never be filled; the perplexities may never be resolved. But it is probably safe to assume that a picture of England based on the Domesday Book, while neither complete nor accurate in all its details, does reflect some of the major elements in the geography of the eleventh century. The broader features of the land utilisation of the time emerge, and with those we must be content. The remarkable thing after all is not that there are tantalising obscurities, but that King William's men did as well as they did, considering the sheer difficulty of making a survey at a time when the central government was without many of the aids we now associate with the administrative machinery of an organised state.

THE MAKING OF THE DOMESDAY BOOK

The story of the making of the Domesday survey is told briefly, but with feeling, in the Anglo-Saxon Chronicle under the year 1085:

Then at midwinter was the King at Gloucester with his wise men, and held there his court five days....Afterwards the King held a great council and very deep speech with his wise men about this land, how it was held, and with what men. He then sent his men over all England, into each shire, and caused them to find out how many hundred hides were within that shire, and what the King had himself of land and of cattle, and what rights he ought to have yearly from that shire. Also he caused them to write down how much land belonged to his archbishops, to his bishops, his abbots and his earls, and, though I tell it at length, what or how much each man that was settled on the land in England held in land and cattle, and how much it was worth. So very narrowly did he cause the survey to be made that there was not a single hide nor yardland, nor— it is shameful to relate that which he thought no shame to do—was there an ox, or a cow or a swine left out, that was not set down in his writing. And all these writings were brought to him afterwards.[1]

[1] J. Earle and C. Plummer, *Anglo-Saxon Chronicle, sub anno* 1085, 2 vols. (Oxford, 1892–9).

LIST OF MAPS

NOTE TO THIRD EDITION

The text of the second edition has been considerably revised to take account of recent research and new place-name identifications. The treatment of the statistics for the boroughs has been brought into line with that in the more recent volumes of this series. The resulting changes in the densities of some units are not great, but they, together with the revision in general, have meant the alteration of a number of maps. A short new section on 'Vineyards', with an additional map, has been added to the final chapter. The first edition appeared in 1952, and in the light of the experience of editing the four subsequent volumes of the series, I probably would present some facts and ideas a little differently today. But I have kept changes in the wording to a minimum and have tried to limit the revision to strictly factual material.

I am greatly indebted to Mr G. R. Versey who has not only altered the maps but has helped at all stages in the checking and revision of the material.

H. C. D.

KING'S COLLEGE,
CAMBRIDGE
St Eligius' Day, 1970.

shore where Time casts up its stray wreckage, we gather corks and broken planks, whence much indeed may be argued and more guessed; but what the great ship was that has gone down into the deep, that we shall never see.' The scene that King William's clerks looked upon has gone, and the most we can do is to try to obtain some rough outline of its lineaments; this chapter in the history of the English landscape can only be a very imperfect one.

The drawing of the maps for this and the subsequent volumes has been made possible through the generosity of the Trustees of the Leverhulme Research Fellowships and of the University of Liverpool. My first duty, therefore, is to thank these two authorities for their kindness and help. The maps in this volume have been drawn by Miss Helen Freestone to whose skill and care I am much indebted. Among others who have been most helpful, I owe particular thanks to Mr Alan Hodgkiss for a great deal of general assistance, to Mr R. Welldon Finn for comments on the whole proof, to Miss Barbara Dodwell for comments on the chapters dealing with Norfolk and Suffolk, to Mr S. Inskip Ladds for comments on that dealing with Huntingdonshire. For other help from time to time I owe particular thanks to Sir Frank Stenton and Professor V. H. Galbraith. I am also indebted to my wife for much help over tedious calculations and for constant encouragement. Finally, I must thank the officials of the Cambridge University Press for their skill and care.

H. C. DARBY

UNIVERSITY COLLEGE
LONDON
Shrove Tuesday, 1952

PREFACE

The Domesday Book has long been regarded as a unique source of information about legal and economic matters, but its bearing upon the reconstruction of the geography of England during the early Middle Ages has remained comparatively neglected. The extraction of this geographical information is not always as simple as it might appear to be from a casual inspection of the Domesday folios. Not only are there general problems of interpretation, but almost every county has its own peculiarities. There is, moreover, the sheer difficulty of handling the vast mass of material, and of getting a general view of the whole. The original survey was made in terms of manors, villages and hundreds, but the Norman clerks reassembled the information under the headings of the different landholders of each county. Their work must therefore be undone, and the survey set out once more upon a geographical basis.

The information that such an analysis makes available is of two kinds. In the first place, the details about plough-teams and about population enable a general picture of the relative prosperity of different areas to be obtained. In the second place, the details about such things as meadow, pasture, wood and salt-pans serve to illustrate further the local variations both in the face of the countryside and in its economic life. An attempt has been made to set out this variety of information as objectively as possible in the form of maps and tables. This volume is intended to be the first of a number covering the whole of Domesday England. When all the maps have been drawn and all the tables compiled, we may begin to have a clearer idea of both the value and the limitations of the survey that has so captured the imagination of later generations.

But great though the bulk of the Domesday Book is, it is only a summary. The making of it not only omitted much, but has, too often, resulted in obscurity. No one works for long on the text before discovering how fascinating and tantalising that obscurity is. In reflecting over many Domesday entries I have been reminded, time and again, of some remarks in Professor Trevelyan's inaugural lecture at Cambridge in 1927: 'On the

CONTENTS

A century hence the student's materials will not be in the shape in which he finds them now. In the first place, the substance of Domesday Book will have been rearranged. Those villages and hundreds which the Norman clerks tore into shreds will have been reconstituted and pictured in maps, for many men from over all England will have come within King William's spell, will have bowed themselves to him and become that man's men.

From the concluding paragraph of F. W. MAITLAND'S
Domesday Book and Beyond (Cambridge, 1897)

TO
MY PARENTS

There is a contemporary account written by Robert Losinga, bishop of Hereford, who may have been present in the winter of 1085 when the project was discussed:

In the twentieth year of his reign by order of William, King of the English, there was made a description of the whole of England, of the lands of the several provinces thereof and of the possessions of all the great men. This was done in respect of ploughland and habitations, and of men both bond and free, both those who dwelt in cottages and those who had their homes and share in the fields, and in respect of ploughs and horses and other animals, and in respect, finally, of the services and payments due from all men in the whole land. Other investigations followed the first; and men were sent into provinces which they did not know, and where they themselves were unknown, in order that they might be given the opportunity of checking the first description and if necessary of denouncing its authors as guilty to the King.[1]

Interesting though these and other contemporary accounts are, they do not throw much light upon the actual operation of compiling the original returns.[2] There are, however, other documents, besides the Domesday Book itself, that must have been composed in part from the original returns. It is true that these documents represent only fragments, but they throw much light upon the larger survey and they are of supreme importance in Domesday interpretation.[3] Among the subsidiary documents is the so-called Exeter Domesday, covering Cornwall, Devon, Somerset, part of Dorset and one manor in Wiltshire. F. H. Baring, in 1912, showed that it was from this Exeter Domesday that the relevant portions of the main Domesday Book were made.[4] In the process of making it, much was omitted, e.g. details of livestock (sheep, swine, etc.). Obviously, any account that is nearer to the original returns than the Domesday Book itself must be of very special interest.

Another of these subsidiary documents is the *Inquisitio Eliensis*, a survey of the estates of the abbey of Ely in the counties of Cambridge,

---

[1] W. H. Stevenson, 'A Contemporary Description of the Domesday Survey', *English Historical Review* (1907), XXII, p. 74; the translation is that of D. C. Douglas, see n. 3 below.

[2] For an account of some early references to the survey, see J. H. Round, 'An early reference to Domesday', in *Domesday Studies*, ed. P. E. Dove (London, 1891), II, pp. 539–59.

[3] For the importance of these, see D. C. Douglas, 'The Domesday Survey', *History* (1936), XXI, pp. 249–57.

[4] F. H. Baring, 'The Exeter Domesday', *Eng. Hist. Rev.* (1912), XXVII, pp. 309–18.

Hertford, Essex, Norfolk, Suffolk and Huntingdon. It opens with an explanatory paragraph which is usually regarded as referring to the operation of the survey:

This is the description of the inquiry concerning the lands which the King's barons [i.e. the Domesday Commissioners] made according to the oath of the sheriff of the shire and of all the barons and their Frenchmen and of the whole hundred court—the priests, reeves and six villeins from every village. In the first place [they required] the name of the manor; who held it in the time of King Edward, and who holds it now, how many hides are there, how many ploughs in demesne and how many belonging to the men, how many villeins, cottars, serfs, freemen and sokemen; how much wood, meadow and pasture; how many mills and fisheries; how much has been added to or taken away from the estate; how much the whole used to be worth and how much it is worth now; and how much each freeman or sokeman had or has there; all this three times over, with reference to the time of King Edward, and to the time when King William gave the land, and to the present time. And if more can be got out of it than is obtained now.[1]

Whether these were the 'official instructions' for all counties, we cannot say; but, at any rate, they, or a similar set of questions, must also have been asked elsewhere. Out of the representative assembly for each hundred a small body of eight jurors were chosen, and the *I.E.* gives a list of the jurors for a number of the hundreds in which the Ely estates lay. Round showed that half the jurors were English and the other half Norman. 'Conquerors and conquered were alike bound by their common sworn verdicts.'[2] We cannot say whether the Commissioners themselves attended every hundred court as Round suggested,[3] or whether, as Maitland thought, they merely held one session in the county town;[4] but a number of entries make it clear that they sometimes heard conflicting evidence.[5] There are also appendices dealing with disputes about ownership in several counties.

[1] N. E. S. A. Hamilton, *Inquisitio Comitatus Cantabrigiensis* (London, 1876), p. 97.
[2] J. H. Round, *op. cit.* pp. 120–3.
[3] *Ibid.* pp. 118–19.
[4] F. W. Maitland, *Domesday Book and Beyond* (Cambridge, 1897), p. 11.
[5] For instance at the end of the account of Geoffrey de Mandeville's manor of Chippenham there is this paragraph: 'Orgar the sheriff himself had 3 hides of this land, and could give [it] to whom he would. Orgar put this land in pledge for 7 marks of gold and 2 ounces, as Geoffrey's men say, but the men of the hundred have seen neither any writ nor any messenger of King Edward concerning it, nor do they [i.e. Geoffrey's men] produce evidence' (197).

Interesting though the *I.E.* is, it is limited in the sense that it does not refer to all the lands in a particular hundred or area; moreover, in its present form it may date from as late as 1093.[1] Even more interesting is the *Inquisitio Comitatus Cantabrigiensis*, which is a twelfth-century copy of a document from an early stage of the Inquest proceedings. It covers a large part of southern Cambridgeshire, and so gives us a complete picture of a substantial number of hundreds. At the beginning of the account of each hundred is a list of jurors, and then each village is described separately. Whatever the exact questions the Commissioners asked, it seems that they conducted their operations upon a geographical basis, county by county and hundred by hundred. Separate bodies of commissioners visited different groups of counties, and a number of attempts have been made to reconstruct their respective circuits according to differences in the phraseology of the record. R. W. Eyton in 1878 thought that the country was covered by nine circuits, each marked by a similarity of language.[2] In 1906, Adolphus Ballard reduced them to seven.[3] More recently, Carl Stephenson has also thought that there were 'at least seven', but has grouped the counties differently from Ballard.[4]

These circuits did not cover the whole of England as we now know it. The northern counties of Northumberland, Durham, and most of Cumberland and Westmorland, were not surveyed. Lancashire likewise is not mentioned by name, but its southern portion is rather sketchily described in a sort of appendix to the Cheshire folios dealing with 'the lands between the Ribble and the Mersey', while much of its northern portion is included with the Yorkshire folios. A great deal of Rutland is described partly under Northamptonshire and partly under Lincolnshire. Finally, the four counties of the Welsh border—Gloucester, Hereford, Shropshire and Cheshire—included lands which are now parts of Wales or Monmouth. For some reason or other, the Domesday Book omits to give any account of some towns, including London and Winchester. In any case, the information about the towns it does describe is far from systematic or complete.[5]

[1] For the statistics of the *I.E.*, see pp. 99–101 below.
[2] R. W. Eyton, 'Notes on Domesday', *Trans. Shropshire Arch. and Nat. Hist. Soc.* (1878), I, p. 10.
[3] Adolphus Ballard, *The Domesday Inquest* (London, 1906), p. 12.
[4] Carl Stephenson, 'Notes on the Composition and Interpretation of Domesday Book', *Speculum* (Cambridge, Mass., U.S.A., 1947), XXII, p. 3.
[5] See Adolphus Ballard, *The Domesday Boroughs* (Oxford, 1904).

What was the purpose of the Inquest? The older generation of scholars, including Round and Maitland, believed that its main object was fiscal, and that King William wished to collect data about the distribution of the geld with a view to correcting anomalies by a new assessment. Thus Maitland, speaking of the Domesday Book itself, wrote: 'One great purpose seems to mould both its form and substance; it is a geld-book.'[1] More recent work, however, has laid greater emphasis upon its feudal and judicial character. Its object, according to Professor V. H. Galbraith, was 'a return by manors and by tenants-in-chief'.[2] As Sir Frank Stenton has said, 'in the last resort the one motive which will adequately explain so great an undertaking is the Conqueror's desire to learn the essential facts about his kingdom.... In searching for the ultimate purpose of the Survey, it is unnecessary to go behind the contemporary opinion that it was undertaken because the king wished to know more about England—"how it was peopled, and with what sort of men".'[3] In this connection it is interesting to note the view held by Richard Fitz-Neal, Treasurer of England, who wrote within a century of its compilation (c. 1179). As Professor Galbraith has pointed out, he quotes a man whose memory went back to within a generation of the Inquest:

The book about which you inquire is an inseparable companion of the royal seal in the Treasury: and how this came about, as I was told by Henry, formerly Bishop of Winchester, was as follows:

When William the Conqueror (a blood relation of Bishop Henry) had subdued the whole island, and by terrible examples tamed the minds of the rebels, to prevent further trouble he decided to place the government of the conquered people on a written basis and to subject them to the rule of law. The laws of the English were therefore considered, according to their three-fold division—the Mercian Law, the Dane Law and the West Saxon Law. Some of these were discarded and some approved, with the addition of such of the imported laws of Neustria as would most effectually keep the peace. Finally, to round off the work, after consulting his council, he sent men of proved discretion on circuit through the Kingdom. A careful description (*descriptio*) was made of the whole country by these men, of its woods, pastures, and meadows, employing the ordinary agricultural terminology. This was gathered

---

[1] F. W. Maitland, *op. cit.* p. 3.
[2] V. H. Galbraith, 'The Making of Domesday Book', *Eng. Hist. Rev.* (1942), LVII, p. 177. Professor Galbraith's views are developed in his *The Making of Domesday Book* (Oxford, 1961).
[3] F. M. Stenton, *Anglo-Saxon England* (Oxford, 1943), pp. 648–9.

into a book so that every man, sure of his own right, should not usurp that of another. This description was done by counties, by hundreds and by hides—beginning with the name of the king at the head and then one by one the names of the other great men who held in chief of the king according to their rank. These were all numbered consecutively so that one can more easily refer to what concerned each in the body of the book. This book is called by the natives Domesday—that is, metaphorically speaking, the day of judgement.[1]

And so it has been known ever since, although the word never appears in the Book itself.

The preliminary work of collecting the facts and of arranging them preparatory to the making of the Domesday Book must have been immense. One view is that the information was sent to the king's treasury at Winchester, and there summarised and rearranged. Round suggested that the returns for Essex, Norfolk and Suffolk were summarised first, and that when the compilers saw how large and unwieldy the result was, they decided to continue the summary for the rest of England in a simpler manner. Hence, according to this view, the distinction between the main Domesday Book (known as vol. I or as the Exchequer Domesday) and the Little Domesday Book covering the three eastern counties, and known as vol. II.[2]

Professor Galbraith, however, regards the process of summarising as being more complicated. He believes that local summaries on a feudal basis were made for groups of counties, and that it was these, and not the original returns, that were submitted to Winchester for final assembling and editing: 'the transforming of the geographical return into a feudal return was done not, as is generally assumed, at Winchester, but locally and hard upon, if not actually during the actual inquest'.[3] The so-called Exeter or Exon Domesday would thus be the first draft of the local summary for the south-west.[4] Professor Galbraith disagrees with Round about the Little Domesday Book. This, he suggests, occupies an intermediate position between the Exeter Domesday and the main Domesday Book,

---

[1] V. H. Galbraith, *Studies in the Public Records* (London, 1948), pp. 103–4. The original is in the *Dialogus de Scaccario*, ed. by A. Hughes, C. G. Crump and C. Johnson (Oxford, 1902), pp. 107–8.

[2] J. H. Round, *op. cit.* p. 141.

[3] V. H. Galbraith, *loc. cit.* p. 166. This view, however, is contested by Professor D. C. Douglas in *The Domesday Monachorum of Christ Church Canterbury* (London, 1944), pp. 19 *et seq.*

[4] See p. 3 above.

'and it is tempting to explain it as the fair copy sent by the commission to Winchester, the original draft of which (corresponding to Exon Domesday) has disappeared'.[1] The stages in the making of the digest we now have might therefore have been as follows:

(1) The information collected in terms of manors, villages and hundreds, and sent to some local centre.

(2) Rearrangement of the returns on a feudal basis made locally for each circuit (Exeter Domesday).

(3) A fair copy (or revision) of the local summary, sent to Winchester (Little Domesday Book).

(4) Main Domesday Book compiled from the local summaries.

Mr R. Welldon Finn believes that the Inquest was perhaps started before the Gloucester meeting in the winter of 1085, and that many Domesday entries bear the mark of a double enquiry—on a geographical and a feudal basis respectively. 'This may be due to either or both the following causes: the despatch of more than one set of Commissioners on each circuit, mentioned by Bishop Robert Losinga, or the provision of both hundredal and feudal returns and their comparison. It is however improbable that all landowners recorded in Domesday Book made a return for their own fees, possible that only those who had an obligation to supply *milites* for the feudal host did so.' The first enquiry may have been made in 1084–5, and its results discussed at the Gloucester Gemot. The second enquiry (perhaps that on a feudal basis) checked and examined discrepancies about ownership. In the meantime the results of the first enquiry had been, or were being, digested into a number of local summaries, and these were amended in the light of the second enquiry. 'It is certainly significant that almost all the material, in the Exeter Domesday, which deals with dispute about ownership, illegal occupation, and similar topics, comes at the end of the appropriate manorial account or is marginal, interlined, or postscriptal.' It is, for the most part, likewise situated in the Exchequer text. The local summaries, of which the Exeter Domesday Book and the Little Domesday Book are examples, may have been the 'writings' which, according to the Chronicle, were brought to the king. From them, perhaps, the Exchequer Domesday was made.[2]

---

[1] V. H. Galbraith, *Eng. Hist. Rev.* (1942), LVII, p. 167.

[2] R. Welldon Finn, 'The making of the Wiltshire Domesday', *Wilts. Arch. and Nat. Hist. Mag.* (Devizes, 1948), LII, pp. 318–27.

The length of time taken over the process of compilation and the date of the Domesday Book itself are also controversial matters. Some place it not long after King William's death in 1087;[1] others place its final completion not before 1100.[2]

Whatever the stages of compilation, the fact remains that the result was very different from the original returns. The new form was more condensed, and, for example, the information about stock was omitted. But apart from this general condensation, there was a much more fundamental difference. Compare, for instance, the account of the Cambridgeshire village of Abington Pigotts as given in the *I.C.C.* and in the Domesday Book itself. In the *I.C.C.* there is a clear statement about the village.[3] It was rated at 5 hides, made up as follows:

	Hides	Virgates
Hugh Pincerna holds of the bishop of Winchester	2½	½
The King	½	—
Ralph and Robert hold of Harduin de Scalers	1	1½
Earl Roger	—	1
Picot the sheriff	—	½
Alwin Hamelecoc the beadle holds of the king	—	½
Total	5	0

In the Domesday Book, however, there is no such account of Abington Pigotts. The information has been rearranged under the headings of the main landholders of the county. We have therefore to turn to a number of folios to assemble the details for Abington Pigotts, and not until all are assembled do we know that it was a 5-hide vill. The contrast between the account of Abington Pigotts in the *I.C.C.* and that in Domesday Book can be seen on pp. 10 and 11. The geographical basis of the original returns has been destroyed, and their information reconstituted upon a feudal basis. For Cambridgeshire, as for other counties, the royal estates are first described; then those of the ecclesiastical lords, first the bishops then the abbots; then again, those of the lay lords; and finally

---

[1] F. M. Stenton, *Anglo-Saxon England* (Oxford, 1943), p. 647.

[2] D. C. Douglas, 'The Domesday Survey', *History* (1936), XXI, p. 255. For reference to the controversy, see D. C. Douglas, *The Domesday Monachorum of Christ Church Canterbury*, pp. 23 et seq.

[3] *I.C.C.* pp. 60–1. See F. W. Maitland, *op. cit.* pp. 11–12.

ABINGTON PIGOTTS

(Inquisitio Comitatus Cantabrigiensis, pp. 60–1)

In hoc hundredo Abintona pro v hidis se defendit tempore regis edwardi. Et modo pro iiii. Et de his v hidis tenet hugo pincerna de episcopo Walkelino Wintoniensis ii hidas et dimidiam et dimidiam virgatam. v carucis est ibi terra, iii carucae in dominio et ii carucae villanis. ix bordarii, iii cotarii, unusquisque v acris. Pratum v carucis et ii solidis. iiii animalia ociosa, lii oves, xxxi porci, i runcinus. In totis valentiis valet vii libras et quando recepit lx solidos, tempore regis edwardi viii libras. Hoc manerium iacet et iacuit in ecclesia sancti petri Wintoniensis. Et in hoc manerio fuit quidam sochemannus qui tenuit dimidiam virgatam sub archiepiscopo stigando tempore regis edwardi. Potuit recedere et vendere cui voluit absque ejus licentia. Et de his v hidis tenet rex dimidiam hidam quae jacet in litlintona. i carucae est ibi terra, et est caruca. Et haec dimidia hida est appretiata cum litlintona. Et de his v hidis tenet Radulphus et Robertus de Hardeuuino i hidam et virgatam et dimidiam. ii carucis est ibi terra, et sunt ibi carucae. v bordarii. Pratum iiii bobus. i animal ociosum. quatuor xx oves. lxviii porci. unus runcinus. Inter totum valet lv solidos et quando recepit xxv solidos, tempore regis edwardi lx solidos. Hanc terram tenuerunt ii sochemanni, homines comitis algari fuerunt. potuerunt dare et vendere cui voluerunt tempore regis edwardi. Et tertius sochemannus, homo regis edwardi, unam virgatam et inveniebat i averam vicecomiti regis. Et de his v hidis comes Rogerus i virgatam quae iacet in sceningeie in proprio suo manerio. xiii solidos et iiii denarios valet et semper valuit. Hanc terram tenuit goda homo comitis algari. Et de his v hidis tenet picotus vicecomes dimidiam virgatam. ii bobus est terra. Haec terra valuit et valet ii solidos. Hanc terram tenuit osgotus de archiepiscopo stigando et iacet semper et iacuit in morduna. De his v hidis tenet aluuinus hamelecoc bedellus Regis dimidiam virgatam de rege. iiii bobus est terra ibi. Et sunt ibi. unus porcus. v solidos valet, tempore regis edwardi x solidos, et istemet tenuit tempore regis edwardi non potuit dare nec vendere extra Litlintonam.

ABINGTON PIGOTTS

(Domesday Book, folios 190, 190, 198, 193, 200b, 190)

190 In Abintone tenet Hugo de W episcopo ii hidas et dimidiam et dimidiam virgatam. Terra est v carucis. In dominio iii carucae et ix bordarii unusquisque de v acris cum ii carucis. Pratum v carucis et ii solidis. Valet vii libras. Quando recepit iii libras. Tempore Regis Edwardi viii libras. Hoc manerium iacuit et iacet in ecclesia sancti Petri Wintoniensis, et ibi unus sochemannus tenuit dimidiam virgatam sub archiepiscopo Stigando et potuit absque licentia eius recedere.

190 In Abintone tenet Rex dimidiam hidam quae jacet in Lidlingtone. Terra est i carucae et ibi est atque cum eodem manerio appreciata.

198 In Abintone tenet ii milites de harduuino i hidam et i virgatam et dimidiam. Terra est ii carucis et ibi sunt cum v bordariis. Pratum iiii bobus. Valet lv solidos. Quando recepit xxv solidos. Tempore Regis Edwardi lx solidos. De hac terra tenuit i virgatam unus homo Regis Edwardi et unam Averam inveniebat vicecomiti, et alii ii sochemanni, homines Algari comitis, potuerunt dare terra sua et vendere cui voluerunt.

193 In Abintone tenet comes Rogerus i virgatam terrae quae jacet in Scelgei suo proprio manerio. Valet et valuit semper xiii solidos et quatuor denarios. Hanc terram tenuit Goda sub Algaro comite.

200b In Abintone tenet Picot dimidiam virgatam. Terra est ii bobus. Valet et valuit semper ii solidos. Hanc terram tenuit Ansgot homo Stigandi Archiepiscopi. jacet et jacuit in Mordune.

190 In Abintone tenet Aluuinus cocus bedellus dimidiam virgatam de rege. Terra est dimidae carucae et ibi est. Valet v solidos. Tempore Regis Edwardi x solidos. Isdem tenuit Tempore Regis Edwardi nec dare nec vendere potuit. In Ichelintone jacuit.

those of the lesser landowners. The original returns have thus been torn into shreds to produce a bewildering collection of statistics. Fortunately, the material for each county is dealt with separately, otherwise it would be more bewildering than it is.

A number of attempts have been made to set out a general view of the information thus assembled, county by county. The most famous is the 'abstract of the population' published by Sir Henry Ellis in 1833.[1] This distinguishes between different categories of people, and represents a gigantic labour. It has been used again and again by a succession of Domesday students. Ellis' 'total of recorded population' came to 283,242. This, of course, is not the number of human beings, and must be multiplied by four or five or perhaps even six before the total population is reached. Another general view is C. H. Pearson's attempt in 1867 to calculate the 'values' or renders in twenty-one counties,[2] but the implication of these 'values' is very uncertain.[3] Yet another general view is Maitland's calculation of the total number of plough-teams, teamlands and hides (or carucates) for each county.[4] All these have proved of inestimable value in obtaining a preliminary view of the contents of the Domesday Book, and in calculating rough densities for each county. But they give only a very general picture, and are capable of being very misleading. They are compiled in terms of the Domesday counties; and they make no allowance for the fact that Cheshire and Yorkshire included parts of what is now Lancashire, that some of Rutland was in Lincolnshire and Northamptonshire, that the counties along the Welsh border were larger then than they are now, and that the boundaries of many other counties have also changed. Moreover, any densities calculated on a county basis must always be misleading. How can an average figure for Cambridgeshire, for example, be of value when a great part of the county was occupied by undrained fen? Or again, the heaths of Surrey complicate any averages for that county. These figures need to be recalculated in terms of smaller units. The most convenient unit for most counties is the hundred, but for some counties other units have to be devised. The other items of information—woods, meadows and the like—need

[1] Henry Ellis, *A General Introduction to Domesday Book*, 2 vols. (London, 1833). The abstract occupies pp. 417–514 of the second volume.

[2] C. H. Pearson, *A History of England during the Early and Middle Ages* (London, 1867), I, pp. 661–70.

[3] See the discussion in F. W. Maitland, *op. cit.* p. 411.

[4] *Ibid.* pp. 400–3.

also to be set out in some general view. These considerations bring us to the problems of analysing and mapping the information of the Domesday Book.

DOMESDAY MAPPING

In order to obtain a view of the English countryside in the eleventh century, the first task must be to undo the work of King William's clerks, and to restore the geographical basis of the survey by piecing together the severed fragments of each vill. The general development of Domesday scholarship in the latter part of the nineteenth century was accompanied by a number of attempts at such restoration. The Rev. R. W. Eyton's 'analysis and digest' of the Dorset folios appeared in 1878,[1] of the Somerset folios in 1880,[2] and of the Stafford folios in 1881.[3] Valuable as these were, they did not tabulate all the items of the survey, and, of course, Eyton's arguments were complicated by his now obsolete views on Domesday mensuration. As early as about 1874 the Rev. William Airy had completed his 'digest of the Domesday of Bedfordshire', but it was not published until 1881.[4] It won even Round's approval:

It was, most happily, pointed out to the author by the Rev. Joseph Hunter 'that what we want is not translations but analyses of the surveys of the several counties' (p. viii). To this most true remark we owe it that Mr Airy resolved to give us a 'digest' instead of that usual 'extension and translation', which is perfectly useless to the Domesday student.[5]

In 1884 came the 'tabular analysis' of the Cambridgeshire folios by the Rev. Bryan Walker; it was a detailed analysis, hundred by hundred and village by village.[6] All this was a beginning, but Thorold Rogers was

---

[1] R. W. Eyton, *A Key to Domesday...exemplified by an analysis and digest of the Dorset survey* (London, 1878).

[2] R. W. Eyton, *Domesday Studies: analysis and digest of the Somerset survey,* 2 vols. (London, 1880).

[3] R. W. Eyton, *Domesday Studies: analysis and digest of the Staffordshire survey* (London, 1881).

[4] W. Airy, *A Digest of the Domesday of Bedfordshire* (Bedford, 1881).

[5] J. H. Round, *op. cit.* p. 55.

[6] Bryan Walker, 'On the measurements and valuations of the Domesday of Cambridgeshire', *Communications of Cambridge Antiquarian Society*, v, pp. 93–129, and Supplement (Cambridge, 1886). The paper was read in 1881, and was published as a part of vol. v in 1884, but the volume was not completed until 1886 which is the date on its title-page.

still able to say in his lectures at Oxford in 1887–8 that 'Domesday Book
has never been analysed from the statistician's point of view, and especially
from that before me, the distribution of wealth in England'.[1] One of the
papers read at the Domesday Commemoration of 1886 had stressed the
need for a 'tabulation' in 'statistical columns'.[2] But the work of analysis,
county by county, was slow. In 1887–9 came the Rev. C. S. Taylor's
'analysis' of the Gloucester folios, an excellent study applying, as it
confesses, 'the methods of interpretation used by the Rev. R. W. Eyton'.[3]
In the decades that followed came the analyses of the Devonshire material
by O. J. Reichel[4] and T. W. Whale.[5] The turn of the century (1899–1901)
also saw the appearance of William Farrer's analysis of the folios relating
to Lancashire.[6] Progress was slow, however, and by the end of the
century most counties were still without analyses or digests; even the
tables that had been constructed were frequently far from providing
a comprehensive view of all the information of the Domesday entries.
As Maitland wrote in 1897, 'Well would it be if the broad features of
Domesday Book could be set out before us in a series of statistical tables.
The task would be gigantic and could hardly be performed except by a
body of men who had plenteous leisure and who would work together
harmoniously.'[7] The nearest answer to Maitland's wish are the *Domesday
Tables* published by F. H. Baring in 1909. They cover the counties of
Surrey, Berkshire, Middlesex, Hertford, Buckingham, Bedford and also
the New Forest; the tables are clearly set out, and are accompanied by
a valuable note on each county. The introduction to the whole confesses
that 'tables are horrible to most of us and many things are to be found in
Domesday besides figures, but after all the main object of Domesday was
to record statistics, and it is well to have them in a convenient form;
indeed without tables it is almost impossible to appreciate the facts re-

---

[1] J. E. Thorold Rogers, *The Economic Interpretation of History* (London, 1888),
p. 142.

[2] P. E. Dove (ed.), *Domesday Studies* (London, 1888), I, p. 23.

[3] C. S. Taylor, *An analysis of the Domesday Survey of Gloucestershire*, 4 parts,
Bristol and Gloucester Archaeological Society (Bristol, 1887–9).

[4] O. J. Reichel, various articles, *Trans. Devon Assoc. Adv. Sci.* (Plymouth, 1894–
1912), XXVI–XLIV *passim*.

[5] T. W. Whale, 'Analysis of Exon Domesday', *Trans. Devon Assoc. Adv. Sci.*
(Plymouth, 1896–1904), XXVIII, XXXIV, XXXV, XXXVI *passim*.

[6] William Farrer, 'Domesday Survey of Lancashire', *Trans. Lanc. and Ches.
Antiq. Soc.* (Manchester, 1899–1901), XVI, pp. 1–38; XVIII, pp. 38–113.

[7] F. W. Maitland, *op. cit.* p. 407.

corded, for it is very difficult by merely reading the text to get a general view of even one feature in a single county'.[1]

In addition to these analyses, digests and tables, there are many other attempts to set out Domesday statistics for particular counties, but most of these attempts deal only with selected items, e.g. hides or population. They usually do not go beyond hundred totals. Such, for example, are John Brownbill's tables for the Cheshire hundreds published in 1901,[2] or Miss Beatrice Lees' table of carucates and population for Suffolk (1907),[3] or George Rickword's tables for Essex (1911–13).[4] Invaluable though many of these are, they do not profess to be comprehensive reconstructions covering all items vill by vill. Maitland's hope of 1897 still remains unsatisfied, and no large-scale analysis covering England has yet been published.

From the making of analyses, it is only one step forward to the construction of maps. Frederic Seebohm in 1883 had published some most interesting maps showing the distribution of freemen, villeins, bordars and serfs as percentages of the total population, but these were based upon Ellis' figures and were only upon a county basis.[5] F. H. Baring's diagram of the New Forest showing the distinction between the villages wholly afforested and those only partially so was first published in 1901, and is an illuminating example of cartographic method applied to Domesday evidence.[6] But such maps as these, drawn *ad hoc* to illustrate particular theses, hardly represent even the beginnings of Domesday mapping. Bishop Stubbs had envisaged the problem when he wrote:

Among the day dreams in which I have indulged in the intervals of terminal courses, has been one of a Domesday Society: a devoted little band of forty savants of research, who might each undertake a separate county, and by adding up the sums, arranging the names and measurements, and identifying the localities, pave the way for a really true Domesday map.[7]

[1] F. H. Baring, *Domesday Tables* (London, 1909).
[2] J. Brownbill, 'Cheshire in Domesday Book', *Trans. Lanc. and Ches. Hist. Soc.* n. ser. (Liverpool, 1901), xv, pp. 1–26. [3] *V.C.H. Suffolk* (1907), I, p. 360.
[4] George Rickword: (1) 'The Kingdom of the East Saxons and the Tribal Hidage', *Trans. Essex Arch. Soc.* (Colchester 1911), N.S. vol. XI, pp. 246–65; (2) 'The East Saxon Kingdom', *ibid.* (1913), N.S. vol. XII, pp. 38–50.
[5] F. Seebohm, *The English Village Community* (Cambridge, 1883), p. 85.
[6] F. Baring, 'The Making of the New Forest', *Eng. Hist. Rev.* (1901), XVI, pp. 427–38. This is reprinted in *Domesday Tables*, pp. 194–205.
[7] W. Stubbs, *Lectures on Early English History*, ed. by A. Hassall (London, 1906), p. 184.

F. W. Maitland, to whom all Domesday scholars owe so much, had something of the same sort in mind when he wrote the concluding words of *Domesday Book and Beyond* in 1897:

A century hence the student's materials will not be in the shape in which he finds them now. In the first place, the substance of Domesday Book will have been rearranged. Those villages and hundreds which the Norman clerks tore into shreds will have been reconstituted and pictured in maps, for many men from over all England will have come within King William's spell, will have bowed themselves to him and become that man's men.[1]

While no maps seem to have been published for over a generation after this, some writers must either have constructed such maps for their private delight, or, at any rate, have had such maps in their 'minds' eye'. One of the earliest of these attempts to plot Domesday data was that of J. H. Round in 1903. It is true that no map was printed, but he certainly had one in mind. Writing of Essex, he declared that 'the only way in which to gauge the distribution of woodland at the time of King Edward's death is to mark down on a map of the county the amount, reckoned in swine, as given for each parish'.[2] The method of Round's cartography, however, leaves much to be desired, and his attempt to calculate the density of wood per hundred acres of each parish is unsatisfactory.[3] Round's discussion of the pasture entries of Essex in relation to the coastal marshes also implies what we may term a 'distributional approach', but he mentioned no map in this connection.[4] Domesday studies for other counties sometimes stressed the distributional aspect of the returns. Round's *V.C.H.* introduction to the Berkshire text (1906) traced 'the fisheries up the rivers of the county' and noted some of the features of the distribution of meadow and wood.[5] Miss Beatrice Lees' introduction to the Suffolk text, likewise noted the most thickly wooded districts.[6] Similar points are to be found in many other articles on the 'Domesday Survey' in the *V.C.H.*, but by no means in all of them. The main preoccupation of these valuable articles is with feudal matters, and none of them carries the discussion of a distribution to its logical conclusion by mapping it.

The first substantial effort to map Domesday information for a county was that of G. H. Fowler in 1922. Following Airy, he analysed afresh the folios for Bedfordshire, 'reconstituting every vill and hundred as far as

[1] F. W. Maitland, *op. cit.* p. 520.   [2] *V.C.H. Essex* (1903), I, p. 375.
[3] See pp. 235–7 below.   [4] See p. 242 below.
[5] *V.C.H. Berkshire* (1906), I, pp. 304–9.   [6] *V.C.H. Suffolk* (1907), I, p. 408.

possible'.[1] He drew maps to show the distribution of Saxon and Norman estates, and others to show the fall in value of many estates between 1066 and 1086 as a result of devastation by marching armies. The maps most concerned with rural economy are those showing wood, meadow and mills—all on a scale of 2 miles to the inch. It is a most interesting experiment, all the more so because Fowler wrote the accompanying text with his eye on the geographical features of the county and on the variation in its soils. Indeed, the volume as a whole forms an extremely good general introduction to the Domesday Book. But Fowler's cartography, like that of Round, is not above reproach. In the first place, he converted the plough-teams, by which the Bedfordshire meadow was measured, into modern acres on the assumption that 24 acres of meadow were sufficient to support a team of 8 oxen; the swine by which the wood was measured were likewise converted at the rate of $1\frac{1}{2}$ statute acres for each head of swine. These assumptions may be correct, although Fowler was careful to point out the 'difficulties and dangers of the method';[2] but in view of the inevitable doubts associated with such conversions it would have been better to plot the Domesday units directly on to the map. In the second place, the percentage of land occupied by meadow and wood was calculated on the basis of each parish. In view of the fact that the acreages of many parishes have changed, it would have been better to use a method that by-passed this problem. In spite of these criticisms, Fowler's maps will always remain a most interesting experiment.[3]

The present experiment in Domesday mapping began in 1934, and seeks to avoid some of these pitfalls by plotting the information with as few assumptions as possible. There are, of course, inevitable difficulties.

[1] G. H. Fowler, *Bedfordshire in 1086* (Bedfordshire Historical Record Society. 1922), p. 4.   [2] *Ibid.* p. 107.

[3] Four other early experiments in Domesday mapping are:

(1) A map of Norfolk showing places with wood for 100 swine and over— H. Beevor, 'Norfolk woodlands from the evidence of contemporary chronicles', *Quart. Jour. of Forestry* (London, 1925), XIX, pp. 87–110.

(2) Four maps of Domesday Shropshire—Dorothy Sylvester, 'Rural settlement in Domesday Shropshire', *Sociological Rev.* (London, 1933), XXV, pp. 244–57.

(3) A map showing the arable, forest and marsh of Domesday Essex by Rupert Coles, 'The Past History of the Forest of Essex', *Essex Naturalist* (Stratford, Essex, 1935), XXIV, p. 128. See p. 238, n. 1 below.

(4) A map of the woodland of Gloucestershire by G. B. Grundy who attempted to convert the Domesday measurements into modern acres—'The ancient woodland of Gloucestershire', *Trans. Bristol and Gloucs. Arch. Soc.* (Gloucester, 1936), LVIII, pp. 65–155.

One difficulty is inherent in the statistics. Tantalising as it may seem, it is sometimes impossible to arrive at a definitive total for a vill or a hundred. Maitland himself was aware of the difficulty. 'As matters now stand', he wrote, 'two men not unskilled in Domesday might add up the number of hides in a county and arrive at very different results, because they would hold different opinions as to the meaning of certain formulas which are not uncommon.'[1] But where two or more sets of statistics relating to the same county or area are available, it is interesting to note that the percentage difference between them is usually not very great. Even if all the dubious phrases could be resolved, and if the perfect computer of Domesday statistics were employed, many queries would still remain, for, as we shall see, the Domesday clerks made mistakes. Some of these mistakes become apparent in the light of the information contained in the satellite documents, but the corrections thus possible are fortuitous. All the maps and calculations in this experiment are therefore based upon the Domesday Book itself.

Another general difficulty must also be mentioned here. The foundation of Domesday study is the exact identification of place-names. All Domesday scholars are indebted to the vast amount of spade-work accomplished by generations of editors and commentators; and, more recently, the work of the English Place-Name Society has given an inestimable advantage to the modern study of the Domesday Book. But even when the place-names of an area have been identified with certainty, some difficulty frequently remains. Broadly speaking, the villages of the Domesday Book are those we know today, but there are many exceptions. Maitland went as far as to say that 'a place that is mentioned in Domesday Book will probably be recognised as a vill in the thirteenth, a civil parish in the nineteenth century'; but he qualified this assertion in a number of ways.[2] Some Domesday vills have not survived the hazards of time and chance; they have become hamlets of neighbouring vills, or have declined until they are represented on the modern map merely by the names of solitary farmhouses; a few places and their names have disappeared so completely that they cannot now be identified with certainty. On the other hand, new names have appeared. Some of these represent new settlements of post-Domesday origin. Others represent old settlements already in existence in the eleventh century, but only as hamlets subsidiary

[1] F. W. Maitland, *op. cit.* p. 407.
[2] *Ibid.* p. 12. For J. H. Round's criticism, see *V.C.H. Essex*, I, pp. 400 *et seq.*

to other vills, so that the information about them lies concealed under the names of their neighbours.

There may also be other reasons why eleventh-century settlements were not specifically mentioned in the Domesday Book. Maitland instanced the case of Farnham in Surrey:

> In Surrey there is now-a-days a hundred called Farnham which comprises the parish of Farnham, the parish of Frensham and some other villages. If we mistake not, all that Domesday Book has to say of the whole of this territory is that the Bishop of Winchester holds Farnham, that it has been rated at 60 hides, that it is worth the large sum of £65 a year and that there are so many tenants upon it. We certainly must not draw the inference that there was but one vill in this tract. If the bishop is tenant in chief of the whole hundred and has become responsible for all the geld that is levied therefrom, there is no great reason why the surveyors should trouble themselves about the vills.[1]

A somewhat similar example comes from eastern Berkshire where the entry for Sonning covers not only Sonning itself but also Ruscombe, Arborfield, Wokingham and even Sandhurst to the south-east—all in the hundred of Charlton, but none of them named in the Domesday Book.[2] In this case, one of the population maps for Berkshire is inaccurate in the sense that it shows a large symbol for Sonning instead of a group of smaller symbols. But the density per square mile of the hundred remains unaffected, so that the second population map gives a correct picture of the hundred in relation to the rest of the county. Again, the Berkshire woodland map, with its large symbol over Sonning, is also inaccurate, and no corrective can be applied to it. Taking a broad view of the county, what the map does show is that there was woodland at Sonning or thereabouts. It enables us to draw broad regional contrasts, and the small scale of the final map reduces any erroneous impression.

Yet another problem connected with the identification of villages must be mentioned. There are many examples on the modern map of two or more adjoining villages that bear the same surname, e.g. Guilden Morden and Steeple Morden in Cambridgeshire, and the three Tolleshunts in Essex. The Domesday Book rarely distinguishes between the components of these pairs or groups, so that we cannot say therefore whether more than

---

[1] F. W. Maitland, *op. cit.* pp. 13–14.

[2] *V.C.H. Berkshire* (1906), I, p. 301. For a discussion of this area, see also F. M. Stenton, *Introduction to the Survey of English Place-Names* (Cambridge, 1924), p. 39.

one separate unit existed in the eleventh century. It is often possible, however, to trace the subsequent history of the Domesday holdings bearing the same name, and so assign them to one or other of the modern villages. The editors of the Domesday text for many counties have inserted these detailed identifications where possible. But frequently the material is not available for such identifications to be made, and it is

Fig. 1. Eastern Counties.

always possible, as Maitland suggested, that in some places, 'the surveyors saw but one vill where we see two'.[1] In the construction of the maps that follow, the Domesday text has been followed literally. Only where a separate component is specifically mentioned has it been plotted separately. The modern parishes of Great and Little Massingham in Norfolk, for example, have been treated as one vill with one symbol, because the Domesday Book merely mentions Massingham. The error that this involves on some of the maps is a slight one, and on the scale of the reproduction it is almost negligible.

[1] F. W. Maitland, *op. cit.* p. 14.

These are some of the general difficulties to be borne in mind when reconstituting the information relating to Domesday vills. There are many other difficulties that are discussed in connection with each county (Fig. 1). The counties are considered separately, and the treatment of each follows a more or less standard pattern as set out below. This method inevitably involves some repetition, but, after some experiment, it has been chosen because of its convenience. It enables the account of each county to be read or consulted apart from the rest, and it also has the advantage of bringing out the peculiar features that characterise the text of each county. For although the Domesday Book is arranged on a more or less uniform plan, there are many differences between the counties, both in the nature of their information and in the way it is presented. The relevance of each of the items to a reconstruction of Domesday geography is examined, and any peculiar features that occur in the phrasing of the Domesday text are also noted. A final chapter sums up some of the salient features of the Domesday geography of the eastern counties as a whole. All the standard maps have been reproduced on the same scale to facilitate comparison between one county and another.

Plan of each chapter on Domesday Geography

All the information does not exist for every county. Slight modifications have occasionally been made: e.g. owing to the nature of the returns, meadow and marsh have been considered together for Essex.

1.	Introduction.	9.	Salt-pans.
2.	Settlements and their distribution.	10.	Waste.
3.	The distribution of prosperity and population.	11.	Mills.
		12.	Churches.
4.	Woodland.	13.	Urban Life.
5.	Meadow.	14.	Livestock.
6.	Pasture.	15.	Miscellaneous Information.
7.	Marsh.	16.	Regional Summary.
8.	Fisheries.	17.	Bibliographical Note.

BIBLIOGRAPHICAL NOTE

(1) This is a list of some general works dealing with the Domesday Book as a whole. Accounts of the folios relating to different counties are noted in the relevant bibliographical notes to each chapter; but some of these accounts, particularly those dealing with Cambridgeshire, contain much that is of more than local interest.

(2) The only complete edition of the text is *Libri Censualis vocati Domesday Book*, vols. I, II (no title), ed. by A. Farley (London, 1783); vols. III, IV, ed. by Henry Ellis (London, 1811, 1816). Vol. I covers the greater part of England; vol. II is known as the 'Little Domesday', and covers Essex, Norfolk, Suffolk. Ellis tells us that Abraham Farley 'had almost daily recourse to the Book for more than forty years', and his remarkable work made the text generally accessible; the folios are numbered to agree with those of the MS. which makes reference easy. Vol. III contains Indexes and an Introduction by Sir Henry Ellis; vol. IV contains four documents that are supplementary to the main Domesday Book—Exon Domesday, Inquisitio Eliensis, Liber Winton and the Boldon Book.

Facsimiles of the folios relating to each county were produced in 35 parts by the Ordnance Survey Office, Southampton, 1861–3.

Extensions and/or translations of the text have been published for a variety of counties, and these are noted in the appropriate places below. But a general mention must be made here of the translations in the *Victoria County Histories*; these are accompanied by introductions that provide a very valuable and convenient approach to Domesday problems.

(3) The following general works, arranged in chronological order, should be consulted:

ROBERT KELHAM, *Domesday Book Illustrated* (London, 1787). An interesting example of older Domesday scholarship, with a long glossary (pp. 145–399) of difficult words and passages.

HENRY ELLIS, *A General Introduction to Domesday Book* (London, 1833), 2 vols. Invaluable for its indexes to personal names and for its statistics of population (see p. 12 above).

W. DE GRAY BIRCH, *Domesday Book* (London, 1887; 2nd edit. 1908). A short popular account.

P. E. DOVE (ed.), *Domesday Studies* (London, 1888–91), 2 vols. These were the papers read at the meetings of the Domesday Commemoration in 1886. They vary in value; but some, especially those of J. H. Round, are valuable.

J. H. ROUND, *Feudal England* (London, 1895; reprinted 1909). A work of fundamental importance that inaugurated a new era in Domesday scholarship. See p. 274 below.

F. W. MAITLAND, *Domesday Book and Beyond* (Cambridge, 1897; reprinted 1907). Many of Maitland's views are now obsolete, but his attractively written book remains a classic. It has been reproduced as a Fontana paperback with an introduction by Edward Miller (1960).

A. BALLARD, *The Domesday Boroughs* (Oxford, 1904).

P. VINOGRADOFF, *The Growth of the Manor* (London, 1904; 4th impr. 1932).

A. BALLARD, *The Domesday Inquest* (London, 1906; 2nd edit. 1923).

P. VINOGRADOFF, *English Society in the Eleventh Century* (Oxford, 1908).

C. STEPHENSON, *Borough and Town: A study of urban origins in England* (Cambridge, Mass., 1933). This has a chapter on the Domesday borough (pp. 73–119).

R. LENNARD, *Rural England, 1086–1135* (Oxford, 1959).

V. H. GALBRAITH, *The Making of Domesday Book* (Oxford, 1961).

R. WELLDON FINN, *The Domesday Inquest and the Making of Domesday Book* (London, 1961).

R. WELLDON FINN, *An Introduction to Domesday Book* (London, 1963).

R. WELLDON FINN, *Domesday Studies: The Liber Exoniensis* (London, 1964).

R. WELLDON FINN, *Domesday Studies: The Eastern Counties* (London, 1967).

(4) Useful papers and articles, arranged in chronological order, include the following:

W. F. ALLEN, 'Rural Population in Domesday', in *Essays and Monographs* (Boston, 1890), pp. 319–30.

W. H. STEVENSON, 'The Hundreds of Domesday', *Eng. Hist. Rev.* (1890), V, pp. 95–100.

F. POLLOCK, 'A brief survey of Domesday', *Eng. Hist. Rev.* (1896), XI, pp. 209–30.

W. STUBBS, 'The Domesday and Later Surveys', in *Lectures on Early English History*, ed. by A. Hassall (London, 1906).

W. H. STEVENSON, 'A Contemporary Description of the Domesday Survey', *Eng. Hist. Rev.* (1907), XXII, pp. 72–84.

F. H. BARING, 'The Exeter Domesday', *Eng. Hist. Rev.* (1912), XXVII, pp. 309–18.

D. C. DOUGLAS, 'Odo, Lanfranc and the Domesday Survey', in *Historical Essays in honour of James Tait* (Manchester, 1933), pp. 47–57.

D. C. DOUGLAS, 'The Domesday Survey', *History* (1936), XXI, pp. 249–57.

M. T. HODGEN, 'Domesday Water Mills', *Antiquity* (Gloucester, 1939), XIII, pp. 261–79.

V. H. GALBRAITH, 'The Making of Domesday Book', *Eng. Hist. Rev.* (1942), LVII, pp. 161–77.

R. LENNARD, 'A Neglected Domesday Satellite', *Eng. Hist. Rev.* (1943), LVIII, pp. 32–41.

R. LENNARD, 'Domesday plough-teams: the south-western evidence', *Eng. Hist. Rev.* (1945), LX, pp. 217–33.

R. LENNARD, 'The economic position of the Domesday *villani*', *Econ. Journ.* (1946), LVI, pp. 244–64.

R. LENNARD, 'The economic position of the Domesday sokemen', *Econ. Journ.* (1947), LVII, pp. 179–95.

C. STEPHENSON, 'Notes on the Composition and Interpretation of Domesday Book', *Speculum* (Cambridge, Mass., 1947), XXII, pp. 1–15.

H. P. R. FINBERG, 'The Domesday plough-team', *Eng. Hist. Rev.* (1951), LXVI, pp. 67–71.

R. LENNARD, 'The economic position of the bordars and cottars of Domesday Book', *Econ. Journ.* (1951), pp. 342–71.

P. H. SAWYER, 'The "Original Returns" and Domesday Book', *Eng. Hist. Rev.* (1955), LXX, pp. 177–97.

P. H. SAWYER, 'The place-names of the Domesday manuscripts', *Bull. John Rylands Lib.* (Manchester, 1956), XXXVIII, pp. 483–506.

J. S. MOORE, 'The Domesday teamland: a reconsideration', *Trans. Roy. Hist. Soc.* (1964), 5th Ser. vol. XIV, pp. 109–30.

R. LENNARD, 'The composition of the Domesday caruca', *Eng. Hist. Rev.* (1966), LXXXI, pp. 770–5.

S. HARVEY, 'Royal revenue and Domesday terminology', *Econ. Hist. Rev.* (1967), 2nd Ser. vol. XX, pp. 221–8.

R. WELLDON FINN, 'The teamland of the Domesday Inquest', *Eng. Hist. Rev.* (1968), LXXXIII, pp. 95–101.

(5) The following papers embody the experiments leading up to the present study of the Domesday geography of England (see p. 17):

C. P. BAYLEY, 'The Domesday Geography of Northamptonshire', *Trans. Northants Nat. Hist. Soc. and Field Club* (Northampton, 1938), XXIX, pp. 1–22.

H. C. DARBY, 'Domesday Woodland in East Anglia', *Antiquity* (Gloucester, 1934), XIV, pp. 211–14.

H. C. DARBY, 'The Domesday Geography of Norfolk and Suffolk', *Geog. Journ.* (1935), LXXXV, pp. 432–52.

H. C. DARBY, 'Domesday Woodland in Huntingdonshire', *Trans. Cambs. and Hunts. Arch. Soc.* (Ely, 1937), V, pp. 269–73.

H. C. DARBY, 'The Domesday Geography of Cambridgeshire', *Trans. Cambs. Antiq. Soc.* (Cambridge, 1936), XXXVI, pp. 35–57.

H. C. DARBY, 'The economic geography of England, A.D. 1000–1250', in *An Historical Geography of England before A.D. 1800* (Cambridge, 1936), pp. 165–229.

H. C. DARBY, 'Domesday Cambridgeshire', *V.C.H. Cambridge* (Oxford, 1948), II, pp. 49–58.

H. C. DARBY, 'Domesday Woodland in Lincolnshire', *The Lincolnshire Historian* (Lincoln, 1948), I, pp. 55–9.

H. C. DARBY, 'Domesday Woodland', *Econ. Hist. Rev.* (Cambridge, 1950), 2nd ser. III, pp. 21–43.

H. C. DARBY, 'Domesday Woodland', *Econ. Hist. Rev.* (Cambridge, 1950) 2nd ser. III, pp. 21–43.

D. HOLLY, 'The Domesday Geography of Leicestershire', *Trans. Leics. Arch. Soc.* (Leicester, 1938–9), XX, pp. 1–36.

F. W. MORGAN, 'The Domesday Geography of Berkshire', *Scot. Geog. Mag.* (Edinburgh, 1935), LI, pp. 353–63.

F. W. MORGAN, 'Woodland in Wiltshire at the time of the Domesday Book', *Wilts. Arch. and Nat. Hist. Mag.* (Devizes, 1935), XLVII, pp. 25–33.

F. W. MORGAN, 'The Domesday Geography of Wiltshire', *Wilts. Arch. and Nat. Hist. Mag.* (Devizes, 1936), XLVIII, pp. 68–81.

F. W. MORGAN, 'Domesday Woodland in Southwest England', *Antiquity* (Gloucester, 1936), XVI, pp. 306–24.

F. W. MORGAN, 'The Domesday Geography of Somerset', *Proc. Somerset Arch. and Nat. Hist. Soc.* (Taunton, 1938), LXXXIV, pp. 139–55.

F. W. MORGAN, 'The Domesday Geography of Devon', *Trans. Devon Assoc. for Advancement of Sci., Lit. and Art* (Plymouth, 1940), LXXII, pp. 305–33.

N. J. G. POUNDS, 'The Domesday Geography of Cornwall', *Ann. Rep. Roy. Cornw. Polytech. Soc.* (Falmouth, 1942), pp. 1–15.

I. B. TERRETT, 'The Domesday Woodland of Cheshire', *Trans. Hist. Soc. Lancs. and Cheshire* (Liverpool, 1948), C, pp. 1–7.

(6) There is a short bibliographical note in Birch's *Domesday Book* (1887), pp. 315–24; a much longer one, together with notes on MSS., in vol. II of *Domesday Studies* (1891), pp. 621–95; and another in C. Gross, *The Sources and Literature of English History from the earliest times to about 1485* (London, 1915), pp. 407–17. There is also a 'Bibliography of Matter relating to Domesday Book published between the years 1906 and 1923' in the 2nd edit. of Ballard's *Domesday Inquest* (1923). D. C. Douglas' paper in *History* (1936) has a bibliographical note. There are also bibliographies in the four books by R. Welldon Finn listed on p. 23.

(7) An account of the manuscript itself, together with much other interesting information, is provided by *Domesday Re-bound*, issued by the Public Record Office (H.M.S.O., London, 1954).

LIBRARY OF MOUNT ST. MARY'S COLLEGE EMMITSBURG, MARYLAND

CHAPTER II

LINCOLNSHIRE

Even a brief examination of the folios relating to Lincolnshire reveals many of the imperfections of the Domesday record. Some of these obscurities or omissions are probably the result of clerical errors, and a few of the more obvious examples will perhaps be more illuminating than any general statement about them. For five groups of villages, the Lincolnshire folios include a summary relating to each group as a whole. The five groups are the villages comprising the sokelands of (i) Kirton, (ii) Caistor and Hundon, (iii) Gayton le Wold, (iv) Horncastle, (v) Greetham. But the totals recorded in each of these summaries do not always agree with the sum of the entries. The two groups of statistics are brought together in the table on p. 28. Sometimes there is agreement; sometimes there is a difference; and there is a very big difference over the sokemen of Greetham.

In the case of the Kirton group of villages, for example, we can almost see the Domesday clerks making mistakes. First of all, a list of villages is given with the number of carucates in each; then follows, in the same order, a more detailed account of each village—sokemen, villeins, bordars, teams, meadow and so on; finally, the totals for the group as a whole are given. When the first list was written, the village of Morton was left out, but the omission was discovered and a reference to Morton was added in the margin. But the second list omits Morton altogether; whoever corrected the first list, did not complete his work by correcting the second. There is also another discrepancy between the two lists. The first list enters three-quarters of a carucate for Stainton, but in the second list the phrase 'and Waddingham' is added above Stainton, and presumably what follows refers to both. In this case, the second list is more complete than the first. In these two ways does fo. 338 of the Domesday Book bear witness to its own imperfections. This is probably about as near as we can get to looking over the shoulders of the clerks as they progressed with their wearisome task.

It may be that clerical errors also explain the incompleteness of some of the entries. Thus no teamlands are mentioned for Firsby in Aslacoe, but both carucates and teams are recorded as well as other details (342).

LIBRARY
MOUNT ST. MARY'S
COLLEGE
EMMITSBURG, MARYLAND

Fig. 2. Lincolnshire: Domesday wapentakes.

The boundaries between Holland, Kesteven and Lindsey are indicated by thick lines: the three ridings of Lindsey are also shown; see Fig. 6.

At Stainsby in Beltisloe, carucates, teamlands and teams are mentioned, as well as other things, but there is no reference to population (358). If this is not a slip, why were the men omitted? There are other examples of uncertainty. In the entries for Nocton and Dunston in the wapentake of

Summary of Five Sokes

Folio	Soke	No. of vills	Carucates		Teamlands		Teams	
			Domes-day	Correct	Domes-day	Correct	Domes-day	Correct
338 338b	Kirton (Corringham)	27†	59	61⅓	68	*	50	54¼
338b	Caistor and Hundon (Yarborough)	15	28½	28 43/48	58	*	30	33⅞
338b 339	Gayton le Wold (Louthesk)	9	25¾	24¾	38	*	34	35
339	Horncastle (Horncastle)	16	42	41⅛	58	*	55	53¼
349	Greetham (Hill)	32	131	129¾	144	143¾	156	157

Folio	Soke	No. of vills	Sokemen		Villeins		Bordars	
			Domes-day	Correct	Domes-day	Correct	Domes-day	Correct
338 338b	Kirton (Corringham)	27†	223	223	15	31	16	18
338b	Caistor and Hundon (Yarborough)	15	211	211	24	24	28	31
338b 339	Gayton le Wold (Louthesk)	9	167	167	37	37	27	27
339	Horncastle (Horncastle)	16	212	211	66	65	70	70
349	Greetham (Hill)	32	376	492	148	148	168	168

† This includes Morton.
* Information about teamlands is not given for individual entries.

Langoe, there are blanks, obviously intended for the subsequent insertion of the number of teamlands, but these insertions were never made (362); at Canwick (likewise in Langoe), there is another blank intended presumably for the insertion of the word 'villeins' (343b). Occasionally, the clerk has corrected his own figures. Thus an entry of three carucates (iii) for Barnetby le Wold has been altered to six (vi), and there are other examples of correction on the same folio (349). These, and other examples, show how the human element, with its margin of error, must never be forgotten in handling the statistics of the survey.

Another group of difficulties encountered in the Lincolnshire text arises from the fact that the information about two or three or more places is sometimes combined into one statement. Thus Appleby, Risby and Sawcliff, in the wapentake of Manley, are described together (346, 352b, 354b). Amongst other things they had 'wood for pannage half a league in length and one furlong in breadth', but we have no means of apportioning either the wood, or the details of plough-teams, sokemen and the like, among the three villages. For the purpose of constructing maps, the details of these combined entries, when possible, have been divided among all the villages concerned.

Closer inspection of the folios yields a number of less obvious examples of uncertainty. At the end of the Lincolnshire account there is an appendix dealing with matters in dispute (375–7), and, amongst other things, this appendix mentions a dispute about 20 acres of wood at Hanby in the wapentake of Calcewath (375), but the survey itself contains no mention of wood at Hanby; indeed it makes no reference to Hanby at all except incidentally as a place where lay the sokeland and 'inland' of holdings elsewhere. Then again, on the same folio, there is a reference to a dispute about some underwood at Hainton in the wapentake of Wraggoe, but none of the main entries relating to Hainton refers to the existence of any wood or underwood there. On the other side of the folio, there is reference to a dispute about a mill in Ashby by Partney, but, if we are to believe the main survey, there was no mill here; at any rate it is not mentioned. In the face of these and other omissions, it is natural to wonder what else has been left out from the main survey, not only for Lincolnshire, but also for those other counties where there is no appendix to give us a hint of what may be missing.

One other complication must be mentioned. The Domesday county of Lincoln does not appear to have been absolutely identical with the modern county. Eight settlements, now in Rutland, are surveyed both under Lincolnshire and under *Roteland*, and an interesting series of duplicate entries has resulted.[1] Furthermore, the Lincolnshire account of the borough of Stamford (336b) mentions six wards, 'five in Lincolnshire and

---

[1] The villages, with their Lincolnshire folios, are: Ashwell (349b), Burley (355b), Exton (367), Market Overton (366b), Stretton (366b), Thistleton (358b, 367), Whissendine (367) and Whitwell (367). All the Rutland entries are on folio 293b. Three other entries for Thistleton and *alia* Thisleton were described only in the Lincolnshire folios (358b, 366, 367).

the sixth in Northamptonshire which is beyond the bridge'; this sixth ward is not specifically described in the Northamptonshire folios.[1] There were also holdings in the borough pertaining, some to Hambleton in Rutland, others merely to Rutland.[2] In addition to these complications, there were also other arrangements that lay athwart the county boundary. The Lincolnshire folios mention land in Uffington tilled with the teams of Belmesthorpe in Rutland.[3] We are also told of two holdings in Misson (Nottinghamshire) that had connections respectively with the Lincolnshire villages of Kirton in Lindsey and Laughton near Gainsborough (281b).

SETTLEMENTS AND THEIR DISTRIBUTION

The total number of separate places mentioned for Lincolnshire seems to be approximately 754. This figure, however, may not be accurate because, today, there are many instances of two adjoining villages that bear the same surname, and it is not always clear whether both units existed in the eleventh century, e.g. East Firsby and West Firsby. Only when there is some specific mention of a second village in the Domesday Book itself, has it been included in the total of 754; the case of Ravendale in Haverstoe, for example, is an easy one because one of the entries starts off: *In Ravenedal et altera Ravenedale* (347b); another clear case is the distinction between North Stoke (*Nortstoches*) and South Stoke (*Sudstoches*) in Winnibriggs (337b). There is, on the other hand, no indication that, say, the Ludford Magna and Ludford Parva (Wraggoe) of today existed as separate villages in the eleventh century. They may well have been separate, but the relevant Domesday entries refer merely to Ludford.[4]

The total of 754 places includes fifteen which appear only incidentally, and for which practically no information is given. Thus the various properties of the Abbey of Crowland in Lincolnshire are entered; the village of Spalding is also said to be a berewick of Crowland (351b); yet there is no record of the settlement of Crowland itself or of its monks and their agricultural activities. Other places are mentioned as holding sokeland or inland, but no details are given of what these places themselves

---

[1] See p. 80 below for the possibility that it may be *Portland* (219b).
[2] See p. 80 below.   [3] See p. 45 below.
[4] The Domesday Book likewise makes no distinction between the modern parishes of Toynton St Peter and Toynton All Saints in Bolingbroke; they both appear under *Totintune* or *Totintun*. Two of the entries, however, each mention a church (351, 351b), so that it does look as if two separate settlements were concealed under one name.

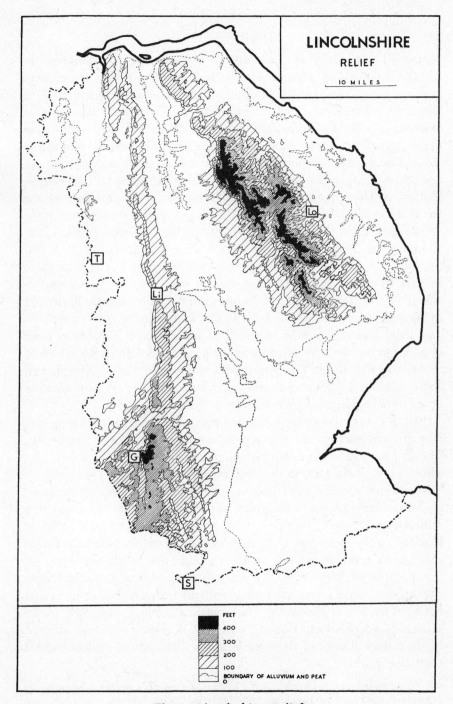

Fig. 3. Lincolnshire: Relief.

Places with Domesday burgesses are indicated by initials: G, Grantham; Li, Lincoln;
Lo, Louth; S, Stamford; T, Torksey.

contained: e.g. Orby in Candleshoe, Upperthorpe in Axholme. In addition to these 15 villages about which the Domesday record says nothing, there are a number of other villages—between 20 and 30—for which the information seems to be incomplete. Coteland in Flaxwell, for example, is entered as possessing 5½ carucates of meadow and some marsh (346b, 369b); there is no mention of arable land or of people. Newton in Well, likewise, has 100 acres of meadow recorded for it (340), but we are told nothing more about it except that it belonged to Laneham in Nottinghamshire (340). We also hear nothing about Winghale beyond the fact that its church held land in Owersby (352); there is no mention of the worshippers or of the land they tilled. Long Sutton is not mentioned at all in the main record but the appendix dealing with disputes tells us that its church lay 'in the king's manor of Tydd' (377b), and it is possible that the land and people of Long Sutton may have been reckoned in with those of Tydd St Mary. Another kind of omission is illustrated by Walmsgate and Stainsby, both in the wapentake of Hill. In Walmsgate there was one carucate assessed to the geld and land for 14 oxen (349b), but we are told no more about it, and yet there is no reference to waste in the village. For Stainsby there is a great deal of information, about teams and mills and meadow and underwood (358), but, whether by accident or design, there is no record of its population.

Not all the 754 names appear as the names of villages on the present-day map of Lincolnshire. Some are represented by hamlets, or by farmsteads, or even by the names of minor topographical features such as woods; thus Otby is now but a farm in the modern parish of Walesby (Walshcroft). The modern parish of Corringham, in north-western Lincolnshire, includes as many as five Domesday names, Corringham itself together with Aisby, Dunstall, Somerby and Yawthorpe which are now names of hamlets or houses. Some Domesday settlements appear merely as mounds or other traces left on the ground; that is all that remains, for example, of West Wykeham now in the parish of Ludford Magna (Wraggoe). Others have left no trace of either their names or sites; that has been the fate of Riskenton which must have stood somewhere in the modern parish of Kirton (Kirton). Canon C. W. Foster's valuable account of the extinct villages of the county brings together the evidence about these changes.[1]

[1] C. W. Foster and T. Longley, *The Lincolnshire Domesday and the Lindsey Survey* (Lincoln Record Society, 1924), pp. xlvii–lxxii, and lxxxvi–lxxxvii.

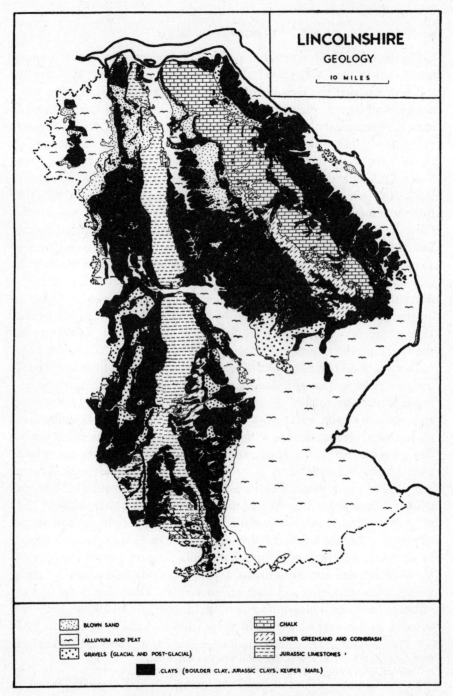

LINCOLNSHIRE
GEOLOGY
10 MILES

BLOWN SAND CHALK

ALLUVIUM AND PEAT LOWER GREENSAND AND CORNBRASH

GRAVELS (GLACIAL AND POST-GLACIAL) JURASSIC LIMESTONES

.CLAYS (BOULDER CLAY, JURASSIC CLAYS, KEUPER MARL)

Fig. 4. Lincolnshire: Surface geology.

Based on Geological Survey Quarter-Inch Sheets 8 and 12, and One-Inch (Old Series) Sheets 70, 83 and 86. This map only gives a general picture. Some of the sheets upon which it is based are very old, and in need of revision.

On the other hand, there are a number of modern villages that are not mentioned in the Domesday Book. Even the Lindsey Survey, scarcely a generation after the Domesday survey itself (1115–18), has a few new names,[1] and later medieval documents contain more. On the analogy of these later records it may well be that details of some of the post-Domesday villages, together with those of the fifteen which are only mentioned by name, were really included under the headings of other villages. Thus South Cadeby and Gayton (both in Louthesk) appear in the Domesday Book but there is no mention of Grimblethorpe. In 1316, however, the three together formed a *villata*.[2] Other examples of such combinations exist. There is one instance of such a grouping explicitly stated in the Domesday Book itself; the entry for Caythorpe (Loveden) is a big one— 40 carucates, 48 teamlands, 48 teams and 170 people (363); but we are told that hereto belong (*huic adjacent*) the adjoining villages of Frieston, Normanton and West Willoughby.[3] Some of the post-Domesday villages, on the other hand, may have been genuinely new creations. As late as 1812, seven new townships were formed in the south of the county as the result of the draining of East Fen, West Fen and Wildmore Fen.

Despite these complications of extinct villages and additional villages, the fact remains that the distribution of Domesday settlements is remarkably similar to that of the modern villages; and it soon becomes apparent that reason was at work when the Anglo-Saxon and Scandinavian invaders laid the foundations of the village geography of subsequent times. The great distinction that appears on Fig. 5 is the contrast between upland and fenland. The settlements of the Fenland were restricted to the silt area and, together with those of Norfolk Marshland, they formed a continuous belt of villages around the Wash; the peat area was without villages. The uplands were fairly uniformly settled, but there are certain features about the distribution that reflect the physical circumstances in a striking manner. In Kesteven, two lines of villages stand out. One runs along the edge of the Fenland, and the pattern of the parish boundaries secures for each village a stretch of fen and a stretch of upland. The other is the line of villages that stretches southwards from Lincoln to Grantham; they are situated to the west of the 'Cliff Edge' and include a stretch of bare

[1] These are indicated on the map which accompanies C. W. Foster and T. Longley's study, e.g. Dalderby in Horncastle, and Stain in Calcewath.

[2] *Feudal Aids* (Public Record Office, 6 vols., 1899–1920), III, 177.

[3] For a discussion of this entry, see F. M. Stenton, *Types of Manorial Structure in the Northern Danelaw* (Oxford, 1910), pp. 12–13.

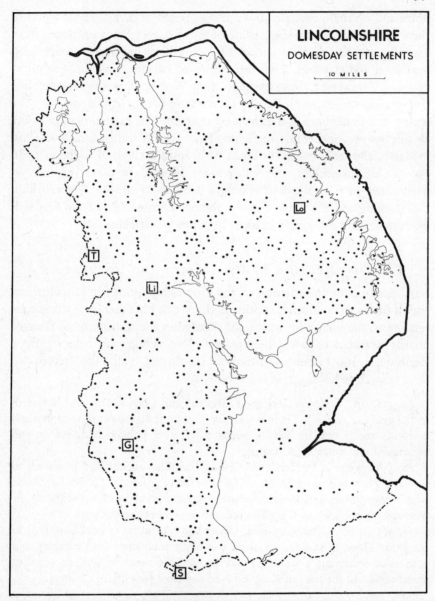

Fig. 5. Lincolnshire: Domesday place-names.

Places with burgesses are indicated by initials: G, Grantham; Li, Lincoln; Lo, Louth;
S, Stamford; T, Torksey. The boundary of alluvium and peat is shown; see Fig. 4.

3-2

heathland on the limestone above and a stretch of damp clay lowland to the west. In Lindsey, a similar line of villages stretches northwards from Lincoln, and the parish territory of each village likewise includes both heathland and clayland. Two other lines of villages flank the Ancholme Marshes. To the east, along the edge of the Wolds, there is yet another line that stretches from South Ferriby on the Humber to Sixhills, marking the spring-line at the base of the chalk escarpment. The eastern margin of the Wolds has yet another line, stretching from Ulceby southwards to Welton le Marsh, and set between the chalk wold and the clayland to the east. In the Wolds themselves, the villages are situated in the river valleys, particularly in the valleys of Hatcliffe Beck, the Lud, the Withern Eau, the Steeping and the Bain. Finally, the northern margin of the Fenland, like the western margin, is marked by a line of settlements.

THE DISTRIBUTION OF PROSPERITY AND POPULATION

Some idea of the information in the Domesday folios for Lincolnshire, and of the form in which it is presented, may be obtained from the entries relating to the village of Stixwould situated in the wapentake of Gartree on the northern edge of the Fenland. The village was held by three landholders, Ivo Taillebois, Alfred of Lincoln and Waldo the Breton, and their respective holdings were as follows:

Fo. 351. In Stixwould there are 2 carucates and 2 bovates of land [assessed] to the geld (*ad geldum*). There is land for 2 teams and 2 oxen. 10 sokemen and 3 villeins and 4 bordars have 3 teams there, and 40 acres of meadow, and 80 acres of wood [land] for pannage.

Fo. 358 (manor). In Stixwould, Siward had 6 bovates of land [assessed] to the geld. There is land for 12 oxen. The same has of Alfred [of Lincoln] 4 villeins with 1 team there, and 20 acres of meadow, and 40 acres of wood [land] for pannage. In the time of King Edward and now worth 10 shillings.

Fo. 365 (manor). In Stixwould, Ulviet had 1 carucate of land [assessed] to the geld. There is land for 10 oxen. He has 1 team there [in demesne], and 2 fisheries rendering 4 shillings, and 40 acres of meadow, and 80 acres of underwood. In the time of King Edward and now [worth] 20 shillings.

These three entries do not include all the items of information that are given for some other places; there is no mention, for example, of mills or salt-pans or of a church. But they are representative enough, and they do contain the recurring standard items that are found in entry after entry.

These standard items are carucates, plough-lands, plough-teams, population and value. Their usefulness in indicating the relative wealth of different localities in 1086 must now be examined.

(1) *Carucates*

The carucate was the unit of assessment in Lincolnshire as in the other northern counties, and the Danegeld was levied at so many shillings on each carucate of an estate. In origin the word 'carucate' was derived from 'caruca', a plough, and just as the Domesday plough-team comprised 8 oxen, so did the carucate comprise 8 bovates. It does not follow, however, that the number of carucates at which an estate was assessed was equal to the number of plough-lands it contained. 'The Old English state had not yet developed the administrative machinery which could make assessment correspond with reality.'[1] There was always a large element of artificiality about an assessment imposed from above.

It was J. H. Round who threw light upon the method of the assessment. Each county was assessed at a round number of carucates or hides.[2] A county then apportioned these among its wapentakes or hundreds; and the men of a wapentake or hundred in turn distributed them among their villages. But, as we shall see, whereas the assessment in southern England was distributed in fives and tens of hides, that of the Danelaw counties was distributed in sixes and twelves of carucates. Thus Langtoft in Ness was assessed at 6 carucates (346b), and Welbourn in Boothby was assessed at 12 carucates (368). We are able to discern the duodecimal system so clearly in these two villages because each was held by a single lord. The assessments of those villages held by more than one owner become clear when the different holdings are assembled, as the examples on p. 39 show. Frequently, the sum of the holdings in a village do not come to such convenient totals. Occasionally, however, it is clear that two adjoining villages formed a 12-carucate block; thus Gedney in Elloe was assessed at 8 carucates and Lutton at 4 carucates (338). Elsewhere, allowance must be made for complications that are hidden from us, and, not least, for clerical errors.

It is clear that there must have been much that was artificial about such a conventional system of reckoning. In some places, it is true, the assess-

---

[1] F. M. Stenton in C. W. Foster and T. Longley, *The Lincolnshire Domesday and the Lindsey Survey*, p. xi.

[2] J. H. Round, *Feudal England*, p. 69. See p. 274 below.

ment may have corresponded with the agricultural realities of the time. A group of villages around Bolingbroke had the same number of carucates, plough-lands and plough-teams, but this was exceptional. For the most part there was divergence. Why, for example, should the wapentake of

Fig. 6. Lincolnshire: Historic divisions.

The parts of Holland, Kesteven and Lindsey are separately distinguished, and also the three ridings of Lindsey.

Graffoe be assessed so heavily when all the indications point to a comparatively low prosperity? Its carucates numbered 167, yet it had land for but 110¼ plough-teams, and only 97⅜ teams appear to have been actually at work in the wapentake. All the considerations that entered into the relative distribution of taxation are lost for ever from our view. The table on p. 39 shows that Kesteven and Holland were assessed much more heavily than Lindsey in relation to their respective amounts of arable land, and arable land at this time was probably a fairly good index

Assessment of Ludford in Wraggoe

	Folio	Carucates	Bovates
(1)	351	—	5
(2)	354	1	6
(3)	354	3	0
(4)	354	—	2
(5)	356b	—	2
(6)	364	—	1
	Total	6	0

Assessment of Barkston in Threo

	Folio	Carucates	Bovates
(1)	337b	8	0
(2)	351b	1	2
(3)	366b	1	0
(4)	370b	—	6
(5)	370b	1	0
	Total	12	0

Carucates, Plough-lands and Ploughs in Lincolnshire

Division	Carucates	Plough-lands	Demesne ploughs	Other ploughs	Total ploughs
LINDSEY					
S. Riding	846	1,119	261	903	1,164
N. Riding	514	1,003	256	583	839
W. Riding	674	764	229	515	744
Total	2,034	2,886	746	2,001	2,747
KESTEVEN	1,881	1,848	388	1,388	1,776
HOLLAND	290	294	45	242	287
Grand total	4,205	5,028	1,179	3,631	4,810

The totals include figures for the boroughs; they are given to the nearest whole number, and refer to the area covered by the modern county. Where nothing is said of plough-lands or where there are blanks, e.g. for Nocton and Dunston (see p. 28), we have assumed them to be equal to the number of recorded teams.

F. W. Maitland's totals for the Domesday county, are as follows: Carucates, 4,188; Plough-lands, 5,043; Plough-teams, 4,712—*Domesday Book and Beyond*, pp. 400–1.

of general economic capacity.[1] The five boroughs of the county have been included in the table although some of their figures are very fragmentary. Even in Lindsey itself the assessment was very uneven. The North Riding came off extremely lightly, but we are given no indication of why this should be so.

(2) Plough-lands

With plough-lands (*terra carucis*) we might hope to be nearer the agricultural realities of the eleventh century. At first sight, there is something concrete about the statement that there is land for, say, 10 plough-teams. The Domesday Book is apparently telling us that the cultivable land of a holding was such that it could be ploughed by 10 teams, and this implication is strengthened by the occasional use of the term 'arable land' instead of just 'land', e.g. in the entries for Foston (348) and Kingthorpe (351). But the formula for plough-lands is not as obvious as at first sight it seems to be. It varies from county to county, and there is a variety of opinion about its precise significance. It may indicate the number of ploughs in 1066, as opposed to those in 1086. Or again, it may indicate potential arable land as opposed to the existing arable. At Wilsford, to the north-east of Grantham, there was land for 16 plough-teams, but only 12 teams were at work there (366, 368); or again at Tathwell, on the Wolds to the south-west of Louth, there was land for 24 plough-teams, but only 11 teams were there (349 b, 363 b). In these, and similar entries, it is tempting to regard the difference between the two sets of figures for plough-lands and plough-teams respectively as indicating the prospect, or at any rate the possibility, of further cultivation.

The plough-land in Lincolnshire, however, as in some other counties, more particularly in Derbyshire and Nottinghamshire, presents a special difficulty. Although for the county as a whole, the number of plough-lands was somewhat greater than the number of teams, yet in some places, the number of plough-lands was very much less than the number of teams. That was the situation, for example, in the village of Fiskerton to the east of Lincoln; there were 3 carucates of land assessed to the geld, and there was land for 3 teams, yet a total of 7 teams were at work in the village—3 in demesne and 4 with 18 villeins and 3 bordars (345 b). There is no

---

[1] For a discussion of the low assessment of Lindsey, see F. M. Stenton, 'Lindsey and its Kings' in *Essays in History presented to Reginald Lane Poole*, ed. H. W. C. Davis (Oxford, 1927), p. 147.

question of any potential arable land being indicated here. What then can be the explanation of this excess of teams over plough-lands?

One explanation is that the manors with excess teams were overstocked, and that this was the result of the large free element among the population of Lincolnshire; that is to say, as Maitland wrote, were these lands to come into 'the hands of lords who held large and compact estates, the number of plough-teams would be reduced'.[1] Freedom and individualism meant an uneconomic use of teams; a fully fledged manorial regime would have been more efficient. But if this explanation were true (and it sounds reasonable enough), the excess of teams should be greatest in those areas where the free element (i.e. the sokemen) is most prominent. This, however, is not the case. There are areas with a high percentage of sokemen that have no excess of teams, and the reverse is also true; the village of Fiskerton, instanced above, had four excess teams but had no sokemen. There is likewise no correspondence between the areas with excess of teams and those with a low percentage of demesne teams (i.e. with a low degree of manorialisation). The demesne teams in the county as a whole amount to about 25 per cent. of the total teams. There is, however, much local variation, but in no way does this variation seem to bear any relation either to the distribution of sokemen or to the incidence of excess teams. One possibility is that the excess of teams simply registers an increase in the arable since 1066. In this case, we should expect to find an increase in value. This is frequently so, but no reasoned correspondence seems possible between (1) variations in value, and (2) differences between plough-teams and plough-lands. Occasionally, as Sir Frank Stenton has suggested, the excess may be due to the creation of new demesne farms. Thus, Sibsey, in Bolingbroke, contained 6 plough-lands, but there were 7 teams there, 1 in demesne and 6 among the men of the village (351). 'The lord's team appears here very plainly as an innovation. In this and in similar cases it should not be assumed that the creation of new demesne was accompanied by the cultivation of new lands. In most cases, the new home farm must have arisen on the ancient arable. Its establishment meant the employment of new teams without any corresponding increase in the number of village teamlands.'[2] But while individual examples may thus

---

[1] F. W. Maitland, op. cit. pp. 428–9. See also P. Vinogradoff, English Society in the Eleventh Century, pp. 164–5, and F. M. Stenton in C. W. Foster and T. Longley, op. cit. p. xix.

[2] F. M. Stenton in C. W. Foster and T. Longley, op. cit. p. xix.

be explained, no general explanation of the occasional excess of teams seems to emerge from the Lincolnshire evidence.

There is another complication, for in some places the incidence of plough-lands seems to be as 'remote from real agrarian life' as that of carucates, and the number of plough-lands corresponds with the number of carucates in such a way as to suggest artificiality.[1] The village of East Deeping (Ness), for example, was held by three landholders, and the coincidence between the assessment in carucates and the number of plough-lands is apparent in each entry.[2] In other places, the number of plough-lands is exactly double that of the carucates; the figures are usually left to speak for themselves but occasionally the fact is explicitly stated. An entry for Minting and Little Minting (351) says that 'there are 7 carucates of land [assessed] to the geld, and 5 bovates and the fifth part of a bovate [assessed] to the geld. There is arable land for twice as many [teams and oxen] (*terra arabilis duplex*)'. The corresponding phrase for Rothwell was *dupliciter ad arandum* (365). It may be that in these and similar cases, the number of plough-lands gives a general and not an exact indication of the arable; it means in effect either that the assessment was just about right in relation to the cultivated area, or that it was only about one-half of what it should be. In all these entries that suggest artificiality, the figure for plough-teams varies quite independently, being sometimes the same, as in Langtoft (346b), sometimes more, as in East Deeping (358, 366 *bis*), sometimes less, as in Harmston (349b, 363). Moreover, it is not possible to generalise about the artificial character of the estimates for plough-lands because there are many other villages, like Ulceby near Brigg, where the number of carucates, plough-lands and plough-teams all differ, and where there is no reason to doubt that the two latter figures represent some agricultural reality.

In the light of these uncertainties, it is really impossible to say exactly what the Lincolnshire 'plough-land' really implied. It may have meant different things to different juries in different places; certainly no comprehensive definition can be found to cover all the variations. Sometimes it is impossible even to imagine what logic and what processes of thought

---

[1] F. W. Maitland, *op. cit.* pp. 471 and 427. See also F. M. Stenton in C. W. Foster and T. Longley, *op. cit.* pp. xv–xix. The relation between the carucates, plough-lands and plough-teams of the Lincolnshire entries is set out in Appendix IX of P. Vinogradoff's *English Society in the Eleventh Century*, pp. 510–56 (Oxford, 1908).

[2] See table on p. 43.

lay behind the figures that now confront us. What, for example, can the entry for a manor in the village of Keisby (Beltisloe) really mean? 'Offram had 4 bovates [assessed] to the geld. There is land for 4 oxen. It is waste except for 3 villeins with 6 oxen' (371); the plough-lands agree with the assessment, and so may only be a rough estimate, an artificial figure, but, despite the fact that the land was waste, 3 villeins were apparently at work there with 6 oxen; the value of the manor was, incidentally, the same in 1086 as in 1066.

Faced with these difficulties, all we can do is to hazard the guess that the Domesday plough-lands of Lincolnshire approached agricultural reality more nearly than did the assessment. For what it is worth, our count shows that there was a deficiency of teams in 42%, and an excess in another 42% of the entries which record both plough-lands and teams.

Some Representative Lincolnshire Villages

	Assessment (carucates)	Plough-lands	Demesne ploughs	Other ploughs	Total ploughs
EAST DEEPING					
358	$\frac{1}{2}$	$\frac{1}{2}$	—	$1\frac{1}{2}$	$1\frac{1}{2}$
366	$3\frac{3}{4}$	$3\frac{3}{4}$	2	7	9
366	$2\frac{3}{4}$	$2\frac{3}{4}$	$1\frac{1}{2}$	$3\frac{1}{2}$	5
Total	7	7	$3\frac{1}{2}$	12	$15\frac{1}{2}$
GOXHILL					
344	1	2	2	1	3
357b	$1\frac{1}{4}$	$2\frac{1}{2}$	1	2	3
360	2	4	—	3	3
362	$1\frac{1}{4}$	$2\frac{1}{2}$	$\frac{1}{2}$	$2\frac{1}{2}$	3
371	$\frac{1}{2}$	1	—	1	1
Total	6	12	$3\frac{1}{2}$	$9\frac{1}{2}$	13
LANGTOFT					
346b	6	6	1	5	6
HARMSTON					
349b	$20\frac{1}{2}$	$20\frac{1}{2}$	—	10	10
363	$3\frac{1}{2}$	$3\frac{1}{2}$	1	1	2
Total	24	24	1	11	12
ULCEBY					
344	$\frac{3}{4}$	2	1	—	1
362	$\frac{3}{4}$	$2\frac{1}{4}$	1	$\frac{1}{2}$	$1\frac{1}{2}$
362	4	10	4	9	13
371	$\frac{1}{2}$	$1\frac{3}{8}$	1	—	1
Total	6	$15\frac{5}{8}$	7	$9\frac{1}{2}$	$16\frac{1}{4}$

(3) *Plough-teams*

Whatever the uncertainties of carucates and plough-lands, the number of plough-teams in a village does seem to bring us nearer to agricultural reality and to the soil itself. Both Round and Maitland came to the conclusion that the Domesday plough-team consisted invariably of 8 oxen. It is, wrote Round, 'as absolutely certain that the Domesday *caruca* was composed of eight oxen as that our own sovereign is composed of twenty shillings',[1] and his conclusion has been generally accepted by a succession of Domesday scholars. This view, it must be emphasised, does not conflict with the fact that the teams to be seen in the field may have varied in size. Indeed, it is unlikely that a uniform team of 8 oxen was at work on all the different soils throughout the length and breadth of England—on heavy clayland and chalk alike.[2] Faced with variation in the size of the working team, the Domesday clerks found it convenient to reckon at the rate of 8 oxen to 1 team, otherwise, argued Maitland, the survey would have been 'a collection of unknown quantities.'[3] Instead of saying, for instance, that 27 sokemen had 38 oxen at North Thoresby and Autby (Haverstoe), they said that '27 sokemen had 5 teams less 2 oxen' (342b). Alternatively they might have said '4 teams and 6 oxen'. At Holton Beckering (Wraggoe), they did say that 4 sokemen had '1 team and 6 ploughing oxen' (339b).

According to Mr Reginald Lennard, the Domesday plough-team in south-west England was variable, comprising 4, 6, 8 or even more than 8 oxen. He counters Maitland's argument about unknown quantities by saying that 'it may even be possible that, in view of local differences of soil and *terrain*, a measurement in terms of the ploughs usual in the locality would be more uniform for practical agricultural purposes than one made in terms of the numbers of oxen employed'.[4] Whether these considerations apply to the rest of England, we cannot say.

---

[1] J. H. Round, *Feudal England*, p. 36. See also J. H. Round in *Domesday Studies*, I, p. 209. See p. 286 below.
[2] H. G. Richardson, 'The Medieval Plough-team', *History* (1942), XXVI, pp. 287–96.
[3] F. W. Maitland, *op. cit.* p. 417.
[4] Reginald Lennard, 'Domesday Plough-teams: the South-western Evidence', *Eng. Hist. Rev.* (1945), LX, p. 233. But for a confirmation of 'the traditional reckoning of eight oxen to the full team', see H. P. R. Finberg, 'The Domesday Plough-team', *Eng. Hist. Rev.* (1951), LXV, pp. 67–71. See also Reginald Lennard, 'The composition of the Domesday caruca', *Eng. Hist. Rev.* (1966), LXXXI, pp. 770–5.

In Lincolnshire we are quite frequently told that there was land for 'n teams and n oxen', and it was this feature that Maitland had in mind when he wrote: 'The theory of a variable *caruca* would in our eyes reduce to an absurdity the practice of stating the capacity of land in terms of the teams and the oxen that can plough it.'[1] Moreover, arithmetic involved in the duodecimal assessment of many Lincolnshire villages seems to indicate that 1 carucate comprised 8 bovates, and the number of entries that link assessment and plough-lands do so on the assumption that 1 plough-team comprised 8 oxen. It may well be that this equation holds good for Lincolnshire as a whole.

There are a number of entries which indicate that ploughing arrangements were sometimes complicated, and which deserve special mention. Eight of these entries are as follows:

(1) At *Elsthorpe and Bulby* in Beltisloe (368), we are told that 'Offram had 2 bovates of land [assessed] to the geld. Guy has them, and they are vacant, but none the less they are tilled (*et uacuae sunt sed tamen coluntur*)'. There is no mention of men or teams on Guy's holding, so that his bovates must have been tilled by another man's men or by the men of some other village.

(2) At *Uffington* in Ness (366b), the Countess Judith had 60 acres of land; 'on it she has no cattle, but tills it as belonging to the manor of Belmesthorpe' in Rutland (*In ea nil pecunie habet, sed colit eam in belmestorp*). In the section dealing with disputes at the end of the Lincolnshire folios (376b), we are told that the Countess tilled these 'with the teams of Belmesthorpe (*et colit cum carucis de belmestorp*)'.

(3) At *Houghton* in Winnibriggs (370b), Colegrim had land for 10 oxen; 'Abbot Thorald holds this land of Colegrim, and ploughs it with his own demesne (*et arat eam cum suo dominio*)'. Abbot Thorald was abbot of Peterborough.

(4) At *Brattleby* in Lawress (340b), the bishop of Durham had land for 6 oxen; 'Colswen has it of him and cultivates it (*et colit eam*)'. But there is no mention either of plough-teams or of the men who used them. This land must likewise have been tilled by outsiders.

(5) At *Fotherby* in Ludborough (354), William de Perci had land for 12 oxen; 'Fulk, William's man, has it and tills it (*et colit*)', but, again, there are no details of how and by whom. Fulk, incidentally, also had 3 teams in the adjoining villages of Little Grimsby and Elkington and he may have used these to work his land in Fotherby.

---

[1] F. W. Maitland, *op. cit.* p. 414. For a Lincolnshire team of 8 oxen, see also Reginald Lennard, 'The economic position of the Domesday *villani*', *Economic Journal* (1946), LVI, p. 250 n.

(6) At *North Stoke* in Winnibriggs (360b), Drew de Beurere had land for 1 team; 'Colegrim has it of Drew, and the rent-payers ploughing (*arantes censores*) there render 7 shillings'. But we are not told how many were these rent-payers, and with what teams they ploughed.

(7) At *Little Grimsby* in Ludborough (340b), the bishop of Durham had land for 3 oxen; 'it was waste, now it is cultivated (*wasta fuit modo colitur*)'; but we are not told by whom or with how many oxen.

(8) At *Claxby by Normanby* in Walshcroft (350), Ivo Taillebois had land for 6 oxen; 'Geoffrey, Ivo's man, has one team there [in demesne] and 2 villeins who do not plough (*non arantes*)'. The villeins had no ploughs of their own, but presumably they worked the demesne team.

It may be that the obscurity of these passages is due to some omissions by the clerks, or to the telegraphic form in which all Domesday entries are cast. Or it may be that the work of the teams recorded for a manor or holding was not necessarily restricted to that manor or holding, and that there was a certain amount of inter-manor or inter-village borrowing and exchange.

To these unusual and curious entries must be added those which mention the existence of teams but make no reference to any population which might work those teams. In these cases, again, the omissions must have been slips of the pen or the teams must have been worked by men from outside. Thus at North Kyme in Langoe there was land for 2 teams and on this 'Colsuain has 1 team there [in desmesne]' (357b), but there is no mention of any men. There is the same omission at Stainby in Beltisloe (358), at Itterby in Bradley (365b), at Binbrook and Irford in Walshcroft (367) and at other places.[1] We can do no more than guess at the reason for the omissions.

Occasionally, the extent of the arable is expressed not in terms of plough-teams and oxen but in terms of dimensions. At Wood Enderby (Horncastle), for example, Siward had '9 acres of arable land' (363b), although, incidentally we are not told whether the arable was actually tilled, and, if so, who tilled it. Some entries mention dimensions as well as plough-teams. At Horbling (Aveland), where there was land for 4 teams, and where 4 teams were actually at work, we are told 'that the arable land is 1 league in length and 1 in breadth' (340). At Osgodby (Beltisloe), where there was land for 5 teams, and where 6 teams were at work, 'the arable land is 14 furlongs in length and 6 in breadth' (345b).

[1] See p. 50 below.

At Cranwell (Flaxwell), where there was land for 12 teams, and where
9 teams were at work, we are told that 'the arable land is 22 furlongs in
length and 7½ in breadth' (355). There are other similar entries to be found
scattered among the more usual formulae. One entry for Lavington
(Beltisloe) is especially unusual; there was land for 5 teams, and 8 teams
were at work there, and we are told that 'the arable land and the feedings
(*pascuæ*) are 2 leagues in length and 6 furlongs in breadth' (340). Sometimes the whole of a holding was described in terms of linear dimensions.
At Bassingham (Graffoe), for example, where there was land for 16 teams,
and where 8 teams were at work, we are told that 'the whole [is] 16½ furlongs in length and 15 furlongs in breadth' (338); it would seem that other
things besides the arable are included in the Bassingham measurements.
In all these examples no amount of arithmetical dexterity can equate
plough-teams with area in any reasonable fashion. Like the similar entries
for woodland, these dimensions raise difficulties of interpretation (see
p. 56). Moreover, there seems to be no reason why they should be
recorded for some places and not for others.

(4) *Population*

The main bulk of the population was comprised in the three categories
of sokemen, villeins and bordars. In addition to these main groups, there
were burgesses and a miscellaneous group that included a substantial
number of priests together with *homines, censores* (rent-payers), *francigenae* and others. No serfs are mentioned for the county.[1] The details of
these groups are summarised in the tables on p. 51. The totals set out in
those tables are smaller than those given by Sir Henry Ellis, even making
allowance for the fact that his figures cover the whole of Domesday
Lincolnshire (i.e. including a portion of Rutland), whereas these are
restricted to the area covered by the modern county.[2] The figures on
p. 51 also differ, but to a very much less extent, from those given by
W. O. Massingberd.[3] From the nature of the Domesday Book, it is likely

[1] But see p. 331 below. Following the practice of the *V.C.H.*, the Domesday word
servus has been translated as 'serf', and not as 'slave'. No view about the status
of *servi* in the eleventh century is implied.

[2] Sir Henry Ellis, *General Introduction to Domesday Book* (London, 1833), II,
p. 465. See p. 5 above.

[3] W. O. Massingberd, 'The Lincolnshire Sokemen', *Eng. Hist. Rev.* (1905),
XX, pp. 699–703.

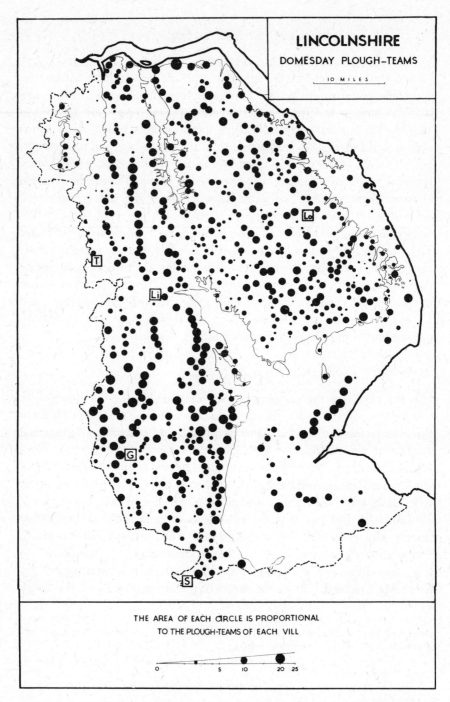

Fig. 7. Lincolnshire: Domesday plough-teams in 1086 (by settlements).

Places with burgesses are indicated by initials: G, Grantham; Li, Lincoln; Lo, Louth; S, Stamford; T, Torksey. The boundary of alluvium and peat is shown; see Fig. 4.

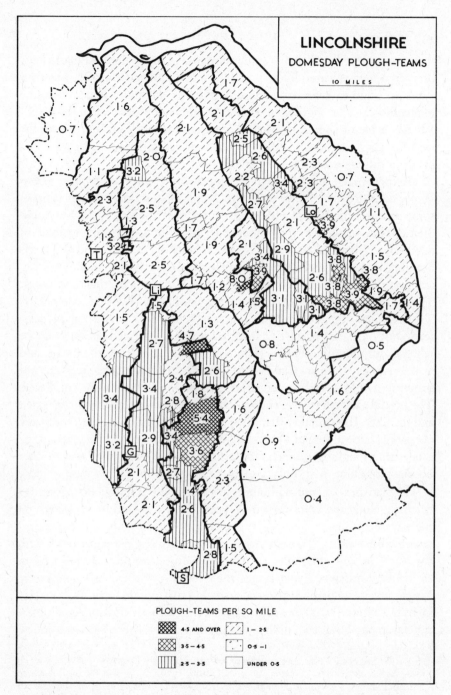

Fig. 8. Lincolnshire: Domesday plough-teams in 1086 (by densities).

Places with burgesses are indicated by initials: G, Grantham; Li, Lincoln; Lo, Louth; S, Stamford; T, Torksey. The thicker lines mark the regions as shown on Fig. 19. For the blank areas of East, West and Wildmore Fens, see p. 92.

that no two people will arrive at identical totals; the present estimates have been compiled as carefully as possible, and have been checked, but they make no claim to definitive accuracy. Finally, one point must always be remembered. The figures presumably indicate heads of households. Whatever factor should be used to obtain the *actual* population from the *recorded* population, the proportions between different categories and between different areas remain unaffected.

The percentage of sokemen was unusually high. It averaged about 50 per cent. for the county as a whole, and ranged up to 80 per cent. in some areas on the Wolds and in the central parts of Kesteven. Sir Frank Stenton has explained the importance of sokemen in the history of northern England. They were the descendants of 'the rank and file of the Scandinavian armies which had settled in the district in the ninth century',[1] and the numerous Scandinavian place-names in the area tell their own story. Today, there are nearly 250 place-names ending in '-by' in Lincolnshire. The sokemen, together with the villeins, were the owners of the plough-teams not on the demesne of a lord; there are a few references to 'villeins who do not plough'; thus there were 4 such villeins in Addlethorpe, and 3 in Friskney, both in Candleshoe (370b), but such references are not many, and they give no indication of how the villeins were employed. The bordars were less free, and may have been labourers, small craftsmen and the like. It is unlikely that many of them owned oxen, but there were occasional exceptions; at Owersby (Walshcroft), for example, there were 2 bordars ploughing (*arantes*) with 2 oxen (352), and there was another bordar ploughing with only 1 ox at Lobingham in Yarborough (350b).

The statistics are not without perplexities. At Stainby (Beltisloe), for example, along the Leicestershire border, there was land for 8 teams, and there were 2 teams in demesne, together with some meadow, some under-wood and 2 mills (358), but there is no record of any people at work with the teams or with the mills; we can only conjecture that this must be an accidental omission. Then again, there were 3½ villeins at *Sudtone*, an extinct village in Great Sturton (Gartree) (359b); there were also 3½ soke-men at Roughton near Horncastle (363b), and half a sokeman at Scredington not far from Sleaford (368b). In Laythorpe by Kirkby (Aswardhurn)

---

[1] F. M. Stenton, 'The free peasantry of the northern Danelaw', *Bulletin de la Société Royale des Lettres de Lund, 1925–26* (Lund, 1926), p. 79. But for doubts about the Scandinavian origin of sokemen, see P. H. Sawyer, 'The density of the Danish settlements', *Birmingham Hist. Journ.* (1958), v, pp. 1–17. See also p. 114 n. below.

there was half a church with half a priest (357). If the Domesday Book were a complete record, we should expect to find the other halves of these people also recorded. But, on the whole, these perplexities are comparatively few, and the main categories of workers stand out clearly.

Recorded Population of Lincolnshire in 1086

A. Rural Population

Sokemen	10,882
Villeins	7,029
Bordars	3,379
Miscellaneous	172
Total	21,462

Details of Miscellaneous Rural Population

Priests	122	*Francigenae*		7
Men (*homines*)	27	*Francus homo*		1
Rent-payers (*censores*)	14*	Knight		1
		Total		172

* There were also an unspecified number at North Stoke (360b).

B. Urban Population

Sokemen, villeins and bordars are also included above.

LINCOLN	900 *mansiones*, together with 36 'outside the city (*extra civitatem*)'; 3 burgesses; 240 *wastae mansiones*.
STAMFORD	Estimated at 500 *mansiones* (including the Northamptonshire ward); 9 burgesses; 6 *wastae mansiones*.
TORKSEY	'102 burgesses dwelling there'; 111 *wastae mansiones*.
GRANTHAM	111 burgesses; '77 tofts of the sokemen of the thegns'; 72 bordars.
LOUTH	80 burgesses; 40 sokemen; 2 villeins.

Above the mass of the population came the landowners, ranging from the king himself down to thanes like Sortebrand. In between the landowners and the agricultural workers came the under-tenants, men named Ilbert, William, Geoffrey and the like. Neither group—landowners nor

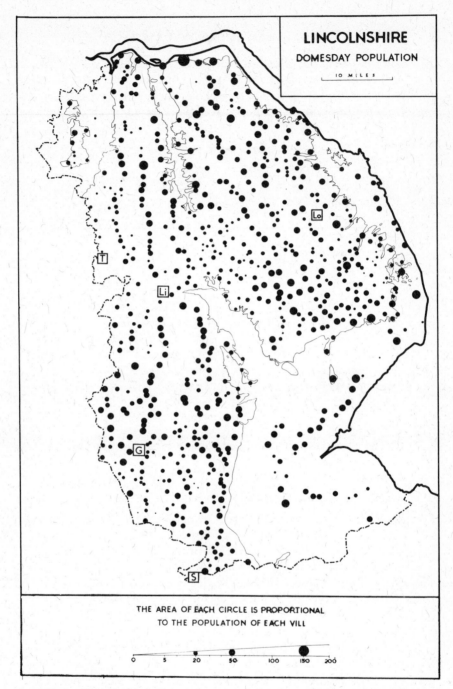

Fig. 9. Lincolnshire: Domesday population in 1086 (by settlements).

Places with burgesses are indicated by initials: G, Grantham; Li, Lincoln; Lo, Louth; S, Stamford; T, Torksey. The boundary of alluvium and peat is shown; see Fig. 4.

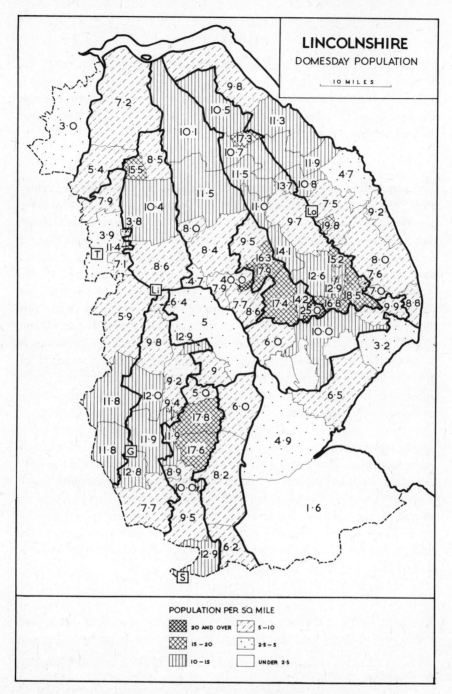

LINCOLNSHIRE

DOMESDAY POPULATION

10 MILES

POPULATION PER SQ MILE

- 20 AND OVER
- 15 – 20
- 10 – 15
- 5 – 10
- 2·5 – 5
- UNDER 2·5

Fig. 10. Lincolnshire: Domesday population in 1086 (by densities).

Places with burgesses are indicated by initials: G, Grantham; Li, Lincoln; Lo, Louth; S, Stamford; T, Torksey. The thicker lines mark the regions as shown on Fig. 19. For the blank areas of East, West and Wildmore Fens, see p. 92.

under-tenants—has been included in the totals of population on p. 51, because it is often difficult to locate the places of their residence. Indeed, it is difficult to say exactly how many under-tenants there were because it is not always possible to know whether the repetition of the same name implies one man or more than one.

(5) *Values*

The concluding entry for a Domesday holding usually states its 'value' both in 1066 and 1086, but not for an intermediate date as in some counties; the value of many holdings remained the same at the two dates, that of others changed, showing sometimes an increase, sometimes a decrease. On some holdings, the value had decreased to nothing or almost nothing, and the land was said to be waste (see p. 70 below). If this 'value' were the rent of an estate or a yearly payment to the lord, we should at once have an index of the productivity of different areas. But the precise meaning of the term is obscure, and any attempt at definition raises difficulties.[1] Quite apart from these general difficulties, however, it is impossible to use this item for estimating the relative prosperity of different areas in the county for the simple reason that the 'values' of the different holdings forming a soke are usually not given separately but are included in the total value of the chief manor to which they belonged.[2] One of the main features of the county was the existence of great sokes stretching over ten, twenty or more villages; thus the 'value' of Greetham on the southern Wolds was £60 in 1086, but this figure covered not only Greetham itself but parcels of sokeland in 33 other villages around (349). There are many similar examples both on a large and small scale. As often as not, a Lincolnshire holding has no 'value' entered specifically for itself. Thus, whatever is possible for some other counties, the form of the information for Lincolnshire makes it impracticable to construct a distribution map of 'values' over the county.

Conclusion

The basic factor in the land utilisation of England in 1086, as of England today, was the soil, and the Domesday information must be interpreted

---

[1] For a discussion of the values, see F. M. Stenton in C. W. Foster and T. Longley, *op. cit.* pp. xxii–xxiii.

[2] See F. M. Stenton, *Types of Manorial Structure in the Northern Danelaw* (Oxford, 1910), p. 31.

in terms of the variations of soil and relief. For this purpose, Lincolnshire can be divided into fourteen regions, each with its own characteristics. The limits of the regions as indicated on Fig. 19 are very artificial, for they have been drawn to coincide with the boundaries of civil parishes in order to make possible a statistical analysis of the information. How far these fourteen regions depart from the realities of the soil may be seen by comparing the map of regions with the geological map (Fig. 4). Many parishes stretch across more than one kind of soil, e.g. from clay upland down to peat fen, or from light chalk soils on to clay. It becomes therefore impossible to distinguish, on this basis, regions that are absolutely homogeneous. Even so, the basis adopted in Fig. 19 is much closer to reality than, say, one which would plot Domesday information merely in terms of the administrative unit of the wapentake. In Figs. 8, 10 and 11 the averages for each portion of a wapentake falling into a region have been kept separate in order to bring the whole picture as near to reality as possible.

Of the five recurring standard formulae discussed above, there are two that stand above the rest in giving something that may reflect the distribution of prosperity throughout the country in Domesday times. These are the formulae for plough-teams and population. Even they are not without some degree of uncertainty, but, if they cannot be trusted in detail, they are, at any rate, useful enough for drawing broad regional contrasts. When the two distributions are compared, certain features stand out as common to both. The main feature is the contrast between (a) the low densities of the Fenland and the Isle of Axholme on the one hand, and (b) the high densities of most of central Kesteven and the Wolds on the other hand. In the Fenland, the most intensively occupied area was that to the north of Boston—the wapentake of Skirbeck. This area seems to have been as prosperous as some parts of the upland. One of the poor upland areas was the district to the south-west of Lincoln city, where there were stretches of infertile sands and gravels; another poor area of sands and gravels was that around Tattershall on the northern margin of the Fenland; a third poor area was the sandy country to the east of Axholme; and, finally, some of the coastal areas of Lindsey had few plough-teams for they must have been marshy. In general, the areas of sparse population coincide with the areas of few plough-teams. The map showing the distribution of plough-lands confirms the other two in a general way (Fig. 11); but, in view of the doubtful nature of the plough-land entries, the implications of this map are uncertain.

Figs. 7 and 9 are supplementary to the density maps, but it is necessary to make one reservation about them. As we have seen on p. 30, it is possible that some Domesday names may have covered two or more settlements. Only where the Domesday evidence specifically indicates the existence of more than one settlement have they been distinguished on Figs. 7 and 9. A few of the symbols should, therefore, appear as two or more smaller symbols. But this limitation does not affect the general character of the maps.

Types of entries
WOODLAND

The Lincolnshire folios give information both for wood itself (*silva* or *silva pastilis*) and for underwood (*silva minuta*). In each case the dimensions are normally expressed in one of two ways, most frequently in terms of acres, but sometimes in terms of linear measurements. Where the wood is described in terms of acres the precise form of the expression varies, but the most frequent formula is '*n* acres of wood for pannage' (*n acrae silvae pastilis*) and/or '*n* acres of underwood' (*n acrae silvae minutae*). The mention of pannage is sometimes omitted, but, on the other hand, the phrase 'throughout the territory' (*per loca*) is occasionally added, and this may imply a scattered distribution. In one case an attempt seems to have been made to locate the position of the wood within a village; the entry for Butyate (Wraggoe) mentions '200 acres of wood for pannage in the middle (*ex media parte*)' (363b). The quantities vary from one acre to many hundreds, and, in one entry, to over a thousand.[1] The detail of many of the entries (e.g. 3, 63, 117), suggests that they were intended to be exact figures rather than estimates. No attempt has been made to equate Domesday 'acres' with those of the present day.

The second method of description usually runs like this: there is wood, or it may be underwood, '*n* leagues in length and *n* furlongs in breadth'. One of these entries, that for Swinderby in Graffoe, takes a unique form: 'there is wood for pannage 8 furlongs in length and 5 in breadth, a moiety of it being feeding land (*pascuæ*) and the other moiety underwood' (367).[2] The exact significance of all these linear measurements is not known—whether they are extreme lengths, or averages, or whether they

---

[1] Thus for Corby (Beltisloe), one entry records '1100 acres of wood for pannage' (344b), and another also records 30 acres for pannage (371).

[2] A combined entry for Withern, Aby, Haugh and Calceby (Calcewath) refers to '92 acres of wood for pannage and underwood' (349).

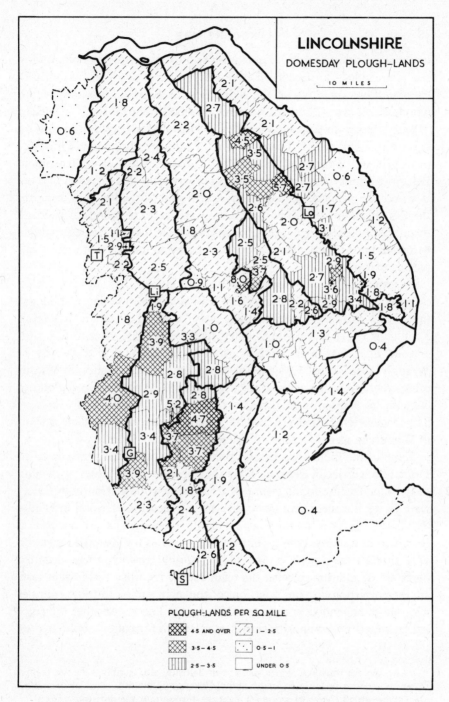

Fig. 11. Lincolnshire: Domesday plough-lands (by densities).

Places with burgesses are indicated by initials: G, Grantham; Li, Lincoln; Lo, Louth; S, Stamford; T, Torksey. The thicker lines mark the regions as shown on Fig. 19. For the blank areas of East, West and Wildmore Fens, see p. 92.

imply some other notion.[1] Sometimes two or more holdings of wood in the same village are recorded differently, one in acres and another in lengths. Thus three out of the six entries for Bourne (Aveland) record wood as follows: (i) 358b: '30 acres of wood for pannage.' (ii) 364b: 'There is wood for pannage 1 league and 8 furlongs in length and 1 furlong in breadth.' (iii) 364b: 'There is wood for pannage 1 league and 8 furlongs in length and 4 furlongs in breadth.' Occasionally, as at Irnham in Beltisloe, both types of measurement occur within a single entry: 'there is wood for pannage 1 league in length and 10 furlongs in breadth. Besides this there are (*extra hanc adhuc*) 200 acres of wood for pannage throughout the territory' (363).[2] Can we assume that the first entry refers to a solid mass of woodland, and that the second entry denotes scattered parcels of wood?

In addition, there are some miscellaneous entries that fall into neither category. At Langtoft in Ness there was 'a wood rendering 2 shillings' (346b); at Spalding in Elloe there was 'a wood of alders rendering 8 shillings' (351b); at Tydd St Mary, likewise in Elloe, 'one fishery with a wood used to render 70 shillings less 4 pence' (338); at Bleasby in Wraggoe there were '2 bovates of wood' (352); at Harlaxton in Winni-briggs there were '60 acres of thicket (*spineti*)' (337b); at Great Ponton, likewise in Winnibriggs, there was 'a wood of thorns (*Silva spineti*) 8 furlongs in length and 1 in breadth' (360b); while finally at Gate Burton in Well there were '70 acres of brushwood (*broce*)' (347).

Some of the difficulties raised by the wood entries are common to all Domesday entries in general. Thus the appendix on disputes at the end of the Lincolnshire folios mentions 20 acres of wood at Hanby in Calce-wath (375), but the main survey itself has no mention of wood in Hanby (351b *bis*). There is another dispute about 'the fourth part of a wood' at Reepham in Lawress (376b), but the main entries for Reepham mention only underwood (345b, 356b, 364b). Quite feasibly, these disputed items are in addition to what the main survey records. But in that case, are the corresponding items left out of the main survey in those counties without an appendix on disputes? We do not know. Another difficulty is that raised by composite entries when the information about two or

---

[1] See p. 335 below.
[2] An entry for Burton Coggles, likewise in Beltisloe, also combines the two forms: 'There is wood 7 furlongs in length and 5½ furlongs in breadth. Besides this (*extra hanc*) there are 280 acres of wood for pannage throughout the territory' (362b).

three places is combined in one statement; thus Burton Coggles and
Bitchfield (Beltisloe) had 150 acres of wood for pannage between them
(357b). These composite entries have been divided between their respective
components. When the wood of a composite entry is measured lineally,
it has been allocated to the first-named village. Whatever minor inaccuracies are thus introduced, they certainly do not affect the general
picture of the distribution of woodland as given on the accompanying
map.

Distribution of woodland

When plotted on a map these wood entries are seen to be disposed in
three main groups (Fig. 12). One is on the clay country to the south-east
of Louth, extending on to the margin of the Wolds. A second and more
densely wooded area is that stretching southwards from Market Rasen to
the northern borders of the Witham Fens as far as Tattershall. The
greater part of this area lies in the Clay Vale of Lindsey; the rest extends
eastward on to the Clay Wolds, and southward on to the sands and gravels
around Tattershall, near the edge of the Fenland. The third area of wood
is on the clays of southern Kesteven, to the south-east of Grantham; this
was the most extensive and most densely wooded area. Kesteven is spelt
'Chetsteven' in the Domesday Book, and the first element, 'Chet,' is
probably derived from the British *cēto* which is cognate with the modern
Welsh *coed* meaning wood.[1]

In all three areas, the bulk of the wood entries were in terms of acres.
Apart from these, there were some scattered woods, more particularly on
the western border of the county in Lindsey, and these, as Fig. 12 shows,
have the peculiarity of being for the most part in terms of linear dimensions; the woods of the Isle of Axholme were entered entirely in this way.
All three main areas, and also the western borders of Lindsey, had some
underwood, and there were in addition a number of isolated localities
with underwood. In general, the underwood was more widely and
sporadically scattered than the woodland itself.

Beyond and around the main woodlands stretched the open areas of
Lincolnshire—on the Wolds, along the oolite belt that runs north of
Grantham past Lincoln to the Humber, and in the Fenland. Some of these
empty areas may always have been but lightly wooded. Others, more

[1] E. Ekwall, *The Concise Oxford Dictionary of English Place-Names*, 3rd ed. (Oxford,
1947), p. 261.

especially the clay lands, must have carried heavy wood at some earlier time, but it is difficult to explain why previous centuries of clearing should have left these particular three patches of clay still covered with wood. All we can say is that by the eleventh century the historic process of clearing had reached the stage represented in Fig. 12. Since Domesday times, further clearing has taken place, although all three areas still carry a moderate amount of intermittent wood cover today. The reverse process has taken place in some localities; plantations have been made on areas that seem to have borne no wood at all in Domesday times, e.g. in the country around Brocklesby on the northern Wolds, and on the sandy areas to the east of the Axholme Level.

MEADOW AND PASTURE

Types of entries

Meadow and pasture were important elements in village economy in an age when root crops and artificial feeding stuffs were not available, and when the winter feed of the village animals depended largely upon hay from the meadows. The distinction between meadow and pasture was clear. Meadow (*pratum*) implied land bordering a stream, liable to flood, and producing hay; pasture (*pastura*) denoted land available all the year round for feeding cattle and sheep. For some counties, the Domesday Book gives separate entries—'there is so much meadow and there is pasture for the cattle of the village'. For the whole of Lincolnshire, however, any mention of pasture is very rare; at Boothby Pagnell and Somerby in Threo there were '2 acres of meadow and 30 acres of pasture' (368); at West Ashby (Horncastle) there were '500 acres of meadow and pasture' (339); and at Cranwell (Flaxwell) 'the pasture (*pascua*) is 10 furlongs in length and 7½ in breadth' (355), and there were also 29 acres of meadow there. Meadow, on the other hand, was recorded for by far the greater number of villages in the county. The usual formula is just '*x* acres of meadow' (*x acrae prati*), and the amounts vary from half an acre to many hundreds of acres; the figures are sometimes round numbers that suggest estimates, e.g. 10, 360, 700; but quite as often they give the impression of being actual amounts, e.g. 22½, 94, 121½. The meadow in composite entries has been divided among the component villages in order to construct Fig. 13. No attempt has been made to equate Domesday 'acres' with those of the present day.

In one portion of the county, in the wapentake of Graffoe, to the south-

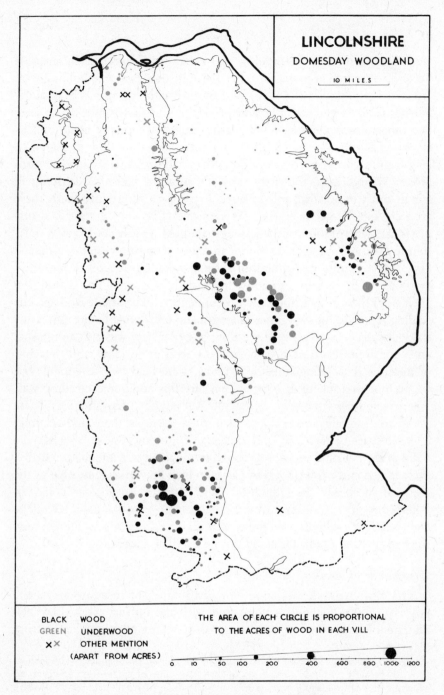

BLACK   WOOD
GREEN   UNDERWOOD
x x   OTHER MENTION
(APART FROM ACRES)

THE AREA OF EACH CIRCLE IS PROPORTIONAL
TO THE ACRES OF WOOD IN EACH VILL

Fig. 12. Lincolnshire: Domesday woodland in 1086.

The boundary of alluvium and peat is shown; see Fig. 4. Where the wood of a village
is entered partly in terms of acres and partly in some other way, only the acres are
indicated.

west of Lincoln city, the meadow was occasionally specified in terms of
linear dimensions; at Stapleford, for example, there was one holding with
'1½ furlongs of meadow' (343b), and another with '5 furlongs of meadow
in length and 60 perches in breadth' (366b). Outside Graffoe, there were
two other places where meadow was measured in terms of linear dimensions; at South Kelsey (Walshcroft) there was 'meadow 1 league in
length and 2½ furlongs in breadth' (338b); and for South Stoke and North
Stoke (Winnibriggs) the entry runs 'Of meadow there is 9 furlongs in
length and 3 in breadth, and 20 acres' (337b). In addition to these, there
are some miscellaneous entries. At Coteland (Flaxwell) there was a total
of 5½ 'carucates of meadow [assessed] to the geld' (346b, 369b); at Wools-
thorpe (Winnibriggs) there were '30 acres of meadow and 3 virgates'
(353); at Heckington (Aswardhurn) there were '2½ bovates of meadow'
(370) as well as other meadow measured in acres. For Lavington
(Beltisloe) there is a curious and obscure entry: 'The arable land and the
feedings (*pascuæ*) are 2 leagues in length and 6 furlongs in breadth'; this
entry also records 36 acres of meadow (340).[1] There was also an unusual
entry for South Carlton in Lawress: '30½ acres of meadow, and 100 acres
of meadow in Nottinghamshire' (370b), were held by Sortebrand, but
we are not told where in Nottinghamshire this additional meadow was.
There is another strange entry for Silk Willoughby (Aswardhurn) where
we are told, amongst other things, that 'there is a priest there, and a church,
and 140 acres of meadow, and 24 acres of meadow' (365); this may be
a slip of the pen, and perhaps 24 acres of woodland was intended. Finally,
there is one entry for Uffington (Ness) which may give some clue to the
value of meadow: 'In Uffington Saint Peter of Burgh [the abbey of
Peterborough] has 48 acres of meadow exempt from the geld. Geoffrey
and the abbot's villeins hold these. *T.R.E.* it was worth 90 shillings; now
the like amount' (346). Or could this be a scribal error?

Distribution of meadowland

The most striking fact about the distribution of meadowland is the
poverty of the Fenland as compared with the upland areas (Fig. 13).
Despite the importance of meadow in the economy of the Fenland during

---

[1] There is another mention of 'feedings' in the section on disputes: 'The men of
Navenby forcibly withhold 16 shillings of customary dues of the feedings (*pascuarum*)
which are in Scopwick and Kirkby Green; and they did not give them in King Edward's
day' (376b). For feeding land (*pascuæ*) in a wood at Swinderby, see p. 56 above.

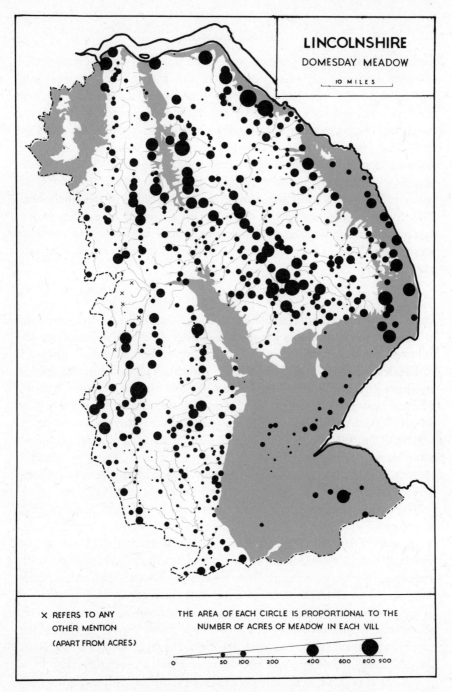

LINCOLNSHIRE
DOMESDAY MEADOW
10 MILES

X REFERS TO ANY
OTHER MENTION
(APART FROM ACRES)

THE AREA OF EACH CIRCLE IS PROPORTIONAL TO THE
NUMBER OF ACRES OF MEADOW IN EACH VILL

0   50   100   200   400   600   800 900

Fig. 13. Lincolnshire: Domesday meadow in 1086.

The areas of alluvium and peat are indicated; see Fig. 4. Rivers passing through these areas are not shown. Where the meadow of a village is entered partly in acres and partly in some other way, only the acres are shown.

the later Middle Ages, it seems to have been relatively unimportant in the eleventh century; and what was true of the Fenland proper was even more true of the Axholme Level. On the upland, the distribution was fairly general, but four areas had particularly large amounts; in each of them there were a number of villages with well over 300 acres of meadow each. The first, and most extensive area, was in the neighbourhood of Horncastle, along the valleys of the Bain and of some smaller streams that also flow southward into the Witham across the chalky Boulder Clay country. The second area was around the upper valley of the Ancholme. The third area extended from the northern silt-lands along the coastal flats of eastern Lindsey. Lastly, there was a moderate amount of meadow along the valleys of the Witham and the Brant in the western lowlands of Kesteven.

MARSH

Marsh is mentioned in connection with 14 places in Lincolnshire, and, in addition to these, the holdings of Geoffrey de Wirce in Axholme are followed by a general entry: 'To this island belong marsh (*maresc*) 10 leagues in length and 3 in breadth' (369b). The other marsh entries are either in terms of linear dimensions like this one, or in terms of acres. Thus at Baston (Ness) there was 'marsh 16 furlongs in length and 8 in breadth' (346b), while at South Kyme (Aswardhurn) there were '700 acres of marsh' (337b). The combined entries that cover a number of places complicate the mapping; thus 30 acres of marsh at Ewerby Thorpe, Howell, Heckington and Quarrington in Aswardhurn (337) have been divided equally between the four villages on Fig. 14.

The marsh villages in the south of the county fall into three groups. A group of 2 villages overlooked Deeping Fen in the extreme south. A group of 8 villages overlooked the Middle Witham fens; a number of these villages, like Evedon with 185 acres of marsh and Old Sleaford with 330 acres, were some distance from the fen border, but their marsh must have been located in the Fenland itself. The third group of 3 villages lay in the extreme north-east corner of the Fenland; here again, the 100 acres of marsh at Candlesby must have been a little distance away on the coastal silts. In the north of the county, apart from the large entry for Axholme, there was an isolated entry of 260 acres of marsh at South Ferriby.

Fig. 14 at once suggests the question whether these entries represented all the marshland of Lincolnshire in 1086. It is impossible to believe that

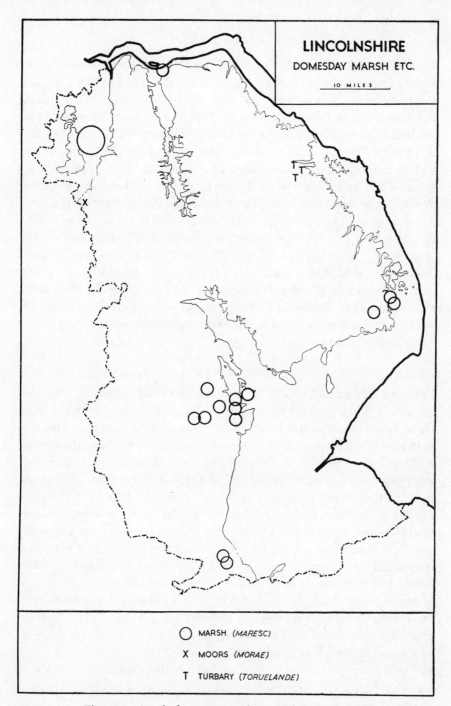

MARSH (*MARESC*)

X MOORS (*MORAE*)

T TURBARY (*TORUELANDE*)

Fig. 14. Lincolnshire: Domesday marsh, etc., in 1086.

The areas of alluvium and peat are indicated; see Fig. 4. The marsh of the Isle of Axholme is indicated by the large circle; see p. 64.

the Fenland did not contain many more stretches of marsh of some value in the economy of the villages of the county. To take but one example, a twelfth-century charter from the reign of Henry II refers to dry marsh and deep marsh in Toynton near Bolingbroke on the northern edge of the Fenland.[1] It is possible that the 'dry marsh' did not exist in 1086, but the 'deep marsh' must certainly have been there, and yet the Domesday Book tells us nothing of it. Some marsh, of course, may have been rated as meadowland, and there was a substantial amount of Domesday meadow in the upper Ancholme valley and along the coastal belt of Lindsey. Apart from this possibility there are three isolated entries from which the existence of marsh may be inferred. In North Thoresby and Autby (Haverstoe), on the edge of the coastal belt of Lindsey, there was 'turbary (*toruelande*) rendering 10 shillings' (342b); at Grainsby (Haverstoe) nearby there was also turbary rendering 5s. 4d. (347). Finally, there were moors (*morae*) at Morton in Corringham (350), but there is no means of telling whether these referred to the Trent marshes or to the moors of the sandy upland close at hand.

FISHERIES

Fisheries formed an important item in medieval economy, and the surprising thing is that they are not more frequently mentioned in a fenland county like Lincolnshire. Altogether, they are mentioned for the year 1086 in the entries relating to 42 places; but besides these, there were 2 villages that had sites of fisheries, and for another village a render of eels is mentioned in connection with half a mill. The appendix on disputes also mentions a toll in respect of fish at Barton on Humber and South Ferriby in Yarborough (375b), but the regular entries relating to these places contain no mention of fish. The value of a fishery is normally stated, sometimes in terms of money, sometimes in terms of eels; but occasionally no value is given and only the presence of a fishery is indicated. In a few entries, as in the case of mills and salt-pans, the value is given in some multiple of 16d.; thus at Heckington (Aswardhurn) there were '3 fisheries rendering 5 shillings and 4 pence' (355). Sixteen pence was the value of the Danish *ora*, and its use is yet another indication of the strong Scandinavian element in Lincolnshire.

The fisheries, as plotted on Fig. 15, fall into three main groups—those

---

[1] F. M. Stenton, *Documents illustrative of the Social and Economic History of the Danelaw* (London, 1920), p. 378.

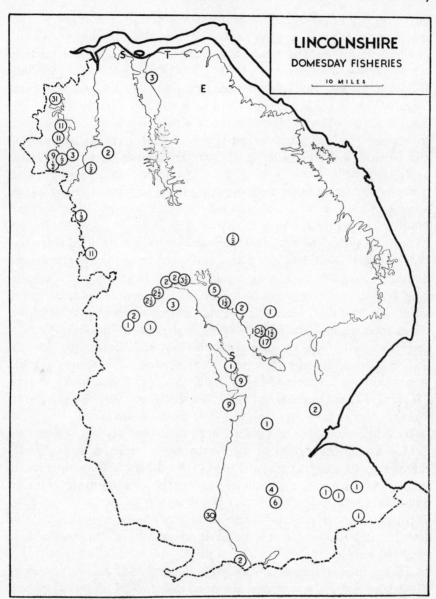

Fig. 15. Lincolnshire: Domesday fisheries in 1086.

The figure in each circle indicates the number of fisheries; 'S' indicates the site of a fishery; 'T', toll in respect of fish at Barton on Humber and South Ferriby; 'E', render of eels from half a mill. The boundary of alluvium and peat is indicated; see Fig. 4.

of the southern Fenland, of the Witham, and of the Trent marshes. The most important centre in the southern Fenland was at Bourne (Aveland) on the western edge of the Fenland, where there were 30 fisheries rendering a total of 72*d*. and 2,500 eels (351b, 358b, 364b, 368b, 370);[1] Spalding (Elloe) to the east had 6 fisheries rendering 30*s*. (351b), and there were other villages in the Fenland with a smaller number. The second area lay along a stretch of the Middle Witham; Tattershall Thorpe (Horncastle), for example, had 10½ fisheries rendering 10*s*. (340b, 341, 343, 359b, 360), and Coningsby (Horncastle) nearby had 17 fisheries rendering 19*s*. 2*d*. (339, 349b, 363b, 370b). South Kyme (Aswardhurn) had 3 *piscariae* and 6 *piscinae* rendering 6*s*. between them (355b, 337b), and at Billinghay in Langoe (340) there were 3 sites of fisheries (*sed' piscar'*). In this neighbourhood, too, there was a fishery at Roughton (Horncastle) on the river Bain (363b), and also the fishery that appears in the joint entry for Barkwith and Southrey (352); the latter was most likely situated in Southrey, although on Fig. 15 a half has been assigned to each village. The Witham fisheries extended up the river beyond Lincoln, but there were no large centres here. The third group of fisheries were those of the Trent marshes, more particularly those in the Isle of Axholme. Crowle had 31 rendering 31*s*. (369b); Epworth (369) and Belton (369) had 11 each, rendering 5*s*. and 7*s*. respectively; Haxey had 9 rendering 7*s*. (369). Among the smaller centres, Lea (Corringham) had half a fishery of 10*d*. (347b) and Laughton also had a half rendering 2*s*. (352). To the south, Torksey had 11 fisheries (337), but their render is not stated.

In addition to these three main groups there were some miscellaneous entries around the mouth of the Ancholme—3 fisheries at Saxby All Saints in Yarborough (350b) and the site of a fishery at Winteringham in Manley (354b), together with the reference to the toll at Barton on Humber and South Ferriby (375b). Farther east, the half mill at Ulceby in Yarborough rendered 10*s*. and, apparently, 500 eels as well (362). It is possible, indeed likely, that some of the other mills of Lincolnshire also rendered eels, but we are not told of them.

Taking the evidence as a whole, it is impossible to believe that these Domesday entries represented the total fisheries of eleventh-century Lincolnshire. There must have been many other places with fisheries.

---

[1] Comprising 21 *piscariae* and 9 *piscinae*. The two terms imply the same thing—see p. 367 below.

SALT-PANS

Salt-pans are recorded in entries relating to 34 villages in Domesday
Lincolnshire (Fig. 16). One of the entries for Gosberton in Kirton is
typical: '2 salt-pans rendering 12 pence' (348b); frequently the amount
rendered, as in the case of mills, was 8 pence, or 16 pence or some multiple
of these sums;[1] occasionally no render was given but merely the number
of pans stated. The two entries for Spalding (Elloe) are exceptional in
form; one stated '20s. from the salt-pans' (351b); the other merely recorded 'a plot of land with salt-pans (*aream salinarum*) rendering 4 pence'
(368). Among the salt-pans of Bicker (Kirton) there was one which was
'waste' (340). At Stallingborough (Yarborough) there were, amongst
others, $2\frac{1}{2}$ salt-pans rendering 2s. (356), but there is no clue to the missing
half.

The salt-pans lay mainly in two areas. The first area was in the Fenland
along the borders of the Wash. There were 15 villages with pans, some of
them with a considerable number of pans; Leake (Skirbeck) had 41
(fo. 348); Donington (Kirton) had 27 (345b, 348*bis*); Bicker (Kirton)
had 22 apart from the one which was waste (340, 348b, 367, 368);
Frampton had 15 pans (348). Later medieval references show the continued importance of salt-making in the Fenland, not only in the villages
for which the Domesday mentions salt-pans, but in others as well.[2] The
second area with salt-pans lay along the coastal marshes of Lindsey. There
was a cluster of salt villages to the north of Louth; Fulstow (Haverstoe)
had as many as 25 pans (340b, 347, 363b), and North Thoresby and Autby
(Haverstoe) had 26 between them (342, 342b, 347b, 356, 357b, 365); and
there were 13 at Tetney in Bradley (350). One interesting point in Lindsey
is the mention of salt-pans for some villages on the Wolds where it was
physically impossible for them to have been located. Thus Maidenwell
(Louthesk), lying at about 350 ft. or so in the Wolds, had one salt-pan
(349b); Fotherby (Ludborough) at 100 ft. and Thorganby (Walshcroft)
at 160 ft. together had 4 pans (353). We can only suppose that while the
holdings in these villages were responsible for the profits of the salt-pans,
the pans themselves lay in the marsh below. It is difficult to apportion the
pans in the joint entries that cover a number of villages. Thus the 5 villages
of Wainfleet (Candleshoe), Haugh, Calceby, Theddlethorpe and Mable-

[1] See p. 66 above.
[2] See H. C. Darby, *The Medieval Fenland* (Cambridge, 1940), pp. 37 *et seq.*

thorpe (Calcewath) were together responsible, amongst other things, for 20 salt-pans (349). On Fig. 16, 4 pans have been allotted to each village, but Haugh and Calceby lie up in the Wolds at 150 and 350 ft. respectively, and the 20 pans must have been in the other three coastal villages. Finally, there is the very curious entry of 2 salt-pans for North Witham (Beltisloe), far away from the sea in the extreme south-west corner of the county (366b); they rendered 10s. to which the scribe seems to have altered the figure from 2s. It is impossible to say where they really were, or why the Countess Judith held them there. They remain an isolated peculiarity among the salt-pans of Lincolnshire.

WASTE

Apart from the waste houses in the three boroughs of Lincoln, Stamford and Torksey, and from an occasional waste salt-pan, holdings described as being 'waste' were recorded in connection with 52 places in Lincolnshire. The real number of villages with waste may have been slightly less owing to the complication of composite entries. There are variations in the form of the entry, but that for Marton (Well) is typical of the general run of 'waste' entries: 'There is land for one team. It is waste' (347); some entries omit a reference to plough-land and connect the waste directly with the assessment, e.g. that for Santon (Manley): '1 bovate assessed to the geld. It is waste' (354b). At Addlethorpe (Candleshoe) there was a variation: 'there are 1 carucate and 1 bovate assessed to the geld. There is land for 9 oxen. Of these 4 bovates are waste' (360). There were also other indications of land that was almost or partly waste. The land for 2 oxen at Bicker (Kirton) was 'waste except for 1 salt-pan' (367); likewise the land for 1 team at Stubton (Loveden) was 'waste except for 1 bordar and 34 acres of meadow' (361b); at Garthorpe and Luddington (Axholme) there was waste land, but 'nevertheless (*tamen*) it renders 3 shillings. *T.R.E.* it was worth 10 shillings' (369b); and there was also the mysterious reference to the land for 4 oxen at Keisby (Beltisloe) which was 'waste except for 3 villeins with 6 oxen' (371). Not included in the 52 places marked on Fig. 17 is the village of Helpringham (Aswardhurn), but it is obvious that conditions on one of its holdings were marginal (357): 'There is land for 2 oxen. There is 1 villein there, and 2 acres of meadow. This land is almost waste (*pene wasta*).' Another entry not marked on Fig. 17 is that relating to a three-carucate holding at

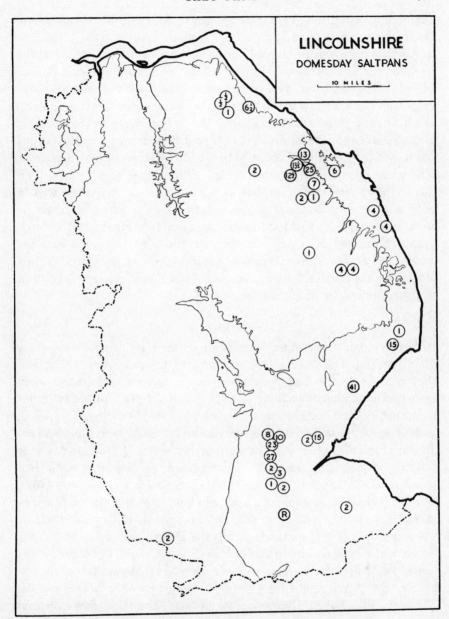

Fig. 16. Lincolnshire: Domesday salt-pans in 1086.

The figure in each circle indicates the number of salt-pans. 'R' indicates a render from salt-pans. For a caution about the location of some of these pans, see pp. 69–70. The boundary of alluvium and peat is shown; see Fig. 4.

Blyton in Corringham (338b); we are merely told that there was nothing (*nihil*) there, but the word 'waste' is not used.

All this waste was presumably not the waste of marsh, heath and the like, and the Domesday folios give no indication of the stretches of land of little value that lay in the Fenland and on the chalk and limestone outcrops and elsewhere. What the Domesday waste entry seems to indicate is a lapse from former land utilisation. But only at Wrangle (Skirbeck) is a reason given for the lapse: 'There is land for 1 team. Guy [of Craon] has it, and it is waste on account of the action (*fluxum*) of the sea' (367b). The waste in some of the other coastal villages may likewise have been due to the ravages of the sea, but we are not told so. Elsewhere we can only assume that the waste entries reflected the hazards of farming or were due to some special local cause. At Little Grimsby in Ludborough (340b), there had been recovery; for, we are told, 'there was land for 3 oxen. It was waste; now it is cultivated (*Wasta fuit, modo colitur*)'. Taken as a whole, the distribution of places with 'waste' entries bears no relation to the natural waste of fen and heath (Fig. 17).

MILLS

Although some corn must have been ground by hand, water-mills played an important part in the economy of the eleventh century, and they were frequently a significant item in the revenue of a manor. They were mentioned in connection with 255 out of the 754 Domesday settlements in Lincolnshire. Their annual value was stated in shillings and pence, and ranged from mills rendering only a shilling each up to the 3 mills at Ruskington (Flaxwell) which were together worth £4. 12s. 8d. a year (369b). Occasionally, no value was returned; on the other hand, half a mill at Ulceby apparently yielded 500 eels as well as a money rent (362), but this is the only example of a render in kind from mills in the Lincolnshire folios. It is interesting to note that a number of mills yielded 16d. or some multiple of this sum, which was the Danish *ora* (see p. 66 above). Some of the mills do not appear to have been working, and merely their 'sites' or 'half-sites' were mentioned. Evedon (Aswardhurn), for example, had 'a mill rendering 5 shillings and 4 pence [i.e. 4 *ora*] and the site of 1 mill' (337b). No renders were made for these sites except at Hougham (Loveden) where the site of one mill was worth as much as 13s. 4d. (366b). Thirteen out of the 255 settlements had mill-sites but not mills. There is one puzzling entry in the appendix dealing with disputes;

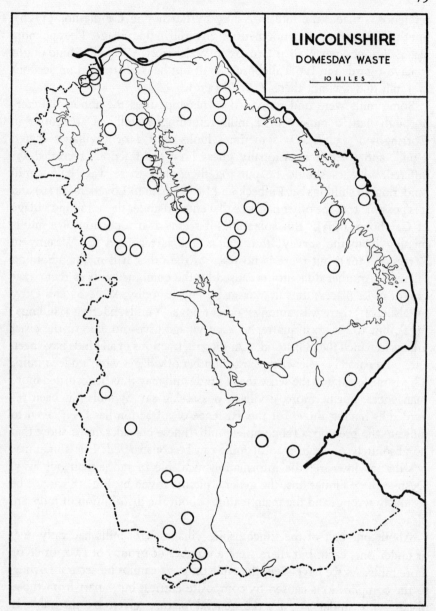

Fig. 17. Lincolnshire: Domesday waste in 1086.

The waste houses in the boroughs of Lincoln, Stamford and Torksey are not indicated. The boundary of alluvium and peat is shown; see Fig. 4.

reference is made to a mill in Ashby by Partney in Candleshoe (375 b), but the main survey does not mention any mill in this village. The appendix also mentions a new mill at Croxby in Walshcroft: 'William Blund ought to have 1 garden in Ivo Tallebosc's land: but he is obstructed on account of a mill that was not there *T.R.E.*' (376).

Some mills were under divided ownership; thus the abbot of Peterborough had 'a moiety of 2 mills returning 8 shillings at Scotter in Corringham' (345 b). It sometimes looks as if 2 or 3 villages shared a mill, and we can occasionally guess how the fractions recorded for different villages should be put together; thus there was 'half a mill rendering 10 shillings' at Fulbeck and Leadenham in Loveden (347 b) and it is possible that the other half was that entered under the adjoining village of Caythorpe (363). But sometimes it seems as if a portion of a mill is missing from the survey; thus half a mill is recorded for Wragby in Wraggoe (362), but there is no trace of the other half in the adjoining villages. Another difficulty is caused by the combined entries that cover two or more places; thus in Market Rasen, Osgodby, Walesby and Otby (Walshcroft) there was, amongst other things, '1 mill rendering 3 shillings' (352), but to assign a quarter to each village gives no clue to the exact village in which the mill stood. On Fig. 18, fractions of all kinds have been entered separately—hence the large number of villages with 'under 1 mill'. This is misleading in the sense that a single mill may thus be recorded more than once. Furthermore, a village possessing say 2½ mills has been regarded as having three, for the existence of a fraction has been taken to indicate the presence of a complete mill. These considerations show that no absolutely accurate map of mills can be constructed; it is sometimes possible to interpret the information available in more than one way. Despite these limitations, the general picture given by Fig. 18 cannot be seriously wrong, and the main features about the distribution of mills are clear.

About one-half of the Lincolnshire villages with mills had only one, or under one, each, but there were a number of groups of two, three or more mills. As we have seen, the table on p. 75 cannot be accurate owing to the complications caused by composite entries; but, apart from those places with 'under 1 mill', the general picture given by the table is probably not very far from the truth, and, in particular, it does show how some villages seem to have had many more than one mill at work. The numbers were out of all proportion to the population of their respective villages, and they suggest some interesting reflections upon the movement of grain between different villages.

Domesday Mills in Lincolnshire in 1086

Under 1 mill	48 settlements		6 mills	4 settlements	
1 ,,	91 ,,		7 ,,,	1 settlement	(Thorganby)
2 mills	55 ,,		8 ,,	1 ,,	(Old Sleaford)
3 ,,	16 ,,		9 ,,	1 ,,	(Nettleton)
4 ,,	18 ,,		13 ,,	1 ,,	(Louth)
5 ,,	5 ,,		15 ,,	1 ,,	(Tealby)

Some of the above villages had mill-sites which have not been included in the computation. There were also 13 villages for which 'sites' alone are mentioned, making a total of 255 villages mentioned in connection with mills.

The figure for Thorganby is an estimate. Six out of the seven entries for Thorganby mention mills as follows: 1 mill (340b); three parts of 1 mill rendering 5s. (350); 1½ mills rendering 8s. (361b); four parts of 1 mill rendering 2s. (365b); 1 mill rendering 3s. (365b); 1 mill rendering 3s. (366).

The 8 mills at Old Sleaford were worth £10 a year; the 9 at Nettleton were worth only £1; the 13 at Louth were worth 60s.; and, finally, no render was recorded for 3 of the mills at Tealby, but 11½ yielded 47s. 10d., and there were also the sites of 3 mills there.

The location of the mills depended on the streams, and Fig. 18 shows that mills were very frequent in two areas—along the upper Witham where there were many clusters of three or more mills, and along the streams of the Wolds, particularly along the Steeping and the Bain. There were no mills in the Fenland except for one at Fishtoft (Skirbeck).

CHURCHES

Lincolnshire, like Norfolk and Suffolk, is one of the counties for which the Domesday Book makes frequent mention of churches. They are recorded in connection with some 245 Lincolnshire villages in addition to those of Lincoln, Stamford and Grantham. This, however, is an arbitrary figure because the composite entries that cover two or more villages provide no clue as to where a church was really situated. Thus the three places of Appleby, Risby and Sawcliff (Manley) had 2 churches between

LIBRARY OF MOUNT ST. MARY'S COLLEGE EMMITSBURG, MARYLAND

them (352b, 354b), while Great Grimsby and Swallow (Bradley) together
had 1 church (363). It is impossible in these and similar instances to say
in which the church really stood. The figure of 245 is obtained by dividing
all composite entries mathematically; without making such division, the
number of places would come to about 220. But little is gained by being
too precise, for even in single-entry villages the statistics are frequently
very puzzling. For some villages the Domesday records only half a
church, or only a third of a church, or, in the case of Laughton (Aveland),
'half a church' and 'a fourth part of two churches' (353, 364b), or in the
case of Scremby (Candleshoe), 'four parts of half a church' (359b). In
none of these cases are we given any clue as to the remaining fractions.
The extreme case of division is Threekingham (Aveland) which had
2 churches—St Mary and St Peter; the following fractions are recorded
for the former: $\frac{1}{12} + \frac{1}{6} + \frac{1}{12}$; and these for the latter: $\frac{1}{6} + \frac{1}{3} + \frac{1}{6}$. Nothing
is said of the remaining two-thirds of St Mary's and of the remaining
one-third of St Peter's.[1] Such divisions may have been the result of
the partition of an estate, or they may reflect the original foundation
of a church by two or more people. Some aspects of this division
have been discussed by Sir Frank Stenton.[2] Standing in contrast to
these fractions, there were a number of places with 2 churches, and
there were two places with more; Lincoln seems to have had $6\frac{1}{2}$ and
Stamford had 4. Curiously enough, no church is mentioned for such
large settlements as Torksey and Louth. Even more puzzling is the fact
that the appendix dealing with disputes at the end of the main survey
refers to a church at Long Sutton (Elloe) which lay 'in the king's manor
of Tydd' (377b), but it is not mentioned in the survey itself.[3] The
disputes also mention a church 'in the soke of Thorpe on the Hill' in
Graffoe (377), but the main survey again does not appear to record it.
Finally, two villages, Ingleby (Lawress) and Fulletby (Hill), had a priest
each but no church (354, 349b).

From some of these complications it is clear that the information is very
unsatisfactory, and that not all the churches of Lincolnshire may have been
recorded. It follows from this that the distribution of those churches that
were recorded gives no clue to the distribution of prosperity.

[1] The folios with entries for the churches of Threekingham are: 341b, 365b
and 370.
[2] F. M. Stenton in C. W. Foster and T. Longley, *op. cit.* pp. xxi–xxii.
[3] See p. 32 above.

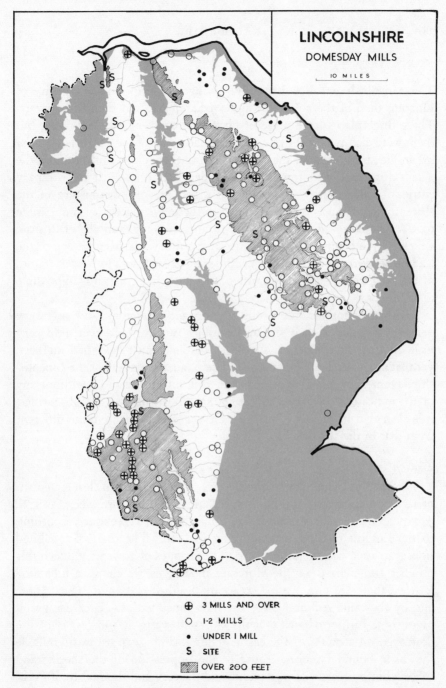

LINCOLNSHIRE

DOMESDAY MILLS

10 MILES

⊕ 3 MILLS AND OVER

○ 1-2 MILLS

• UNDER 1 MILL

S SITE

OVER 200 FEET

Fig. 18. Lincolnshire: Domesday mills in 1086.

The area of alluvium and peat is indicated; see Fig. 4. Rivers passing through these areas are not shown. Some villages with mills also had sites of mills, but these latter are not shown.

URBAN LIFE

The Lincolnshire folios begin by giving a description of the city of Lincoln, then of the royal borough of Stamford, and then of Torksey. These three places have pride of place in the survey of the county, but there were also two other places which had some of the characteristics of urban life; burgesses are mentioned at Grantham and Louth, though the details for these two towns are recorded later on amidst the ordinary entries for the county. Whether the urban life of Lincolnshire in the eleventh century was really restricted to these five places, it is impossible to say. The Domesday entries make no mention, for example, of Boston, which by the beginning of the thirteenth century had become one of the leading seaports in the kingdom. Either its growth was to be very rapid, or the king's commissioners omitted it from their record; it is impossible to say.

The figures for the five towns are very unsatisfactory, and only very general estimates of their size are possible. We are, moreover, told very little about their urban activities. All of them must have had markets, yet that at Louth alone is recorded. The other $5\frac{1}{2}$ markets of the Lincolnshire Domesday Book were in places without burgesses or without any of the indications of urban life (see p. 83). But whatever the obscurities, it is clear that in these five places there was a kind of life quite different from that in the surrounding villages.

Lincoln

The page and a half devoted to the city (*civitas*) gives no clear statement of its population (336–336b), but we are told that there were ' *T.R.E.* 970 inhabited messuages (*mansiones*). This number is reckoned according to the English method, 100 counting for 120.' The total of inhabited houses in 1066 was therefore 1,150. The changes of 20 years reduced this number somewhat; 'of the aforesaid messuages which were inhabited *T.R.E.*, there are now waste 200 by the English reckoning, that is 240; and by the same reckoning 760 are now inhabited'. A later paragraph gives some further details: 'Of the aforesaid waste messuages, 166 were destroyed on account of the castle. The remaining 74 are waste outside the castle boundary, not because of the oppression of the sheriffs and officers but by reason of misfortune and poverty and the ravage of fires.' This figure of 760 in 1086 gives a total of 900 messuages. The number of churches in the city is not clearly stated, but there seem to have been at least 4½ within the city as well as 2 recently built outside (see below).

It is impossible to be sure that the figure of 900 really included all the houses of the city in 1086.[1] A number of property-owners are mentioned by name, and some details are given about them because there was something special about them or some problem connected with their holding. Apparently they were all included in the total, but we cannot be absolutely certain. Despite the waste houses within the city, its limits were expanding; a certain Colsuen had recently built beyond the city-walls; 'outside the city (*extra civitatem*) he has 36 houses and 2 churches to which nothing belongs, which he built on the waste land that the king gave him, and that was never before built upon'. Sir Frank Stenton declares that these new houses almost certainly 'stood in the tract of low-lying land immediately to the south of the Witham'.[2] Presumably they must be added to the 900 houses within the city in order to obtain a complete picture of the settlement at Lincoln. It is interesting to note, incidentally, that an entry for Scotton (Corringham) says that in Lincoln there were 3 burgesses rendering 5s. (345b), and these were presumably additional.[3] The total of 939 houses and burgesses implies a population of between 4000 and 5000, or even more; Lincoln was one of the most important cities of the realm.

The Domesday account gives no explanation of what sustained and nourished this city. It tells us, it is true, that 'in the fields of Lincoln outside the city' there were 12½ carucates of land, and that, in addition, the bishop of Lincoln had 1 little manor with one carucate 'near the city'; there were also 100 acres of meadow. But many villages in the county had more than 13½ carucates, and they could not have supported a settlement of this size. We can only assume that the citizens of Lincoln lived largely by trading and its associated activities; the Domesday Book certainly mentions a mint rendering as much as £75, but that is all. The famous reference to the twelve lawmen (*lagemanni*) also provides a hint of the city as a centre of jurisdiction.[4]

---

[1] The total of 900 for 1086 (and that of 1,150 for 1066) has been calculated on the assumption that English reckoning (*anglico numero*) counted a whole 100 as 120 and then added the remainder.

[2] F. M. Stenton in C. W. Foster and T. Longley, *op. cit.* p. xxxiii.

[3] For the connection between some towns and nearby villages, see p. 251 below.

[4] Lawmen (*lagemanni*) are mentioned in the Domesday accounts of Lincoln, Stamford and Cambridge; the accounts of Chester and York mention judges.

Stamford

It is impossible to be clear about the size of Stamford (336b). There were six wards in the borough, 'five in Lincolnshire, and the sixth in Northamptonshire which is beyond the bridge'. But the sixth ward is not described in the Northamptonshire folios, unless the entry for *Portland* refers to it (219b).[1] The five Lincolnshire wards had, in 1066, '141 messuages which used to render all customs'. They were still there in 1086 'except 5 which are waste on account of the work of the castle (*propter opus castri sunt wastae*)'. But these were not the only messuages (*mansiones*); there were also 278½ others and one waste messuage held by various people, including the king himself; 77 of these were 'messuages of sokemen'. This makes a total of 414½ in 5 wards; if the sixth ward was as large as the others, the whole township must have included nearly 500 inhabited messuages and also at least 6 waste messuages. Furthermore, an entry for Uffington (Ness) nearby mentions 9 burgesses at Stamford who rendered 4s. (385), and these were presumably additional.[2] All this implies a population of between 2000 and 3000 or more. Stamford was clearly one of the most important of the midland towns in 1086.

As in the case of Lincoln there is little clue to the activities of this population. What detail is given is meagre enough. Seventy messuages belonging to the king had 2½ carucates of land (*carucatae terrae*), 'and 1 ploughing team (*caruca arans*), and 45 acres of meadow outside the vill'.[3] The king also had '600 acres of arable land outside the vill in Lincolnshire'. Then there was another half-carucate, and there were mills, one rendering 40s., another rendering 30s., and two halves, one of which rendered 15s. Four churches are also mentioned. Like Lincoln, the borough contained lawmen (*lagemanni*), and this fact provides a hint of the town as a centre of jurisdiction. But these items of information are mere stray fragments, the by-product of other information. There is no mention, for example, of a market, and yet we know that one existed here in earlier times, for it is mentioned in a charter of 972.[4] Standing where the Great North Road crossed the Welland, Stamford was in a favourable position for trading, but on this matter the Domesday entries are absolutely silent.

[1] *V.C.H. Northamptonshire* (London, 1902), I, pp. 277–8 and 304.

[2] For the connection between some towns and the surrounding villages, see p. 251 below. Some holdings in Stamford 'belonged' to Rutland, others to Hambleton in Rutland. [3] And 12 acres in *Portland*.

[4] W. de G. Birch, *Cartularium Saxonicum* (London, 1893), III, p. 580.

Torksey

The Witham and the Trent are connected by the Foss Dyke, an artificial channel 7 miles long constructed by the Romans.[1] It leaves the Witham at Lincoln, and joins the Trent at Torksey, now a small village with only about 200 inhabitants but with the ruins of a castle. It was in its location that the early importance of Torksey lay, and its fortunes were, of course, very susceptible to the state of the waterways upon which it depended, and in particular to any obstruction in the Foss Dyke.

In 1066 there were 215 burgesses in Torksey (337). The Domesday account describes some of their obligations thus: 'If the king's messengers should come hither, the men of the same town should conduct them to York with their ships and their means of navigation, and the sheriff should find the messengers' and sailors' food.' By 1086, 111 messuages were waste, and there were only '102 burgesses dwelling there', which implies a total population of 500 or so, probably more. It may be that the decline was due to some obstruction in the Foss Dyke; at any rate, we hear of its being cleared in 1121. The king held both Torksey and 'the manor of Hardwick adjoining it'. There were 2 carucates outside the town, and 20 acres of meadow, 60 acres of underwood and 11 fisheries. Both Torksey and Hardwick were valued together at £18 in 1066 and £30 in 1086—an increase which is surprising in view of the decayed condition of the town. Not only were Torksey and Hardwick thus grouped together, but both were connected fiscally with Lincoln. When geld was levied upon Lincoln, Torksey and Hardwick together contributed one-fifth, Torksey's share being two-thirds and Hardwick's share one-third. Obviously the connection was close, but there are no details of the traffic that passed along the Foss Dyke. We know that in pre-Domesday times Torksey had a mint, but the Domesday Book makes no mention of this, or of the other activities of this little inland port, or of any church.[2]

Grantham

In 1066 there were 111 burgesses and '77 tofts of the sokemen of the thanes (*Toftes sochmanorum teignorum*)' in Grantham (337b). The meaning of this latter phrase is obscure; in any case, the same number was likewise

[1] See C. W. Phillips, 'The Present State of Archaeology in Lincolnshire', *Arch. Journ.* (1934), XCI, p. 117.
[2] See F. M. Stenton in C. W. Foster and T. Longley, *op. cit.* p. xxxv.

there in 1086 when the king held the town. In addition to these, there were 72 bordars. This would make a total recorded population of 260. Although not one of the three towns that prefaced the Domesday account of Lincolnshire, it was obviously a place of considerable size with a population of at least 1,200. It was assessed at 12 carucates. The information about plough-lands and teams is confused, but it looks as if at least a few teams were there in 1086, although we are specifically told that there was no arable land 'outside the vill'. Still, 3 teams had been there in 1066, and at least one remained in 1086. There were 8 acres of meadow and 4 mills rendering 12s.; a church is also mentioned. But many other things must have been there as well. All we can say is that Grantham was a settlement lying on the Great North Road, probably a trading settlement, at any rate quite a different settlement from the surrounding villages of Kesteven.

Louth

Louth seems to have been a smaller township (345). It was held by the bishop of Lincoln and assessed at 12 carucates; and there was land for 12 teams. The bishop had 3 teams in demesne, and the population comprised 80 burgesses, 40 sokemen and 2 villeins—which imply a total population of at least 600. These men had 13 teams between them, and 2 knights (*milites*) also had 2 teams, making a grand total of 18 teams. There was a market rendering 29s., and 13 mills rendering 13s., together with 21 acres of meadow and 400 acres of woodland for pannage. We are also told that Louth was '1 league and 8 furlongs in length and 10 furlongs in breadth' though it is difficult to see what these dimensions implied.[1] Its value had increased from £12 in 1066 to £22 in 1086. No church is mentioned, which is surprising. All this is not very much to go on, but it is enough to show that Louth was a mixture of town and village, and that it stood out as the main settlement of the Wolds and the area around in the eleventh century.

[1] See pp. 46–7 above.

MISCELLANEOUS INFORMATION
Markets

The entries relating to markets are seven in number:

(1) Thealby, Derby and Burton upon Stather (Manley): half a market belonging to (*pertinet ad*) Kirton in Lindsey (338b).
(2) Louth (Louthesk): 1 market rendering 29*s*. (345).
(3) Bolingbroke (Bolingbroke): a new market (351).
(4) Spalding (Elloe): a market; '40 shillings' is interlined above (351b).
(5) Barton upon Humber (Yarborough): 1 market (354b).
(6) Partney (Candleshoe): a market rendering 10*s*. (355).
(7) Threekingham (Aveland): a market (*forum*) rendering 40*s*. (356).

Of these places, only Louth had burgesses or other signs of town life, though at Barton upon Humber there was a ferry which must have been a factor in its commercial activity. It is impossible to say in which of the three places in the first entry the half-market was situated, nor is there any record of the other half. In the first six places the word market is a translation of *mercatum*, but at Threekingham, the word *forum* was used; perhaps 'fair' would be a more accurate translation, and Threckingham certainly had a large and well-known fair in later times. The seven entries form a meagre list, made all the more mysterious by the absence of any reference to markets at Lincoln, Stamford, Torksey and Grantham.

Ferries

The entries relating to ferries are seven in number, and they refer to six places:

(1) Great Grimsby (Bradley): the customs and the ferry render 40*s*. (343).
(2) Great Grimsby and Swallow (Bradley): 1 ferry rendering 5*s*. (363).
(3) Lea (Corringham): 1 ferry rendering 12*d*. (347).
(4) South Ferriby (Yarborough): 1 ferry rendering 60*s*. (354).
(5) South Ferriby (Yarborough): 1 ferry rendering £3 (354b).
(6) Winteringham (Manley): 1 ferry rendering 13*s*. (354b).
(7) Barton on Humber (Yarborough): a ferry rendering £4 (354b).

The ferry in the second entry must have been at Great Grimsby because Swallow is situated up in the Wolds. The location of all of them is understandable enough. Winteringham, South Ferriby and Barton were crossing places on the Humber; that at Lea must have been across the Trent; the ones at Great Grimsby must have been in connection with the sea, though we are told nothing of the early port of Grimsby beyond the fact that there was a new toll there (376). Like the list of markets, it is meagre.

Tolls

The section on 'disputes' at the end of the Lincolnshire survey contains a few meagre references to the trade of the small ports and havens on the east coast:

1. 'In Saltfleet Haven and in Mare and in Swine [Louthesk] a new toll has been established, and Ansger of Skidbrook [nearby] has taken it, and Raynald and Humphrey and Geoffrey also; and the wapentake of Louthesk says, and the whole South Riding also, that this toll did not exist *T.R.E.* . . . Archil of Withern testifies that he saw Ansger receive the toll in respect of 24 ships from Hastings' (375 b).

2. 'In Saltfleet [Louthesk] Hugh the serjeant takes the customs of ships which come there, whether it is admitted or not, which custom did not exist *T.R.E.*' (375 b).

3. 'In Barton upon Humber and South Ferriby [Yarborough] Gilbert de Gand's men take another toll than they took *T.R.E.* in respect of bread, fish, hides, and very many other things, for which nothing was ever given *T.R.E.*' (375 b). It was Gilbert de Gand who held the ferry rendering £4 (see above).

4. 'Ralph de Mortemer's men and Losoard's men take a new toll in Great Grimsby [Bradley] which did not exist *T.R.E.*; but Losoard denies that his men took it on his account' (376). It was Ralph de Mortemer who held the ferry at Great Grimsby and Swallow (see above).

Apart from these, the only other tolls mentioned were those at Lincoln, Stamford and Torksey.

Iron-works

There are three entries relating to iron-works and iron-workers:

(1) Stow in Well (344): 3 iron-works (*ferrarie*).
(2) Castle Bytham in Beltisloe (360b): 3 iron-workers' shops (*fabricas ferri*) rendering 40s. and 8d.
(3) Little Bytham in Beltisloe (360b): an iron-worker's shop (*fabrica ferri*) rendering 40s.

It is impossible to obtain any idea of the scope of the activities implied by these entries. None of the three places is on iron-stone outcrops and it is unlikely that the entries imply the smelting of iron ore.[1] They must

---

[1] I am indebted to Professor S. H. Beaver for information about the iron deposits of Lincolnshire.

therefore have meant the working-up of iron by the forging of iron smelted elsewhere, and in the Bytham area a plentiful supply of wood was certainly available for this purpose; the two entries themselves mention wood. The area around Stow was not well wooded, but even so there was a little wood in the neighbourhood.

Horse provender

Four entries include a mention of provision for horses (*ad victum equorum*) together with its value. The places are Hough on the Hill, 50s. (347b); Brant Broughton, 50s. (347b); Fulbeck and Leadenham, 100s. (347b); and Long Bennington, 100s. (348). All five places are situated in the wapentake of Loveden, and the entries may simply reflect some idiosyncrasy in the returns for that wapentake.

Other references

There is a solitary reference to a warren for hares (*warenna leporum*) at Gelston in Loveden (347b). There is another solitary reference to half a shearing house (*dimidiam laninam*) at Stallingborough in Yarborough (340). There is also one reference to sheep; *Sudtone*, in Gartree, was held by Gilbert de Gand and we are told that 'Gilbert has a flock of sheep there' (354b). There were castles at Lincoln and at Stamford (336b).

REGIONAL SUMMARY

This regional description is intended to supplement the account of the main items of information that the Domesday Book records. The regions number fourteen (Fig. 19); their boundaries are very largely artificial for the reasons indicated on p. 55. Other boundaries, equally valid, could no doubt be drawn, but at any rate the account which follows represents one attempt to assemble the Domesday information against the background of the physical variations in the county.

(1) *The Wolds*

The Wolds form an upland of some 45 miles long and from 5 to 8 miles wide. This upland is essentially a dissected chalk plateau bordered by a steep escarpment on the west that rises to a height of 548 ft. south of Caistor. Southwards, the scarp becomes lower and less pronounced, and it is broken by springs and by a number of small streams flowing into either the Ancholme or the Witham. To the east, the dip slope is much dissected by streams that flow eastwards to reach the North Sea. In the south, the plateau surface is much broken by the various tributaries of the Steeping which flow south-eastwards and which have cut down through the chalk to the underlying clays and sandstones. In places, the chalk is covered by glacial deposits—by sands and gravels and particularly by Boulder Clay.

Despite their fundamentally uniform character, the Wolds have different characteristics in the north, the centre and the south. The northern Wolds are comparatively devoid of Boulder Clay and have few streams and valleys. Today, as in Domesday times, villages are relatively scarce. The central Wolds have a more complicated relief. The western scarp is less steep; the dip slope is more broken by watercourses; and the countryside is more varied. Villages are more numerous, and are to be found nestling in the valleys beneath the bare Wolds above. This variety is further emphasised in the southern Wolds, where the chalk has disappeared over considerable areas, and where the villages lie particularly thick along the southern edge, and in the valleys of the Steeping basin.

Today, the Wolds form very largely an arable area, but before their enclosure in the late eighteenth and early nineteenth centuries, much of the land was given over to sheep walk, warren and gorse.[1] It is difficult to think back from this evidence to its condition in Domesday times. The landscape of the Wolds during the intervening years has still to be delineated. But it is clear that the Domesday density of plough-teams and of population was highest in the south—on alluvial strips in the basin of the Steeping and along the southern edge generally. It is also clear that the northern Wolds had both fewer villages and fewer teams, and that the central Wolds to the west of Louth, where Arthur Young was to note so many warrens, had likewise a relatively low density of teams and population. Some indication of the agriculture carried on in the valleys that broke the surface of the Wolds is furnished by the distribution of Domesday mills. They were strung along the Hatcliffe Beck, the Lud, the Withern Eau, and, of course, along the Steeping streams. Whatever may have been the condition of the high Wolds, the valleys were obviously cultivated.

Taken as a whole, the Wolds carried but little woodland, and their meadowland was likewise small in amount; what little meadow there was,

[1] Arthur Young, *General view of the agriculture of the county of Lincoln* (London, 1799), *passim*.

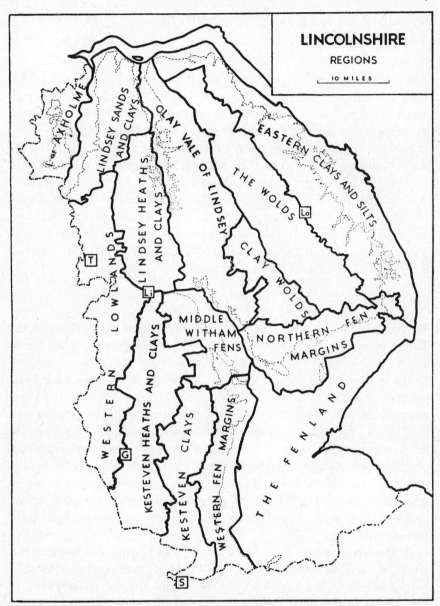

LINCOLNSHIRE

REGIONS

10 MILES

AXHOLME

LINDSEY SANDS AND CLAYS

CLAY VALE OF LINDSEY

LINDSEY HEATHS AND CLAYS

EASTERN CLAYS AND SILTS

THE WOLDS

CLAY WOLDS

T

Li

WESTERN LOWLANDS

MIDDLE WITHAM FENS

NORTHERN FEN MARGINS

Lo

KESTEVEN HEATHS AND CLAYS

KESTEVEN CLAYS

WESTERN FEN MARGINS

THE FENLAND

G

S

Fig. 19. Lincolnshire: Regional subdivisions.

The limits of these regions are defined by means of parish boundaries; see p. 55 above. Places with burgesses are indicated by initials: G, Grantham; Li, Lincoln; Lo, Louth; S, Stamford; T, Torksey. The boundary of alluvium and peat is shown; see Fig. 4.

lay in the south, along the upper reaches of the streams that drained into the Bain and Steeping.

(2) *The Clay Wolds*

The south-western part of the Wolds is covered by chalky Boulder Clay through which run the Bain and its tributaries. The elevation of much of the region—rising to well over 300 ft.—links it with the Wolds proper; its clay soil links it with the Clay Vale of Lindsey to the west. It forms a distinct area between the two; its Domesday density of teams and population was higher than that of the Wolds proper and was comparable with conditions in the Steeping valley. The Bain valley, too, was marked by mills and by an abundance of meadow. Woodland was absent from the higher areas, but in the lower areas—in the villages of the Bain valley below Horncastle—there were considerable quantities of wood that adjoined the wooded areas of the Clay Vale of Lindsey to the east, and the woodlands of the Fen margin to the south.

(3) *Eastern Clays and Silts*

Between the Wolds and the sea is a belt of country extending from Barton upon Humber to Burgh le Marsh. For the most part, it lies below 100 ft., and includes two types of land at different levels known respectively as the 'Middle Marsh' and the 'Marsh'. Both types have been grouped together because the parishes very frequently extend to the coast across both kinds of soil. The Middle Marsh, sometimes known as the 'Clays', forms a zone some 3–6 miles wide flanking the Wolds. It lies between 20 and 100 ft. above sea-level, and consists of an undulating Boulder Clay surface varied occasionally by patches of glacial sands and gravels. At one place, south of Grimsby, this Boulder Clay zone broadens to reach the coast. The 'Marsh' proper is a coastal belt of silt lying almost entirely below 20 ft., and, of course, draining has done much to give it its present character.

In Domesday times, the density of teams and population was, on the whole, somewhat lower than on the Wolds. It was highest where the belt of Boulder Clay was widest, in the neighbourhood of Grimsby. It was lowest in the south, where there was still much woodland. Here, between Louth and Alford, was one of the three main tracts of woodland in Domesday Lincolnshire, and intermittent stretches of wood are also to be found here today. Meadow was generally abundant throughout the whole region, and some villages had very considerable quantities. Mills were frequent but not abundant. A distinctive feature of the area was its salt-pans; the village of Fulstow alone had 25, and salt-making must have been an important activity in the life of the marsh villages. Much of the area, particularly along the coast, must have been very marshy, but, as Fig. 14 shows, the Domesday record is practically silent about this.

(4) *The Clay Vale of Lindsey*

To the west of the Wolds lies the Clay Vale of Lindsey, a depression in the Oxford and Kimmeridge Clays through which run the Ancholme to the Humber and the Langworth to the Witham; the watershed between the northward and southward flowing streams is only about 50 ft. above sea-level. The depression is covered over much of its surface by glacial sands, gravels and Boulder Clay. In the north, there are considerable stretches of blown sand along the foot of the Wold escarpment, and the parishes extend from the Wolds, across the Boulder Clay and sands, down to the Ancholme marshes or 'carrs'. Place-names and other names in this locality frequently include the element 'moor' which is indicative of the condition of the sandy stretches. In the southern area, Boulder Clay is extensive, with villages along the streams that run through it.

Today, both areas have intermixed arable and grassland; but, as might be expected, both areas had a low team density in Domesday times. The density in the Boulder Clay area might have been higher but for a considerable quantity of woodland; here was one of the most heavily wooded areas in Domesday Lincolnshire, and the density of population was lower than to the north. This southern area had a little meadow, well distributed over its surface, but the main area of meadow was to be found in the villages bordering the Ancholme valley, and the meadows themselves were presumably located in the Ancholme carrs. Mills were fairly frequent. In the south, along the border of the Middle Witham fens, there were fisheries.

(5) *Lindsey Sands and Clays*

Blown sand forms an important element in the landscape and economy of this region. The sand covers much both of Oolitic Limestone and of Boulder Clay, and gives a distinctive character to the area. It is not surprising that in Domesday times it was a region of comparatively few teams per square mile, especially in the south, where the density was not much above one, compared with over two per square mile on, say, the Wolds; mills were not very abundant. Its population was likewise but thinly scattered. The villages of the area had only small amounts of meadow—usually under 100 acres; where there was more, it most probably lay in the marsh to the west and north and east. The region had a little wood, but this was almost entirely *silva minuta* (underwood). Today there is a considerable stretch of woodland to the east of Scunthorpe, but this is the result of recent afforestation upon the sandy soil.

(6) *The Isle of Axholme*

The distinction between the island itself and the surrounding lowland was even more important before the drainage and warping of the seventeenth and later centuries. The island proper is about 12 miles long and from 2 to 4 miles wide, and it rises to a height of 133 ft. It is formed for the most part of Keuper Marls covered in places by drift and blown sand, and its soil is largely a clay loam. Around the island is an expanse of silt with areas of peat in the west. This low-lying area in Domesday times must have been a fenny tract of little value; the Domesday entry briefly says 'to this island belong marsh lands (*maresc*) 10 leagues in length and 3 in breadth' (369b); what exactly is implied by this we cannot say, except that the marsh was evidently of considerable extent. For the wapentake as a whole, the density of teams and population was very low. There was some wood on the island itself, but its villages contained only very small amounts of meadow.

(7) *Lindsey Heaths and Clays*

To the west of the Clay Vale of Lindsey are the Oolitic Limestone heights that extend from north to south throughout the county, broken only by the gaps at Lincoln and Ancaster. The features of the belt are particularly clear to the north of Lincoln; the country is for the most part over 100 ft. above sea-level, and the escarpment itself (known as the 'Cliff' or 'Edge') rises to just over 200 ft. with a sharp drop on the west and a more gentle slope to the east. Along the western edge, at the junction of the limestone with the underlying clays, there are a series of springs and a line of villages whose parish territories extend west-east from clayland to limestone. On the eastward slope, a series of similar west-east villages stretches from limestone to clay and so to the Ancholme marshes. The limestone belt is commonly called the Heath. Before the enclosures and improvements of the latter part of the eighteenth and early nineteenth centuries, this belt, like that of the Wolds, was largely a zone of heaths, sheep-walks and rabbit warrens.

It is impossible to differentiate between the condition of the limestone and clay areas in Domesday times; the group of parishes extending across both must be taken as a whole. In density of population and of teams, the region was similar to the Wolds. There were comparatively few mills in the area, and these were in the east, on the tributaries of the Ancholme and Langworth. Like the Wold area it was a district without woodland, but its villages included a considerable amount of meadow—situated presumably on the clay areas on either side of the Heath.

(8) *Kesteven Heaths and Clays*

The Heath country of Kesteven is a continuation of that in Lindsey to the north of Lincoln. The limestone escarpment is likewise known as the 'Cliff', and here also is a double line of villages separated by a belt of Oolitic Limestone that was formerly a tract of heath, warrens and sheep runs. It, too, has undergone a great transformation as a result of enclosure and improvement in the eighteenth and early nineteenth centuries. The soil of the limestone belt is light and thin; the eastern parishes stretch on to Boulder Clay, and those on the west to the Liassic clays and alluvium of the Trent valley. For the most part, we can only guess at the state of the countryside in Domesday times, and the guessing is not made easier by the fact that each parish includes such diverse soils. The densities of teams and population in the group of parishes as a whole resemble those on the Wolds and on the similar country to the north of Lincoln. In the south of the area, several clusters of mills mark the course of the upper Witham. There was a fair sprinkling of meadowland, particularly in the north, and this meadow must have been located on the clay portions of the parishes. But whether limestone or clay, the northern parishes were almost bare of woodland; on the more extensive claylands of the south, however, there were outliers of the extensive woodland to the east.

(9) *The Western Lowlands*

Along the western border of the county lies an undulating lowland, drained by the upper Witham, by its tributary, the Brant, and by smaller streams that flow westward to join the Trent. The area as a whole is one of Liassic clays, but there are considerable tracts of alluvium, sands and gravels that mark the former courses of streams. The southern part of the belt is higher and better drained, and it is richer both in Domesday teams and in population; here, too, mill clusters are most frequent—along the upper Witham and its tributaries. Northwards, in the wapentakes of Graffoe, Well and Corringham, these densities drop to nearly one-half. For the villages of the northern area there were a number of entries of wood and underwood, and stretches of woodland are also found here today; 'the old gravel spreads are sometimes marked by poor soil with much wood—as to the south-west of Lincoln and on the old moorland stretch, now wooded, of Stapleford Moor'.[1] Meadow was frequent throughout the area as might be expected from the numerous streams that cross it.

(10) *Kesteven Clays*

The dominant characteristic of the surface of this region is its clay (Boulder Clay and Oxford Clay), although there are also areas of lighter soils. Water and streams are plentiful, and villages are scattered throughout the area without that marked parallelism of parish boundaries which is such a feature of so many other parts of Lincolnshire. The fertility of the claylands in Domesday times was reflected in a high density of teams and population per square mile, especially in the northern portion, although there was an unexplained low density in the wapentake of Flaxwell to the north of Sleaford. In the south, the density was lower than in the north, for here was to be found a considerable amount of woodland. This still is the most wooded part of Kesteven. Mills were not frequent in the area except in the extreme south along the Glen and the Welland. Most of the villages of the belt had some meadow, but the greatest amounts of meadow were to be found where there was least wood, in the lower area (below 200 ft.) towards Sleaford.

(11) *Northern Fen Margins*

This region includes those parishes whose territory extends from the Wolds into the Fenland. It also includes the territory of the new townships formed in 1812 as a result of the drainage of the East Fen, West Fen and Wildmore Fen. The area covered by these new townships is indicated on Fig. 8 and has been excluded from the calculation of the densities within the region. This must mean some inaccuracy, but, in view of the 'drowned'

[1] L. Dudley Stamp, *The Land of Britain: Parts 76–7, Lincolnshire* (London, 1942), p. 505.

condition of these Fens in pre-drainage times, the inaccuracy cannot be very great, certainly not great enough to affect the general picture as here given.

There is a great contrast between the eastern and western portions of this marginal area. The eastern area (stretching through the wapentakes of Candleshoe and Bolingbroke) rises quickly to over 200 ft. and is largely a land of clays together with some Greensand and small patches of gravel. It was not, generally speaking, as densely peopled as the Wolds behind nor did it carry as many plough-teams to the square mile. But still it compared quite favourably with the county as a whole. It carried hardly any wood, and comparatively little meadow, except in the extreme east where it merged into the coastal marsh belt. Curiously enough, no fisheries are recorded here, though it is inconceivable that there were not some fisheries in Bolingbroke and Candleshoe. Only occasional villages had mills.

The western area (in the wapentake of Horncastle), on the other hand, stands out as a poor area. Here, in the neighbourhood of Tattershall, there is a flat expanse of gravel and sand lying well below 100 ft. and for the most part below 50 ft. Today, a large part of it is poor woodland or heath, and in Domesday times it carried on every square mile only one-half the plough-teams and population of the adjoining land to the east. Its villages, however, had this in common with those to the east—they contained very little meadow. But, on the other hand, they carried a good deal of woodland, very often in places where we find most woodland today. The proximity of the area to the Fenland is reflected by the presence of fisheries; Horncastle had as many as seventeen worth 19s. 2d. Only occasional villages had mills.

(12) *The Middle Witham Fens*

The parish boundaries of the Middle Witham area show a striking arrangement. The parishes stretch in parallel strips from the upland of clay and limestone across to the peat Fenland. These fens now comprise some of the most fertile land in the county, but before the improvements of the eighteenth century they formed a swampy area of little value. Any average densities for the district as a whole must be misleading. On Figs. 8 and 10 the densities of plough-teams and population for the fen area would be about nil, while those for the upland would therefore be nearly double the averages for the region as a whole. There was but little wood, the most outstanding entry being 150 acres of wood at Potter Hanworth. The amounts of meadow were likewise small apart from the 470 acres that were entered for Metheringham. There were some fisheries here, but not nearly as many as might be expected. Mills were likewise infrequent.

(13) *Western Fen Margins*

Like the Northern Fen Margins and the area of the Middle Witham, this is an area where the parishes stretch from the upland down to the Fenland. The surface of the upland consists mainly of Boulder Clay, but there are also gravels and other soils. The Fenland includes a narrow strip of peat flanking the upland, with silt beyond. The densities of Domesday plough-teams and population, like those of the border areas, are misleading; the most one can say is that they are roughly intermediate between those of the Fenland proper and those of the upland. The villages of the area had small amounts of meadow, never above 200 acres. The northern part of the belt had very little wood, but in the south there was a great deal of woodland which adjoined the well-wooded area of the Kesteven clays to the west. A little marsh was recorded in the extreme north, and there were also some fishing centres; Bourne had as many as 30 fisheries yielding 6s. and 2,500 eels. But the references to both marsh and fisheries are only a fraction of what must have existed there. There were several mills situated on the streams that cross the region to the Fenland in the east.

(14) *The Fenland*

The Fenland of Lincolnshire, like that of Norfolk, is roughly coincident with the belt of silt that separates the peatlands of Cambridgeshire from the sea. It also includes three separate tracts of peat, but only one of these comes in the district as here defined, and that is in the south, in the wapentake of Holland. Along this silt belt, a line of Domesday villages stretched from the Wolds of Lincolnshire to the uplands of Norfolk. It is impossible to say where the coast was, but it probably ran not far from the line of villages; there is no evidence that the so-called Roman sea-bank was Roman in age.[1] The present-day parishes of the silt belt stretch in narrow bands across it from the Wash to the peat in the interior.

Although more prosperous than the peat area to the south, the silt belt was still a poor country in Domesday times. The low density of plough-

[1] C. W. Phillips, 'The Present State of Archaeology in Lincolnshire, Part II', *Arch. Journ.* (1934), XCI, pp. 123–4.

teams and population in the three wapentakes of Elloe, Kirton and Skirbeck and of the southern part of Candleshoe, stand in contrast with the
later medieval prosperity of the area, and with its present-day wealth.[1]
Not all the Fenland was equally poor; the wapentake of Skirbeck, to the
north of Boston, was the most intensively occupied, and it seems to have
been as prosperous as some infertile upland areas. The particularly low
densities for Elloe are due to the waterlogged nature of its southern portion. Despite its villages, the silt belt was a watery country. Contrary to
expectation, however, there was little meadow there. Fleet, it is true, had
500 acres of meadow, and four other villages had between 100 and
200 acres each, but the remaining villages were either without meadow or
with only small amounts. The belt, as might be expected, had no wood,
apart from one 'wood of alders' at Spalding and another unspecified
'wood' at Tydd. Fisheries were recorded for 8 villages, but there is no
reference to marsh comparable to that entered for the Isle of Axholme.
There were, however, many references to salt-pans, and it is evident that
salt-making was an important and characteristic occupation in the area.
As might be expected from the gradients of the district, no mills were
recorded, except for a solitary one rendering 10s. at Fishtoft.

BIBLIOGRAPHICAL NOTE

(1) There were two nineteenth-century translations of the Domesday text
relating to Lincolnshire:

WILLIAM BAWDWEN, *Dom Boc: A Translation of the Record called Domesday*
(Doncaster, 1809). This covered the counties of Derby, Nottingham,
Rutland, Lincoln, York, and parts of the counties of Lancaster, West-
morland and Cumberland.

CHARLES GOWEN SMITH, *A Translation of that portion of Domesday Book which
relates to Lincolnshire and Rutlandshire* (London, 1870).

These two nineteenth-century translations were superseded by C. W. Foster
and T. Longley's *The Lincolnshire Domesday and the Lindsey Survey* (Lincoln
Record Society, 1924). This edition is extremely valuable for its introduction
by F. M. Stenton and for the careful identification of the difficult place-names
of Lincolnshire. Any student of the Lincolnshire Domesday must owe a very
great debt to the volume. It has formed the basis of the present chapter.

[1] See H. C. Darby, *The Medieval Fenland*, pp. 119 *et seq.*

(2) Three works by F. M. Stenton discuss, amongst other things, various aspects of the Lincolnshire evidence:

Types of Manorial Structure in the Northern Danelaw (Oxford, 1908).
Documents Illustrative of the Social and Economic History of the Danelaw (British Academy, London, 1920).
'The free peasantry of the northern Danelaw', *Bulletin de la Société Royale des lettres de Lund, 1925–6* (Lund, 1926), pp. 73–185.

Doubts about the Scandinavian origin of sokemen are set out in: (1) R. H. C. Davis, 'East Anglia and the Danelaw', *Trans. Roy. Hist. Soc.* (1955), 5th Ser. vol. v, pp. 23–39; (2) P. H. Sawyer, 'The density of the Danish settlements', *Birmingham Hist. Journ.*, (1958), v, pp. 1–17.

The following papers may also be mentioned:

W. O. MASSINGBERD, 'The Lincolnshire Sokemen', *Eng. Hist. Rev.* (1905), XX, pp. 699–703.
H. C. DARBY, 'Domesday Woodland in Lincolnshire', *The Lincolnshire Historian* (Lincoln, 1948), I, pp. 55–9.

(3) The Lindsey Survey (1115–18) was first printed by T. Hearne in his edition of the Black Book of the Exchequer, *Liber niger scaccarii* (Oxford, 1728; 2nd edit., London, 1771; reprinted 1774), 2 vols. It has been translated three times:

R. E. C. WATERS, *A roll of the owners of land in the parts of Lindsey in Lincoln-shire, compared with the Domesday survey of Lindsey* (Lincoln, 1883). This was reprinted from the *Associated Architectural Societies' Reports and Papers* (Lincoln, 1882), XVI.
JAMES GREENSTREET, *The Lincolnshire Survey, temp. Henry I* (London, 1884).
And, thirdly in C. W. Foster and T. Longley's edition of the Lincolnshire Domesday (Lincoln, 1924). This last translation is authoritative, and the place-name identifications are particularly valuable.

The date of the survey was determined by J. H. Round in *Feudal England*, pp. 181–95, which discusses it at length.

CHAPTER III

NORFOLK

The Domesday folios relating to Norfolk are of especial interest for two reasons. In the first place, the county of Norfolk, like the counties of Suffolk and Essex, is described in the so-called Little Domesday Book which is more detailed than the main survey. The Little Domesday Book gives, for example, details about the stock on the demesne, or home farm, of the lord of the manor. It also gives details about population and other matters for 1066 as well as for 1086; figures for an intermediate date are also frequently given. It is, in fact, much less of a summary than the main Domesday Book, and for this reason its information cannot fail to be of peculiar interest.

But this more detailed information is not without its drawbacks. The entries of the Little Domesday Book are more cumbrous and untidy than those of the main Domesday Book. They give the impression of being more hastily compiled. The comparatively neat and precise entries of the main survey do not tell us as much, but in some ways they are often less ambiguous, or at any rate they appear to be. J. H. Round suggested that the Little Domesday Book was the first volume to be compiled and that when the compilers saw how bulky their digest was becoming, they decided to summarise the information for the other counties in a simpler manner.[1] This view has been rejected by Professor Galbraith who thinks that 'instead of serving as an imperfect model for volume i, it may well be a local compilation made by the commission, and actually posterior to volume i'.[2] Whatever the reason for the more detailed treatment of these three counties, it is clear that the Little Domesday Book is nearer to

---

[1] J. H. Round, *Feudal England*, p. 141.

[2] V. H. Galbraith, *Eng. Hist. Rev.* LVII, p. 167: 'The eastern commissioners, we should then suppose, having to struggle with a region of notoriously intricate tenures, were so late with their return, that the Winchester scribes began without it: and when at last it did come, never bothered to revise or abbreviate it. On the other hand, Exon Domesday is in a more inchoate stage than volume ii of Domesday, which (apart from the details of the animals) has a general similarity to volume i. Little Domesday thus occupies a position intermediate between Exon Domesday and volume i, and it is tempting to explain it as the fair copy sent by the commission to Winchester, the original draft of which (corresponding to Exon Domesday) has disappeared.' See also p. 7 above.

the original returns, and it must therefore always present a particular
challenge to the Domesday student.

The second fact that lends a special interest to the Norfolk folios is
that there is an important subsidiary source of information. This is the
Inquisitio Eliensis, which gives particulars about the lands held or claimed

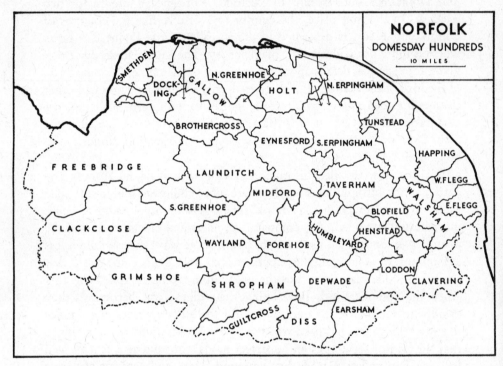

Fig. 20. Norfolk: Domesday hundreds.

The boundaries of the Broadland hundreds in the east of the county are particularly
arbitrary; modern maps show a number of areas where detached portions of parishes
were intermixed, so that it is impossible to draw any lines with accuracy.

by the Abbey of Ely in the six counties of Cambridge, Hertford, Essex,
Norfolk, Suffolk and Huntingdon.[1] Round argued that the information
about some of these counties was copied from the original returns of
the Domesday Commissioners while the information about others was
copied from the Little Domesday Book.[2] Into the latter category he put

[1] The edition of N. E. S. A. Hamilton (1876) is used in all the references that follow.
[2] J. H. Round, *op. cit.* pp. 137 *et seq.*

Norfolk, but this seems impossible, for the Norfolk section of the *I.E.* sometimes mentions names of people that are not in the Little Domesday Book. Moreover, it gives particulars about the village of Bergh Apton (Henstead) which do not appear in the Little Domesday Book.[1] It is clear then that the compilers of the *I.E.* must have had access to information other than that contained in the Little Domesday Book as we now know it. A draft return of the Little Domesday Book may have been revised to produce the *I.E.*, following the death of Abbot Symeon in 1093.[2] Generally speaking the correspondence between the two, as might be expected, is very great. But there are differences. The *I.E.* includes among the possessions of the abbey a number of estates which the Little Domesday Book attributed to other holders. Such monkish zeal is understandable, especially in view of the many disputes about land-ownership that followed the Norman settlement. What is more relevant to our purpose is that the statistics sometimes differ. This is not the place for an exhaustive collation, but a comparison of two sets of figures relating to the village of Cranwich in Grimshoe shows the kind of difference:

(*a*) *Little Domesday Book* (fo. 163)

...always 2 ploughs on the demesne, and 9 villeins and 5 bordars and 2 serfs; and 4 acres of meadow. Then and afterwards 4½ ploughs belonging to the men, now 3; and 2 ploughs on the demesne, half a mill and half a fishery....

(*b*) *Inquisitio Eliensis* (pp. 138–9)

...always 2 ploughs on the demesne, and 11 villeins, and 5 bordars and 2 serfs; and 2 acres of meadow; then and afterwards 4 ploughs belonging to the men, now 3½; and one mill; and half a fishery....

Sometimes, the three manuscripts of the *I.E.* are not all in agreement. In an entry relating to Mundford (Grimshoe), two manuscripts say 'then 3 men now 2' (p. 132), while the third agrees with the Little Domesday Book (213b) in saying 'then 3 ploughs belonging to the men now 2'. Another example of discrepancy and of the sort of slip that might easily

---

[1] *V.C.H. Norfolk* (London, 1906), II, p. 138. See p. 102 below. These objections do not 'destroy Round's main conclusion that the *Inquisitio Eliensis* was derived from *a* Domesday Book which was ninety per cent. identical with the existing Little Domesday. The true inference is, surely, that the *Inquisitio Eliensis* is based on an earlier version of volume II, something analogous perhaps to the Exon Domesday.' V. H. Galbraith, *op. cit.* p. 167.

[2] V. H. Galbraith, *The Making of Domesday Book* (Oxford, 1961), pp. 140–1.

occur in copying comes from Islington (Freebridge). The Little Domesday Book records amongst other things '18 sokemen with 17½ acres'
(213); the *I.E.*, on the other hand, records '18 sokemen with 17 acres of

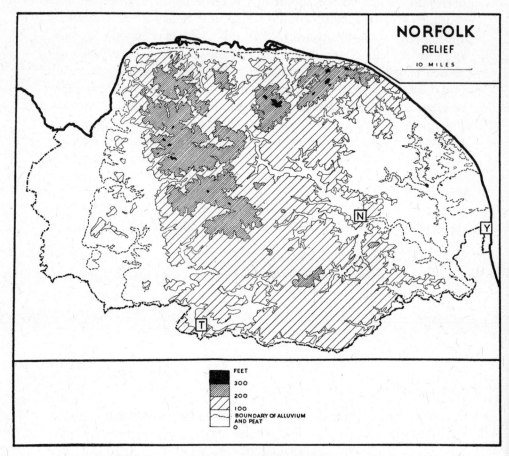

Fig. 21. Norfolk: Relief.
Places with Domesday burgesses are indicated by initials:
N, Norwich; T, Thetford; Y, Yarmouth.

land and half a plough' (p. 131). In this particular case, the latter entry
sounds more probable. For Cranwich, on the other hand, the Domesday
figures may well be the correct ones. We cannot tell. But in view of the
possible revision which produced the *I.E.* in the form in which we know

it, the statistics may not always be exactly comparable with those of the Little Domesday Book.[1]

There is one further consideration that must be mentioned. The Domesday county of Norfolk corresponds more or less with the modern county, but there are some differences along the border with Suffolk. Gorleston is surveyed under Suffolk (283, 283b, 284b), quite naturally because it was in Suffolk until quite recently. There is also reference in the Suffolk section to twenty-four fishermen in Yarmouth (283). Farther west, there is reference in the Suffolk folios to the Norfolk village of Gillingham (Clavering); and we are told that 'in Gillingham are 30 acres and 1 villein and half a plough (283b). Then again the reference in the Suffolk folios to one mill at 'Belingesfort' (436) may refer to the modern Billingford which appears in the Norfolk section under the name of 'Prelestuna', and which was known by its alternative names (Billingford or Pirleston) until quite recently. Farther west still, the main entry relating to the parish of Diss occurs under the heading of the adjoining hundred of Hartismere in Suffolk (282). Burston to the north of Diss is surveyed, on the other hand, under Norfolk, but we are told that it 'belongs to Diss in Suffolk and is there valued' (114). Thetford seems to have been partly in one county and partly in the other, but it is surveyed under Norfolk.[2] Some other places also seem to have belonged to both counties. The Norfolk village of Rushford[3] and the Suffolk village of Mendham[4] are described partly in one county and partly in the other, and it is interesting to note that until recently their parishes straddled the county boundary. Finally, there are some places in Suffolk that have entries in the Norfolk folios—Mildenhall, Knettishall and Rumburgh—but these will be referred to again.[5]

SETTLEMENTS AND THEIR DISTRIBUTION

The total number of separate places mentioned for Norfolk seems to be approximately 731. This figure, however, may not be quite accurate because today there are many instances of two or more adjoining villages bearing the same surname, and it is not always clear whether more than

[1] V. H. Galbraith, *The Making of Domesday Book*, p. 141.
[2] See p. 140 below.
[3] Rushford: Norfolk (214 *bis*, 270b); Suffolk (421).
[4] Mendham: Suffolk (310b, 329b, 349, 349b, 355b, 368, 379b); Norfolk (195b, 210b).   [5] See pp. 155 and 158 below.

one existed in the eleventh century. Only when there is specific mention of a second village in the Domesday Book itself, has it been included in the total of 728. Thus the existence of North and South Pickenham in the eleventh century is indicated by the mention of *Pichenham* and *Altera Pichenham*, of at least two Raynhams by the mention of *Reineham* and *Sut Reinham*, of two Snarehills (Great and Little) by the mention of *Snareshella* and *Alia Snareshella*, of two Meltons by the mention of *Meltuna* and *Parva Meltuna*. There is, on the other hand, no indication that, say, the Great and Little Massingham of today existed as separate villages. They may well have been separate, but the relevant Domesday entries refer merely to Massingham. The information about churches seems to suggest that some Domesday names may have covered two or more settlements.[1]

The total of 731 includes a number of places—between 20 and 25— about which very little information is given. The Domesday record may be incomplete, or, as we shall see, the relevant details may have been included with those of some other village. Thus we are told that *Rippetuna* (Rippon Hall) is included in the measurement (*mensura*) of the neighbouring vill of Hevingham (241 b), and that it rendered 5½d. for geld; but we are left to conjecture whether its men and ploughs, and wood and meadow (if any) are included in the totals of these items in Hevingham. Or again, the size and geld of the vill of Reepham are stated (247b); men (*homines*) are also mentioned, and we are told that they are valued (*appreciati*) in the neighbouring vill of Kerdiston, but we are not told how many they were or what were the resources of the place in which they lived. In the village of Colton, there were likewise 2 freemen with 30 acres that were included in the valuation (*pretio*) of Barnham Broom (166), but that is all we are told about Colton. There were holdings in many other localities that were 'valued' elsewhere.[2] *Snora* (Snore Hall in Fordham) is another example of an apparently incomplete entry; we are merely told that it had half a carucate worth 10s. (215b). The case of Pattesley is rather different. It was a manor of 2 carucates, with wood, with half a fishery and with stock. In 1066 there was a 'plough-team belonging to the men' there; by 1086 this had disappeared, but who the men were, and whether they too had disappeared, is something that the Domesday entry does not mention (256b). Perhaps the most interesting of all these problematical entries is that relating to Bergh Apton. On fo. 215 we are

---

[1] See p. 138 below. [2] See p. 119 below.

told that some sokemen and their property in *Torp* (unidentified) were valued in Bergh Apton (*Berc'*), but about Bergh Apton itself the Domesday Book is completely silent. Fortunately, it belonged to the monastery of Ely and, consequently, the *I.E.* tells us about its population, its ploughs, its meadow, its mill, its wood and its stock (p. 136). Were it not an Ely manor, we should have no idea of what it contained.[1] For the most part, however, these twenty or more problematical localities do not seem to have been very large places; maybe that is why they were so summarily treated.

Not all the 731 Domesday names appear as the names of villages on the present-day map of Norfolk. Some are represented by hamlets, by individual houses, or by the names of topographical features. Thus Bickerston is now a hamlet in Barnham Broom (Forehoe); Fodderstone is another in Shouldham Thorpe (Clackclose) and Toombes appears on the modern map as the name of a wood in that parish. The Domesday *Boielund* is represented by Boyland Hall in the parish of Morningthorpe (Depwade); and *Clipestuna* is represented by Clipstone House and Lower Clipstone in Croxton, which has itself been united with the adjoining parish of Fulmodeston (Gallow). Glosthorpe is hardly more than a name in the parish of Bawsey (Freebridge), and even Bawsey is now very decayed. Portions of some Domesday places have been devoured by the sea. The outstanding example is Shipden (North Erpingham), the predecessor of the modern Cromer. In 1086 it was a moderately substantial village with a recorded population of 17, with 4½ plough-teams at work, with 3 acres of meadow and with wood for 36 swine, but its site today lies out in the sea. Cromer is not mentioned in the Domesday Book, though its territory was presumably surveyed with that of Shipden. Its name was first recorded in 1262, and from then onwards it replaced Shipden until before 1500 the name Shipden had fallen out of use. It is said by some that the modern Blakeney bears a similar relation to the Domesday Snitterley (Holt). The Domesday village of Whimpwell (Happing), to the south of Happisburgh, has also disappeared though there is now a hamlet of Whimpwell Green in the parish. Portions of other parishes along the north Norfolk coast (e.g. Overstrand and Eccles) have likewise disappeared beneath the sea.[2] Finally, there is a very small category of

[1] For a comparison of the entries, see *V.C.H. Norfolk*, II, p. 138.
[2] For a summary see J. A. Steers, *The Coastline of England and Wales* (Cambridge, 1946), pp. 375–6.

Domesday names that remain unidentified or that cannot be identified with certainty, e.g. *Letha* in Blofield, and *Iarpestuna* and *Naruestuna* in Clavering. For the most part, these must have been very small settlements.

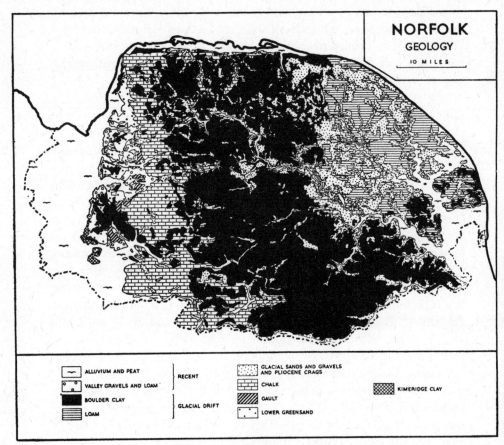

NORFOLK
GEOLOGY
10 MILES

ALLUVIUM AND PEAT	RECENT	GLACIAL SANDS AND GRAVELS AND PLIOCENE CRAGS
VALLEY GRAVELS AND LOAM		CHALK
BOULDER CLAY	GLACIAL DRIFT	GAULT
LOAM		LOWER GREENSAND

KIMERIDGE CLAY

Fig. 22. Norfolk: Surface geology.
Based on Geological Survey Quarter-Inch Sheets 12 and 16.

On the other hand, there are a number of villages on the modern map that are not mentioned in the Domesday Book. They are scattered here and there throughout the county, and their names do not appear until the twelfth and thirteenth centuries. Thus Irstead in Tunstead seems to have been first recorded about 1140, Geldeston (Clavering) in 1242, and

Needham (Earsham) not until as late as 1352.[1] Before these times their respective territories must have been surveyed with those of neighbouring villages. The most striking change has occurred in the Marshland part of

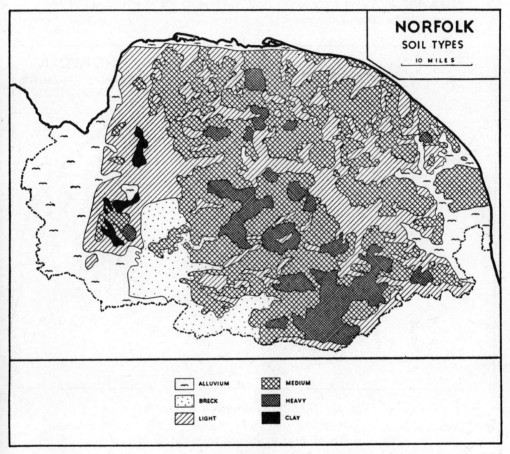

Fig. 23. Norfolk: Soil types.

Redrawn from the map in *An Economic Survey of Agriculture in the Eastern Counties of England*, p. viii (Heffer, Cambridge, 1932). This is Report No. 19 of the Farm Economics Branch of the Department of Agriculture in the University of Cambridge.

Freebridge hundred. Here, the names of the two new parishes of Emneth and Tilney are first recorded in 1170, and, more particularly, the Domesday

[1] The dates in this paragraph are taken from E. Ekwall, *The Concise Oxford Dictionary of English Place-Names*, 3rd ed. (Oxford, 1947).

localities of Terrington, Walpole and Wiggenhall each appear now as divided into a number of parishes named after their respective churches, e.g. Wiggenhall St Germans, St Mary the Virgin, St Peter, and St Mary Magdalen. Medieval documents bear witness to the colonisation of the marsh in post-Domesday times.

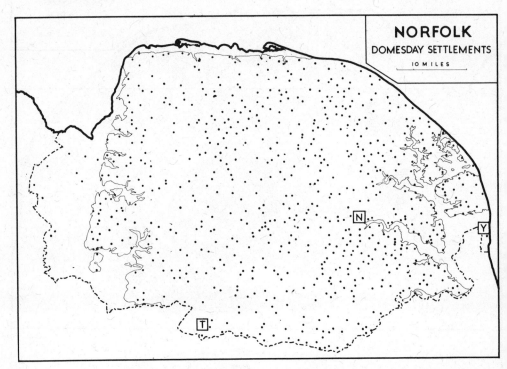

Fig. 24. Norfolk: Domesday place-names.

Places with burgesses are indicated by initials: N, Norwich; T, Thetford; Y, Yarmouth. The boundary of alluvium and peat is shown; see Fig. 22.

Despite the complications of extinct villages and additional villages, the fact remains that the distribution of Domesday names is remarkably similar to that of the present-day villages (Fig. 24). For the most part, the villages are scattered generally over the central upland, making full use of the river valleys that break its surface. There are no outstanding lines of villages as in Lincolnshire where the geological outcrops frequently resulted in linear arrangements of village sites. Generally speaking, villages are fewer on the light soils of the west of the county, and are especially few in the Fenland. What villages there were in the Fenland were all on the silt area, and, as we have seen, they are more numerous now than they were in Domesday times. The peat area was devoid of villages apart from those of Hilgay and Southery situated on an island in the peat. On the marshes of the Broadland in the east of the county, there were belts of unoccupied territory; but the 'island' of the two hundreds of Flegg, with its fertile soil and strong Scandinavian element, stood out as a densely settled area.

The Distribution of Prosperity and Population

Some idea of the nature of the information in the Domesday folios for Norfolk, and of the form in which it is presented, may be obtained from the entry relating to the village of Bircham Newton situated on the uplands of north-western Norfolk, in the hundred of Docking (225b–226). The village was held entirely by Ralph de Bellofago and so it is covered by a single entry:

NIWETUNA (Bircham Newton) was held *T.R.E.* by Toue, a freeman, [as] 2 carucates (*car' terrae*). Then as now 4 villeins and 3 bordars. Then 3 serfs, afterwards and now 1. Then 1 plough on the demesne, afterwards 2, now 3. Then and afterwards 4 ploughs belonging to the men, now 2½. Then as now 2 rounceys and 10 swine. Then 220 sheep, now 540. To this manor belong (*Hic iacent*) 11 freemen [with] 1½ carucates and 11½ acres. Then 4 ploughs belonging to the men, now 2½. [There is] 1 church [with] 20 acres, worth 16 pence. These freemen his predecessor Eudo had; Stigand [had] the soke. It was then worth 60 shillings, afterwards and now 100. The whole is half a league in length and a half in breadth, and renders 15 pence out of 20 shillings of geld.

The general items relating to the village as a whole are six in number: (1) carucates, (2) plough-teams, (3) population, (4) values, (5) dimensions and (6) assessment. There are two peculiar features about these basic items. In the first place, there is no reference to plough-lands; in this Norfolk resembles Suffolk and Essex.[1] The second peculiar feature is characteristic only of Norfolk and Suffolk and consists of the reference at the end of the entry to the length and breadth of the holding and to the amount of geld for which it was liable. The bearing of these six items of information upon regional variations in prosperity must now be considered.

---

[1] There is also no systematic mention of plough-lands for the counties of Gloucester, Worcester and Hereford.

(1) *Carucates*

The normal entry in Norfolk, as in Suffolk, states the number of carucates and/or acres that belonged to a landholder. The phrase *ad geldum* is not added here as it is in other carucated counties, and, as we have seen, information about geld is given us in quite a different formula that is unique to Norfolk and Suffolk. In view of this other formula we might for the moment believe that the East Anglian carucate (*car' terrae*) was equivalent to the plough-land of other counties. Maitland, however, gave good reason for believing that this was not so, but that it referred to the apportionment of the geld among the various landholders within each vill.[1] The division of the carucate into acres instead of bovates is another peculiar feature of East Anglia. Some of the holdings were very small; there was, for example, 1 freeman with only 1 acre at Aslacton (190), and another with 5 acres at Diss (276b); at Gissing, 8 freemen held 60 acres (130), and at Dickleburgh 4 sokemen held 20 acres (211). The large number of these small tenements reflects the peculiar economic and social structure of the East Anglian peasantry and we shall return to the point in considering the Domesday population.[2] There is only one clear case of a virgate being mentioned—at Merton in Wayland (252) where there was a holding of 3 carucates and 1 virgate (*virgata*). Three sokemen at Litcham (Launditch) held 4 acres and 1 *virgata* (207b), but this probably means a rood; the references to a *virga* among the meadow entries likewise imply roods.[3]

On some holdings the number of carucates was the same as the number of plough-teams at work, but, generally speaking, the number of carucates and acres on a holding bore no constant relation to the actual number of teams at work. Four entries from the hundred of Depwade will show the complete lack of correspondence. At Boyland there was a total of 3 teams on a holding of 1 carucate (249), while a similar holding at Forncett carried 4 teams (180b); and at Hardwick a freeman's holding of 30 acres had 2 ploughs while another of 30 acres at Hempnall had only 1 plough. There seems likewise to be no relationship between the number of carucates and the amount of the assessment, but this will be discussed later on.[4] Whatever its obscurity, and whatever its previous history, it

---

[1] F. W. Maitland, *op. cit.* pp. 429–31. See also P. Vinogradoff, *English Society in the Eleventh Century* (Oxford, 1908), p. 199, n. 1.

[2] See p. 114 below.　　　　[3] See p. 129 below.　　　　[4] See p. 122 below.

is obvious that the East Anglian carucate implied not what was real but what was rateable.

Maitland, making many reservations, estimated the total number of carucates in Domesday Norfolk at 'about 2,422'.[1] The present count, for the area covered by the modern county, has produced 2,428. But both sets of figures are subject to one limitation; there are many entries which omit any reference to carucates. In the hundred of South Greenhoe, for example, no carucates or acres are recorded for many holdings, e.g. at Bodney (237), Bradenham (252), Cockley Cley (120), Hilborough (167b), Langford (237) and Narford (144). In view of the very high degree of incompleteness it is obviously impossible to compare the incidence of carucates, hundred by hundred or region by region. Both estimates of the total number of carucates given above have assumed that 1 carucate comprised 120 fiscal acres, and Maitland gave his reasons for believing this equation to be true.[2] Many people have come to the same conclusion, but, on the other hand, it must be pointed out that a case for a 100-acre carucate has been made out,[3] though in Suffolk the evidence seems to be in favour of a 120-acre carucate.[4]

(2) *Plough-teams*

The Norfolk entries, like those of other counties, usually draw a distinction between the teams held by the lord of a manor in demesne and those held by the peasantry. But at times the distinction is not made, especially on the very small manors; at other times, it is not clear, and occasional entries seem to be defective. The present count has yielded a total of $5,033\frac{5}{8}$ teams in 1086 for the area covered by the modern county.[5] Frequently there had been changes between 1066 and 1086. Thus at Hedenham (Loddon) there were 'then 3 ploughs on the demesne, afterwards none, now 2. Then and afterwards $1\frac{1}{2}$ ploughs belonging to

---

[1] F. W. Maitland, *op. cit.* p. 430.

[2] *Ibid.* p. 483.

[3] See (a) G. J. Turner, *A calendar of the feet of fines relating to the county of Huntingdon*, p. lxxxiii (Camb. Antiq. Soc., Cambridge, 1913); (b) J. C. Tingey, 'Some Notes on the Domesday Assessment of Norfolk', *Norfolk Archaeology* (1923), XXI, pp. 134–42; (c) D. C. Douglas, *The Social Structure of Medieval East Anglia* (Oxford, 1927), p. 50.   [4] See p. 164 below.

[5] F. W. Maitland's total, for the Domesday county, came to 4,853 teams; *Domesday Book and Beyond*, p. 401.

the men, now 2' (152b). There are occasional departures from the normal
formula about these matters, and five of these are given below:

(1) *Plumstead* in Blofield (224b). 'Now as then the ploughing is done
    with 2 oxen (*semper aratur cum ii bovibus*).'
(2) *Sharrington* in Holt (112b). 'These (men) plough with 2 ploughs
    (*Hi arant ii carucis*).'
(3) *Barningham* in North Erpingham (184b). 'Then he ploughed with 2
    oxen, now with half a plough (*tunc arabat cum ii bovibus modo cum
    dimidio carucae*).'
(4) *Thurgarton* in North Erpingham (185). 'Then as now he ploughed with
    half a plough (*semper arat cum dimidio carucae*).'
(5) *Murlai* in North Greenhoe (192b). 'Then he ploughed with one plough,
    now with 2 oxen (*Tunc arabat i caruca modo ii bovibus*).'

When the existing teams in 1086 were fewer than those in times past,
we are sometimes told that the deficit could be made good, and a contrast
between actual and potential arable is implied. One of the entries for
Briningham in Holt (198) states: 'Then 3 ploughs on the demesne, now
2½ and half a plough might be made good (*posset restaurari*).' Nor was
the addition always limited to the restoration of what had once been; thus
two entries for Osmondiston in Diss (176b, 263) both say: 'Then as now
1 plough on the demesne but there might be 2 (*possent esse*).' Or again,
there was a holding at Holkham in North Greenhoe (113) that was waste
in 1086 but three ploughs could be employed there (*est vastata et iii
carucae possent ibi esse*). A little lower down on the same folio we are told
about a holding at Egmere where there was nothing, but 1 plough could
be employed (*et nichil est ibi aliud sed i caruca posset esse*). Over the county
as a whole, there was a decrease of teams in 34 per cent., and an increase
in 6 per cent., of the entries with details for both 1066 and 1086.

To sum up: although the Norfolk folios do not give us information
about plough-lands in the sense that it is recorded for some other counties,
we can often infer this from these details about the increase or decrease
in the teams, and from the possibilities of further cultivation that are
thus indicated. In this way were the local fortunes of agriculture, varying
from place to place, put on record. It is, however, sometimes difficult
to envisage what had really happened; thus at Buxton in South Erpingham, the total number of ploughs had fallen from 16 to 7½, yet the number
of men seems to have increased and a lot of wood had also been cut down
(229).

Recorded Population of Norfolk in 1086
A. Rural Population

Freemen	5,250
Sokemen	5,410
Villeins	4,617
Bordars	9,910
Serfs	977
Miscellaneous	206
Total	26,370

Details of Miscellaneous Rural Population

Men (*homines*) .	160	Priests	11
Fishermen . .	24	*Consuetudinarii* . .	11
		Total . . .	206

B. Urban Population

Sokemen, bordars, serfs, fishermen and the villein, are also included above.

NORWICH   665 English burgesses; 124 French burgesses; 480 bordars; 297 *mansurae vacuae*; 1 *mansura vasta*.

THETFORD   725 burgesses; 1 villein; 2 sokemen; 3 serfs; 30 bordars; 33 men; 224 *mansurae vacuae*.

YARMOUTH   70 burgesses; 24 fishermen.

(3) Population

The main bulk of the population was comprised in the five categories of freemen, sokemen, villeins, bordars and serfs. In addition to these main groups were the burgesses, together with a miscellaneous group that included *homines*,[1] fishermen and others.[2] The details of these groups are summarised above. The tenants-in-chief and the under-tenants have been omitted for the reasons stated on pp. 51–4. There are two other estimates of the Domesday population of Norfolk, a recent one by

---

[1] Many of these unspecified 'men' may have been freemen.

[2] An unusual category is that of 6 free villeins (*vi liberi villani*) at Barford (145) counted here among the villeins.

Miss Barbara Dodwell,[1] and, of course, the old one by Sir Henry Ellis.[2] The present estimate is not strictly comparable with either of these for

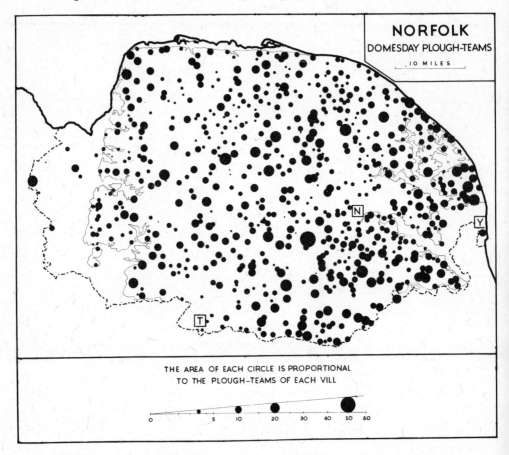

NORFOLK
DOMESDAY PLOUGH-TEAMS
. 10 MILES

THE AREA OF EACH CIRCLE IS PROPORTIONAL
TO THE PLOUGH-TEAMS OF EACH VILL

0   5   10   20   30   40   50   60

Fig. 25. Norfolk: Domesday plough-teams in 1086 (by settlements).

Places with burgesses are indicated by initials: N, Norwich; T, Thetford; Y, Yarmouth.
The boundary of alluvium and peat is shown; see Fig. 22.

a variety of reasons, one reason being that it has been made in terms of the modern county boundary; Miss Dodwell's estimate, moreover, refers

[1] Barbara Dodwell, 'The free peasantry of East Anglia in Domesday', *Norfolk Archaeology* (Norwich, 1941), XXVII, p. 156.
[2] Sir Henry Ellis, *General Introduction to Domesday Book* (London, 1833), II, pp. 469–70.

to conditions in 1066. One thing is certain; no one who counts Domesday
population can claim definitive accuracy. Varying interpretations of many

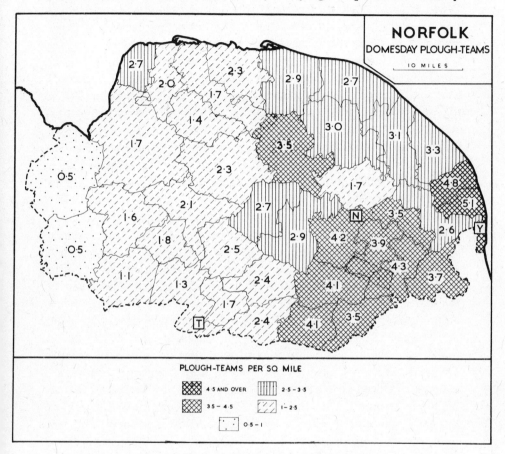

Fig. 26. Norfolk: Domesday plough-teams in 1086 (by densities).
Places with burgesses are indicated by initials: N, Norwich; T, Thetford; Y, Yarmouth.

entries are inevitable, especially in the Little Domesday Book. Finally,
one point must always be remembered. The figures presumably indicate
heads of households. Whatever factor should be used to obtain the *actual*
population from the *recorded* population, the proportions between the
different categories and between different areas remain unaffected.[1]

[1] See p. 360 below for the position of the serfs.

One of the outstanding characteristics of the county was the presence of large numbers of freemen and sokemen. Taken together, they amounted to 41 per cent. of the total recorded population, the number of freemen being slightly below that of sokemen. The distinction between the two categories is obscure, and has given rise to much discussion.[1] In this connection it is interesting to note that, in an entry relating to Methwold, the Domesday Book records four freemen (136) where the *I.E.* records four sokemen (p. 138), but this may have been a slip of the pen. Taken together, the two groups constituted the free element in the population as opposed to villeins, bordars and serfs. Like the single category of sokemen in Lincolnshire, they may be a witness to the Scandinavian influence in eastern England. Miss Dodwell, who has discussed their distribution, finds that 'there is a close correspondence between the regions where Scandinavian place-names are to be found and those where the free peasantry form a high proportion of the population'.[2]

The striking feature about the property of these freemen and sokemen is that their holdings were frequently so very small, often less than 10 acres and sometimes less than 5 acres. Thus at Barningham in North Erpingham there was one freeman with 3 acres (185), and at Beckham, in the same hundred, one sokeman held 4 acres, another held 2½ acres, while a third held only 1 acre (185, 198b, 128). Frequently, no ploughs or oxen are recorded in connection with these small holdings, and we are driven to ask how the holders of these small tenements got a living. As Miss Dodwell has shown, they do not seem to have supplemented their resources by sheep-farming, at any rate not on any large scale:[3] and Sir Frank Stenton has suggested that 'some of them may well have eked out the produce of their acres by finding employment on the farms of noblemen or of wealthier members of their own class'.[4] The implications of these minute holdings in relation to the social structure of medieval East Anglia has been discussed at length by Professor Douglas who points to 'the existence of a free peasant class which discharged all or most of its obligations by means of money payments'.[5] Here, I am simply

[1] F. W. Maitland, *op. cit.* pp. 66 *et seq.*
[2] B. Dodwell, *loc. cit.* p. 152. But doubts have been cast upon the connection between Scandinavians and free peasantry in Norfolk and Suffolk—see R. H. C. Davis. 'East Anglia and the Danelaw', *Trans. Roy. Hist. Soc.* (1955), 5th Ser. vol. v, p.32.
[3] *Ibid.* p. 150.
[4] F. M. Stenton, *Anglo-Saxon England* (Oxford, 1943), p. 510.
[5] D. C. Douglas, *Medieval East Anglia*, p. 97.

concerned with the bearing of these facts upon the Domesday population of the county, and it must be pointed out that it was with these small holdings in mind that Maitland wrote: 'We think it highly probable that in the survey of East Anglia one and the same free man is sometimes mentioned several times; he holds a little land under one lord, and a little under another lord.'[1] Professor Douglas likewise points out that much reduplication is to be expected.[2] On the other hand, Mr Lennard has noted the occasional mention of half-sokemen which suggests that 'Domesday Commissioners endeavoured to distinguish sokemen who held under more than one lord, while the fact that these "half-sokemen" are very few in number seems significant';[3] half-freemen are more frequent than half-sokemen, but are still not very many. Miss Dodwell has also come to the conclusion that, while the wealthier peasants did occasionally possess more than one tenement, 'it does not seem likely that in very many instances a man had several holdings and so has been counted more than once'.[4] I shall return to this point in connection with the Suffolk freemen and sokemen, but here all I can do is to point out this uncertainty about their numbers. It may involve a large error; on the other hand, it seems more likely to involve a small one.[5]

It is just possible that there may be another complication about the East Anglian figures. At the very end of some entries, after the measurement and the geld have been noted, words to the effect that others held there are added. The precise wording varies, e.g. *Alii ibi tenent* or *Plures ibi tenent*, and there are other variants, e.g. *Plures habent ubi* (sic) *terram* (271). Ellis thought that this implied additional 'agricultural tenantry'.[6] Maitland, on the other hand, suggested that it meant 'that the vill is divided between several tenants in chief'.[7] In this connection a variant of the phrase that occurs for 3 villages in the hundred of South Greenhoe may be relevant. Following the measurement and geld for Bodney (237), comes the statement 'with those who hold there (*cum tenentibus in ea*)'. The same phrase is found at the end of an entry relating to Caldecote, except that it is placed differently—*in geldo cum tenentibus in ea v denarii*

[1] F. W. Maitland, *op. cit.* pp. 20 and 106–7.

[2] D. C. Douglas, *op. cit.* p. 122.

[3] Reginald Lennard, 'The Economic Position of the Domesday sokemen', *The Economic Journal* (1947), LVII, p. 195.

[4] B. Dodwell, *loc. cit.* p. 157.   [5] See p. 170 below.

[6] Henry Ellis, *op. cit.* II, pp. 490–1.

[7] F. W. Maitland, *op. cit.* p. 20 n.

(235b). It also appears in one of the entries for Cressingham—*totum simul cum tenentibus in ea reddit xiiii denarii* (191). It is most unwise to base a Domesday theory on a few entries, but these three may point the way to a solution that is not inconsistent with *plures* and *alii*. These words

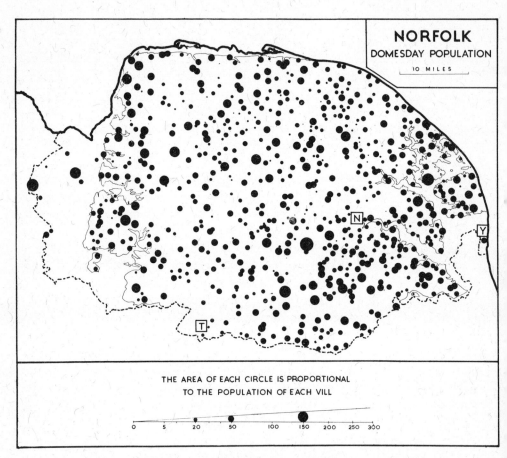

NORFOLK
DOMESDAY POPULATION
10 MILES

THE AREA OF EACH CIRCLE IS PROPORTIONAL
TO THE POPULATION OF EACH VILL

Fig. 27. Norfolk: Domesday population in 1086 (by settlements).
Places with burgesses are indicated by initials: N, Norwich; T, Thetford; Y, Yarmouth.
The boundary of alluvium and peat is shown; see Fig. 22.

may simply refer to other holdings mentioned elsewhere but included in one assessment. As the measurement and geld is attached only to one of the entries relating to a village, it would only be natural to add that others held land within the assessment.[1] The phrase may even have included holdings in other villages for it is not every village that has a statement of measurement and geld attached to it. This may be the answer, but we cannot be sure.

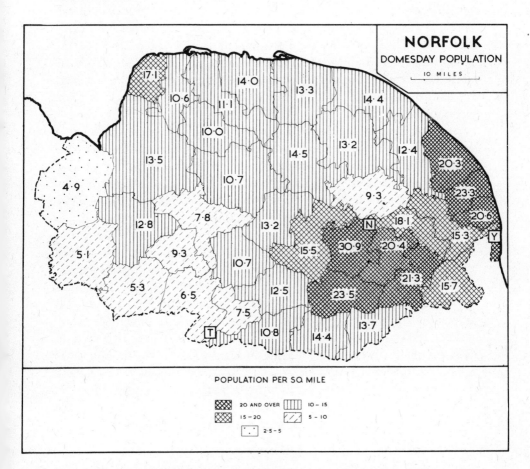

Fig. 28. Norfolk: Domesday population in 1086 (by densities).

Places with burgesses are indicated by initials: N, Norwich; T, Thetford; Y, Yarmouth.

[1] For a discussion of the phrase *plures ibi tenent* in an entry relating to Martham in West Flegg (195b), see W. H. Hudson, 'Status of "Villani" and other tenants in Danish East Anglia in pre-Conquest times', *Trans. Roy. Hist. Soc.* 4th ser. (1921), IV, p. 27. Hudson concludes that the phrase refers to other holdings in the vill.

Finally, some uncertainty occasionally arises from the fact that the text frequently does not state categorically whether the numbers of freemen and sokemen refer to 1066 or to 1086; the difference between *tenet* and *tenuit* is sometimes obscure. In such entries, however, it is often possible to infer which date is meant from the general character of the entry, or from the addition of the words *T.R.E.*; sometimes both dates are meant. Thus one entry for Porringland, in Henstead, states: '1 freeman of Edwin *T.R.E.* with (*de*) 12 acres and 1 bordar and half an acre of meadow. Then as now half a plough' (203). Presumably the freeman and his bordar continued to live there in 1086 as they had done 20 years previously.

Some of these doubts may be unjustified, but, in any case, it is impossible to assess the degree of error they involve. Fortunately, we are not confined to the data about recorded population in estimating the relative prosperity of different regions. The statistics for plough-teams form a useful check, and comparison of the two maps of population and plough-teams may prompt some interesting reflections.

The information about the unfree population involves far fewer problems, at any rate from our point of view. Changes between the various categories are frequently specified. Thus in an entry relating to Somerton in West Flegg we read: 'Then 4 villeins, afterwards and now 2. Then as now 11 bordars. Then 6 serfs, afterwards and now 2' (146b). The total population on a holding in 1086 was sometimes less, sometimes more, than in 1066, and there was frequently no change. The approximate ratio between the three groups of villeins, bordars and serfs for the county as a whole in 1086 was 4:9:1. Half-villeins and half-bordars are occasionally mentioned. A few entries seem to be defective, and contain either no reference, or only a vague reference, to population, but it is impossible to be really certain about the significance of these omissions.[1]

(4) *Values*

The valuation of an estate or holding seems to have been carried out with care. At any rate the figures seem to suggest that. When we read, for example, that a holding in Titchwell (Docking) was worth 13s. 4d. in 1066 and 12s. in 1086, it seems to suggest a careful appraisal (183). Generally speaking, the greater the number of ploughs and people on a holding, the higher its value, but there are all kinds of anomalies and no equation is

---

[1] See p. 102 above.

possible. Moreover, when we attempt to assess the relative prosperity of different localities, we immediately come face to face with great difficulties. There are many holdings and even some places for which no value is recorded. Presumably they are accounted for under other totals. The value of a berewick, or an outlying estate, is often included with the total for its parent holding. Thus on fo. 109b no value is given for Southmere, but the account of this holding is immediately followed by that of its berewick in Titchwell, and the value at the end of Titchwell is obviously a total for both holdings. Frequently there is no need for any assumption; the value of a holding is specifically stated to be included in that of another vill, which may even be in another hundred. Four berewicks in Brinton, Saxlingham, Beckham and Hempstead were reckoned (*computatae sunt*) in Thornage (192); two bordars with half a plough in Antingham were valued (*appretiati sunt*) in Suffield (184b); the estate of four sokemen in Coltishall was included in the valuation (*in pretio*) of Frettenham (244). Examples could be multiplied at great length. Furthermore, we sometimes read of men and possessions in one place 'belonging' to another place. There were 2 freemen with half a plough in Shingham who belonged to (*jacent in*) Nacton (236). There were 19 sokemen who lived in (*manent in*) Warham, but who belonged to (*pertinent in*) Wells (271). A more explicit illustration for our purpose comes from Holkham (170b); there, a holding of half a carucate with 1 bordar belonged to Burnham, was of the fee of Frederic, and was there valued (*pertinet ad brunaham et est de feudo frederici et ibi est appretiata*). Or again, there were some men in Reepham who belonged to Kerdiston and were there valued (247b): *Huic terrae* [i.e. in Kerdiston] *jacent homines in Resham et sunt appretiati cum ipsa terra*. Personal, feudal and manorial ties thus cut across the geographical arrangement of people in villages.[1] In view of these complexities, and of the general uncertainty about the exact implications of the term 'value', it is clear that any interpretation of the figures upon a geographical basis is impossible.

(5) *The Measurement and* (6) *the Geld*

At or near the end of many entries may be found a statement about size followed almost invariably by another about geld assessment; only

---

[1] For the bearing of 'the confused terminology of the Little Domesday' upon the organisation of sokes in East Anglia, see D. C. Douglas, *Medieval East Anglia*, pp. 173–91 and 210–11.

very rarely are the two statements separated by other information.[1] The
words that introduce the statements vary, as can be seen from these seven
examples taken from the hundred of Clackclose:

(1)	Barton Bendish (230b)	*Totum hoc manerium*...
(2)	Beechamwell (251b)	*Tota becheswella*...
(3)	Denver (160)	*Tota*...
(4)	Hilgay (215)	*Hoc manerium*...
(5)	Marham (212b)	*Haec terra*...
(6)	Stradsett (206b)	*Haec villa*...
(7)	Wimbotsham and Stow Bardolph (206b)	*Hae villae*...

One of the entries for Barton Bendish contains a curiosity that may be
either a slip of the scribe's pen or an attempt to distinguish the vill as
a whole from a manor within it: 'All this manor (*Totum hoc manerium*) is
1 league in length, half a league and 3 furlongs in breadth. When the
whole hundred renders 20s. of geld, the whole of this vill (*tota haec villa*)
16d.' (230b). One of the entries for Fincham, in the same hundred,
draws a similar distinction between *Totum hoc manerium* and *haec·villa*
(159b). Whether the information be indicated in terms of manors, vills
or land, it is clear that these liabilities for payment were grouped into
larger units for the purpose of assessment. This larger unit was known as
the leet, and it has been discussed at length by a succession of Domesday
scholars. The Domesday Book explicitly tells us that the hundreds of
Clackclose (212b) and South Greenhoe (119b) comprised respectively
10 and 14 leets, and Charles Johnson made an attempt to reconstruct the
Domesday leets of the county as a whole.[2] Occasionally, but not as
frequently as in Suffolk, no measurements are given for some vills, and
their liability for geld is presumably hidden in the totals of neighbouring
vills.[3] 'Probably the hundred or half-hundred was assessed as a whole,
and the geld was then partitioned among the smaller fiscal areas or leets,
and through them again it would fall on the selected vills, which may have
been tax-centres for a district.'[4] In a few rare instances we are told that

---

[1] They are separated, for example, in an entry for Marham (212b), and in an entry
for Cockley Cley the geld comes first (120).

[2] *V.C.H. Norfolk*, II, pp. 204–11. See p. 122 below.

[3] The Domesday Book omits the measurement and geld for Alpington in Henstead
(203b), which is supplied by the *I.E.*, p. 141.

[4] *V.C.H. Suffolk*, I, p. 362.

one estate was measured in another vill; thus Salthouse was measured (*mensurata*) in Sheringham (223b), Runton in Beeston Regis (224), and Rippon in Hevingham (241b). A variant of this is a single set of figures for two vills jointly, e.g. Holt and Cley (111b), Panxworth and Ranworth (129), Wells and Warham (271).

The size is usually stated in leagues and furlongs, but the detail sometimes descends to perches and even feet. Measurement in terms of miles and furlongs is, generally speaking, rare, though in the entries relating to the hundred of South Greenhoe, for example, it is encountered fairly frequently. The meaning of all these measurements is obscure.[1] It is difficult to see what exactly is implied by such statements as 'it is half a league in length and half in breadth' (258) or 'the whole is 1 league 10 perches in length and 1 league 4½ feet in breadth' (160b).[2] Whatever the length of a league was, it seems to have comprised 12 furlongs or 480 perches.[3] But this does not take us far. How did the Commissioners envisage shape in estimating length and breadth? What relation did these linear measurements bear to area? We cannot tell. That they seem to have comprised some sort of sum total is shown by a peculiarity in an entry for Marham in Clackclose (212b): 'This land is 1 league and 100 perches in length and half a league and 1 furlong in breadth. And in marsh the measurement is unknown (*in Maresc nescit mensuram*).' A similar curiosity is to be found in an entry for Well, now represented by Well Hall in Gayton (Freebridge). Both these places were measured together: 'Well and Gayton are 1½ leagues in length and a half in breadth and render 16 pence of geld whoever holds there. To Well also belongs (*jacet adhuc*) pasture 5 furlongs in length and 4 in breadth' (221b). A similar type of measurement is used in some counties to measure woodland. It is also used to measure estates in Yorkshire, and it is sometimes found in other connections, e.g. in occasional entries relating to arable and meadow in Lincolnshire.[4] But in no other county, except Suffolk, is this type of

[1] It has been suggested that they might refer to pasture—R. Welldon Finn, *The Eastern Counties* (London, 1967), p. 59. For a discussion of linear measurements relating to woodland, see p. 335 below.

[2] Weeting (Grimshoe) is described merely as '1½ leagues in breadth' (162b), but this may well be due to an omission and perhaps should read '1 league in length and half a league in breadth'.

[3] F. W. Maitland, *op. cit.* p. 432. See also p. 176 below. But note that in the measurement of Thelveton (Diss), the Domesday Book speaks of 'half a league' where the *I.E.* says '5 furlongs'; there is also another discrepancy between the two entries.

[4] See pp. 46 and 62 above. For Huntingdonshire, see p. 332 below.

measurement linked with a statement about geld. It is a feature peculiar to East Anglia.

The geld is stated in shillings and pence, and is the amount that was contributed to every twenty shillings paid by the hundred as a whole; sometimes the phrase 'of a geld of 20s.' is explicitly added, as we have seen in an entry for Barton Bendish; occasionally, it is specified as 'the king's geld', and there are minor variants. Theoretically, therefore, the sum of these amounts in each hundred should add up to 20s. In the reconstruction of the leets attempted by Charles Johnson, they rarely come to so exact an amount, but the amounts for many hundreds come very near it. The difference may be a measure of the imperfection either of the record or of our understanding of it.

As the measurement and the geld liability are so closely linked in the text, we might expect some correspondence between them. But this is not so. There seems to be no constant relation between them even in the same hundred, as the figures from half a dozen entries relating to the hundred of Diss will show:

	Measurements	Geld liability
Burston (130b)	8 × 4 furlongs	12d.
Dickleburgh (211)	5 × 4 „	6d.
Frenze (154b)	5 × 4 „	3d.
Osmondiston (263)	5 × 4 „	2d.
Roydon (228b)	10 × 8 „	9d.
Winfarthing (130)	1 × ½ league	9d.

No amount of arithmetical ingenuity will make any intelligible order out of this. The relationship between measurement and geld seems to be an unfathomable mystery. Moreover, any attempt to compare these figures with the carucage is complicated by the fact that both the measurement and the geld of any specific entry may include concealed totals belonging to neighbouring estates. But, as far as we can judge, there is no correspondence. Areas of equal assessment seem to have widely differing carucage.

Conclusion

For the purpose of calculating densities, Norfolk has not been subdivided so minutely as Lincolnshire. The reason for this is that the geological outcrops in Norfolk are not arranged in the linear fashion of those of Lincolnshire. Generally speaking, the hundreds themselves form fairly convenient units in the sense that the soil of each hundred is moderately uniform in character (Figs. 22 and 23). This is only a generalisation, and some modifications have had to be made in order to make the units that form the basis of the calculations correspond more closely with differences in soil. In the first place, the hundreds that border the Fenland have been divided into two, an upland and a fenland portion; these hundreds are those of Freebridge, Clackclose and Grimshoe. Then again, Shropham has been divided into an eastern and a western portion in order to separate the sandy Breckland from the rest; the hundred of South Greenhoe has likewise been divided into a northern and southern portion. In the second place, some of the small outlying portions of hundreds in the north of the county have been thrown into other hundreds in order to make more compact areas. In the third place, the Domesday Book records the information for some villages partly in one and partly in another hundred; these have been included wholly within one of the hundreds. The result of these modifications is 38 units which form a rough and ready basis for distinguishing variations over the face of the county. It does not enable us to arrive at as perfect a regional division as a geographer could wish for, but it is probably adequate for our purpose.

From the preceding discussion of the six recurring formulae, it is obvious that only two can be relied upon to give something that reflects the distribution of wealth and prosperity throughout the county in Domesday times. These are the statements about plough-teams and population. Neither is without uncertainty, but, taken together, they provide a check upon one another, and when the distributions of plough-teams and population are compared, certain common features stand out. The first of these features is the contrast between the east and the west of the county. The lighter soils of the west, particularly those of the sandy Breckland, had fewer plough-teams, and there were still fewer in the Fenland (Fig. 26). The general contrast is not as clearly seen on the population map (Fig. 28), but the low densities of Breck and Fen stand out on both maps. In the eastern half of the county, the two most densely occupied areas were (a) the island of the two Flegg hundreds, and (b) the country to the south and south-west of Norwich. In both areas, there are substantial tracts of moderately heavy soils, and the villages lay thick upon the ground. These high densities are even more striking when it is remembered that a considerable acreage in some of these hundreds must

have been under water or marsh. Thus the densities for the hundred of
Walsham would be very much higher if the Broads were excluded. One
curiosity in the east is the low density, both of teams and population, for
the hundred of Taverham to the north of Norwich. Closer examination
will show that this was a hundred with comparatively few villages, and
these were for the most part small. East of Felthorpe, for example, there
was a tract of village-less country, and the modern land utilisation map
of the area shows that the whole hundred includes considerable stretches
of heath situated upon glacial sands and gravels. Moreover, Mousehold
Heath, now within the limits of the city of Norwich, is only a relic of
a much greater stretch of heath that extended north-eastwards towards
Woodbastwick. Most of this heathland is now arable, but in Domesday
times, it must have been very different. There must also have been similar
patches of heath in the hundreds to the north of Taverham, and these may
help to explain why the north-eastern area ranked behind the Flegg area
and the country to the south of Norwich both in plough-teams and in
population. If we could only bring unit areas into closer accord with
soil variations, a much clearer picture would result, but these rough-and-
ready divisions enable us to see the main contrasts.

Figs. 25 and 27 are supplementary to the density maps, but it is necessary to make one reservation about them. As we have seen on p. 102, it is
possible that some Domesday names may have covered two or more
settlements, e.g. the present-day villages of Great and Little Massingham
are represented in the Domesday Book by only one name. Only where the
Domesday evidence specifically indicates the existence of more than one
settlement have they been distinguished on Figs. 25 and 27. A few of the
symbols should, therefore, appear as two or more smaller symbols. But
this limitation does not affect the general character of the maps.

WOODLAND

Types of entries

In the Little Domesday Book the extent of woodland on a holding is
usually indicated by the number of swine which it could support, for the
swine fed upon the acorns and the beech mast, and so provided a convenient measure. The normal formula in the Norfolk entries runs 'wood
for *n* swine'—*silva ad n porcos, silva de n porcis,* or just *silva n porcos.* The
number of swine range from just a few (one, two or three) up to many
hundreds and in a few entries to over a thousand. The larger entries are

frequently given in round numbers that may indicate estimates rather than actual amounts, but, on the other hand, the many instances of very detailed figures (e.g. 3, 7, 9, 49) suggest exactness. Occasionally, the record is extremely precise; at Strincham in South Erpingham (196b) there were two sokemen who had 'wood for 18 swine and two-thirds of another (*silva de xviii porc' et ii part' alti*)'.[1] When 'wood for *n* swine' is recorded for any particular holding, it may not follow that *n* swine were actually there; the swine were merely used as units of measurement. Conversely, the Norfolk folios, as we shall see, sometimes record swine for places in which there was no wood.[2]

While swine form the normal unit of measurement, there are some exceptional entries that measure woodland in other ways. The hundred of Clackclose included a group of places with these exceptional entries: there was half an acre of wood at Westbriggs (206); 1 acre at Stow Bardolph (206); 8 acres at Barton Bendish (205b, 230); 16 acres at South Runcton (209); while at Fincham, there was half a league of wood (205b). A few similar entries are scattered through the folios relating to the other hundreds. Bittering, in Launditch, had 7 acres (137). Pickenham, in South Greenhoe, had 1 acre as well as wood for 30 swine (232). East Dereham, in Midford, had 3 acres, as well as wood for several hundred swine (214). Sparham, in Eynesford, had 6 acres, likewise in addition to wood for swine (204). At Colkirk (197b), in Brothercross, Bishop Ærefastus appropriated the wood of *Fangeham* which was 60 acres in length (*silva de fangeham, et est in longo lx acrae*). This may refer to wood at Fakenham (Gallow) some three miles or so to the north of Colkirk; whatever it was, it is difficult to see the point of measuring its length in acres.[3] There is one definite instance of a wood in Norfolk being specifically named. At Hempnall, in Depwade, there was wood for 200 swine which (or part of which) was called *Schieteshaga* (248b). Finally, the list of unusual entries is completed by the reference to a deer park (*parcus bestiis*) at Costessey in Forehoe (145).

---

[1] Comparison with the 'semibos' of F. W. Maitland suggests itself; *op. cit.* p. 142. Here it must be sufficient to say that feed for 'half a cow is known in law as feed for a cow for half the year'; Joshua Williams, *Rights of Common* (London, 1880), p. 49. On the other hand, the sentence could be expanded to read: 'wood for 18 swine and two-thirds of another (wood)'.   [2] See p. 144 below.

[3] For 'linear acres', however, see: (1) O. J. Reichel in *V.C.H. Devon* (London, 1906), I, p. 387; (2) R. W. Eyton, *A Key to Domesday: the Dorset Survey* (London, 1878), p. 25.

One feature of the wood entries in the Little Domesday Book is the
contrast that is sometimes drawn between conditions in 1066 and 1086.
Thus, on a holding at Blickling, in South Erpingham, we are told: ' *Tunc
silva cc porcos modo c*' (196b). The number of distinct places in Norfolk
where woodland thus decreased was thirty-three, and the details are
summarised in the table on p. 128. The Norfolk folios give no indication
of the purpose of this clearing. Mr Reginald Lennard has recently shown,
however, that the destruction of the wood was not accompanied by any
extension of the arable. Many of the holdings from which the wood had
disappeared show not an increased number of plough-teams, as one might
perhaps expect, but a smaller number in 1086 than in 1066. Thus at Buxton,
in South Erpingham, the number of swine which the wood could support
had dropped from 1,000 to 200, but the number of plough-teams at work
showed no complementary increase. On the contrary they had decreased
from 16 to 7½ (229). Only occasionally was there an increase of plough-
teams on the holdings where the wood had been reduced. 'Here and
there', writes Mr Lennard, 'the plough may have penetrated the bounds
of the former woodland. But in general the Domesday record points
unmistakably, not to "assarting", but to "waste". The tall trees had gone
and with them the acorns and beech mast on which the pigs of the
peasantry had fed. But the tree stumps, one suspects, remained and they
must have been a serious obstacle to cultivation, while thickets of scrub
must have taken the place of the standing timber.'[1]

Distribution of woodland

The most notable feature of Fig. 29 is the concentration of wood on
the medium soils of mid-Norfolk, where there were many villages each
with wood sufficient to feed several hundred swine; some with even
enough for a thousand swine. These relatively heavy soils continue south-
eastwards in a belt to the southern boundary of the county, and one might,
perhaps, expect the wood cover in this southern area to have been more
dense than it apparently was. The population and plough-team maps,
however, show that the district to the south of Norwich was a closely
settled arable area (Fig. 28), and the absence of dense wood is therefore
all the more understandable. In the north-east of the county, in the loam

[1] Reginald Lennard, 'The Destruction of Woodland in the Eastern Counties under
William the Conqueror', *Econ. Hist. Rev.* (1945), XV, p. 39.

region, there was a moderate amount of wood, but nothing to compare
with that of mid-Norfolk. The closely settled Flegg hundreds, for example,
were particularly devoid of wood. Curiously enough, the village with

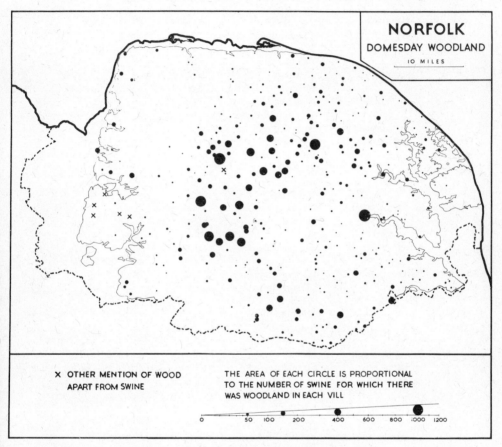

Fig. 29. Norfolk: Domesday woodland in 1086.

The boundary of alluvium and peat is shown; see Fig. 22. Where the wood of a village
is entered partly in terms of swine and partly in some other way, only the swine are
shown.

the largest amount of wood was in this eastern part of the county; Thorpe
next Norwich had wood sufficient to support 1,200 swine (137b) and
it stands out on Fig. 29. Finally, the light soils of the north-west of the
county, and the even lighter soils of the Breckland to the south, formed

Reduction of Woodland in Norfolk, 1066–86

The numbers refer to swine for which there was wood in 1066 and 1086 respectively
The folios are those of the Little Domesday Book.

Hundred	Place	1066	1086	Folio
Diss	Thelveton	60	30	*215*
,,	*Watlingseta*	20	0	*114*
,,	Winfarthing	250	200	*129b*
Earsham	Earsham	300	200	*138b*
,,	Pulham	600	300	*214b*
,,	Redenhall	60	20	*125*
,,	Thorpe Abbots	60	40	*210b*
N. Erpingham	Sheringham	160	100	*223b*
S. Erpingham	Aylsham	400	300	*132*
,,	Baconsthorpe	40	30	*255*
,,	Blickling	200	100	*196b*
,,	Buxton	1,000	200	*229*
,,	Cawston	1,500	1,000	*115*
,,	Colby	12	8	*115b*
,,	Mannington	60	30	*132b*
Eynesford	Hindolveston	600	300	*192b*
Forehoe	Wymondham	100	60	*137b*
,,	,,	60	16	*137b*
N. Greenhoe	Hindringham	10	8	*192*
Launditch	North Elmham	1,000	500	*191b*
,,	Gateley	300	80	*239*
,,	Mileham	100	50	*136b*
,,	*Suttona*	200	100	*232b*
Midford	East Dereham	600	300	*214*
,,	Flockthorpe	60	40	*122*
,,	Shipdam	60	40	*166b*
,,	,,	40	20	*277*
,,	*Berch* (? Southburgh)	8	4	*166b*
,,	Swathing.	60	40	*121b*
,,	*Torp*	800	600	*214*
,,	Whinburgh	150	110	*207b*
,,	Wood Rising	200	160	*167*
Shropham	Buckenham	120	60	*126b*
Taverham	Horsford	160	60	*155*
,,	Horsham	160	60	*155b*

On one holding at Denton (Earsham) we are told: ' *Modo silva xxx porcis*' (246),
but there is no indication of what had been there '*tunc*'. It may be just a clerical error.

very open country, and this in spite of the fact that the western area was
not densely peopled. It is interesting to see how the comparatively dense
woodland of mid-Norfolk thinned out along the margins of this western

area. There were, it is true, some local patches of wood here, but so were there patches of heavier soils. In a very general way, the map of wood is complementary to that of demesne sheep (Fig. 34). Where there was most wood, there were fewest sheep. Fig. 29 shows the distribution of wood in 1086. The cutting that had gone on since 1066 had not affected the general pattern of the distribution. A map of woodland in 1066 would present similar features, except that the most densely wooded areas would appear even a little more wooded.

MEADOW

Types of entries

The entries for meadow in Norfolk are uniform and comparatively straightforward. On holding after holding, the same type of entry repeats itself monotonously, 'n acres of meadow' (n acrae prati). The amount of meadow in each vill varied from under 1 acre to over 100 acres, and indeed to over 200, but figures above 50 are comparatively rare. The amounts under 1 acre usually consist of half acres of meadow, but 'three parts of one acre' are entered for Anmer in Freebridge (151b), 1 rood (virga) for Holkham in North Greenhoe (264b), another for Roudham in Shropham (239b), and 3 roods for Hanworth in North Erpingham (184). As in the case of Lincolnshire, no attempt has been made to translate the Domesday figures into modern acreages. The Domesday acres have been treated merely as conventional units of measurement, and Fig. 30 has been plotted on that assumption.[1]

Distribution of meadowland

The main fact about the distribution of meadow is its concentration in and around the Broadland. The winter floods must have meant good crops of hay along the margins of the more permanent stretches of water. On the other side of the county, on the other hand, in the Fenland, there was not as much meadow as might be expected, but many of the streams that drained into the Fenland were bordered by fair quantities. What meadow there was in the middle of the county, was naturally associated with the streams, and particularly with the Waveney that bounds the county on the south.

[1] A charter of 1068 mentions meadow at Sporle, but the Domesday entry for Sporle records none—H. M. Cam, 'The English lands of the abbey of St Riquier', Eng. Hist. Rev. (1916), XXXI, pp. 443–7.

PASTURE

Pasture, unlike meadow, is not regularly mentioned in the Norfolk folios. There are only eleven places for which information is given, and

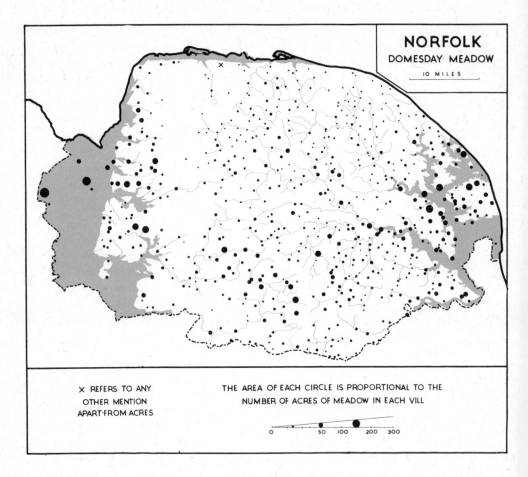

Fig. 30. Norfolk: Domesday meadow in 1086.

The areas of alluvium and peat are indicated; see Fig. 22. Rivers passing through these areas are not shown. Where the meadow of a village is entered partly in acres and partly in some other way, only the acres are shown.

perhaps the simplest thing is to make a list of these places. The first five specifically mention pasture for sheep; the others do not.

(1) At Haddiscoe in Clavering there was pasture capable of supporting a total of 170 sheep: 80 (fo. 181b), 50 (fo. 182) and 40 (fo. 190) respectively. It is, incidentally, interesting to note that none of these three entries records the presence of sheep themselves, although another entry for the village records 100 sheep (141).

(2) At Wheatacre, also in Clavering, there was pasture for 200 sheep (250). The same entry adds that there had been 200 sheep there in 1066 but that there were only 100 in 1086. On the same folio another entry for Wheatacre records an increase from 160 to 176 sheep.

(3) At Herringby in East Flegg there was pasture for 100 sheep (273), but no sheep were recorded as actually being in the village.

(4) At Wells-next-the-Sea (North Greenhoe) there was pasture sufficient for a total of 300 sheep, 100 (fo. 192) and 200 (fo. 271) respectively; but only 200 sheep were actually there in 1086 and previous to that the figure had been as low as 60 (fo. 271).

(5) In Houghton St Giles (North Greenhoe) there was pasture for 1,000 sheep (113), but no sheep are recorded for the village.

(6) To Well (near Gayton Thorpe in Freebridge) belonged '5 furlongs of pasture in length and 4 in breadth' (221b).

(7) At Wimbotsham in Clackclose there was 'pasture worth 18 pence' (215b).

(8) At Breckles in Wayland (110b) there was 'a certain customary due in pasture (*quedam consuetudo in pastura*)' which was in dispute.

(9) At Fodderstone in Clackclose (274) 6 freemen rendered custom because they could not do without their pasture (*non possunt carere sua pastura*).

(10) In the account of the town of Norwich, 16 acres of pasture are mentioned (117). This seems to be repeated on fo. 234b where 16 acres of pasture, amongst other things, are said to be in the 'hundred ot Norwich'.

(11) There are two references to pasture on the entry relating to Thetford (118b). The first entry says that 2 ploughs remain in pasture (*ii carucae remanent in pastura*). Its meaning is obscure; one suggestion is that 'ploughs' should read 'plough-lands'.[1] The other entry merely records the presence of pasture in that part of Thetford that lay in Norfolk.[2]

---

[1] *V.C.H. Norfolk*, II, p. 47.
[2] See p. 141 below.

The first five places suggest analogy with the Essex entries that refer to pasture for sheep.[1] The pasture of Haddiscoe and Wheatacre must have been on the Waveney flats; that of Herringby on the Bure flats; while that of Wells and of Houghton St Giles may have been on the coastal flats of the north. But it is difficult to believe that these comprised all the pasture there was on the marshy flats of Norfolk. If, for example, there was pasture for sheep in Herringby, why not in other villages of the Broadland? Furthermore, it is impossible to believe that the other five entries account for all the remaining pasture in the county. It does look as if the pasture of the Norfolk villages was entered sporadically, and maybe accidentally, whereas in Essex or in Cambridgeshire it was regularly entered wherever it existed. We cannot get behind the imperfections of the survey; all we can do is to register the idiosyncrasies of different counties.

MARSH

Marsh is mentioned in connection with only three places in Norfolk:

(1) *Fo.* 205. Heckingham (Clavering): marsh for 60 sheep (*maresc lx oves*).
(2) *Fo.* 273b. Raveningham (Clavering): one marsh (*i maresc*).
(3) *Fo.* 212b. Marham (Clackclose): and in marsh the measurement is unknown (*et in maresc nescit mensura*).

The first two villages lie near the marshes of the lower Yare and Waveney; the third extends into the valley of the Nar which is an extension of the Fenland in the west of the county. It is at once obvious that these three entries cannot have represented all the marsh in a county that includes part of the Fenland in the west and the Broadland in the east. Marshland must have played an important part in the economy of many more villages. The reference to sheep at Heckingham suggests some analogy with the pasture entries we have already discussed. As we have seen, the 'pasture for sheep' that is recorded for five villages presumably referred to marshy flats on which the sheep fed. But the addition of these five localities does not affect the fact that the greater part of the Norfolk marshland remains unaccounted for in the Domesday text.

It is possible that the entry relating to Marham throws a little light (but only a very dim light) on the problem. That entry follows a statement about the dimensions of Marham—its length and breadth—and is

---

[1] See p. 241 below.

introduced in such a way as to suggest that it is drawing attention to the incompleteness of the information conveyed by those dimensions. Presumably for other places, the information about marsh is, in some way, included in the total measurement of the village. But this does not take us very far, because, as we have seen, the meaning of these dimensions is wrapped in complete obscurity. All we can do is to say that here is another example of the incompleteness of the Domesday information.

FISHERIES

Fisheries are recorded for 1086 in connection with 61 places in Norfolk. For each of these places the number of fisheries only is stated, and no reference is made to their value as is the case in some other counties. Usually there was but one fishery in a vill, but two and three and even six and seven are occasionally recorded. At the other end of the scale, there is mention of half-fisheries and even of quarter-fisheries. Sometimes, it is possible to guess how the half-fisheries came to be recorded, e.ġ. two adjacent villages must have shared one fishery, and a half is recorded for each. But it is frequently impossible to combine the fractions in this way; thus Gayton Thorpe in Freebridge had a quarter of a fishery (274b), but we hear nothing of the other three-quarters. The usual Latin word used is *piscaria*, but there are variations; *piscina* occurs, for example, at South Runcton (209), and *piscatio* at Kilverstone (153b). A distinction is occasionally made between conditions in 1066 and 1086; Harling (Guiltcross) had 5 fisheries in 1066 but only 1½ in 1086 (149b): while at Ingoldisthorpe (Smethden) we are simply told 'then one fishery' (256b).

As Fig. 31 shows, these fisheries, for the most part, lay in the west of the county—in and near the Fenland and along the westward-flowing streams, Babingley River, the Nar, the Wissey, the Little Ouse and the Thet. Elsewhere (e.g. along the Yare, the Waveney and the Wensum), the distribution is sporadic, and, quite often we hear nothing of fisheries in places where we should expect them to be. None is mentioned, for example, in the Broadland. There is, moreover, no reference to sea-fisheries, though we cannot be certain that the fisheries recorded for Hunstanton and Heacham, in the north-west of the county, were not sea-fisheries. The Norfolk folios are silent even about the Yarmouth fisheries, yet among the Suffolk entries there is a reference to 24 Yarmouth

fishermen (283). It is not impossible that the rent of 2,000 herrings paid by
Thorpe next Norwich really came from Yarmouth (137b).

SALT-PANS

Salt-pans are recorded in connection with 62 villages in Norfolk. For
each of these villages the number of pans only is stated and no estimate of

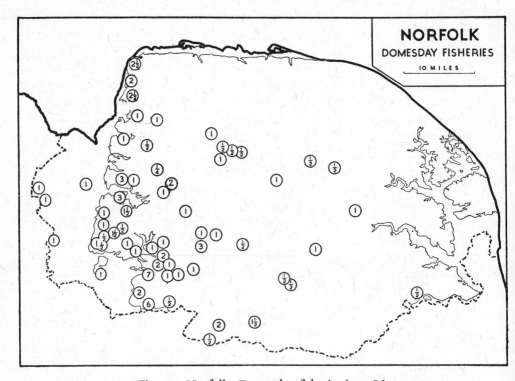

Fig. 31. Norfolk: Domesday fisheries in 1086.
The figure in each circle indicates the number of fisheries. The boundary of alluvium
and peat is shown; see Fig. 22.

their value is given. The number of pans in a village varies from under 1 to
over 40. Where fractions of a pan are mentioned, it is occasionally possible
to fit them together in a way that suggests that adjacent villages shared
a pan. But only too frequently this is impossible; thus at Shernborne
(Docking) there was one-twelfth of a pan (268), but we are given no clue
as to the other eleven-twelfths. In some villages there had been changes

between 1066 and 1086. Three examples from Freebridge hundred will show the amount of variation involved:

	1066	1086
Gaywood (191)	30 salt-pans	21 salt-pans
West Walton (160, 213)	30½ ,,	37 ,,
Wootton (126)	20 ,,	14 ,,

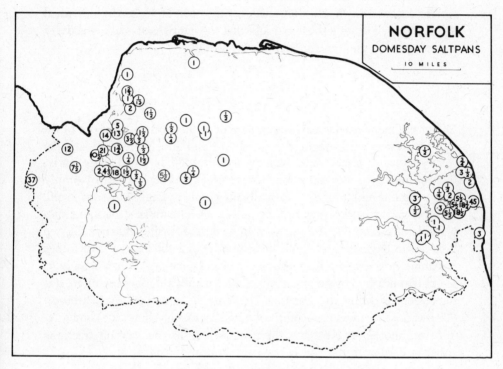

Fig. 32. Norfolk: Domesday salt-pans in 1086.

The figure in each circle indicates the number of salt pans. For a caution about the location of some of these pans, see p. 136. The boundary of alluvium and peat is shown; see Fig. 22.

Fig. 32 shows that the distribution of the salt-making industry was very limited, being confined almost exclusively to two areas around the eastern and western marshlands respectively. The outstanding villages in each area were Caister in East Flegg with 45 pans, and West Walton in Freebridge with 37. The two concentrations of east and west were separated by quite a big gap. Burnham was the only place along the north coast for which a salt-pan was entered. Some of these pans, particularly those in the west, could not have been located in the villages for which they are recorded. Thus it is physically impossible that there could have been a salt-pan in any of the three villages of Helhoughton (122), Rainham (237b), and Rudham (169). The salt-pans of these and other upland villages must have been situated elsewhere—in the Fenland, or along the eastern coast of the Wash. But whatever the uncertainty about individual distributions, Fig. 32 leaves no doubt that substantial salt-making activity was centred on the Fenland and the Broadland.

MILLS

Mills were mentioned as existing in 1086 in connection with 302 out of the 731 Domesday settlements in Norfolk. In addition, there were another thirteen places where mills had existed in 1066 but had, apparently, disappeared by 1086; thus for Hedenham (Loddon) the record simply says 'then one mill' (152b). Normally the number of mills only was stated, and this varied from a fraction of a mill up to nine mills. It is sometimes possible to reassemble the fractions in a comprehensible manner; of two holdings in Bayfield (Holt), one had a quarter of a mill (112) and the other had three-quarters (242b), presumably of the same mill. Occasionally, it seems that nearby villages must have shared a mill, but, only too often, it is impossible to bring the fractions conveniently together. At Tasburgh (Depwade) there was one-eighth of a mill on one holding (202) and one-third on another (225b), but there is no clue to the missing fractions either in Tasburgh itself or in the neighbouring villages.

Domesday Mills in Norfolk in 1086

Under 1 mill	33 settlements		5 mills	8 settlements
1 ,,	129 ,,		6 ,,	1 settlement
2 mills	86 ,,		7 ,,	2 settlements
3 ,,	28 ,,		8 ,,	1 settlement
4 ,,	13 ,,		9 ,,	1 ,,

Over one-half of the villages with mills had only 1 mill or a fraction of a mill. The above table cannot be accurate owing to the complications caused by the fractions. Apart from those places with 'under 1 mill', an outstanding fraction of a mill for a village has been counted as a whole mill, and the proportion of villages in each category may be affected. But the general picture given by the table is probably not far wrong, and, in particular, it does show how some villages seem to have had many more

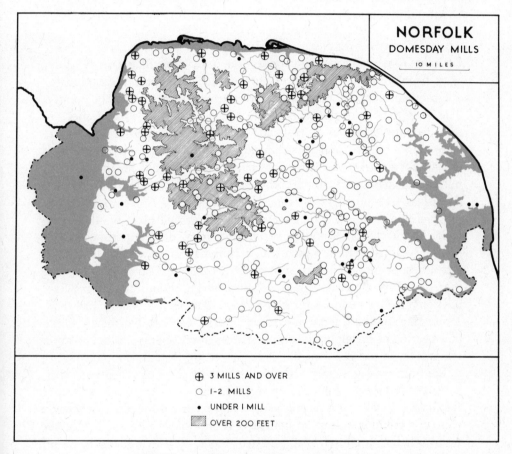

Fig. 33. Norfolk: Domesday mills in 1086.
The areas of alluvium and peat are indicated; see Fig. 22. Rivers passing through these areas are not shown.

than one mill at work. The group of 6 mills was at Wymondham (Forehoe); those of 7 mills at Acre and at Snettisham (Freebridge); that of 8 at Thetford; that of 9 mills at Barsham (Gallow).

The mills were water-mills, and Fig. 33 shows how they were aligned along the streams. But the general distribution, as opposed to the location of individual mills, is not what might be expected. The areas with most arable and with the most dense population, are not the areas with either the most mills or the largest clusters of mills. What, for example, happened about milling in the two hundreds of Flegg with only two half-mills?

CHURCHES

Churches are mentioned in connection with 217 villages in Norfolk, apart from those of Norwich, Thetford and Yarmouth. We cannot for one moment suppose that these were the only churches in the county. The weight of probability is against such an idea. No churches are recorded, for example, at Holt and at Dunham (Launditch) yet there were markets there, and it is difficult to believe that a place important enough for a market was without a church. Moreover, there are a number of hundreds with but 1 church each—Earsham, Forehoe, North Greenhoe, Grimshoe, Smethden. Then again, for 7 places, the *I.E.* records churches not mentioned in the Domesday text.[1] A few villages, on the other hand, had 2 churches, and some of these form double parishes today. Thus Tivetshall (Diss), which had 2 churches, is now represented by 2 parishes, St Margaret and St Mary. Wheatacre in Clavering is likewise represented by 2 parishes, All Saints and Burgh, though the latter parish has come to be known as Burgh St Peter. Barsham in Gallow had three Domesday churches, and today it forms 3 parishes, East, North, and West. The bearing of this upon the double-names discussed on p. 102, and upon the process of parish formation as envisaged by Round, is interesting.[2]

For some villages only a fraction of a church is recorded (one-half, a quarter or a third), and it is impossible to find any clue to the remaining fractions.[3] Finally, priests are occasionally recorded for places where no church is mentioned, but, of course, it is impossible to do anything but guess whether a church really existed there. At Hevingham, in South Erpingham, the chances seem to be that there was a church, for we are told that a priest, with 40 acres of land, sang 'three masses every week' (133).

[1] *I.E.* pp. 136–7, East Dereham, *Torp*, Pulham, Bridgham, Northwold, West Walton, Terrington. The *I.E.* also includes Feltwell in the list, but its church may be the same as that in a Domesday entry for the vill under William de Warenne (162).

[2] See J. H. Round in *V.C.H. Essex*, I, pp. 400 *et seq.*

[3] For the nature of these fractions, see p. 76 above.

Normally, the value of a church was stated together with the number of acres it held; thus at Appleton, in Freebridge, we are told that there was 'one church with 12 acres, and it is worth 12 pence' (173b). In some cases no value was entered and we are left to infer that the value was included in that of the holding as a whole. Indeed this is stated explicitly more than once. Thus on fo. 172 we are told that 'all the churches on the land of William de Warenne are valued with the manors'. It was the same on the lands of Hermer de Ferrières (208), and elsewhere.

URBAN LIFE

Only three places in the Norfolk folios are recorded as possessing burgesses—Norwich, Thetford and Yarmouth. The information recorded for each of these places is very unsatisfactory. All three must have possessed markets, yet none is recorded; the markets of the Norfolk Domesday Book were in places without burgesses. All we can do is to summarise the information such as it is; although unsatisfactory, it does at any rate tell us something.

Norwich

The account of Norwich (116–18) starts off clearly enough by saying that in 1066 there had been 1,320 burgesses in the town. It then goes on to give more detailed particulars, but these soon become hopelessly involved. It is difficult to fit the isolated pieces of information into one coherent picture, and, very frequently, the details relating to 1066 seem to be intermixed with those of 1086. A few general features emerge. Seventy-two acres of meadow are recorded, and these reflect the location of the town in the moist alluvial valley of the Wensum before it joins the Yare to enter the region of the Broads; there were also 16 acres of pasture. Numerous churches are mentioned, and they give the impression of a well-populated town. In one place we are told that the burgesses used to hold (*tenebant*) 15 churches; in another place that they were then holding (*tenent*) 43 chapels. Some of the churches are mentioned by name— All Saints, St Martin, St Michael, Holy Trinity, St Simon and St Jude, and, finally, St Lawrence. There is also reference to the houses which King William had given 'for the principal seat of the bishopric'; and, we are also told that the bishop could have one moneyer (*monetarius*) if he wished, but there is no mention of a mint. Mills are also mentioned, all of them in fractions—a half of one, a quarter of another and three parts of a third. Holdings of acres are mentioned as belonging to various people and churches, but the information is too incomplete to add up. The mention of 3 ploughs and a render of honey serves to remind us that the towns of the early Middle Ages still had the flavour of rural communities about them. A hint of the amenities of the time is given by the reference to 'one bear and six dogs for bear [baiting]'. From unsatisfactory fragments such as these two facts stand out fairly clearly.

In the first place, the town had fallen upon evil days. There is a tantalising statement to the effect that 'now there are in the borough 665 English burgesses and they pay the customary dues (*consuetudines*); and 480 bordars who on account of poverty pay no customary dues'. The relation of these bordars to the population of 1066 is not stated, yet there are several indications that the total population of the town had decreased. A total of 297 empty messuages (*mansurae vacuae*) is mentioned together with '50 houses from which the king has not his custom'. Ninety-eight of these empty dwellings were *in occupatione castelli*, which may imply that they had been cleared to make way for building the castle. Twenty-two burgesses had gone to live in Beccles, and another ten had also quitted (*dimiserunt*) the borough. 'Those fleeing and the others remaining have been entirely ruined (*vastati*) partly by reason of the forfeitures of Earl Ralf, partly by reason of a fire, partly by reason of the king's geld, partly by Waleram.' But despite its many misfortunes, Norwich must have been a substantial settlement in 1086, with probably nearer 5,000 than 4,000 inhabitants, and quite possibly with more than 5,000.

In the second place, it is clear that the conquerors had added a new borough (*novus burgus*) to the old. By 1086 this addition seems to have included 124 French burgesses and one waste messuage. There was also a church which Earl Ralf had built in the new borough. But on the topographical relation of the new borough to the old, the Domesday Book is silent.

Thetford

The main account of Thetford is given on fos. 118b–119, but there are three additional entries relating to the town, on fos. 136, 137 and 173. The figures are no less perplexing than those of Norwich. One thing is clear. Although it was described entirely in the Norfolk section of the Domesday Book, the town lay partly in Norfolk and partly in Suffolk, as indeed it continued to lie until the boundary changes of the nineteenth century.

'Of the king's land in Thetford, on the Norfolk side of the river (*ultra aquam versus Norfolc*) is 1 league of land in length and half [a league] in breadth.... Of all this land, one half is arable, and the other half is pasture.... On the other side [of the river] towards Suffolk, there is half a league of land in length and a half in breadth.... All this land is arable and 4 ploughs can till it.' There were 943 burgesses in the borough in 1066, but by 1086 there were only 720 burgesses 'and 224 empty messuages'. Other people were also enumerated, but in a rather sporadic and untidy fashion. Thus in 1086 there seem to have been 5 burgesses in addition to the 720 already mentioned; there were also 1 villein, 2 sokemen, 3 serfs, 30 bordars, and 33 men, but even the grand total of these categories may well not represent all the adult male population of the town. A picture of a populated centre sharply differentiated from the countryside around is also given by the fact that 12½ churches are mentioned as being in the town, and some of them are specifically named, St Peter's, St John's, St Martin's, St Margaret's and St Helen's; there was also a monastery. A mint (*moneta*) tendering £40 to the king is also mentioned. We are not told what commercial activity, if any, sustained and nourished this community, but some reference is made to the agricultural element in it. A total of 9 plough-teams seems to be mentioned for 1086, and there was land for four further teams, while 2 plough-lands remained in pasture (*in pasture*).[1] The meadow amounted to 34 acres, and there seems to have been a substantial amount of pasture around the town. A total number of 163 sheep is mentioned, together with 1 horse. The resources of the town also included 7⅔ mills, and the render of the town included honey, goat-skins and ox-hides.

These stray fragments of information leave much to be desired, and the figures are very unsatisfactory. From them we must envisage a substantial community, not, it is true, as large as it had been, but still quite considerable for these early days. It numbered at least 4,000, and probably more. Around the settlement lay the arable and pasture, together with meadow along the courses of the Little Ouse and Thet, and it is clear that agriculture must have played an important part in the lives of its inhabitants.

Yarmouth

The Domesday account of Yarmouth is brief (118). In 1086, as in 1066, there were 70 burgesses there; they were served by at least one

[1] See p. 131 above.

church, that of St Benet. No mention is made of other categories of population, and no clue is given to the activities of the community as a whole. In the Suffolk section of the Little Domesday Book, however, we are told that 24 fishermen in Yarmouth belonged to the manor of Gorleston (283); from this hint we must imagine the rest. Altogether, Yarmouth must have included at least 400 people and probably considerably more.

LIVESTOCK

The Norfolk folios, like the rest of the Little Domesday Book, record information about livestock—not about the total stock on a holding but only about that held on the demesne land. Sometimes this restriction is explicitly stated; the enumeration of the stock at Wilton (Grimshoe), for example, is prefaced by the phrase 'on the demesne' (162). But elsewhere, that is to say in the bulk of entries, we can only assume that it is the stock on the demesne that is recorded. Where no stock is recorded for a village, such a village is usually without demesne. Some places with demesne land, it is true, have no stock, but no place without demesne has any stock recorded for it. The total number in each category of stock in 1086 is as follows:[1]

Sheep	46,458	Rounceys	767
Swine	8,074	Horses	50
Goats	3,020	Mares	56
Animals	2,107	Wild Mares	139
Cows	23	Foals	25
Donkeys	2	Mules	1

The figures for 1086 are sometimes very different from those of 1066, but the form of an entry is occasionally so obscure that it is impossible to say whether the stock on a holding in 1066 was also there in 1086 and vice versa. Two entries from South Greenhoe will illustrate this obscurity. Of Newton by Castle Acre, we are merely told 'when Godric received it he found 9 animals and one rouncey, 30 swine, 30 sheep' (120). Were

[1] There is another count of the Norfolk livestock in M. E. Seebohm's *The Evolution of the English Farm* (London, 1927), p. 156:

Sheep	43,848	Cows	26
Swine	7,824	Rounceys	584
Goats	3,016	Horses	242
Animals	2,125		

these numbers there in 1066? Were they still there in 1086? It is impossible to say. Or again, we are told that at Sporle there were 'then 6 animals and 2 rounceys and 60 swine and 180 sheep' (119b). Probably all these figures refer to 1066, but it is just possible that the 'then' may govern 'animals' only and that the rounceys, swine and sheep were there in 1086 as well as 1066. On the other hand, nothing could be more definite than the statement for Fritton in Depwade: 'Then 6 animals and 60 sheep, now nothing' (260). That for Snoring in North Greenhoe is equally clear: 'Always 30 swine, afterwards and now 180 sheep' (122b). There is a curious entry for Hempnall in Depwade. After giving particulars about stock and other matters, the entry goes on to say: 'Besides all this the manor renders (*reddit*) 6 cows and 20 swine and 20 rams' (249). What was the relation of these to the stock already enumerated? We can only say that the earlier enumeration does not mention cows or rams. There is yet another curiosity recorded for Halvergate in Walsham. The entry enumerates all the details of the manor (including the stock) and then closes with this statement: 'And besides the sheep aforesaid there belong to this manor 700 sheep and they render 100 shillings' (128b). It must be a witness to some peculiarity in the arrangements of the manor, but what that was we cannot tell. These few examples will show some of the difficulties raised by the enumeration of stock.

Horses are fairly frequently recorded. Sometimes the words *in aula* (131), *in dominio* (186) or *in aula dominica* (257b) are added. At other times, the word for horse is followed by the adjective *silvestres* or *silvaticae*, and it is clear that groups of these wild or unbroken mares were to be found in a number of Norfolk parishes. Foals are occasionally mentioned; at Great Ellingham (Shropham) there were 6 mares with foals (207). But of all the varieties of horse, the most frequently mentioned is the rouncey (*runcinus*); the usual number recorded for the demesne of a village is 2, 3 or 4, but occasionally it is greater. Donkeys and mules, on the other hand, are only very occasionally mentioned; there was a donkey at Beechamwell in Clackclose (190b) and a mule at Rudham in Brothercross (169b). There must have been many others that were not recorded.

Goats are recorded for a number of holdings, but the flocks were very much smaller than those of sheep. The number on the demesne of a village was usually under fifty and sometimes less than ten.

Swine are very much more frequently mentioned. The number on the demesne of a holding was rarely the same as the number its woodland could support, being sometimes less and occasionally more. Frequently, swine are recorded for holdings without any wood; thus there were 60 swine on the demesne at Snoring in Gallow, but no wood is entered for the village (257).

Animals presumably include all the non-ploughing beasts. Curiously enough cows are very seldom mentioned, certainly not more than about a dozen times. Yet they must have been kept in considerable numbers for breeding the oxen which formed the mainstay of the economic life of the countryside. Possibly they were included under the general heading of *animalia*. These 'animals' are recorded for a large number of villages— usually less than twenty in a village, but occasionally more.

Each of the major groups of stock discussed above was fairly widely distributed over the county, some, of course, more so than others; the distribution of goats, for example, was not as evenly spread as that of the other groups. But none of the distributions presents any special features, and no maps illustrating them have been reproduced. There is one other group of animals, however, that merits more detailed treatment. Sheep are recorded in large numbers and their distribution presents some interesting features.

Sheep

Although Fig. 34 cannot in any way be regarded as a complete map of the sheep of the county, it may give some hint about some of the factors governing the distribution of sheep in general. The first thing that stands out is that there were fewest sheep where there was most wood; the largest number of sheep was to be found on the lighter soils in the west of the county. The second feature is the association of sheep with salt marshes; the largest flock numbered 1,300 and was at West Walton in the Fenland (213). It is possible that some of the sheep in the north-western hundreds of the county may have been pastured on the salt marshes of the coast. At any rate they were certainly associated with the marshy estuaries in the eastern part of the county as Fig. 34 shows. This is not to suggest that geographical conditions alone were important in affecting the distribution of sheep, for social organisation, too, entered into their distribution.

The number of sheep often varied a great deal between 1066 and 1086. In some villages there was a great decline; in others a great increase. Thus at Appleton (Freebridge) there had been a drop from 163 to 16 (fos. 173b, 256), while at Harpley, nearby, there had been a rise from 180 to 308 (fo. 161b). But the reason for all these changes lies beyond our reach.

The existence of other sheep in the county is shown by the frequent reference to 'fold-soke (*soca faldae*)'. This was one of the services ren-

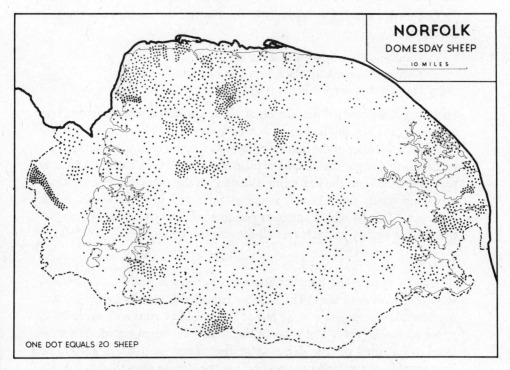

NORFOLK
DOMESDAY SHEEP
10 MILES

ONE DOT EQUALS 20 SHEEP

Fig. 34. Norfolk: Domesday sheep on the demesne in 1086.
The boundary of alluvium and peat is shown; see Fig. 22.

dered by a man to his lord. 'The man must not have a fold of his own; his sheep must lie in the lord's fold. It is manure that the lord wants; the demand for manure has played a large part in the history of the human race.'[1] Six men in the village of Hellington (Loddon) owed fold-soke (203b), yet no sheep are recorded there. They were not on the demesne of a manor and so escaped record. Many other examples could be given. We cannot even guess at the numbers of these unrecorded sheep although,

[1] F. W. Maitland, *op. cit.* p. 76.

if thirteenth-century evidence is anything to go by, the flocks of the tenants were frequently as great as, and sometimes very much greater than, those of their lords.[1]

Markets

The entries relating to markets in the Norfolk folios are only three in number:

(1) Dunham (Launditch): half a market (137).
(2) Litcham (Launditch): the fourth part of a market (207b).
(3) Holt (Holt): one market (111b).

Sir Henry Ellis omitted the market at Holt, but stated that there was one at Colney (204b);[2] this inclusion, however, seems to be due to a misreading of the text. Neither of the first two places has record of any special activity or group of people that might explain the presence of a market, nor is there any clue as to the remaining fractions of the markets. For Holt, on the other hand, there is a mysterious reference to what seems to be 'one port' (111b) which suggests commercial activity. It is a short list that cannot by any means cover all the markets of Domesday Norfolk.

Beehives

Associated with the statistics about stock, there is occasionally a statement about hives of bees. The number recorded is usually under 10, and sometimes it is only 1, 2 or 3; but at Methwold (Grimshoe) as many as 27 are recorded (136). The value of the beehives is never stated. The total number recorded on the demesne of the county in 1086 is 421.[3] The keeping of bees was far more important in the Middle Ages than now—for mead, for wax and for sugar. These entries cannot represent all the hives in the county, and occasionally a render of honey is stated for places where no beehives are mentioned, e.g. for Foulsham in Eynesford (114).

Other references

There was a deer park (*parcus bestiis*) at Costessey (145), a castle at Norwich (116b), and waste land (*est vastata*) at Holkham (113).

---

[1] Eileen Power, *The Wool Trade in English Medieval History* (Oxford, 1941), pp. 30–1.
[2] Sir Henry Ellis, *op. cit.* I, p. 252.
[3] M. E. Seebohm, *op. cit.* p. 156, gives the number as 446.

REGIONAL SUMMARY

The regional division of Norfolk, shown on Fig. 35, follows in the main that of P. M. Roxby,[1] but incorporates some details from the maps of Dr J. E. G. Mosby.[2] The regions number eight and, while their boundaries do not agree with those of the unit areas of Figs. 26 and 28, they are sufficiently near to enable generalisations to be made. The main basis of the division can be seen from the maps of Geology (Fig. 22) and Soil Types (Fig. 23). Comparison of these two maps shows the limitations of geological nomenclature for our purpose. The 'Boulder Clay' of the geological map, for example, is seen to include a wide variety of soils, varying from light to heavy. And, moreover, the light sandy Breckland that forms such a feature of the soil map does not stand out distinctively upon the geological map.

(1) Mid-Norfolk

This is largely a Boulder Clay area, lying for the most part between 150–250 ft. above sea-level and rising to just over 300 ft. in the north-west. The soils vary a great deal but are mainly between medium and heavy, and perhaps they can best be described as strong loams. The long eastward slope is varied with wide and deep valleys that supported numerous villages, each with anything up to two dozen acres of meadow. The general prosperity of the area, as indicated by plough-teams and population, was about average for the county as a whole—not as great as that of the north-eastern loam area, but a good deal higher than that of the western sandy regions. The upland as a whole was originally wooded, and in Domesday times still carried a substantial amount of wood cover. Sheep, at any rate demesne sheep, were comparatively few in the region.

(2) South Norfolk

This region is a continuation of mid-Norfolk and it is difficult to draw a line separating them. But there are many differences between the two. South Norfolk is lower; its highest point reaches only 230 ft., and for the

---

[1] P. M. Roxby, 'East Anglia', in A. G. Ogilvie (ed.), *Great Britain: Essays in Regional Geography* (Cambridge, 1928), p. 164.

[2] J. E. G. Mosby: (1) 'Norwich in its Regional Setting: The Geography of Norfolk', in R. H. Mottram (ed.), *A Scientific Survey of Norwich and District* (British Association, London, 1935), p. 20; (2) J. E. G. Mosby, *Norfolk* (London, 1938), p. 193, being Part 70 of *The Land of Britain*, ed. L. Dudley Stamp.

most part it lies between 50 and 150 ft. Its soils, too, are distinctly heavier than those of mid-Norfolk, though there is much variation. Presumably the area was at one time as heavily wooded as mid-Norfolk, perhaps even more heavily wooded, but Fig. 29 shows that by the eleventh century

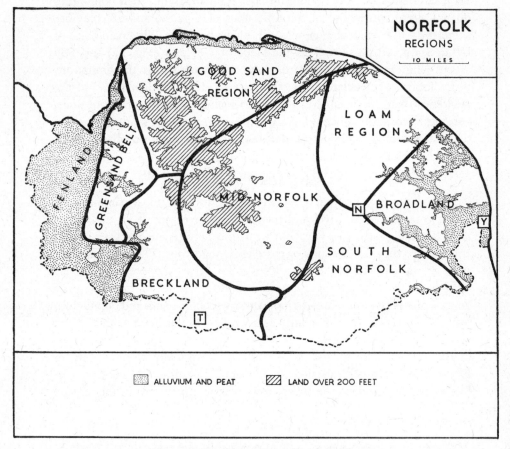

Fig. 35. Norfolk: Regional subdivisions.
Places with burgesses are indicated by initials:
N, Norwich; T, Thetford; Y, Yarmouth.

a great deal of clearing had been carried on, and that only a small amount of wood remained. An explanation of this clearing may lie in the fact that the villages here lie thick upon the ground, especially in the area immediately south of Norwich. This is reflected in the high density of both teams and population. Sheep were relatively few except in the east along the margins of the Broadland. Meadow, as might be expected, was most extensive partly on the Broadland margins and partly in the south along the Waveney.

(3) Broadland

The Broadland includes two types of country. In the first place, there is the alluvial area which must have been even more watery and marshy in Domesday times than it is today. In the second place, there is the 'island' of the two hundreds of Flegg, the greater part of which lies below 60 ft. above sea-level. The soil of the island is a medium loam, very fertile, and closely settled with numerous villages. The densities of teams and population are among the highest for Norfolk, and are particularly striking when it is remembered that the acreages of the two hundreds included substantial amounts of marshy alluvium. Many of the village names are Scandinavian, and it is interesting to note, as Miss Dodwell has pointed out, that the free element is particularly high in the population. In view of the high density of population, it is not surprising to see that there was very little wood in the area. Sheep, on the other hand, were numerous, and they may have fed upon the marshes, though the Domesday Book does not say so. The distinctive physical characteristics of the area are reflected in the large number of salt-pans; salt-making must obviously have been an important industry here. There was abundant meadow.

(4) The Loam Region

This is a low-lying comparatively featureless area for the most part below 150 ft. above sea-level. Its main characteristic is the presence of glacial loams yielding fertile light to medium soils. The advantages of the area for early settlement and early agriculture have often been stressed, but, taking the county as a whole, it may well be that its attractions have been overrated. It has been asserted, for example, that the loam area around Walsham and Aylsham was open country, easily settled, with an outstandingly large number of villages. But the map of Domesday settlements shows that the Boulder Clay area to the south of Norwich was considerably more densely occupied than the Loam Region. The fact is that intermixed with the loams, there are considerable stretches of infertile sands and gravels that locally give rise to heaths. Many have disappeared before the advances of scientific farming, but the modern Land Utilisation map still showed a considerable amount of heath and rough pasture to the south of Aylsham. In view of these facts, it is not surprising that the density of Domesday plough-teams was below that of South Norfolk, but higher than those of the light soils of the west; the averages for population reflect these differences in a general way. The curiously low figures for the hundred of Taverham have been discussed on p. 124. The original wood-cover was probably lighter than that of mid-Norfolk and South Norfolk, and the Domesday villages carried relatively small amounts of wood. Sheep were comparatively rare except towards the Broadland. Meadow was likewise small in amount.

(5) *The Breckland*

The Breckland is mostly a low plateau rising to between 50 and 150 ft. above sea-level. It owes its character to a remarkable cover of sand that lies over a complex subsoil of Chalk and Boulder Clay. The sand is so light that it has been known to blow away in the wind; much of its surface is occupied by heath and warren. The few villages of the region are set in the valleys of the Wissey, the Little Ouse and their tributaries. Either these streams or the adjoining Fenland supported a large number of fisheries; the valleys, too, carried a moderate amount of meadow.

The density of both teams and population was low. There was hardly any wood in the region, and this is one of the few areas in England where there is more wood today than there was in Domesday times. Tree-planting on a large scale started in the middle of the nineteenth century, and since 1921, the Forestry Commission has greatly changed the appearance of the region. But in 1086 the heaths presumably were still bare, and it is interesting to see that they seem to have carried a fair number of sheep.

(6) *The Good Sand Region*

The greater part of this upland country averages between 150 and 300 ft. above sea-level. Some of it is Chalk; the rest of it is covered by Boulder Clay which here consists of light soils—sands and gravels together with medium and light loams. Arthur Young gave it the name 'Good Sand' in opposition to the 'Light Sand' of the Breckland. The term 'good' was only justified by the agricultural improvements of the eighteenth century, and this is the region most closely associated with the development of the 'Norfolk Husbandry'. Before the eighteenth century, it must have included great stretches of heath and sheep-walk; some still remain. Villages were fairly frequent, but occasional villageless tracts testify to the one time poverty of the country. It can hardly have been initially attractive to agriculturalists, and, generally speaking, the density of teams is lower than that of the Loam Region. The area was almost completely lacking in wood, and so stood in contrast with mid-Norfolk to the south-east. Sheep, on the other hand, were widespread. The little valleys (e.g. of the Babingley and the Stiffkey) carried a certain amount of meadow. Salt-pans are entered for some villages, but the pans themselves must have been situated along the coast to the west.

(7) *The Greensand Belt*

This has been marked as a distinct region because of its geological formation, but its soil resembles that of the Good Sand Region in being light; tracts of heath are still to be found here today. Patches of heavier soil, particularly between the Nar and the Wissey, form exceptions to this generalisation. Villages were fairly frequent, and the general densities of teams and population resembled those of the Good Sand Region. Sheep, too, were numerous here. There was also some wood, associated possibly with the tracts of clay. A distinctive feature was the large number of salt-pans associated with the villages of the northern part of the area— bearing witness to the proximity of the sea. The lower course of the streams before they entered the Fenland proper, seem to have been bordered by appreciable quantities of meadow.

(8) *The Fenland*

This low-lying area comprised silt in the north and peat in the south. Like the rest of the fen country, it must have been a poor area in the eleventh century. The few settlements were situated upon the silt except for Hilgay and Southery which lay upon islands in the peat. The densities of teams and population were low, and form a contrast to the great prosperity of the siltlands in the later Middle Ages. As might be expected, the region had no wood entered for it, but the presence of fisheries and salt-pans reflected the geographical peculiarity of the area. Sheep seem to have been fairly numerous. Like those of Essex, they may have fed upon the marsh, but the Domesday Book says nothing of this. Some of the Fenland villages had a good deal of meadow.

BIBLIOGRAPHICAL NOTE

(1) The text of the Norfolk folios has been translated by Charles Johnson and E. Salisbury in *V.C.H. Norfolk* (1906), II, pp. 38–203. There is also an introduction by Charles Johnson (pp. 1–37).

(2) An older study of the Norfolk Domesday is the Reverend George Munford's *An analysis of the Domesday Book of the county of Norfolk* (London, 1858). It is not a geographical analysis hundred by hundred or vill by vill, and much of it is devoted to an account of the tenants-in-chief.

(3) Two works by D. C. Douglas discuss, among other things, various aspects of the Norfolk evidence:

The Social Structure of Medieval East Anglia (Oxford, 1927).
Feudal Documents from the Abbey of Bury St Edmunds (London: British Academy, 1932).

The following also deal with various aspects:

K. J. ALLISON, 'The Lost Villages of Norfolk', *Norfolk Archaeology* (Norwich, 1955), XXXI, pp. 116–62.

H. BEEVOR, 'Norfolk woodlands from the evidence of contemporary chronicles', *Quart. Journ. of Forestry* (1925), XIX, pp. 87–110. This contains a map on p. 91 showing places which had wood for 100 or more swine.

H. C. DARBY, 'Domesday Woodland in East Anglia', *Antiquity* (Gloucester, 1934), XIV, pp. 211–14.

H. C. DARBY, 'The Domesday Geography of Norfolk and Suffolk', *Geog. Journ.* (1935), LXXXV, pp. 432–52.

R. H. C. DAVIS, 'East Anglia and the Danelaw', *Trans. Roy. Hist. Soc.* (1955), 5th Ser. vol. V, pp. 23–39.

BARBARA DODWELL, 'The free peasantry of East Anglia in Domesday', *Norfolk Archaeology* (Norwich, 1941), XXVII, pp. 145–57.

BARBARA DODWELL, 'The making of the Domesday Survey in Norfolk: the hundred and a half of Clackclose', *Eng. Hist. Rev.* (1969), LXXXIV, pp. 79–84.

R. WELLDON FINN, *Domesday Studies: The Eastern Counties* (London, 1967).

J. C. TINGEY, 'Some Notes on the Domesday Assessment of Norfolk', *Norfolk Archaeology* (Norwich, 1923), XXI, pp. 134–42.

(4) The method and contents of the Little Domesday Book and of the *Inquisitio Eliensis* are discussed in many of the general works upon the Domesday Book (see pp. 3 *et seq.* and pp. 7 *et seq.* above, and p. 264 below).

CHAPTER IV

SUFFOLK

The Domesday folios relating to Suffolk share the double distinction of those relating to Norfolk. In the first place, they form part of the Little Domesday Book, with its greater detail, its information about conditions in 1066 as well as those in 1086, and its particulars about livestock on the demesne lands. The account of Suffolk comes last, and it is followed by a sentence that forms the concluding paragraph to the book as a whole. This is the famous colophon: *Anno millesimo octogesimo sexto ab Incarnatione Domini vigesimo vero regni Willelmi facta est ista descriptio, non solum per hos tres comitatus sed etiam per alios.* Round believed that the word *descriptio* refers not to the making of the book, but to the making of the survey; and that the book itself, as we now know it, was not completed until much later.[1] Professor Galbraith, however, does not draw this distinction between the *descriptio* and the Little Domesday Book, and he believes that the latter was itself completed in 1086.[2]

In the second place, the *I.E.* again provides an important subsidiary source of information. Indeed, it is more important for Suffolk than for Norfolk because the abbey of Ely held more estates here, and the opportunities of comparing the two sets of information are correspondingly greater; the Ely estates were particularly numerous in the hundreds to the north and east of Ipswich. As in the case of Norfolk, a minute comparison makes it unlikely that the *I.E.* was copied from the Little Domesday Book, for it is clear that the compilers of the *I.E.* must have had access to sources of information other than the Little Domesday Book as we now know it.[3] The footnotes to the Domesday text as edited in the *Victoria County History* for Suffolk show how it differs in detail from that of the *I.E.*: the former puts 7 where the latter puts 8, or 18 where the latter puts 16, and so on.[4] The figures relating to Undley, now in the

[1] J. H. Round, *Feudal England*, pp. 139–40.
[2] V. H. Galbraith, 'The Making of Domesday Book', *Eng. Hist. Rev.* (1942), LVII, p. 177. But this view is contested by Professor D. C. Douglas in *The Domesday Monachorum of Christ Church Canterbury* (London, 1944), p. 24.
[3] For the statistics of the *I.E.*, see pp. 99–101 above.
[4] *V.C.H. Suffolk* (London, 1911), I, pp. 518–26.

parish of Lakenheath (Lackford), illustrate the kind of discrepancy to be found:

(*a*) *Little Domesday Book* (fo. 382)

(At) *Lundale* Saint Etheldreda held 1 carucate of land. And 3 bordars and 4 serfs. Always 2 ploughs on the demesne. And 13 acres of meadow. And 2 fisheries. And 1 horse, 24 beasts, and 62 sheep.

(*b*) *Inquisitio Eliensis* (p. 154)

(At) *Undelai* Saint Etheldreda held *T.R.E.* 1 carucate of land. Always 5 bordars and 4 serfs. Always 1 plough on the demesne. And 13 acres of meadow. And 2 fisheries. Always 1 rouncey, and 23 beasts, and 62 sheep.

Sometimes the three manuscripts of the *I.E.* disagree with one another; thus in the account of Undley one manuscript records 60 sheep instead of the 62 noted above. Such minor variants are fairly common. It all bears out what has already been said about the human factor that always enters into Domesday statistics.

These two features are not the only ones that give a special flavour to the Suffolk section of the Domesday Book. There is a third feature that makes parts of the Suffolk text of peculiar interest. This is the existence of an independent survey based upon an enquiry made at a time near that of the Domesday Inquest, and covering the estates of the abbey of Bury St Edmunds. A number of these estates lay in Norfolk, but most were in Suffolk, and especially in the western part of the county. A portion of the survey has been preserved in the twelfth-century Feudal Book of Abbot Baldwin, and it has been discussed at length by Professor D. C. Douglas. Its bearings upon Domesday criticism and upon the social structure of East Anglia are of unique importance. It gives for some villages, according to Professor Douglas, nothing other than 'the names, estates, and rents of the Domesday freemen and sokemen'.[1] The attempt to compare the two sets of statistics is, however, frequently disappointing, and it has been suggested that the names are those of the successors of the Domesday holders and that the list was completed probably not later than 1119.[2]

There is one further consideration that must be mentioned. While the Domesday county of Suffolk corresponds more or less with the modern

---

[1] D. C. Douglas, *Feudal Documents from the Abbey of Bury St Edmunds* (London: British Academy, 1932), p. lix.

[2] R. Lennard, *Rural England, 1086–1135* (Oxford, 1959), p. 359.

county, there are some differences. Thus, one holding in Mildenhall was described among the Norfolk entries (263), another holding in Knettishall was likewise included in the Norfolk section (120b), while the curious Norfolk references to the Suffolk village of Rumburgh are discussed below.[1] Moreover, as we have seen, the Norfolk village of Rushford and the

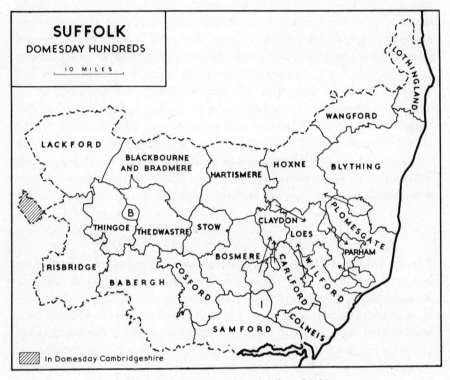

Fig. 36. Suffolk: Domesday hundreds.
I is the half-hundred of Ipswich. B is the *villa* of Bury St Edmunds.

Suffolk village of Mendham seem to have straddled the county boundary in Domesday as in later times; and a further complication is caused by the fact that holdings in a few Norfolk villages were described in the Suffolk section of the Domesday Book.[2] Rather similar features are to be found in some of the villages along the Suffolk-Essex border.[3] *Eilanda* (Nayland) lay athwart the River Stour and was surveyed partly in Suffolk

---

[1] See pp. 101 and 158.   [2] See p. 101 above.
[3] See J. H. Round in *V.C.H. Essex*, I, p. 408.

and partly in Essex.[1] A little higher up the river, Bures likewise lay in both counties; there is a further complication here, in that the eastern portion of the Essex half lay in the hundred of Lexden, while the western portion lay in that of Hinckford. But although in Essex, this western portion is today a hamlet of the Suffolk Bures, and it is interesting to note that the anomaly goes back to Domesday times; its entry in the Essex section reads: *Hec terra est in comitatu de Sudfolc* (84b). Farther up the river, Ballingdon and Brundon lie on the south side of the Stour and were surveyed in Essex, but boundary changes have now brought them into Suffolk. Not far away, the two Essex villages of Hedingham and Henny had connections with Sudbury.[2] Finally, the Essex village of Toppesfield seems to have had some of its holdings surveyed in the Suffolk folios (372b), unless, of course, there was an unidentified village of that name in Suffolk. There have also been changes along the western boundary where Suffolk marches with Cambridgeshire. Here, Exning formed part of Domesday Cambridgeshire, but it seems to have become part of Suffolk as early as the twelfth century.[3]

SETTLEMENTS AND THEIR DISTRIBUTION

The total number of separate places mentioned for Suffolk seems to be approximately 640. This figure, however, may not be quite accurate because, today, there are many instances of two or more adjoining villages bearing the same surname, and it is not always clear whether both units existed in the eleventh century. Only when there is specific mention of a second village in the Domesday Book itself, has it been included in the total of 640. Thus the existence of Great and Little Thornham (Hartismere) in the eleventh century is indicated by the mention of *Thornham* and *Parva Thornham*, of two Fakenhams (Great and Little) by the mention of *Fachenham* and *Litla Fachenham* (Blackbourne), and of two Waldingfields (Great and Little) by the mention of *Waldingfelda* and *altera Walingafella* (Babergh); the existence of two Fornhams (St Martin and St Genevieve) is likewise indicated by the mention of *Fornham* and *Genonefae Forham* (Thedwastre), and there is another *Fornham* (presumably All Saints) in the adjacent hundred of Thingoe. There is, on the other hand, no indication that, say, the Great and Little Blakenham

---

[1] See p. 211 below. [2] See p. 253 below.
[3] See L. F. Salzman in *V.C.H. Cambridgeshire*, I, p. 340 n.

(Bosmere) of today existed as separate villages; the Domesday information about them is entered under only one name, though they may well have been separate settlements in the eleventh century. The seven present-

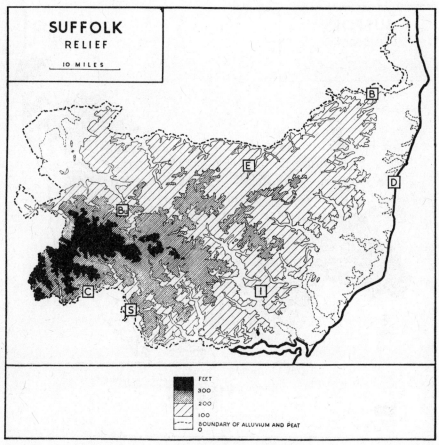

Fig. 37. Suffolk: Relief.

Places with Domesday burgesses are indicated by initials: B, Beccles; Bu, Bury St Edmunds; C, Clare; D, Dunwich; E, Eye; I, Ipswich; S, Sudbury.

day parishes of South Elmham (Wangford) are likewise entered under only one name, but the large size of its recorded population in 1086 (fo. 109) suggests that the one name covered more than one settlement; the same applies to the four modern parishes of Ilketshall, likewise in

Wangford. The information about churches seems to suggest that some Domesday names may have covered more than one settlement.[1]

The total of 640 includes a number of places—between 30 and 40—

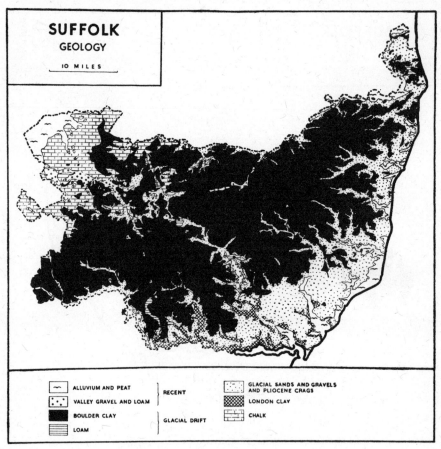

SUFFOLK
GEOLOGY
10 MILES

ALLUVIUM AND PEAT — RECENT
VALLEY GRAVEL AND LOAM
BOULDER CLAY
LOAM — GLACIAL DRIFT
GLACIAL SANDS AND GRAVELS AND PLIOCENE CRAGS
LONDON CLAY
CHALK

Fig. 38. Suffolk: Surface geology.
Based on Geological Survey Quarter-Inch Sheets 12 and 16.

about which very little information is given. Either the Domesday record is incomplete or the relevant details have been included with those of some other village. An outstanding example is the village of Rumburgh in the hundred of Blything. Curiously enough it is mentioned incidentally

[1] See p. 191 below.

twice in the Norfolk folios; some land at Alburgh (149b) and Mundham (177) is said to belong to Rumburgh. We might, therefore, expect to find some account of Rumburgh in the Suffolk folios, but all we are told

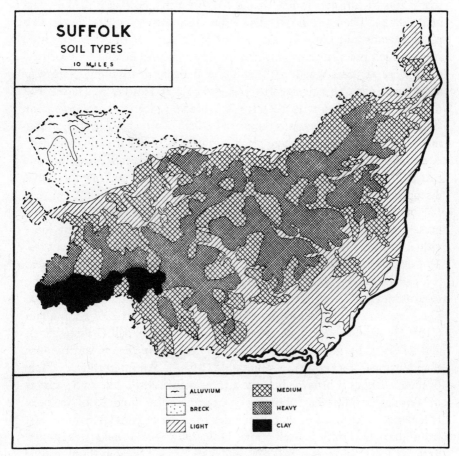

SUFFOLK
SOIL TYPES
10 MILES

ALLUVIUM   MEDIUM

BRECK   HEAVY

LIGHT   CLAY

Fig. 39. Suffolk: Soil types.

Redrawn from the map in *An Economic Survey of Agriculture in the Eastern Counties of England*, p. viii (Heffer, Cambridge, 1932). This is Report No. 19 of the Farm Economics Branch of the Department of Agriculture in the University of Cambridge.

of it is that some land in Elmham belonged to the church of Rumburgh (298), and that a holding of 60 acres at Stone was included in its valuation (292b). There is no statement about its people, its plough-teams or its other resources. These details may have been included with those of some neighbouring village or the village as a whole, like that of Bergh Apton in Norfolk, may have been left out.[1] Another curious example is that of Chattisham in the hundred of Samford. All we are told about it is that it was 8½ furlongs in length and 6 in breadth, and that it paid 6½d. in geld (287b). There are no details of the village itself—of its people and plough-teams and the rest. Then there are a number of other localities about which practically no information is given. At Foxhall in Carlford there were 15 acres worth 2s. (386b); at Benacre in Blything there was a sokeman with 10 acres worth 16d. (371b); at Hestley in Hartismere there were 2 freemen with 10 acres worth 20d. (429); and at *Burgesgata* (unidentified) in Plomesgate there was 1 acre worth 3d. (317); nothing more is said about any of these places. The list could be greatly extended. A number of these localities have not been identified, and it would seem that they must have been very small places whose name and memory have disappeared.

Not all the 640 Domesday names appear as the names of villages on the present-day map of Suffolk. Some are represented by hamlets, by individual houses, or by the names of localities or topographical features. *Forlea* is now the hamlet of Fordley in Middleton (Blything). *Hinetuna* is a hamlet in Blythburgh (also in Blything), and it has given its name to a number of local features, e.g. Hinton Springs and Hinton Walks. *Colestuna* is now represented by Colston Hall in the parish of Badingham (Hoxne); *Duniworda* by Dunningworth Hall in Blaxhall (Plomesgate); and *Mertlega* by Martley Hall in Easton (Loes). *Citiringa* is hardly more than a name (Chickering) in Wingfeld (Hoxne). An interesting example of these changes is provided by the area now included in the two parishes of Trimley St Mary and Trimley St Martin in the hundred of Colneis. It is rather exceptional in that it includes so many Domesday names apart from that of Trimley itself. The Domesday *Alteinestuna* was united with Trimley St Martin in 1362, and its church has now disappeared; *Grimestuna* and *Morestuna* are represented by Grimston Hall and Morston Hall; *Torpa* by Thorpe Common; *Candelenta* by the small hamlet of Candlet. The names of *Nortuna*, *Plugeard*, *Leofstanestuna*, *Mycelegata* and *Turestanestuna* are lost, though it is possible to conjecture where approximately they must have been situated in the two Trimley parishes.[2]

[1] See p. 102 above.
[2] W. G. Arnott, *The Place-Names of the Deben Valley Parishes* (Ipswich, 1946), pp. 34–40.

Portions of some villages along the coast have disappeared where erosion has been active, but only one seems to have completely disappeared; this was Newton to the east of Corton in Lothingland. In Domesday times, a freeman held 30 acres and half a plough here, and his holding was worth 3s. (284b). Moreover, the site of the old town of Dunwich has disappeared, and we are told that the sea had carried away (*abstulit*) some of its lands by 1086.[1]

On the other hand, there are a number of villages on the modern map that are not mentioned in the Little Domesday Book. They are scattered here and there throughout the county, and their names do not appear until the twelfth and thirteenth centuries. Thus Gosbeck (Bosmere) seems to have been first mentioned in 1179, Barnardiston (Risbridge) in 1194, Newmarket (Lackford) in 1200, and Felixstowe (Colneis) in 1254. If any settlements existed in these places in Domesday times, the information about them was presumably included under the headings of other villages. The village of Pettistree (Wilford), for example, is a modern village and parish that was not mentioned in the Domesday Book and that does not appear in records until 1253. Yet this modern parish contains Bing Hall and Loudham Hall that appear as Domesday settlements named *Benges* and *Ludham* respectively.[2]

The distribution of Domesday settlements (as indeed of present-day villages) was fairly uniform over the face of the county (Fig. 40). They were numerous all over the Boulder Clay centre of the county. In the east, in the sandy area, they were perhaps somewhat less frequent, but the only portion of the county that stood in marked contrast to the rest was the north-west. Here, on the Breckland, villages were few and were separated by great empty stretches. The peat fen, that adjoins the Breckland, was, of course, also devoid of settlement.

The Distribution of Prosperity and Population

The Suffolk entries resemble those of Norfolk both in form and in content. The Norfolk example given on p. 107 consisted of a village held by one landholder, and therefore represented by only one entry. The example of a Suffolk village given below comprises a number of entries. They

---

[1] See p. 194 below.
[2] The dates in this paragraph are taken from E. Ekwall, *The Concise Oxford Dictionary of English Place-Names*, 3rd ed. (Oxford, 1947).

relate to Bradley (Risbridge), now represented by the parishes of Great and Little Bradley in the upper valley of the Stour along the western border of the county.

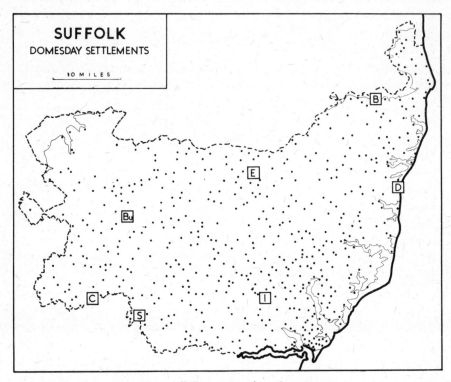

SUFFOLK
DOMESDAY SETTLEMENTS
10 MILES

Fig. 40. Suffolk: Domesday place-names.

Places with burgesses are indicated by initials: B, Beccles; Bu, Bury St Edmunds; C, Clare; D, Dunwich; E, Eye; I, Ipswich; S, Sudbury. The boundary of alluvium and peat is shown; see Fig. 38.

Fo. 371 b. In Bradley 8 freemen [with] 80 acres,[1] and 1 bordar, and 2 ploughs, and 1 acre of meadow, and they are worth 11 shillings and 3 pence. In the same [vill] 4 freemen [with] 60 acres, and 1 bordar, and 2 ploughs, and 1 acre of meadow, and they are worth 10 shillings. Saint Edmund [has] commendation and soke and sake.

Fo. 396 b. In Bradley always 2 freemen [with] 69 acres, and 1 acre of meadow. Always 1 plough, and they are worth 17 shillings and 6 pence.

[1] The figure lxxx is doubtful; it may be lxxv.

Fo. 397. In Bradley 4 freemen, Ulwin, Leuric and Lewin, and they have 15 acres. The fourth is Bundo and he has 1 carucate (*car' terrae*). Always 2 ploughs and 2 acres of meadow and they are worth 22 shillings and 6 pence. Of these, Richard's predecessor had not the commendation *T.R.E.* Saint Edmund had the entire soke.[1]

Fo. 429. Olf the thane held Bradley as a manor (*pro manerio*) *T.R.E.* Now Roger holds [it] in demesne. 7 carucates (*car' terrae*). Always 14 villeins, and 12 bordars and 6 serfs and 3 ploughs in demesne, and 7 ploughs belonging to the men, and 13 acres of meadow. Wood for 500 swine. Always 1 rouncey. Then 12 animals, now 18. Then 60 pigs, now 53. Then 20 sheep, now 63. And 7 goats and 1 hive of bees. A church with 15 acres of free land. Then it was worth 6 pounds, now 8. It is 1 league in length, and 7 furlongs in breadth, and [pays] 6 pence for geld.

The basic items, like those of Norfolk, are six in number: (1) carucates, (2) plough-teams, (3) population, (4) values, (5) dimensions, and (6) assessment. The same two peculiar features are apparent: the absence of any reference to plough-lands, and the presence of a curious reference to dimensions and geld. The bearing of these six items of information upon regional variations in prosperity must now be considered. The main facts have already been discussed in connection with Norfolk. Here, they need only to be outlined in relation to the Suffolk evidence.

(1) *Carucates*

The main features of the Suffolk as of the Norfolk carucate entry are four in number, and they can be briefly summarised as follows. In the first place, the statement about the carucate (*car' terrae*) seems to have a fiscal rather than an agricultural significance. In the second place, the Suffolk carucate is likewise divided into acres and not bovates. In the third place, some of the holdings are very small. In the hundred of Bosmere, for example, there was a freeman with only a quarter of an acre at *Uledana* (446), another with a mere half an acre at Ashbocking (383b), a third with one acre at Coddenham (422b); these are rather extreme examples, but holdings with only 5 or less acres are quite frequent. In the fourth place, the number of carucates and/or acres on a holding usually

---

[1] This entry is repeated at the end, in the section dealing with encroachments (*Invasiones*) upon the king's land (447b). The figures are the same, except that the amount of meadow is stated to be 5 acres. The Domesday text thus convicts itself of inaccuracy.

bears no constant relation to the number of plough-teams at work. Thus in the hundred of Hartismere there was a holding of 80 acres at Redgrave which carried 8 ploughs (361), while another holding of 80 acres at Rickinghall had only 3 ploughs (361). There seems likewise to be no relationship between the number of carucates and the amount of assessment, but this has been discussed above for Norfolk.[1]

The present count, for the area covered by the modern county, has yielded a total of 2,404 carucates.[2] This estimate has been made on the assumption that one carucate comprised 120 fiscal acres. As we have seen, doubt has been cast on this by some people,[3] but a little evidence from Suffolk does seem to indicate that the figure of 120 is correct. An estate in Great Glemham (Plomesgate) is entered in the Domesday Book as 180 acres (430) and in the *I.E.* as '1 carucate and a half' (p. 153). One entry is not enough to support any argument about Domesday figures, but support is given to the idea of a 120-acre carucate by a collation of some Domesday figures with those of the Feudal Book of Abbot Baldwin of Bury St Edmunds.[4]

(2) *Plough-teams*

The Suffolk entries, like those of other counties, usually draw a distinction between the teams held by the lord of a manor in demesne and those held by the peasantry. But at times the distinction is not made, especially on the very small manors; at other times it is not clear, and occasional entries seem to be defective. The present count has yielded a total of 4,501 $\frac{5}{24}$ teams in 1086 for the area covered by the modern county.[5] Frequently there had been changes between 1066 and 1086. Thus at Henham (Blything) there were 'then 2 ploughs on the demesne, afterwards 1, now 2. Then and afterwards 5 ploughs belonging to the men, now 3' (fo. 415). There are occasional departures from the normal formula about these matters, and two examples of variation are given

---

[1] See p. 122 above.

[2] Miss Lees' estimate, for the Domesday county, came to 2,348 carucates; *V.C.H. Suffolk*, 1, p. 360. F. W. Maitland gave no estimate for Suffolk.

[3] See p. 109 above.

[4] D. C. Douglas, *Feudal Documents*. Similar evidence is found in the *I.E.*, in two accounts of a holding in Hitcham (Cosford), where *lx acrae* (p. 156) is equated with *dimidia c[arucata]* (p. 178).

[5] Neither Miss Lees nor Maitland gave any estimate of teams for Suffolk.

below:

(1) *Whatfield* in Cosford (369). 'Then they ploughed with 4 ploughs, and now [also] (*Tunc araverunt cum iiii carucis, et modo*).'
(2) *Eruestuna* in Stow (409). 'Then and afterwards 3 ploughs among them all, now they scarcely have 1 plough (*Tunc et post iii carucae inter omnes, modo vix habent i carucam*).'

At Cretingham in Loes (300) there were '8 acres of waste land (*vastata terra*)', and at *Kingeslanda* in Carlford (425) '1 carucate of waste land (*terra guasta*)'.

When the existing teams in 1086 were fewer than those in times past, we are sometimes told that the number could be made good, and a contrast between actual and potential arable is implied. One of the entries for Clopton in Carlford (417b) states: 'then 3 ploughs on the demesne, now 2, but [the other] could be employed (*sed potest fieri*)'. Nor was the addition always limited to the restoration of what had once been there. At Seckford, also in Carlford (373), there were 'then as now 2 plough-teams on the demesne, and a third could be employed (*tercia potest fieri*)'. The phrasing of the formula varied. At Kettleburgh in Loes (293b), for example, there were 'then 4 ploughs on the demesne, now 3, but [the other] could be restored (*sed potest restaurari*)'; at Gusford, in Samford (431), there was also prospect of further cultivation beyond that of 1086, for there were 'then 2 ploughs belonging to the men, now 1, and 3 ploughs could be added (*possent restaurari*)'. Another variant in the phraseology may be illustrated from an entry relating to Boyton in Wilford (318b), where 'the men had then 4 ploughs now 1, but [the others] could be employed (*sed possent esse*)'. Sometimes, the different varieties of phrasing are combined in one entry. At Ilketshall in Wangford (301), there were 'then on the demesne 3 ploughs, now 1, but they [all] could be employed (*sed possent esse*). Then the men had 3 ploughs, now 2, but they [all] could be employed (*sed possent restaurari*)'. These three groups of variants (*fieri, restaurari,* and *esse*) do not exhaust all the possibilities. The entry for Blythburgh in Blything (282) expresses the information in yet a different way: there was 'then 1 plough in demesne; [there was] land [sufficient] for 5 ploughs on the demesne. But Roger received [only] 3 oxen, and now there is a like number'. Over the county as a whole, there was a decrease of teams in 48 per cent., and an increase in 4 per cent., of the entries with details for both 1066 and 1086.

To sum up, although the Suffolk folios do not give us information about plough-lands in the sense that it is recorded for some other counties, we can infer this from these details about the increase or decrease in the

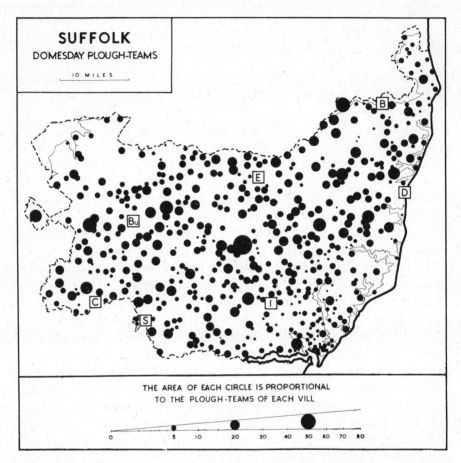

Fig. 41. Suffolk: Domesday plough-teams in 1086 (by settlements).

Places with burgesses are indicated by initials: B, Beccles; Bu, Bury St Edmunds; C, Clare; D, Dunwich; E, Eye; I, Ipswich; S, Sudbury. The boundary of alluvium and peat is shown; see Fig. 38.

teams, and from the possibilities of further cultivation that are thus indicated. In this way were the local fortunes of agriculture, varying from place to place, put on record. It is, however, sometimes difficult to guess what had really happened; thus at Herringfleet, the total number of ploughs had fallen from 1½ to none, yet both the number of men and the value had remained the same (284b).

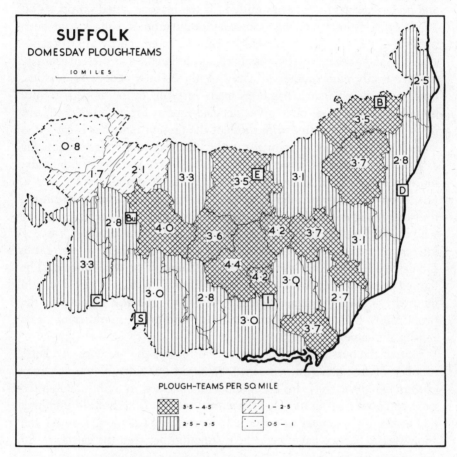

Fig. 42. Suffolk: Domesday plough-teams in 1086 (by densities).

Places with burgesses are indicated by initials: B, Beccles; Bu, Bury St Edmunds; C, Clare; D, Dunwich; E, Eye; I, Ipswich; S, Sudbury.

(3) *Population*

The main bulk of the population was comprised in the five categories of freemen, sokemen, villeins, bordars and serfs. In addition to these main groups were the burgesses, together with a miscellaneous group that comprised *homines*, priests and others.[1] A variety of people are also mentioned in connection with the monastery at Bury St Edmunds.[2] The details of these groups are summarised on p. 169. The tenants-in-chief and under-tenants have been omitted for the reasons stated on pp. 51–4. Three other estimates of the Domesday population of Suffolk have been published, the old one by Sir Henry Ellis,[3] a later one by Miss Beatrice A. Lees,[4] and a recent one by Miss Barbara Dodwell.[5] The present estimate is not strictly comparable with any of these for a variety of reasons, one reason being that it has been made in terms of the modern county boundary. Miss Lees' table gives detailed figures for each hundred, but these cannot be compared with those of the present estimates because the latter involve various adjustments to the hundred boundaries to meet the case of those border villages recorded under two Domesday hundreds; moreover, Miss Lees' figures seem to include urban population. Thirdly, Miss Dodwell's figures refer to 1066. No strict comparison between the four sets of figures is therefore possible; but one thing is certain: no one who counts Domesday population can claim definitive accuracy. Varying interpretations of many entries are inevitable, especially in the Little Domesday Book. Finally, one point must always be remembered. The figures presumably indicate heads of households. Whatever factor should be used to obtain the *actual* population from the *recorded* population, the proportions between different categories and between different areas remain the same.[6]

One of the outstanding features of Suffolk was the presence of a large number of freemen (41 per cent.). Whereas in Norfolk the sokemen outnumbered the freemen, the number of sokemen in Suffolk amounted only to about one-ninth that of freemen; many of the Suffolk hundreds had either no sokemen or practically none, e.g. Claydon, Colneis and Plomesgate. As we have seen, the distinction between the categories of

---

[1] Freemen who were smiths are mentioned: Edwin the smith, and Aluric the smith's son at *Carlewuda* (?) in Colneis (314b); Bunde the smith at Stickland in Blything (334b); Godric the smith at Walton in Colneis (339b); these are counted in the total for freemen. There had also been one smith at Bures in Babergh (435b) in 1066.

[2] See p. 197 below.

[3] Sir Henry Ellis, *A General Introduction to Domesday Book* (London, 1833), II, pp. 488–90.

[4] Beatrice A. Lees in *V.C.H. Suffolk*, I, p. 360.

[5] Barbara Dodwell, 'The free peasantry of East Anglia in Domesday', *Trans. Norfolk and Norwich Arch. Soc.* (Norwich, 1939), XXVII, p. 156.

[6] See p. 360 below for the position of the serfs.

Recorded Population of Suffolk in 1086
A. *Rural Population*

Freemen	7,730
Sokemen	859
Villeins	3,130
Bordars	6,460
Serfs	910
Miscellaneous	34
Total	19,123

Details of Miscellaneous Rural Population

Men (*homines*) . .	24	Priests	4
Franci homines . .	5	*Francus* . .	1
		Total . .	34

B. *Urban Population*

Freemen, villeins, bordars, sokemen and serfs are also included above.

IPSWICH	162 burgesses; 100 poor burgesses; 3 *mansurae*; 6 *domus*; 12 freemen; 32 bordars; 13 villeins; 328 *mansiones vastatae*; 6 *vastatae mansurae*; 10 *mansurae vacuae*.
DUNWICH	316 burgesses; 2 bordars; 24 *franci homines*; 80 *homines*; 178 *pauperes homines*.
EYE	25 burgesses; 9 freemen; 57 sokemen; 21 villeins; 32 bordars.
BECCLES	26 burgesses; 12 freeman; 30 sokemen; 7 villeins; 46 bordars.
CLARE	43 burgesses; 5 sokemen; 30 villeins; 30 bordars; 20 serfs.
SUDBURY	138 burgesses; 2 villeins; 2 serfs.
BURY ST EDMUNDS	See pp. 197–8. Details include 54 freemen and 122 bordars.

freemen and sokemen is difficult to draw; but, taken together, the two groups constituted the free element in the population as opposed to villeins, bordars and serfs. Unlike Norfolk, Suffolk does not present a close correspondence between the geographical distribution of the free peasantry and that of Scandinavian place-names. This is, perhaps, not surprising for, generally speaking, in Suffolk the 'Danish names are more scattered

and contain very few Scandinavian names in the strictest sense'.[1] Marked
Danish influence is most noticeable around the mouth of the Waveney
adjoining the strongly Danish parts of Norfolk, but the main areas of
free peasantry in Suffolk lay elsewhere. Although the correspondence
between place-names and free peasantry cannot be pressed, there are
many other general indications of Scandinavian influence in Suffolk. As
Miss Dodwell has pointed out, the values of many estates show a reckoning
based upon the Danish *ora* of sixteen pence, and the names of many
Domesday peasants are definitely Scandinavian.[2] Moreover, Professor
Douglas has calculated that about 8½ per cent. of the personal names in
the Feudal Book of Bury St Edmunds are Scandinavian.[3]

As we have seen, many of the holdings of the Suffolk freemen and sokemen were minute, and no ploughs or oxen are recorded in connection
with them.[4] Here, as in Norfolk, we are confronted with the peculiar
economic and social structure of East Anglia which has been discussed at
length by Professor Douglas.[5]

The statistics relating to the free peasantry raise the same three doubts
as do those of Norfolk. In the first place, there may be much reduplication, though not as much as some people have supposed. Ballard, however, held that this reduplication was serious. In 315 references to freemen
in the hundred of Colneis, he counted only 122 different names, and he
noted that a certain Blakeman, for example, was recorded as a landholder
in five different places.[6] But he does not appear to have given sufficient
weight to the fact that some names were very common; the name Blakeman is found not only in Suffolk, but in many other counties. Miss
Dodwell came to the conclusion that the number of freemen and sokemen
who held more than one tenement was small, and that while the Domesday
totals are open to suspicion they are 'substantially correct'.[7] Very occasionally, it is true, the record tells us explicitly that a freeman held land
in two places; there was, for instance, a certain freeman named William
who held 60 acres in Dagworth and 15 acres in *Weledana* (427); and

---

[1] Eilert Ekwall in *An Historical Geography of England before A.D. 1800*, ed. H. C.
Darby (Cambridge, 1936), p. 152.
[2] Barbara Dodwell, *loc. cit.* pp. 153–4. But for doubts about the Scandinavian
evidence in Norfolk and Suffolk, see p. 114 n. above.
[3] D. C. Douglas, *Feudal Documents*, p. cxx.   [4] See p. 163 above.
[5] D. C. Douglas, *Medieval East Anglia*.
[6] Adolphus Ballard, *The Domesday Inquest* (London, 1906), p. 144.
[7] Barbara Dodwell, *loc. cit.* p. 157.

another freeman named Siric held land in Wortham, Stoke Ash and Aspall (322b); but this kind of statement is rare. It may be relevant, however, to note that a number of half-freemen are noted, and at Bredfield in Wilford there was even one quarter-freeman (318).

In the second place, the mysterious reference to 'other holders' is as frequent in Suffolk as in Norfolk.[1] The usual formula that follows the statement about geld is *Alii ibi tenent* or *Plures ibi tenent*, with variants of *Alii ibi habent* (365b), *Alii tenent in istis maneriis* (341), and *Alii habent ibi terram* (348b). The Suffolk entries seem to throw no light on the problem. Nor does comparison with the *I.E.* help. It is, however, interesting to note that while the phrase *Alii ibi tenent* appears in the Domesday entries for Chedburgh (384b) and Hitcham (385), it is omitted from the corresponding entries in the *I.E.* (pp. 155–6). The same phrase occurs in the Domesday entries relating to Kingston and Brightwell (386), but it is rendered as *Plures ibi tenent* in the *I.E.* (p. 160). These are but curiosities.

In the third place, uncertainty occasionally arises from the fact that the Suffolk text, like that of Norfolk, does not always categorically state whether the numbers of freemen or sokemen refer to 1066 or to 1086. But it is often possible to infer what is meant. When the entry for *Rodeham* in Stow states that there was a freeman with 10 acres *T.R.E.*, and that there was also 'then as now half a plough' (374) we may reasonably suppose that someone was still there in 1086.

It is impossible to say what these three groups of uncertainties amount to, but, at any rate, we do not have to rely only on the population figures in assessing the relative prosperity of different parts of the county. The figures for plough-teams form a useful check, and the two maps must be considered together.

The information about the unfree population involves far fewer problems, at any rate from our point of view. Changes between the various categories are frequently specified. Thus in the entry relating to Withermarsh in Babergh we read: 'Then 27 villeins, now 24. Then 32 bordars, now 27. Then 2 serfs, now 1' (fo. 401). The total population on a holding in 1086 was sometimes less, sometimes more, than in 1066, and there was frequently no change. The approximate ratio between the three groups of villeins, bordars and serfs for the county as a whole in 1086 was 3:6:1. Half-villeins and half-bordars are occasionally mentioned. A few

[1] See p. 115 above.

entries seem to be defective, and contain either no reference, or only a vague reference to population, but it is impossible to be really certain about the significance of these omissions.[1]

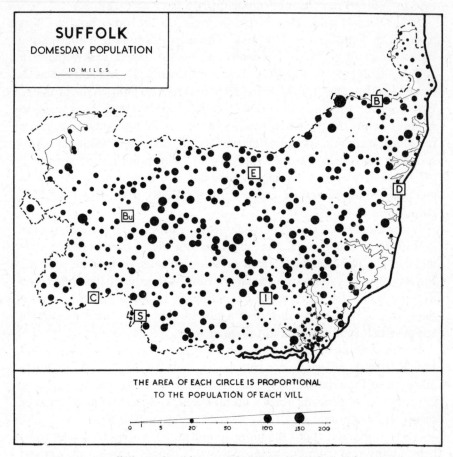

SUFFOLK
DOMESDAY POPULATION
10 MILES

THE AREA OF EACH CIRCLE IS PROPORTIONAL
TO THE POPULATION OF EACH VILL

0   5   20   50   100   150   200

Fig. 43. Suffolk: Domesday population in 1086 (by settlements).

Places with burgesses are indicated by initials: B, Beccles; Bu, Bury St Edmunds; C, Clare; D, Dunwich; E, Eye; I, Ipswich; S, Sudbury. The boundary of alluvium and peat is shown; see Fig. 38.

(4) *Values*

The values of the Suffolk estates exhibit the same general features as those of Norfolk. The figures seem likewise to suggest a careful appraisal;

[1] See pp. 158–60 above.

we read, for example, that a holding in Ubbeston (Blything) was worth
6s. 8d. in 1066 and 8s. in 1086. Generally speaking, the greater the
number of ploughs and people on a holding, the greater its value, but

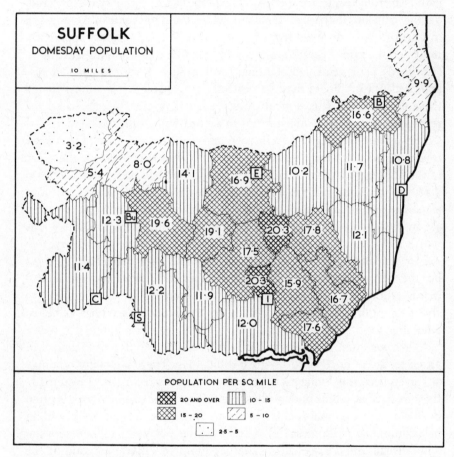

SUFFOLK
DOMESDAY POPULATION

10 MILES

POPULATION PER SQ MILE

20 AND OVER | 10 - 15
15 - 20 | 5 - 10
2·5 - 5

Fig. 44. Suffolk: Domesday population in 1086 (by densities).

Places with burgesses are indicated by initials: B, Beccles; Bu, Bury St Edmunds;
C, Clare; D, Dunwich; E, Eye; I, Ipswich; S, Sudbury.

there were all kinds of anomalies and no equation is possible. For instance,
5 freemen with 50 acres in Marston (Colneis) had 'then 1½ ploughs.
Now 1½ acres of meadow. Then it was worth 10s., now 17s.' (292). Does
this mean that, although the ploughs had apparently disappeared, the

value had risen, or is the text faulty? An entry for Crowfield in Bosmere is more explicit: 5 freemen there held 40 acres with 'then and afterwards 2 ploughs, now none. 1 acre of meadow', but the value of the holding had risen from 16s. to 20s. (374b). The ploughs had certainly disappeared, yet the value had increased. Or again, why should the value of Alnesbourn in Carlford have dropped from 30s. to 10s. when its resources apparently remained the same (347); or why should the value of a holding in Culpho (Carlford) have remained stationary when its solitary plough had disappeared (346)? There may be perfectly reasonable explanations for all these oddities, but it is difficult to see what they are. Occasionally, the record hints that the value was not in accord with reality. The manor of Combs (Stow) rendered £10 in 1066 and £16 in 1086 (291), but we are told that it could hardly yield that amount (*vix potest reddere*); the value of the holdings of 50 freemen in the same village had been increased from £16 to £31 (291), but we are told that they could not endure it without ruin (*non possunt sufferre sine confusione*); a holding at Kembrook rendered £6 in 1086 as in 1066 (343) but the men of the hundred thought it was worth only 48s. (*Homines hundreti habent hanc terram pretiata xlviii solidos*); a holding at Pettaugh in Claydon had been valued at £3. 15s., but the men were thereby ruined (*sed homines inde fuerunt confusi*), and so it was reduced to 45s. (440b). Many an argument must have gone on about the figure the Domesday Book so tersely records as the 'value' of a holding.

When we attempt to assess the relative value of different localities or areas, we are at once faced by great difficulties. There are many holdings and even occasional villages for which no value is recorded. Presumably they are accounted for under other totals. The value of a berewick is often included with the total for its parent holding. The account of a holding in Saxmundham (Plomesgate) is followed by details of its berewicks at Knoddishall and Peasenhall in another hundred (Blything), and at the end of the account, the value of the whole (*totum*) is given (338b). Frequently, a holding is specifically stated to be valued with that of another vill. There were 11 acres in Woodbridge (Loes) included in the valuation (*in pretio*) of Kettleburgh (294). Two holdings in Cavenham and Lakenheath (392) were likewise included in the valuation of Desning in Lackford (*hae ii terrae sunt in pretio de desilinges*). Examples could be multiplied. Occasionally, the value of a whole group of holdings was summed up together in one total. On fo. 317 an account of holdings in six different villages is followed by a statement that they were all included in the valuation (*in pretio*) of Hollesley in Wilford. The phrasing sometimes varied. The men and stock on a holding in Butley in Loes (348) are said to be 'valued with Sudbourne (*sunt pretiata cum sutburna*)'. Another holding in Somerleyton is said to 'belong to (*pertinent ad*)' Gorleston, and was presumably valued there (283b). Thirty acres in Wilford (325) are said to belong to Hollesley and to its valuation (*pertinent ad holeslea et in pretio*). Yet another holding in Stanham in Bosmere (350b) is said to be part of the demesne land of the hall in Creeting (*de dominica terra halle in cratinga*). A holding of 60 acres in Peasenhall (Blything) is said to belong to (*iacet in*) Saxmundham (333b). In view of all these complications it is impossible to say what was the 'value' of many a village, and any interpretation of the figures upon a geographical basis is not feasible.[1]

(5) *The Measurement and* (6) *the Geld*

The peculiar entries relating to measurement and geld have already been discussed in connection with Norfolk.[2] The words that introduce the statement in the Suffolk folios likewise show much variation, as may be seen from the following examples:

(1) Blything: Wrentham and its berewick in Henstead (399b)	*Omnes hae terrae…*
(2) Blything: Ubbeston (415)	*Tota haec terra…*
(3) Cosford: Ealdham and Whatfield (369)	*He due ville…*
(4) Risbridge: Stansfield (396)	*Tota stenesfelda…*
(5) Babergh: Cockfield (359)	*Haec villa…*
(6) Babergh: Edwardstone (304)	*Hoc manerium…*
(7) Bradmere: Ixworth (438b)	*Totum…*

There are some curiosities. In the case of Chattisham, as we have seen, nothing but the measurement and the geld is given.[3] For Southwold in Blything (371b) there is a strange addition to the formula: 'Southwold is 9 furlongs long and 5 broad. This division [extends] from the sea as far as Yarmouth (*haec divisio a mari usque Jernesmua*). And [it pays] 2½ pence in geld.' Or, again, no measurements are given for the villages of the half-hundred of Lothingland, but we are told

---

[1] For the bearing of 'the confused terminology of the Little Domesday' upon the organisation of sokes in East Anglia, see D. C. Douglas, *Medieval East Anglia*, pp. 173–91 and 210–11.

[2] See p. 119 above.   [3] See p. 160 above.

that the half-hundred as a whole was '6 leagues long and 2½ leagues and 2 furlongs broad. And in geld [it pays] 10 shillings' (283b). Very occasionally the amount of the geld is followed by the statement 'in a geld of 20 shillings' (382b). The dimensions are usually stated in terms of leagues and furlongs, but the detail sometimes descends to perches, e.g. in the case of Groton in Babergh (287). A league seems to have consisted of 12 furlongs, for a Domesday entry relating to Rattlesden (Thedwastre) speaks of 16 furlongs (381b) whereas the corresponding entry in the *I.E.* mentions '1 league and 4 furlongs' (p. 153); the Domesday entry relating to *Brihtoluestana* (Colneis) likewise speaks of half a league (406) whereas the *I.E.* mentions 6 furlongs (p. 143).[1] There are also a number of discrepancies between the Domesday text and that of the *I.E.*; the Domesday Book puts the geld of Lakenheath at 20*d.* (382) whereas the *I.E.* puts it at 10*d.* (p. 154); the Domesday Book records 5 bordars at the same place, whereas the *I.E.* puts the figure at 4. All these matters are but details. Like those of Norfolk, they throw no light upon the central problem of what is implied by the measurements.

Reference has already been made to the grouping of villages into units of assessment known as 'leets'.[2] J. H. Round elucidated the leets of some of the Suffolk hundreds,[3] and, following upon this pioneer work, Miss Beatrice A. Lees attempted a reconstruction of the leets of the county as a whole.[4] The details of these attempts must now be modified in the light of the evidence afforded by the early thirteenth century 'Kalendar' of Abbot Samson of Bury St Edmunds which has been discussed by Professor D. C. Douglas.[5] With these details we are not concerned here, but Miss Lees' general statement provides a clear summary of the part played by the leet in the fiscal arrangements of East Anglia:

In this system the vill appears as the gelding unit, but the tax falls on the vill through the hundred. This is proved by the entry relating to Lothingland, where the lineal measurements and geld are given for the whole half-hundred, without distinction of vills. This may help to explain the fact that only certain vills in each hundred were assessed to the geld. Thus in the hundred of Claydon, out of twenty-five vills mentioned in the Survey, the 'geld' falls on eleven; in Wilford hundred, out of thirty-three vills, eleven geld; in Blything twenty-

---

[1] See p. 121 above.   [2] See p. 120 above.

[3] J. H. Round, *Feudal England*, pp. 98–103.   [4] *V.C.H. Suffolk*, I, pp. 412–16.

[5] D. C. Douglas, *Feudal Documents*, pp. clx–clxvii. See also R. H. C. Davis (ed.), *The Kalendar of Abbot Samson of Bury St Edmunds and related documents* (Camden Series, London, 1954), pp. xv–xxx.

nine of the fifty-six vills are assessed; in Risbridge twenty-one out of thirty-seven. Probably the hundred or half-hundred was assessed as a whole, and the geld was then partitioned among the smaller fiscal areas or leets, and through them again it would fall on the selected vills, which may have been tax-centres for a district.[1]

As in Norfolk, there seems to be no standard relation between the measurement and the geld, as the figures for half a dozen places in the hundred of Thedwastre will show:

	Measurements	Geld liability
Pakenham (361b)	16 furlongs × 1 league	$13\frac{1}{2}d.$
Rougham (362)	16 „ × 1 „	20d.
Drinkstone (381b)	8 „ × 7 furlongs	11d.
Hessett (326b)	8 „ × 7 „	18d.
Felsham (326b)	8 „ × 6 „	5d.
Timworth (363)	8 „ × 6 „	14d.

Whatever these statistics may mean, one thing is obvious: they cannot help us in assessing the relative prosperity of different areas.

Conclusion

Suffolk, like Norfolk, has not been as minutely subdivided as Lincolnshire. Generally speaking, the hundreds themselves have been adopted as units for calculating the densities of population and plough-teams, but a number of modifications have been made in order to make units correspond more closely with differences of soil (Figs. 38 and 39). In the north-west, the hundred of Lackford has been divided into two, an upland and a fenland portion; Blackbourne and Bradmere have likewise been subdivided in order to separate very roughly the sandy Breckland from the rest. In the east, the hundred of Blything has also been divided into two in order to separate the light sands of the coastal belt from the heavier soils inland. Plomesgate, Loes and Wilford ought to have been divided in a similar fashion, but the number of unidentified localities within each of these hundreds make this impossible. In the south-east, the hundred boundaries have been modified in order to produce more compact units, and in this process the little hundred of Parham has been absorbed within those of Loes and Plomesgate, the detached villages of Loes have been included in Carlford, and there have been a few other

[1] *V.C.H. Suffolk*, I, p. 362.

minor changes, e.g. a portion of Claydon has been added to Carlford, a portion of Loes to Hoxne, and a portion of Hoxne to Loes. Finally, occasional villages described partly in one and partly in another hundred have been included wholly within one or other. The result of all these modifications is twenty-five units which form a rough-and-ready basis for distinguishing variations over the face of the county. It does not enable us to arrive at as perfect a regional division as a geographer could wish for, but, with the exception of the undivided coastal hundreds, it is probably adequate for our purpose.

Of the six standard formulae, only those relating to plough-teams and population are likely to reflect something of the distribution of wealth and prosperity throughout the county. Neither is without uncertainty, but taken together they supplement one another, and when the distributions of plough-teams (Fig. 42) and population (Fig. 44) are compared, certain common features stand out. The Boulder Clay of Suffolk is a continuation of that of Norfolk, and it covers the whole of the interior of the county. Over this surface, the plough-teams vary between 3 and just over 4 per square mile, and the population between 10 and 20 per square mile. One might expect the densities of the heathy 'sandlings' of eastern Suffolk to be lower than those of the Boulder Clay interior. It is difficult, however, to make a full comparison because these eastern hundreds have not been divided into sandy and clay areas. It is true that the coastal belt of Blything is poorer than the country inland, but it is not very markedly poorer. To the south, the hundred of Colneis lies entirely within the 'sandlings', and yet it has high densities both for teams and population; nor did a second check alter the figures. It is difficult to see from the geological map why these densities should be so high. There are, however, local fertile tracts within the sandy belt, and a remark in Arthur Young's survey of Suffolk is illuminating.

From the river Deben, crossing the Orwell, in a line some miles broad, to the north of the river Stour, to Stratford and Higham, there is a vein of friable putrid vegetable mould, more inclined to sand than to clay, which is of extraordinary fertility: the best is at Walton, Trimley, and Felixstowe, where, for depth and richness, much of it can scarcely be exceeded by any soils to be found in other parts of the county, and would rank high among the best in England.[1]

[1] Arthur Young, *General View of the Agriculture of the County of Suffolk*, 3rd ed. (London, 1804), p. 3.

In the north-east of the county, in the marshy half-hundred of Lothing-land, the densities tend to be low, but really low figures are encountered only in the north-west, on the sterile sands of the Breckland, and even more so in the parishes of the fen margin.

Figs. 41 and 43 are supplementary to the density maps, but it is necessary to make two reservations about them. As we have seen in the case of Norfolk, a few of the symbols should appear as two or more smaller symbols.[1] The second reservation arises from the fact that many Domesday names in Suffolk are unidentified. This is especially true of the south-eastern hundreds. The figures for these unidentified localities are therefore missing from Figs. 41 and 43, though, of course, they have been taken into account in the preparation of the density maps.

WOODLAND

Types of entries

As in Norfolk, the extent of woodland on a holding is almost invariably indicated by the number of swine which it could support. The normal formula is 'wood for n swine'—*silva ad n porcos, silva de n porcis*, or just *silva n porcos*. The number ranged from one to as many as a thousand. The round figures of the larger entries may indicate that they are estimates rather than precise amounts, but, on the other hand, the very detailed figures of some of the smaller entries suggest exactness (e.g. 1, 3, 5, 6 or 7). It does not necessarily follow that these figures indicate the actual number of swine grazing in a wood; the swine were used merely as units of measurement. Conversely, swine were often recorded for places in which there was no wood.[2] The hundred of Lackford is a good example of this; wood is entered for none of its villages, yet swine are frequently mentioned.

While swine formed the normal unit of measurement, there are a few exceptional entries that measure wood in other ways; thus we are told that '14 acres of wood' belonged to *Redles* (unidentified) in Cosford (438). Or, again, the wood entries relating to Stonham in Bosmere are mixed. Some record wood in terms of swine, but there were also '28 acres part woodland part open country (*inter silvam et planum*)' together with another '1½ acres of wood' (294b). There is another curiosity in an entry relating to Gislingham in Hartismere: a certain Lewin held 'the fourth part of a wood' there (322); the other three-quarters are not mentioned unless, that is, they consisted of the wood for a total of 43 swine that was

---

[1] See pp. 124 and 156–8 above. [2] See p. 200 below.

also to be found in the village. Finally, a number of parks are mentioned, one each at Dennington (328), Eye (319b) and Ixworth (438b), and half a park (*dimidius parcus*) at Bentley (287).

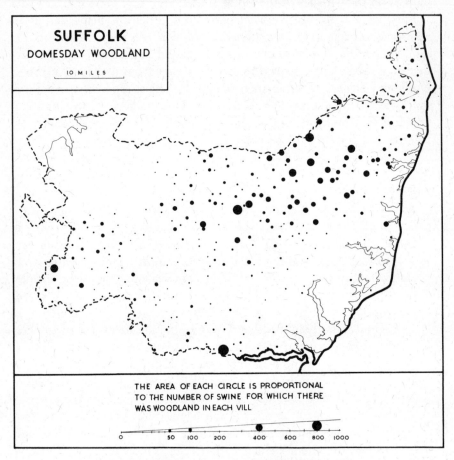

Fig. 45. Suffolk: Domesday woodland in 1086.

The boundary of alluvium and peat is shown; see Fig. 38. Where the wood of a village is entered partly in terms of swine and partly in some other way, only the swine are shown.

The wood entries for Suffolk, as for the other two counties of the Little Domesday Book, often draw a contrast between conditions in 1066 and 1086. The entry for Winston (Claydon) is fairly typical of the way in which the contrast is expressed: *Tunc silva c porcos; modo lx* (383b). For

Reduction of Woodland in Suffolk, 1066–86

The numbers refer to swine for which there was wood in 1066 and 1086
respectively. The folios are those of the Little Domesday Book.

Hundred	Place	1066	1086	Folio
Babergh	Newton	8	6	360
Blything	Halesworth	60	20	293
,,	,,	300	100	299
,,	Huntingfield	150	100	311
,,	Leiston	500	200	311b
,,	Linstead	30	20	310b
,,	Wissett	300	60	293
Bosmere	Battisford	60	10	434b
,,	*Bricticeshaga*	16	4	433b
,,	Coddenham	10	2	375
,,	,,	30	11	375
,,	,,	30	10	338
,,	,,	30	10	338
,,	Ringsett	30	16	393b
,,	Stonham	80	40	337b
,,	*Uledana*	24	?[1]	374b
Claydon	Barham	100	16	383b
,,	Debenham	60	40	305
,,	,,	100	40	305
,,	,,	100	40	417b
,,	Framsden	80	40	298b
,,	Helmingham	20	10	394b
,,	Ulverston	8	4	376b
,,	Winston	100	60	383b
Hartismere	Burgate	100	40	419
,,	Eye	120	60	319b
,,	,,	16	6	320
,,	Mendlesham	1,000	800	285b
,,	Redlingfield	100	50	320
,,	Rishangles	240	120	323
,,	Thorndon	200	120	323
,,	Thornham	30	20	437b
,,	Wetheringsett	500	400	384b
,,	Wortham	6	2	322b
,,	Wyverstone	40	20	436b
Hoxne	Chippenhall	160	100	368
,,	Mendham	360	300	368b
Ipswich	Ipswich	8	4	393
Parham	Parham	20	10	285b
Plomesgate	Rendham	40	30	307b
Samford	Belstead	30	20	430b
Stow	Creeting	40	0	432b
,,	Thorney	30	6	281b
Wangford	Homersfield	600	200	379
Hinckford (Essex)	Brundon	20	6	90

[1] The entry for *Uledana* merely says *Tunc silva de xxiiii porcis*; the omission of any
reference to *modo* may be a clerical error.

the unidentified locality of *Bricticeshaga* in Bosmere (433b), however, we are told that there was 'wood in which 16 swine could be pastured *T.R.E.*, now 4 (*silva qua poterant pasci xvi porci t.r.e. modo iiii*)'. The number of distinct places in Suffolk where woodland thus decreased was thirty-eight, and the details are summarised on p. 181. As in Norfolk, many of the holdings from which the wood had disappeared show not an increased number of plough-teams, as one might expect, but a smaller number in 1086 than in 1066. Thus at Leiston, in Blything, the number of swine which the wood could support had dropped from 500 to 200, but the number of plough-teams at work showed no corresponding increase; on the contrary, they had decreased from 17 to 10½ (fo. 311b). Only occasionally was there an increase of plough-teams on the holdings where the wood had been reduced. As Mr Lennard suggests, the disappearance of the wood must have been due, for the most part, not to assarting but to wasting.[1]

Distribution of woodland

The most notable feature of Fig. 45 is the concentration of wood in a belt stretching south-westwards from Halesworth towards Stowmarket. Here were many villages each with wood sufficient to feed 50 or more swine, and in one village wood for as many as 800 swine is recorded. This is a region of fairly heavy soils that forms part of the central claylands of Suffolk. The rest of these claylands, however, was not heavily wooded, although there was a fairly uniform scatter of small amounts of wood. For the villages on the light soils in the south-east of the county, the wood entries were few in number and small in amount. The even lighter soils of the Breckland in the north-west were completely devoid of wood. In a very general way, the map of wood is complementary to that of demesne sheep (Fig. 50). Where there was most wood, there were fewest sheep. Fig. 45 shows the distribution of wood in 1086. The cutting that had gone on since 1066 had not affected the general pattern of distribution. A map of woodland in 1066 would present similar features, except that the most densely wooded areas would appear even a little more wooded.

[1] See p. 126 above.

Types of entries

MEADOW

The entries for meadow in Suffolk, like those in Norfolk, are uniform and straightforward. The same type of entry repeats itself monotonously

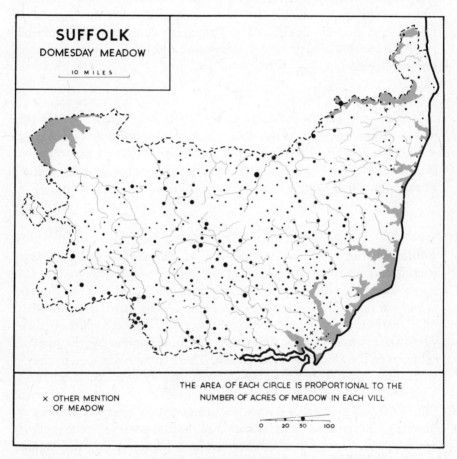

SUFFOLK
DOMESDAY MEADOW
10 MILES

THE AREA OF EACH CIRCLE IS PROPORTIONAL TO THE
NUMBER OF ACRES OF MEADOW IN EACH VILL

✕ OTHER MENTION
OF MEADOW

0   20   50   100

Fig. 46. Suffolk: Domesday meadow in 1086.

The areas of alluvium and peat are indicated; see Fig. 38. Rivers passing through these areas are not shown. Where the meadow of a village is entered partly in acres and partly in some other way, only the acres are shown.

—'*n* acres of meadow' (*n acrae prati*)—except in the case of Exning; this was part of the Domesday county of Cambridge, and its meadow is measured in terms of teams. The amount in each vill varied from half an acre to over 60, but amounts above 30 acres (and indeed above 20 acres) were comparatively rare. At *Mycelegata* (Colneis) there was one rood (*virga*) of meadow (342), and at Blakenham in Bosmere (285) there were 2 acres of meadow less 1 rood (*virga*). As in the case of Norfolk and Lincolnshire, no attempt has been made to translate the Domesday figures into modern acreages. The Domesday acres have been treated merely as conventional units of measurement, and Fig. 46 has been plotted on that assumption.

Distribution of meadowland

Meadow was distributed fairly uniformly in small quantities over the whole surface of the county. There were no areas with outstanding amounts, but some villages with over 40 and as much as 65 acres were to be found along the Waveney in the north, along the Gipping in the centre of the county and along the Stour in the south.

PASTURE

Entries relating to pasture are rare in the Suffolk folios. This is surprising because of the frequency of the entries relating to 'pasture for sheep' along the coastlands of Essex to the south.[1] It is true that Suffolk is without the considerable expanses of alluvial flats that border the coast of Essex, but, at any rate, one might expect such entries for the hundred of Colneis which adjoins Essex and which is flanked by the alluvial estuaries of the Orwell and the Deben. There is, however, one reference to pasture in the hundred (339b), which says that 'in the hundred of Colneis there is a certain pasture common to all the men of the hundred (*In Hundret de Colenes est quedam pastura communis omnibus hominibus de hundret*)'. It is an interesting indication of the practice of intercommoning about which we hear so much for certain localities in the later Middle Ages. Apart from this, there is a solitary reference to pasture in the hundred of Bosmere, where we are told that a freeman held '93 acres and 20 acres of pasture as a manor' in the village of Ashbocking (285). Finally, in the west, the village of Exning is now included within the modern boundary of Suffolk and one of its entries records *pastura ad pecuniam villae* (vol. 1, fo. 195b) in the usual Cambridgeshire manner. Quite

[1] See p. 241 below.

obviously, these few entries cannot represent all the pasture that was in Suffolk in 1086. But whatever the imperfections of the Suffolk folios in this respect, they have at least given us an illuminating insight into the pasture arrangements in Colneis.

FISHERIES

Fisheries are recorded for 1086 in connection with 19 places in Suffolk, one of which (*Turchetlestuna* in Samford) is at present unidentified. For each of these places, the number of fisheries only is stated, and no reference is made to their value as for some counties. The number of fisheries recorded for a village ranges from one third at Erwarton (394b) to $3\frac{1}{2}$ at Mildenhall (289). We cannot tell how the fractions should be completed, and to whom, for example, the missing half of the fourth fishery at Mildenhall belonged. In addition to the 3 fisheries at Lakenheath we are also told that there were 4 fisheries in Ely and one fishing boat (*iiii piscariae in eli et i navis ad piscandum*) belonging to the village (392). The entry for Exning (in Domesday Cambridgeshire) follows the Cambridgeshire pattern and states that the fishery there yielded 1,200 eels (vol. I, fo. 195 b); three mills in the same village also yielded 7,000 eels amongst other things. The usual Latin word is *piscaria*, but there are variations; *piscina* occurs, for example at Erwarton (394b) and *piscatio* at Hollesley (317). A distinction is occasionally made between conditions in 1066 and 1086; Tuddenham (Lackford) had one fishery in 1066 but none in 1086 (fo. 403); the fishery at Walton (Colneis) had likewise disappeared (339b).

As Fig. 47 shows, by far the greater number of these fisheries lay in the hundred of Lackford, on the edge of the Fenland and along the westward-flowing streams, the Little Ouse and the Lark; this concentration of fisheries continued along the edge of the Norfolk Fens. Elsewhere in Suffolk, there were only a few scattered fisheries in the south-east of the county, but whether any of these were sea-fisheries or not, it is impossible to tell.

There was, however, another type of fishing activity in Suffolk, for in the hundreds of Blything, Lothingland and Wangford there are 18 places for which herrings (*allecti*) are recorded. Thus a holding in Kessingland was 'then worth 10 shillings now 22 shillings and 1,000 herrings' (407). In 1086, Southwold returned 25,000 herrings (371 b); and Beccles returned

60,000 (370); and Dunwich 68,000 (312). Five of the places are as yet unidentified, but the other thirteen are marked on Fig. 47. There are also other references to activity along the sea-shore. At Southwold (371b) there was the moiety of a sea-weir and the fourth part of the other moiety

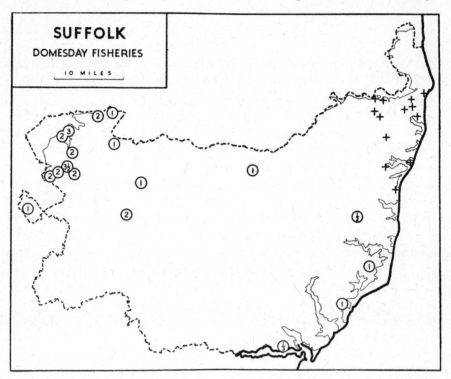

Fig. 47. Suffolk: Domesday fisheries in 1086.

The figure in each circle indicates the number of fisheries; the crosses indicate places for which renders of herrings are recorded. The boundary of alluvium and peat is shown; see Fig. 38.

(*medietas unius heiemaris et quarta pars alterius medietatis*), but there is no reference anywhere to the remaining three-eighths. There also belonged to the manor of Blythburgh the fourth penny from the rent of the haye or hedge of *Riseburc* (*quartus denarius de censu de heia de riseburc*), though we are not told what kind of haye this was (282). It is impossible to say exactly what activity all these references imply, and we can only note the existence of Yarmouth with its fishermen just across the county boundary

(283), and the mysterious reference to a seaport (*portus maris*) at Frosten-den in Blything (414b). Judged by Domesday evidence alone, the sea certainly played a more important part in the life of Suffolk than in that of Norfolk.

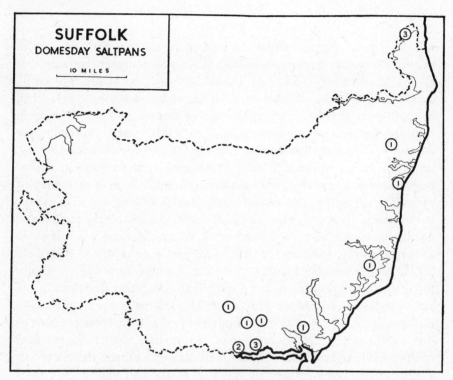

Fig. 48. Suffolk: Domesday salt-pans in 1086.

The figure in each circle indicates the number of salt-pans. The boundary of alluvium and peat is shown; see Fig. 38.

SALT-PANS

There were far fewer salt-pans in Suffolk than in Norfolk. For the year 1086 these were recorded in connection with only 10 villages. The number of pans only is stated, with no estimate of their value. The number of salt-pans in each village was small; only 2 villages had as many as 3 pans. There were also 4 villages each with 1 salt-pan which had disappeared between 1066 and 1086 and which are not marked on Fig. 48: Easton, Frostenden and Wangford in Blything, and Fritton in

Lothingland. Fig. 48 shows that the salt-making villages of 1086 were scattered sporadically along the coast with a tendency to concentration around the estuaries of the Stour and the Orwell.

MILLS

Mills are mentioned as existing in 1086 in connection with 178 out of the 640 Domesday settlements in Suffolk. In addition, there were another eleven places where mills had existed in 1066, but had, apparently, disappeared by 1086; thus an entry for Uggeshall in Blything says 'then one mill now none' (299b), while each of three entries for Belstead in Samford merely says 'then one mill' (306, 411b, 418b). Normally, the number of mills only was entered, and this varied from a fraction of a mill up to 5½. It is sometimes possible to reassemble the fractions in a comprehensible manner; thus at Kembrook (Colneis) there is one entry of 1½ mills (343) and another of half a mill (441b), making a total of 2 mills in the village. It is even possible occasionally to assemble the fractions of neighbouring villages; in the hundred of Wangford, there was half a mill at Barsham (335b) and another half in the adjoining village of Ringsfield (282b), and it may be that these were halves of the same mill. But only too often it is impossible to bring the fractions together like this. In the same hundred there was one-fifth of a mill at each of three nearby places— Elmham (356), Flixton (380) and Linburne (370). Were these portions of one and the same mill? We cannot say. In any case, there is the problem of the remaining fractions. On another holding at Flixton there was half a mill (434b), but whether this was part of the half mill at the neighbouring village of Ilketshall (300b) we cannot be sure. On a holding in the unidentified village of *Langhedana* in Bosmere (404b), there was 'in every third year one quarter of a mill (*in tercio anno quarta pars molini*)', presumably one-quarter of the profits of a mill. At Barking in Bosmere (382b) there was 'then as now one mill and a weir of another mill, and in the weir of the other mill, Robert Malet had a share (*semper i molinum, et unam exclusam alterius molini, et in exclusa alterius molini habet Robertus malet partem*)'; and at Creeting, likewise in Bosmere (304b), there was also one part of a weir (*una pars unius excluse*). Neither values nor renders are assigned to the mills except very occasionally; at Hollesley in Wilford there was a mill which seems to have been worth 12s. (317b), while renders both of money and of eels are stated for the mills at Exning (vol. 1, fos. 189b, 195b), but this was in Domesday Cambridgeshire and follows the normal formula for that county. There were five places with winter mills (*molinum hiemale*)—Cockfield (359), Edwardstone (304)

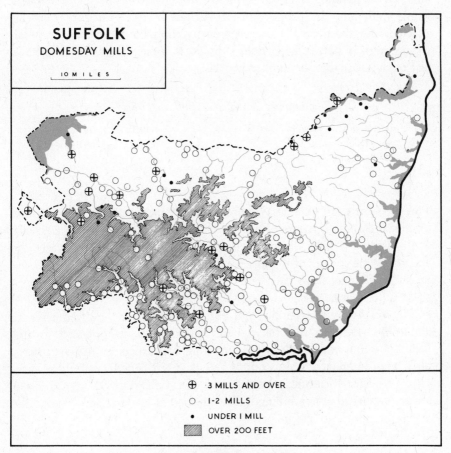

Fig. 49. Suffolk: Domesday mills in 1086.

The areas of alluvium and peat are indicated; see Fig. 38. Rivers passing through these areas are not shown.

and Groton (359b) in Babergh; at Rickinghall (365) in Blackbourne; and at Pakenham (361b) in Thedwastre. Presumably, the little streams on which these were situated had a flow of water sufficient to turn the mill wheels only in winter.

Over two-thirds of the villages with mills had only one or a fraction of one mill. The following table cannot be accurate owing to the complications caused by the fractions. Apart from those places with 'under 1 mill', an outstanding fraction of a mill for a village has been counted as a whole mill, and the proportion of villages in each category may be affected. But the general picture given by the table is probably not far wrong, and, in particular, it does show how some villages seem to have had many more than one mill at work.

Domesday Mills in Suffolk in 1086

Under 1 mill	18 settlements		4 mills	5 settlements
1 ,,	112	,,	5 ,,	1 settlement
2 mills	32	,,	6 ,,	1 ,,
3 ,,	9	,,		

The group of 5 mills was at Weybread; the Domesday Book records only 4 mills and three-quarters of another (329b), but there was a quarter of a mill at the adjoining village of Instead (447) and this may be the missing fraction. The group of 6 mills was at Bungay, or rather 5½ mills; the missing half may have been entered under Ilketshall or Flixton or yet some other place.

The mills were water-mills, and Fig. 49 shows how they were aligned along the streams. But the general distribution, as opposed to the location of individual mills, is not what might be expected. In Hartismere, mills were entered for only 4 out of 34 villages; in Thedwastre there were only 3 villages with mills out of a total of 19 villages. Or what, for example, happened about milling in the hundred of Lothingland where only 2 villages out of 30 had mills?

CHURCHES

Churches are mentioned in connection with 345 villages in Suffolk as well as those of Ipswich, Dunwich, Bury St Edmunds, Beccles, Clare, Eye and Sudbury. They were therefore more numerous than those of Norfolk, but, even so, we cannot believe that the Domesday record included all the churches in the county.[1] In many hundreds, the number of villages with churches fell well below the total number of villages. Some villages,

[1] Thus the *I.E.* (p. 147) alone mentions a church at Harpole.

on the other hand, had two or more churches; and, in view of J. H. Round's theory of the formation of parishes, it is interesting to note that these villages are occasionally represented by two or more parishes today.[1] Cornard, in Babergh, had two churches, and it appears on the modern map as Great Cornard and Little Cornard. The Domesday churches of South Elmham (Wangford) add up to 6⅓, and it now gives its name to six adjacent parishes; but it is impossible to say whether these two sets of facts can be correlated to suggest that six or more separate settlements were grouped under the Domesday name *Elmeham*. On the other hand, many villages with two or more Domesday churches each have always remained single parishes, e.g. Shimpling (Babergh) and Debenham (Claydon). Some of these, moreover, had a surprising number of churches; Bungay (Wangford), for example, had five, Saxmundham (Plomesgate) had three.

For some villages, only a fraction of a church is recorded, e.g. one-half, a third or a quarter. Occasionally it is possible to put the fractions together in an intelligible manner. One entry for Aspall, in Hartismere, mentions 'two parts' of a church (321), while another mentions a 'third part' of a church (418). At Wantisden, in Loes, the fractions similarly add up to a satisfactory total—one-half (306b) and two quarters (307, 344). But it is not always possible to arrive at these convenient and happy totals. At Rickinghall (Hartismere), 14 freemen held the fifth part of a church (361), but there is no clue to the holders of the other four-fifths. For Akenham, in Claydon, there was one entry of 'half a church' (352b) and another of 'three parts of a church' (422b), but it is difficult to see exactly what they signify, apart from the fact that several lords held a church or churches there.[2] Further indication of the division of a church among a number of holders is provided by an occasional statement to the effect that 'others shared in it'. The mention of a church at Kenton (Loes) is followed by the statement: *plures ibi participantur* (326). The church at Loudham (Wilford) was likewise held jointly: *plures ibi parciuntur* (388b). So was the church at Burgh (Carlford): *plures habent partem* (400b).

A number of entries relating to the hundred of Thedwastre speak of the village church (*ecclesia hujus villae*)—Great Barton (361b), Bradfield (362), Fornham St Martin (361b), Pakenham (361b), and Rougham (362). The idea of a parish is also clear from events at Combs and Stow, two

---

[1] See J. H. Round in *V.C.H. Essex*, I, pp. 400 *et seq*. See p. 158 above.
[2] For the nature of these fractions, see p. 76 above.

villages only a mile or two apart: '12 sokemen in Combs used to be parishioners (*parrochiani*) in Stow Church, but now they are in Combs Church' (291 b). The growth of daughter churches or chapels is illustrated by an incident on the royal manor of Thorney (in Stowmarket) where 4 freemen built a chapel 'on their own land near the cemetery of the mother church. And they were inhabitants of the parish of the mother church, [and built this chapel] because it could not take in the whole of the parish (*et fuerunt manentes de parrochia matris ecclesiae, quod non poterat capere totam parrochiam*).' The entry goes on to record the arrangement about burial fees between church and chapel (281 b). Another chapel was built under (*sub*) the church at Wisset in Blything hundred (293). These details do not amount to much, but they enable us to glimpse some of the arrangements that are usually hidden by the terse and telegraphic entries of the Survey.

Normally, the value of a church was stated together with the number of acres it held; in the case of the larger churches the number of tenants and number of plough-teams at work were also added. Thus at Mettingham in Wangford there was 'a church with 12 acres worth 3 shillings' (300 b). Some churches were stated to hold their land freely (*libera terra*) or in alms (*pro elemosina*). At some places a church without land (*sine terra*) is recorded, e.g. at Undley in Lackford (382). No value is assigned to an occasional church, and we are left to infer that this is included in the total valuation of the holding as a whole, e.g. at Stonham (374b) and Burstall (375) in Bosmere.

URBAN LIFE

Burgesses are recorded for as many as six places in Suffolk—Ipswich, Dunwich, Eye, Beccles, Clare and Sudbury. Markets are entered for the last four, but not for Ipswich and Dunwich though it is difficult to believe they were without. The other five places with markets had no burgesses.

Unsatisfactory though the evidence for each of the six boroughs is, it is sufficient to enable us to glimpse something of the character of the Norman town. How rural it was on the one hand, with its arable, and its meadow and its stock. What an air of bustle it must have had on the other hand, with its many churches, its market, its mint and its burgesses. In addition to these six boroughs there was also Bury St Edmunds. Although described as a *villa* in the Domesday Book, it is grouped here with the boroughs since, as we shall see, it may well have been one.

Ipswich

The half-hundred of Ipswich included not only the town (*burgus*) itself, but also the village of *Stoches*; for the purpose of this analysis, the latter has been included in the hundred of Samford. Here we are concerned with the town alone. The main entry relating to it occupies both sides of fo. 290, but this is supplemented by three other important entries (294, 392b and 421b), and there are also thirteen subsidiary entries which provide fragments of information.[1] The main entry summarises briefly the condition of the town: 'In the borough there were *T.R.E.* 538 burgesses rendering custom to the king, and they had 40 acres of land. But now there are 110 burgesses who render custom, and 100 poor burgesses who are unable to render to the king's geld [anything] but one penny a head. And among the whole of them in like manner they have 40 acres of land. And 328 burgages (*mansiones*) within the borough lie waste.' No hint of the cause of this decrease from 538 to 210 is given, but the record goes on to enumerate 8 churches in the city. The other entries bring the total of churches up to 11 which suggests a strong urban flavour; these other entries also mention 52 burgesses, 6 houses (*domus*), 3 *mansurae* and 16 empty or waste *mansurae*. Three of the entries refer to properties belonging to rural manors: a burgess to Playford (314b), a *mansurae* to Nacton (410) and another to *Mosa* (411b), possibly Moze in Essex.[2] Two of the entries tell us that 17 burgesses had died between 1066 and 1086 (289, 402). In addition to the burgesses and the urban properties, Ipswich in 1086 also had 12 freemen, 32 bordars and 13 villeins.[3] On the assumption that the details of the main entry on fo. 290 did not include those of the other entries, the grand total for 1086 amounted to 328 people, houses and *mansurae*.[4] The population of Ipswich at this time must therefore have been about 1600, or maybe more. The presence of moneyers (*monetarii*) and of a mint (*moneta*) is indicative of the commercial activity of the town.

[1] Fos. 289, 295, 304b, 314b, 378b, 402, 410, 411b, 425, 427, 438, 446, 446b.

[2] For the connection between towns and surrounding villages, see p. 251 below.

[3] 'We are accustomed to think of a burgess as being of necessity a free man, but we read of one at Ipswich who is expressly stated to be a slave (*servus*).' A. Ballard, *The Domesday Boroughs* (Oxford, 1904), p. 57. The reference is on fos. 392b–393.

[4] It is a coincidence that this total is the same as the number of waste burgages (328) noted above.

As well as this commercial and urban element, there was also an important agricultural flavour about the settlement—16 plough-teams, woodland for 4 swine (reduced from 8 in 1066) and 7 acres of meadow. No bees are mentioned, but honey is included in the render. The stock comprised 9 animals, 2 rounceys, 7 goats, 9 swine and 93 sheep. There were also 2½ mills. This statement about the mills symbolises the incompleteness of the information as a whole. All we can say, with certainty, is that Ipswich, with its burgesses and its many churches, and its mint, must have been a substantial settlement in 1086 despite the misfortune that had fallen upon it since the Conquest.

Dunwich

The main entry relating to Dunwich, in the hundred of Blything, stretches from the bottom of fo. 311b on to the next page, and there are four subsidiary entries on fos. 312, 331b, 333b and 385b. The encroachment of the sea which was to prove the undoing of the old town had already begun. The record is terse but eloquent enough: 'Then 2 carucates of land, now 1. The sea carried away the other (*mare abstulit alia*).' Despite this loss, there was still one plough-team there in 1086 as in 1066, and there are indications of progress. The number of bordars, it is true, had fallen from 12 to 2, but there were 24 *franci homines* and the burgesses had increased from 120 to 236. There were, however, 178 poor men (*pauperes homines*). There were also 80 men (*homines*) who seem to be additional to these figures; and one of the subsidiary entries refers to 80 burgesses of Dunwich dwelling upon 14 acres, who belonged to the unidentified manor of *Alnet'ne* (385b).[1] If these two additional groups of people be included, the total recorded population for Dunwich in 1086 amounts to 600 which may imply an actual population of about 3,000 or so. The number of churches had increased from 1 in 1066 to 3 in 1086, which again seems to indicate growth. The renders of the town included a total of 68,000 herrings, but we are left to guess exactly what part the sea played in the economic life of the growing centre. No wood, meadow, mills, salt-pans or livestock are mentioned.

---

[1] Connection between Dunwich and the villages of the surrounding countryside is also shown by (1) the 3 acres in Dunwich that belonged to Bridge (331b); (2) the 2 acres in Dunwich that belonged to Thorpe (333b–334). For the connection between boroughs and the surrounding countryside, see p. 251 below.

Eye

The main account of Eye, in the hundred of Hartismere, extends from fo. 319b on to fo. 320; and there are also two other entries relating to the town on fos. 379 and 449b. The general picture that emerges is that of a substantial agricultural settlement with a growing urban element in its midst. The importance of the agricultural background is indicated by the fact that no less than 23½ plough-teams are recorded for 1086. On some of the holdings that went to make up this total, the number of teams had fallen since 1066, but in one case we are specifically told that the other ploughs could be made good (*alie carucae possent restaurari*). There was woodland for a total of 69 swine in 1086 [1], but enough for another 70 swine had disappeared since 1066. There was also a park, 61 acres of meadow, 2 mills and a fishery. The demesne stock had varied between 1066 and 1086; the number of rounceys had decreased from 7 to 1, animals from 24 to none, swine from 50 to 17; on the other hand the number of sheep had increased from 80 to 90. There had also been variations in the population, but in 1086 there were 9 freemen, 57 sokemen, 21 villeins, 32 bordars, and no serfs. There was also a wealthy church dedicated to St Peter.

The rise of the urban element is indicated by the fact that there was a market which does not seem to have been there in 1066 (*modo i mercatum*) and that 25 burgesses lived in or around (*manent*) the market. The total recorded population for 1086 amounts therefore to 144 which may imply a population of anything up to 700 or more. Further information about the market is given in the account of Hoxne (379) about 3 miles away.

In this manor [i.e. of Hoxne] there used to be a market *T.R.E.* and [it went on] after King William came hither; and it was set up (*sedebat*) on Saturdays. And William Malet made his castle at Eye, and on the same day as the market used to be held on the bishop's manor [i.e. of Hoxne] William Malet made another market in his castle and thereby the bishop's market has been so far spoilt that it is of little worth; and now it is set up on Friday. But the market at Eye is set up on the Saturday.

The Conquest had brought prosperity to Eye. With its castle and its market and its burgesses, it was obviously becoming a place of some consequence. The rise was to continue, but only up to a point, for the situation of the little town had few geographical advantages.

[1] Counting 3 swine for Suartric (319b), not 13 as in the duplicate entry (449b).

Beccles

The main information relating to Beccles is entered under the hundred of Wangford where the settlement was situated (369b–370); but three subsidiary entries on fo. 283b give some additional details and are entered under the hundred of Lothingland. Taken together, the information gives the impression of an agricultural village with an urban element. It had at least eleven plough-teams at work, but we cannot say how many more because of what is obviously an omission from the text. In 1086, as apparently in 1066, there were 12 freemen, 30 sokemen, 7 villeins and 46 bordars. Two serfs had disappeared since 1066. There were also 26 burgesses.[1] The total of 121 recorded people implies a population of about 600 or possibly more. There was also a market and a church, together with wood for 8 swine, and 10 acres of meadow. The recorded stock numbered only 2 rounceys. The burgesses and the market were not the only non-agricultural elements in the economy of the settlement, for we are told that whereas in 1066 it rendered 30,000 herrings, in 1086 it rendered 60,000. We can do no more than guess at the significance of this maritime element in the economy of the settlement. We are told nothing, for example, of fishermen.

Clare

The entry relating to Clare, in the hundred of Risbridge, is fairly brief (389b), and it gives the impression of an agricultural settlement that was acquiring something of the flavour of a town. The agricultural element in the settlement was still very strong although the number of plough-teams had dropped from 49½ in 1066 to 32½ in 1086. The population in the latter year comprised 5 sokemen, 30 villeins, 30 bordars and 20 serfs, making a total of 85 as compared with 75 in 1066. This increase in population coupled with the substantial decrease in the number of teams suggests that the inhabitants had been increasingly engaged upon non-agricultural pursuits during the preceding 20 years. In 1086 (*modo*) there were in addition 43 burgesses who are not mentioned as being there in 1066, although there was a market there in 1066 as well as 1086 (*semper*). The grand total of 128 recorded people implies a settlement of some 600

---

[1] The account of Norwich states that 22 burgesses who dwelt there had gone to live in Beccles (117); but it is impossible to say whether these are included in the 26 recorded for Beccles. See p. 140 above.

or more people. The limits of the settlement also included wood for 12 swine, 43 acres of meadow, one mill, 5 arpents of vineyard and 12 hives of bees. There was also a church named after St John. The number of animals had risen from 10 to 14, the number of swine from 12 to 60, and the number of sheep from 60 to 480, while the number of rounceys had remained stationary at 6.

Sudbury

The Domesday account of Sudbury is brief (286b); it is rubricated under the hundred of Thingoe of which it was an outlying portion. Its recorded population in 1086 included 63 burgesses attached to the hall (*halle manentes*), and 55 on the demesne (*in dominio*), together with 2 villeins and 2 serfs. There were also 15 burgesses belonging to Hedingham (76b) and 5 to Hinckford hundred (40), both in Essex.[1] This total of 142 implies a settlement of anything up to 700 or more people. There was a market, and therein were moneyers (*ibi sunt monetarii*), which implies a fair amount of commercial activity over and above weekly trading. There were 7 plough-teams at work, and the arrangement of the items within the entry suggests that most, if not all, of these were held by the burgesses. There were also 34 acres of meadow, a mill, and a church named after St Gregory. The stock on the demesne comprised 2 horses, 17 animals, 24 swine and 100 sheep.

Bury St Edmunds

The account of Bury St Edmunds on fo. 372 of the Little Domesday Book raises many problems that cannot be answered satisfactorily. But it is an extremely interesting entry because it provides a notable example of the growth of a commercial centre, and it has been discussed in some detail by Mrs M. D. Lobel in her study of the borough. The entry describes Bury not as a borough but as a *villa*, and it does not mention burgesses. These facts led Ballard to say that it was not a borough,[2] but Mrs Lobel has questioned this. She points to the loose use of technical terms both in the Domesday Book and in later documents, and says that 'the same argument applies to the word *homines* which is often used as an alternative for *burgesses*'.[3] The fact remains that the settlement around

[1] Moreover, dues from Sudbury were payable to Henny in Essex—see p. 252 below.
[2] Adolphus Ballard, *The Domesday Boroughs*, pp. 119–20.
[3] M. D. Lobel, *The Borough of Bury St Edmunds* (Oxford, 1935), pp. 11–15.

the monastery at Bury was very different in character from the settlements of the surrounding countryside. Here is the Domesday account in full:

In the town (*villa*) where rests enshrined Saint Edmund king and martyr of glorious memory, Abbot B[aldwin] held, in the time of King Edward, towards the provision of (*ad victum*) the monks, 118 men, and they could give and sell their land; and under them 52 bordars from whom the Abbot can have some little aid (*aliquid adjutorii*), 54 freemen quite poor (*satis inopes*), 43 almsmen, each of them has 1 bordar. Now 2 mills, and 2 stews or fishponds (*vivaria vel piscinae*). This town was then worth 10 pounds, now 20 pounds. It is 1½ leagues in length and as much in breadth. And when a pound is levied on the hundred for geld, then there go from the town 60 pence towards the provision of the monks. But this refers to (*est de*) the town as [it was] in the time of King Edward as if [it were still] so. Now the town is contained in a greater circle (*maiori ambitu*), including (*de*) land which then used to be ploughed and sown, whereon are 30 priests, deacons and clerks together (*inter*), 28 nuns and poor people who daily utter prayers for the king and for all Christian people; 80 less 5 bakers, ale-brewers,[1] tailors, washerwomen, shoemakers, robe-makers (*parmentarii*), cooks, porters, agents (*dispensatores*) together. And all these daily wait upon the Saint, the abbot and the brethren. Besides whom there are 13 reeves over the land who have their houses in the said town, and under them 5 bordars. Now 34 knights, French and English together, and under them 22 bordars. Now altogether [there are] 342 houses on the demesne of the land of Saint Edmund which was under the plough in the time of King Edward.

The picture that emerges is that of an older settlement for which 310 people were recorded, on the assumption, that is, that each almsman had a bordar. Around this centre, the built-up area had extended on to the arable, and a total of 207 people are mentioned in connection with this new town. It is unlikely that all these (e.g. priests and washerwomen) were householders, yet the account ends up by saying that 342 new houses had been built. Many householders must therefore have been omitted from the enumeration. If, tentatively, we add this figure of 342 to the recorded figure of 310 for the old town, the total implies a population of over 3,000. Such calculations are obviously very conjectural.

It is clear that the Domesday record is incomplete about other matters as well as about population. Mrs Lobel has shown that Bury very probably had a market and a mint in 1066, yet the Domesday record does not mention them. Nor is there any mention of stock or of meadow, for

---

[1] The Latin is *cervisarii*. The only other Domesday use of this word is in the Cornish folios (120) where it may imply tenants who paid their dues in ale.

example, in spite of the fact that the valleys of the Lark and the Linnet in the east, south and north, may well have had meadow. But, says Mrs Lobel, 'the strangest part about the Domesday entry is not so much its omissions as the fact that it was made at all, for the demesne lands of St Edmund were exempt from geld payments'.[1] Edward the Confessor had granted that whenever other men paid to the geld, the men of St Edmund should pay their contribution to the abbey. Hence the reference to the 60 pence payable for the provision of the monks. But, in spite of the incompleteness of the information, the veil is lifted, for a moment at any rate, to give a glimpse of the growth of a commercial centre. From other sources we can obtain a picture of the remarkable ability of Abbot Baldwin who presided over this growth.[2]

LIVESTOCK

The Suffolk folios, like those of Norfolk and Essex, record information about livestock on the demesne. The total number in each category of stock in 1086 is summarised as follows:

Sheep	37,522	Rounceys	527
Swine	9,843	Horses	127
Goats	4,343	Wild mares	114
Animals	3,083	Donkeys	2
Cows	9		

The figures for 1086 are frequently very different from those for 1066. Thus an entry relating to Acton in Babergh declares 'Then 8 horses at the hall, now 11. Then 34 animals, now 31. Then 200 swine, now 160. Then 300 sheep, now 423 sheep' (416). The stock had entirely disappeared from some holdings. At Eaton in Blything there were 'then 1 rouncey and 3 beasts and 2 swine and 80 sheep. Now nothing' (444b); and it was likewise at Loose in Cosford (416b) and at Crowfield (421b) and Offton in Bosmere (337), and at several other places besides. No clue is given as to the cause of these catastrophic changes, and we can only guess whether they were due to the policy of a landowner or to the accidents of murrain and mortality. Occasionally, as in Norfolk, the form of the Domesday entry makes it difficult to be absolutely certain whether the amount of stock on a holding in 1066 was still there in 1086 and vice versa.

[1] M. D. Lobel, *op. cit.* p. 13.
[2] D. C. Douglas, *Feudal Documents*, pp. lxii *et seq.*

Horses are fairly frequently recorded. Sometimes they are said to be *in halla* (416), which, says Miss Lees, may imply that they were 'riding horses or horses used for breeding purposes, though the different terms were probably not applied with any great precision'.[1] A number of entries refer to *equae silvaticae*, and it is clear that occasional groups of wild and unbroken mares were to be found in Suffolk as in Norfolk; Melford, for example, had forty of these forest mares in 1086 (fo. 359). But of all the varieties of horse, the one most frequently mentioned is the rouncey (*runcinus*); the demesne of a village usually carried 2, 3 or 4, but occasionally the number was greater. Finally, 2 donkeys are mentioned at Brandon (421); there must have been many more.

Goats are recorded on a number of holdings, but much less frequently and in smaller numbers than are sheep. The number of goats on the demesne of a village was rarely above fifty.

Swine are much more frequently mentioned. The number on the demesne of a holding was rarely the same as the number its woodland could support; usually it was less, but occasionally it was more. Swine are sometimes recorded for holdings without any wood; thus, in 1086, there were 55 swine on the demesne at Stansfield in Risbridge, but there is no mention of the wood (390b, 396).

Animals presumably include all the non-ploughing beasts; sometimes they are described as *animalia otiosa*, e.g. at Huntingford (311) and Thorington (400) in Blything. Cows are very seldom mentioned (e.g. 376b and 400), yet they must have been kept in large numbers for breeding the all important ploughing oxen. They may often have been included under the general heading of *animalia*. These 'animals' are recorded for a large number of villages—usually less than twenty in each, but sometimes more.

The distribution of each of these major groups of livestock was fairly widespread, and presents no special features of interest. There is, however, one group that merits more detailed treatment. Sheep are recorded in large numbers, and their distribution must be examined more closely.

Sheep

Fig. 50, of course, is a map only of sheep on the demesne lands; but, although thus limited, it may give some hint about the general distribution of sheep throughout the county. Roughly speaking there were, as

[1] *V.C.H. Suffolk*, I, p. 407.

in Norfolk, fewest sheep where there was most wood. There were, for example, few sheep in the wooded country that extended through Hartismere, Hoxne and western Blything. Sheep were most numerous in the west of the county, and especially in the Breckland hundred of Lackford. Flocks of 1,000 sheep were to be found in 1086 at Mildenhall, of 934 at

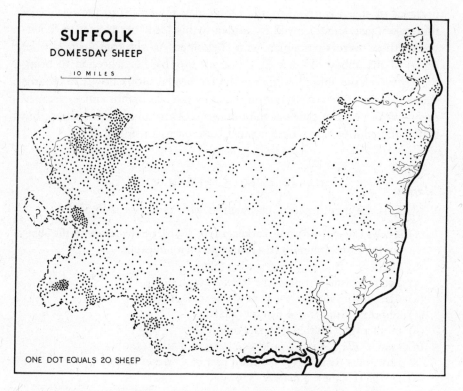

SUFFOLK
DOMESDAY SHEEP

10 MILES

ONE DOT EQUALS 20 SHEEP

Fig. 50. Suffolk: Domesday sheep on the demesne in 1086.

The boundary of alluvium and peat is shown; see Fig. 38. The parish of Exning is queried for it was in Domesday Cambridgeshire and no sheep are therefore recorded for it.

Icklingham, 900 at Santon Downham, 860 at Elvedon and 800 at Eriswell. There were also 880 at *Coclesworda* where there had been 1,200 in 1066.[1]

[1] *Coclesworda* is now represented by Chamberlain's Hall Farm in Eriswell—J. T. Munday, 'The topography of mediaeval Eriswell', *Proc. Suffolk Inst. Arch.* (Ipswich, 1967), xxx, pp. 201-9.

The number of sheep often varied a great deal between 1066 and 1086. In some villages there was a decline; in others the reverse. At Rendlesham in Loes there had been a decrease from 36 to 10 (326b), while at Wratting in Risbridge there had been a great increase from 140 to 800 (fos. 396, 396b). The reason for all these changes lies beyond our reach.

As we have seen in the case of Norfolk, another indication of the presence of sheep is given by the Domesday references to the service of fold-soke (*soca faldae*) owed by a man to his lord. At Hesset in Thedwastre there were 54 freemen who 'belonged' to the fold (*pertinent ad falda*) of the abbey of Bury St Edmunds (362b), i.e. who had to bring their sheep to the abbot's fold. Yet the Domesday Book nowhere records sheep at Hesset; they were not on the demesne of a manor and so escaped mention. We cannot guess at the number of these unrecorded sheep, but taking the county as a whole it must have been considerable.[1]

MISCELLANEOUS INFORMATION

Markets

Markets are mentioned in connection with nine places in Suffolk:

(1) Beccles (Wangford): one market (283b, 369b), three parts with the abbey of Bury St Edmunds and a fourth part with the king.
(2) Sudbury (Thingoe): one market (286b).
(3) Eye (Hartismere): now one market (319b).
(4) Clare (Risbridge): then as now one market (389b).
(5) Thorney (Stow): one market (281b).
(6) Blythburgh (Blything): a market (282).
(7) *Caramhalla* (? Kelsale in Plomesgate): a market (330b).
(8) Haverhill (Risbridge): the third part of a market (428).
(9) Hoxne (Hoxne): a market (379).

The first four of these places also had burgesses, and the presence of markets is therefore not unexpected. The others were all in very substantial villages, judged by eleventh-century standards. There is no clue to the other two-thirds of the market at Haverhill; a subsequent phrase in this entry speaks of the market as being worth 13s. 4d., and it may be that the market as a whole is implied, but we cannot be sure. In any case, the statement of the value of the market is exceptional. Compared with markets recorded for other counties, this is a long list, but, even so, it

---

[1] See pp. 145–6 above.

cannot by any means cover all the markets that must have been held in the county. The entry relating to Hoxne gives an interesting idea of the competition between two markets at Hoxne and Eye respectively.[1]

Beehives

Associated with statistics about stock, there is an occasional statement about hives of bees. The number recorded is usually under a dozen, and sometimes it is a mere two or three. No value is attached to the numbers. The usual form of the entry is *vasa apum* which is what is entered for Acton in Babergh (416); but sometimes the phrase *ruscae apum* is used, e.g. in an entry relating to Camsey (443b). The total number of beehives recorded on the demesne of the county in 1086 is 350. All the entries cannot represent the total number of hives in the county, and occasionally a render of honey is stated for places where no beehives are mentioned, e.g. for Diss in Hartismere (282) and for Ipswich (290b).

Vineyards

Vineyards (*vineae*) are mentioned in connection with four localities in Suffolk, and they are measured in terms of arpents (*arpenni*), a French unit of measurement.[2] There were five arpents at Clare (389b), three at Ixworth (438b), two at Barking (382b) and one (*arpentum*) at Lavenham (418).

Other references

In an entry relating to Frostenden, near the coast in Blything, there is a mysterious reference to a seaport (*i portus maris*), but there is nothing else in the entry which throws light either on the port or its activities (414b).[3] At Aspall in Hartismere there is another mysterious reference to the third part of a fair (*tercia pars feriae*), but no clue is given anywhere to the rest of the fair or to what kind of activities were carried on (418). There must have been other fairs in the county, but they are unrecorded. Parks are entered for four places,[4] waste for two places,[5] and a castle for Eye (379).

---

[1] See p. 195 above.

[2] For a discussion of the arpent see Sir Henry Ellis, *A General Introduction to Domesday Book*, I, p. 117. See p. 258 below.

[3] For the existence of the port, see C. Morley and E. R. Cooper, 'The sea port of Frostenden', *Proc. Suffolk Inst. Arch. and Nat. Hist.* (Ipswich, 1924), XVIII, pp. 167–79.   [4] See p. 180 above.   [5] See p. 165 above.

REGIONAL SUMMARY

The regional division of Suffolk, shown on Fig. 51, follows in the main
that of P. M. Roxby.[1] Basically, it is the same as the regional division of
the Suffolk Report of the Land Utilisation Survey, except that the latter
is more detailed and its regions more numerous.[2] For our purpose,
Roxby's more generalised scheme is adequate, because the Domesday
information enables only broad contrasts to be drawn. The boundaries
of the regions do not agree with those of the unit areas of Figs. 42 and 44,
and, in particular, the unit areas are such that they do not enable the region
of the Sandlings to be separated clearly.[3] But some generalisations can
at any rate be made. The main basis of the division can be seen from the
maps of geology (Fig. 38) and soil types (Fig. 39). Essentially, Suffolk
consists of a large central Boulder Clay area flanked on the east by the
light soils of the 'Sandlings', and on the north-west by the Breckland.
The county boundary also includes small portions of three other regions—
Fenland, Broadland and Chalk Downland.

(1) *High Suffolk*

The general level of the surface lies between 150 and 250 ft. above
sea-level, rising to over 400 ft. in the west. It is largely a Boulder Clay
area that forms a continuation of that of central Norfolk, but the soils are
on the whole heavier than those of Norfolk, especially towards the south-
west. The river valleys cut into the Boulder Clay support numerous
villages, each with anything up to two dozen acres of meadow, and
occasionally with as many as 40–50 acres. The general prosperity of the
region, as indicated by plough-teams and population, resembles that of
much of central Norfolk, and contrasts markedly with that of the Breckland. The region as a whole was originally wooded, and the northern
portion still carried a substantial amount of wood-cover in 1086. Small
amounts of woodland were fairly distributed elsewhere, but the amount of
wood was least in the area to the north of Ipswich, i.e. in those hundreds
with the highest densities of plough-teams and population. Sheep, at any
rate demesne sheep, were comparatively few, especially in the wooded
areas.

[1] P. M. Roxby, 'East Anglia', in A. G. Ogilvie (ed.), *Great Britain: Essays in
Regional Geography* (Cambridge, 1928), p. 164.
[2] R. W. Butcher, *Suffolk* (London, 1941), p. 345, being Parts 72–3 of *The Land of
Britain*, ed. L. Dudley Stamp.   [3] See p. 177 above.

(2) *The Breckland*

This is a continuation of the Norfolk Breckland, and has similar characteristics. The few villages of the region are set either along the fen

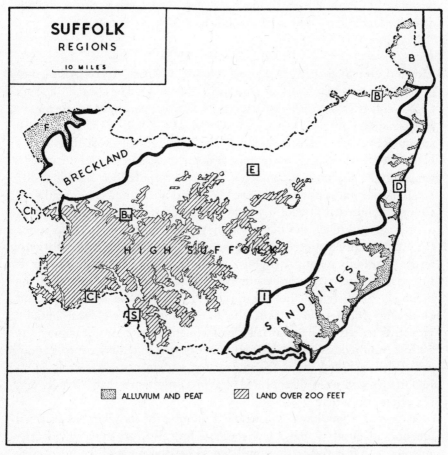

Fig. 51. Suffolk: Regional subdivisions.

The additional regions are as follows: B, Broadland; Ch, Chalk Downland; F, Fenland. The places with burgesses are B, Beccles; Bu, Bury St Edmunds; C, Clare; D, Dunwich; E, Eye; I, Ipswich; S, Sudbury.

margin, or in the valleys of the Little Ouse and the Lark and their tributaries. As in Norfolk, either the Fenland or the streams flowing into it supported a large number of fisheries; the valleys, too, carried moderate amounts of meadow. The densities of plough-teams and population were very low. There was no wood in the region, and not a single entry of wood occurs for the hundred of Lackford. The Forestry Commission has greatly changed the appearance of the region today, but in 1086 the heaths presumably were still bare. It was, however, a great sheep region, and the demesne lands of a number of villages had flocks of 800 and more.

(3) *The Sandlings*

This is a very distinctive area along the Suffolk coast. It consists mainly of glacial sands and gravels, together with the sandy loams of the Pliocene Crags, and it is occupied by large stretches of open heath even today. It is penetrated by long estuaries bordered by silt, and in the south there are numerous patches of London Clay. The regional prosperity of the belt as a whole is difficult to appraise because it has been found impossible to subdivide the coastal hundreds.[1] In the hundred of Blything, the Sandling portion is poorer than the clay interior, but not very greatly so. Colneis hundred lies wholly within the Sandlings, and its prosperity is a striking feature of the maps showing the densities of plough-teams (Fig. 42) and population (Fig. 44); as we have seen, the soil is locally very fertile. The settlement maps (Figs. 40, 41 and 43) do not do justice to Colneis because of the large number of unidentified names within the hundred. Set between the estuaries of the Orwell and the Deben, and possessing some fertile tracts, the hundred must have been initially attractive to settlers. But it has not maintained its position among the Suffolk hundreds. The fact that so many of its Domesday names cannot today be identified is significant; many settlements have declined in importance and even disappeared, leaving little more than a name, and sometimes only that.

Taking the Sandlings as a whole, a number of its villages had small amounts of meadow and a few sheep; a few also had some wood. The references to fisheries in the south and to herring rents in the north give some indication of the estuaries and of the maritime element in the life of the coastlands.

(4) *The Broadlands*

This extension of the Norfolk Broadland is a flat country, mostly below 60 ft. above sea-level. Part of the area is occupied by the Waveney flats and by expanses of water, e.g. Oulton Broad. The soil of much of the

[1] See p. 177 above.

area consists of glacial sands and gravels, and, generally speaking, it is lighter than that of the Flegg hundreds in Norfolk; the densities of plough-teams and of population are also lower than those of the Flegg area. Only small amounts of wood and of meadow are recorded for the villages of the region. No fisheries at all are recorded, and there is only one place (Burgh Castle) with a record of salt-pans. There was also a dearth of mills, the only entry being that of half a mill at Flixton.

(5) Chalk Downland

This little extension of the downland of south-eastern Cambridgeshire comprises the parishes of Exning and Moulton, and also that of Newmarket which is not mentioned in the Domesday Book. The densities of its teams and population resemble those of the surrounding country and call for no special comment. There is a little meadow entered for both places, but wood only for Moulton. Sheep are also entered for Moulton alone; but this is due to the fact that Exning was part of the Domesday county of Cambridge, and its sheep went unrecorded.

(6) The Fenland

Only a small strip of Fenland is included within the county boundary. It is a completely villageless area included in the territories of the nearby Breckland parishes. It is impossible therefore to separate the densities of Fen and Breck, but quite obviously the undrained peat fen cannot have supported any agriculture and only a few people. It played its part, however, in the economy of the fen margin settlements, and the numerous fisheries entered for these marginal settlements reflect the geographical peculiarity of the area. The Domesday record, however, gives no clue to the other occupations of the fen.

BIBLIOGRAPHICAL NOTE

(1) An older translation of the Domesday text relating to Suffolk is John Hervey's *Suffolk Domesday: the Latin text extended and translated* (Bury St Edmunds, 1888–91), 2 vols. This translation was 'adapted' and checked for the *V.C.H. Suffolk* (London, 1911), I, pp. 417–582, and was accompanied by an introduction by Miss Beatrice A. Lees (pp. 357–416).

(2) Two works by D. C. Douglas discuss, amongst other things, various aspects of the Suffolk evidence:

The Social Structure of Medieval East Anglia (Oxford, 1927).

Feudal Documents from the Abbey of Bury St Edmunds (London: British Academy, 1932).

(3) The following also deal with various aspects:

H. C. DARBY, 'Domesday Woodland in East Anglia', *Antiquity* (Gloucester, 1934), XIV, pp. 211–14.

H. C. DARBY, 'The Domesday Geography of Norfolk and Suffolk', *Geog. Journ.* (1935), LXXXV, pp. 432–52.

R. H. C. DAVIS, 'East Anglia and the Danelaw', *Trans. Roy. Hist. Soc.* (1955), 5th Ser. vol. v, pp. 23–39.

BARBARA DODWELL, 'The free peasantry of East Anglia in Domesday', *Norfolk Archaeology* (Norwich, 1941), XXVII, pp. 145–57.

R. WELLDON FINN, *Domesday Studies: The Eastern Counties* (London, 1967).

(4) The method and contents of the Little Domesday Book and of the *Inquisitio Eliensis* are discussed in many of the general works upon the Domesday Book (see pp. 3 *et seq.* and pp. 7 *et seq.* above, and p. 264 below).

CHAPTER V

ESSEX

Essex occupies a special place among Domesday counties. On the one hand, it is described in the Little Domesday Book, and it has, therefore, much in common with Norfolk and Suffolk. Its entries are far more detailed than those of the counties described in the main Domesday Book, although they are also more cumbrous and untidy. But, on the other hand, although Essex has so much in common with Norfolk and Suffolk, it is sharply differentiated from them in one way. Its assessment is stated, in a straightforward fashion, in terms of hides, and not by the peculiar method that distinguishes Norfolk and Suffolk from all other counties in England. As J. H. Round pointed out in his masterly study in the *Victoria County History* for Essex, this is one of the indications that separate Essex from the historic kingdom of East Anglia and links it with the rest of Saxon England.[1]

The abbey of Ely held but few estates in Essex, and so there is no great opportunity, as in Norfolk and Suffolk, of comparing the figures of the Little Domesday Book with those of the *Inquisitio Eliensis*. The few parallel entries that there are seem to agree with one another except that the *I.E.* mentions a sokeman at Amberden in Chelmsford (p. 129) which the Domesday Book does not.[2] A further opportunity for comparison is provided by the fact that the Essex folios of the Domesday Book itself occasionally duplicate an entry, and, in doing this, they sometimes convict themselves of inaccuracy. Compare, for example, the parallel entries relating to *Fenne* which Round identified with Stow Maries in Dengie. The numbers of the hides and of the villeins are given differently; the livestock are entered in the second entry but not in the first; and the second entry, on the other hand, leaves out a holding of one hide.

(1) *Fo.* 62. *Fenne*, which was held by Friebern, a free man, in King Edward's time, as a manor and as 4 hides in King Edward's time, is held of G[eoffrey] by Hugh. Then as now (*semper*) 4 villeins. Then 2 bordars, now 7. Then 2 serfs, now none. Then as now 2 ploughs on the demesne. Then 1 plough belonging to the men, now a half. Wood for 40 swine. Pasture for 30 sheep. Now as then

---

[1] *V.C.H. Essex* (London, 1903), I, p. 333.
[2] For the statistics of *I.E.*, see pp. 99–101 above.

Fig. 52. Essex: Domesday hundreds.

M indicates the half-hundred of Maldon. For *Thunreslau*, see *V.C.H. Essex*, i, p. 405.

it is worth 60 shillings. The same Hugh has also 1 hide which was held by a freeman [and was] worth 20 shillings. And he also has 37 acres, which were held by 1 freeman; then half a plough, now none. It is worth 5 shillings.

(2) *Fo. 63. Phenna*, which was held by Friebern as a manor and as 3 hides, is held by Hugh de Verli. Then as now (*semper*) 2 villeins. Then 2 bordars, now 7. Then 2 serfs, now none. Then as now 2 ploughs on the demesne. Then 1 plough belonging to the men, now a half. Wood for 40 swine. Pasture for 30 sheep. Then 5 swine, 30 sheep, and now 70 swine. It is worth 60 shillings. There also the same [Hugh] holds 37 acres; then half a plough, now none. It is worth 5 shillings.

Or again, there are minor differences in the duplicate entries relating to Hawkswell in Rochford (50 and 51b), while one of the duplicate entries relating to *Haintuna* in Dengie omits any mention of stock (46 and 47).

Such discrepancies are of very great interest for 'the light they throw on the treatment by the scribes of the original returns with which they had to deal'.[1] They emphasise what had already been said about the human element in the Domesday statistics of other counties.

There is one further consideration that must be mentioned. The Domesday county of Essex corresponds more or less with the modern county. But there are some differences along the borders. In the north, the Chishalls (Great and Little) and Heydon were transferred to Cambridge-shire in the nineteenth century; and Ballingdon and Brundon, adjoining Sudbury, were likewise transferred to Suffolk. There are a few other complications. *Eilanda* and Bures lay athwart the Essex-Suffolk boundary, and were surveyed partly in one and partly in the other county.[2] The Essex village of Toppesfield seems to have had some of its holdings surveyed in the Suffolk folios (372b), unless, of course, there was an unidentified village of that name in Suffolk. Moreover, a number of Essex villages had connections with Sudbury in Suffolk, and with London, but these will be discussed later on.[3] Finally, there are a few entries in the Essex folios which refer to holdings in neighbouring counties. There were offshoots of the Essex manor of Chesterford at Babraham and Hinxton in Cambridgeshire, and also an offshoot of the Essex Newport at Shelford in the same county.[4] To Hatfield Broad Oak there belonged, in 1066, the 3 berewicks of Amwell, Hertford and Hod-desdon in Hertfordshire (2). In the north, Brightlingsea had a berewick at Harkstead in Suffolk (6); and an estate in Ardleigh was attached (*jacet*) to 'a certain manor' in Suffolk but belonged to (*pertinet in*) the hundred of Tendring in Essex (68). On the other hand, we read in the Kentish folios that the manor of Chalk had a holding in Essex rightly belonging to it (vol. 1, fo. 9).[5]

---

[1] J. H. Round in *V.C.H. Essex*, 1, p. 410.

[2] See p. 155 above. For a fuller discussion of the complications of the Essex-Suffolk boundary, see J. H. Round, *V.C.H. Essex*, 1, p. 408.

[3] See p. 252 below. A reference to Ipswich in the Suffolk folios mentions a burgess belonging to *Mosa* (411b) which may possibly be identified with Moze in Essex.

[4] See *V.C.H. Essex*, 1, p. 338, and *V.C.H. Cambridge*, 1, pp. 361, 362, 385. See p. 267 below.

[5] *Gravesanda* (26b) was for long a problem, and was even identified with Graves-end on the opposite shore of the Thames in Kent, but Mr W. R. Powell writes that it was clearly in Tilbury.

SETTLEMENTS AND THEIR DISTRIBUTION

The total number of separate places mentioned for Essex appears to be approximately 440. This figure, however, may not be accurate because, today, there are many instances of two or more adjoining villages bearing the same surname (e.g. Great Bromley and Little Bromley), and it is rarely clear whether more than one separate unit existed in the eleventh century. There are eight parishes bearing the name Roding today,[1] and three bearing the name Tolleshunt,[2] but the Domesday Book merely records information relating to *Rodinges* (or *Roinges*) and *Toleshunta* respectively. Essex has many examples of these collective surnames, but only when there is specific mention of a second village in the Domesday Book itself has it been included in the total of 440. Thus there is mention of *Bricceia* and *Parva Bricceia* (Lexden), and separate parishes of Great and Little Birch existed down to the eighteenth century though only one Birch exists today. Under the same hundred there is also mention of *Colun* and *Parva Colun*; there are four parishes of Colne today,[3] and the Domesday Little Colne was part of what is now Colne Engaine. One of the holdings in Colne provides an interesting example of how parish groups with the same name arose. It was a holding of one hide with 7 bordars and 3 ploughs and it was held by a certain *Dimidius Blancus* (77). In the following century there is mention of *Colum Miblanc*, and by the thirteenth century this has become *Whyte Colne*, the modern parish of White Colne.[4] In the hundred of Ongar, distinction was likewise made between *Stanfort* and *Parva Stanfort*, but the second name does not appear in subsequent records, and today there is only one parish of Stanford Rivers. There are also three villages distinguished by *alia* or *altera*—Fyfield, Melesham and Navestock. Such names in Norfolk and Suffolk are today indicated by double parishes. It is not so in Essex. 'In no one of the three cases do we find any trace of two villages of the same name';[5] we can only suppose that here at any rate the *alia*

---

[1] Abbess Roding, Aythorpe Roding, Beauchamp Roding, Berners Roding, High Roding, Leaden Roding, Margaret Roding and White Roding. In the parish of White Roding there was once a Morrell Roding; the name was extant as late as 1848, but is now lost. P. H. Reaney, *The Place-Names of Essex* (Cambridge, 1935), p. 494.

[2] Tolleshunt Major, Tolleshunt d'Arcy and Tolleshunt Knights.

[3] Colne Engaine, Earls Colne, Wakes Colne and White Colne.

[4] P. H. Reaney, *op. cit.* p. 384.

[5] J. H. Round, *V.C.H. Essex*, I, p. 403.

or *altera* refers to another holding that never grew into a separate parish.[1]

The total of 440 includes a number of places—between 15 and 20—about which very little information is given; the record may be incom-

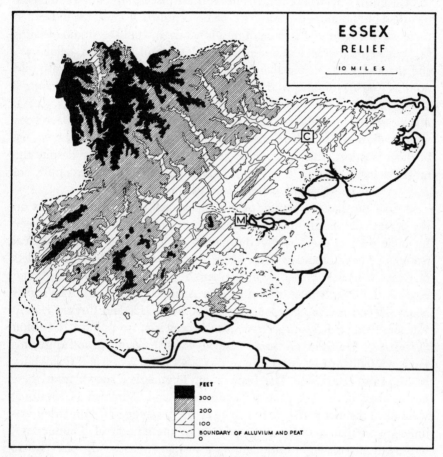

ESSEX
RELIEF

10 MILES

FEET
300
200
100
BOUNDARY OF ALLUVIUM AND PEAT
0

Fig. 53. Essex: Relief.

Places with Domesday burgesses are indicated by initials: C, Colchester; M, Maldon.

plete or the details may have been included with those of another village. Thus a joint entry relating to Stanmer and *Winthelle* in Barstable

---

[1] There is also mention of an *Alia Rodinges* in one MS. of the *I.E.* (p. 128), but the Domesday record does not so distinguish it.

includes ploughs and wood and stock; it also speaks of oxen belonging to 'the men' but it does not say how many men there were, or what they were (92b). No population is likewise entered for Doddinghurst (85) in the same hundred, nor for a few other places elsewhere, and we are left to conjecture who worked the teams at these places. Sometimes, men are recorded but no plough-teams. At the unidentified *Witesworda* in Lexden there was a bordar and an acre of meadow but, it would seem, no ploughs (41); or again, the unidentified place of *Midebroc* in Rochford yielded 4*s*., and there was one villein there, but of its resources (if any) we are told nothing (99b). Similarly, the only statistical information for Braintree (Hinckford) is that three men held 30 acres which yielded 3*s*. (103). Many of these problematical entries refer to places which must have been very small; they never developed into substantial settlements; the memory of them was lost, and their names remain unidentified today despite the most exhaustive researches even of J. H. Round. Such, for example, are *Ulwinescherham* (4b) and *Wringehala* (49b) in Dengie.

Not all the 440 Domesday names appear as the names of villages on the present-day parish map of Essex. Some are represented by hamlets, by individual houses, or by the names of localities or topographical features. The Domesday *Watelea* is now represented by the hamlets of Great and Little Wheatley in the parish of Rayleigh (Rochford), and *Roda* is the little hamlet of Rothend in Ashdon (Freshwell). The names *Assewella* and *Boituna* have survived as Ashwell Hall and Boyton Hall in Finchingfield (Hinckford); *Samantuna* is now Sampson's Farm in Peldon (Winstree). Or again, *Hecham* has survived as Higham Hill and Higham's Park in Walthamstow (Becontree); *Cuica* is Quick Wood and Quickbury in Sheering (Harlow). The history of Thunderley shows how these names may have disappeared. Thunderley and Wimbish (Uttlesford) were once distinct parishes, but in 1425 the vicarage of Thunderley was united with that of Wimbish, and, 'as to the church of Thunderley', wrote Morant, the eighteenth-century historian of Essex, 'the place where it stood is now part of a field'. Thunderley has therefore disappeared as a village, leaving Thunderley Hall to testify to its former existence. Sometimes, the Domesday name has completely disappeared from the map. The parish of Bulmer (Hinckford) contains three Domesday names today—*Bulenemara* itself together with *Goldingham* (Goldingham Hall) and *Smedetuna* (Smeetham Hall)—but it also once contained *Bineslea*; this was a hamlet in the thirteenth century but it has disappeared by today.

And, as we have seen, some names have disappeared so effectively that they can be assigned to no locality.

On the other hand, there are a number of villages on the modern map that are not mentioned in the Domesday Book. They are scattered here and there throughout the county. Some of these missing names go back even to pre-Domesday times.[1] The name Dagenham (Becontree), for example, occurs in charters of as early as the seventh century but it does not reappear until 1218; the name Fingringhoe (Winstree) likewise occurs before the year of the Domesday survey, but it does not appear again until 1202. Other names missing from the Domesday Book do not make their first appearance until the twelfth and thirteenth centuries; Romford (Becontree), as far as record goes, appears in 1177, Inworth (Lexden) in 1206, Roxwell (Chelmsford) in 1291. Before these years, their territories must have been surveyed with those of neighbouring villages. The parish name of Pleshey (Dunmow) is one of those not mentioned in the Domesday Book, but a twelfth-century reference shows that Pleshey was part of the nearby village of Easter, and its resources were presumably included with those of Easter in the Domesday returns. Brentwood is likewise not mentioned in the Domesday Book, and it seems that it was part of the old parish of South Weald (Chafford). Two groups of these post-Domesday names deserve further comment. In the first place, the hundred of Lexden today contains the two parishes of Great and Little Horkesley. J. H. Round has shown that they formed part of the lordship of *Eiland* (the modern Nayland) which stretched across the Stour into Suffolk.[2] It was surveyed partly in Essex and partly in Suffolk under the name *Eiland*, and so the names of its components do not appear; Horkesley is therefore not mentioned in the Domesday Book, and the earliest record of its name is from about 1130. In the second place, there is a group of missing names comprising Thorpe-le-Soken, Kirby-le-Soken and Walton-le-Soken (Tendring). All three parishes belonging to the Dean and Chapter of St Paul's, London, are grouped together in the Domesday Book in the manor of *Ældulvesnasa* which has, incidentally, given part of its name to the nearby Walton-on-the-Naze; the manor was a large one, comprising 27 hides and 36 ploughs and 119 men in 1086, but how these were distributed among the constituent areas it is impossible to say.

[1] For the names in this paragraph, see P. H. Reaney, *The Place-Names of Essex*, *passim*.

[2] J. H. Round, *V.C.H. Essex*, I, p. 408.

In many counties, despite the complications of extinct villages and
additional parishes, the distribution of Domesday names is remarkably
similar to that of the present-day villages. In Essex, this is not entirely

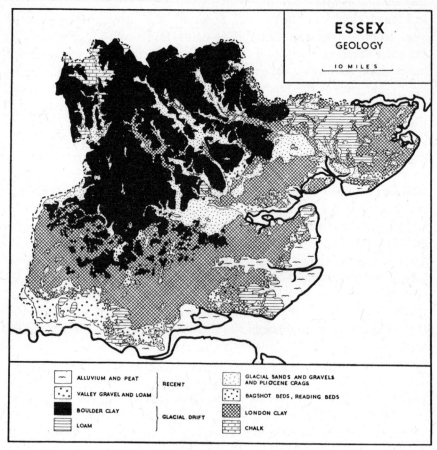

ESSEX

GEOLOGY

10 MILES

⌒ ALLUVIUM AND PEAT	} RECENT	∴ GLACIAL SANDS AND GRAVELS AND PLIOCENE CRAGS	
∴ VALLEY GRAVEL AND LOAM		∴ BAGSHOT BEDS, READING BEDS	
■ BOULDER CLAY	} GLACIAL DRIFT	▦ LONDON CLAY	
≡ LOAM		▤ CHALK	

Fig. 54. Essex: Surface geology.
Based on Geological Survey Quarter-Inch Sheets 16, 20 and 24.

so, for two reasons. In the first place, the great growth of built-up areas
in the south-west corner of the county, and at places along the Thames
estuary, has greatly altered the earlier pattern of settlement. And, in the
second place, as we have seen, very many Domesday names now appear
as subsidiary settlements, hamlets, or farms in parishes that bear another

name. It was Maitland who wrote that a place 'mentioned in Domesday Book will probably be recognized as a vill in the thirteenth, a civil parish in the nineteenth century';[1] but Round, writing of Essex, naturally found

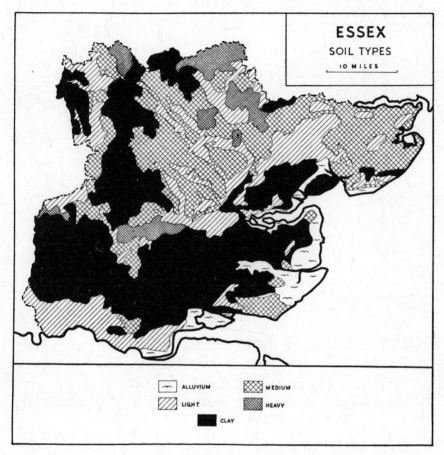

ESSEX
SOIL TYPES
10 MILES

ALLUVIUM   MEDIUM

LIGHT   HEAVY

CLAY

Fig. 55. Essex: Soil types.

Redrawn from the map in *An Economic Survey of Agriculture in the Eastern Counties of England*, p. viii (Heffer, Cambridge, 1932). This is Report No. 19 of the Farm Economics Branch of the Department of Agriculture in the University of Cambridge.

this an unsatisfying generalisation.[2] It may be that so many exceptions to Maitland's statement are found in Essex because its rural settlement is mainly of the dispersed type. Where a parish is centred upon a nucleated

[1] F. W. Maitland, *op. cit.* p. 12.   [2] J. H. Round, *V.C.H. Essex*, I, p. 400.

village, that village is more likely to survive the vicissitudes of the
centuries and so maintain its identity. The distribution of Domesday
names (Fig. 56) is fairly uniform over the face of the county. They are,

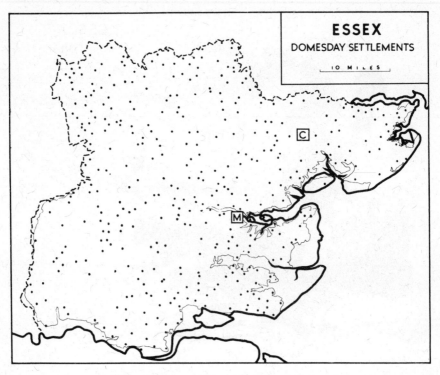

Fig. 56. Essex: Domesday place-names.

Places with burgesses are indicated by initials: C, Colchester; M, Maldon. The
boundary of alluvium and peat is shown; see Fig. 54.

it is true, least numerous in the south-western parts of the county, and it
is in this region that the Forests of Epping and Hainault lay. There are,
too, some empty tracts along the coast, but these are the alluvial areas
which must have been very marshy in the eleventh century.

The Distribution of Prosperity and Population

Some idea of the nature of the information in the Domesday folios for Essex, and of the form in which it was presented, may be obtained from the two entries relating to the village of Gestingthorpe in the hundred of Hinckford, not far from the Suffolk border:

Fo. 39. Gestingthorpe, which was held, in King Edward's time, by Ledmar the priest as half a hide (*pro dimidia hida*), is held of R[ichard] by W. Peche. Then as now (*semper*) 3 ploughs on the demesne, and 3 ploughs belonging to the men, and 8 villeins. Now 9 bordars. Then as now (*semper*) 6 serfs. Wood for 20 swine, 20 acres of meadow. Then 1 mill, now none. To this estate (*terrae*) there belongs then as now (*semper jacet*) 1 sokeman with 15 acres, and he has half a plough and 2 bordars and 1 acre of meadow. Then worth 100 shillings, now 7 pounds.

Fo. 98. Gestingthorpe was held by Earl Ælfgar as half a hide, now Otto holds [it] similarly. Then as now (*semper*) 3 ploughs on the demesne, and 3 ploughs belonging to the men. Then 13 bordars, now 16. Then as now (*semper*) 6 serfs. Wood for 60 swine, 25 acres of meadow. 80 sheep, 32 animals, 88 swine and 3 rounceys, and there were 12 sokemen in King Edward's time—now there are 11—dwelling (*manentes*) on this manor, and they hold half a hide and 30 acres. Then as now (*semper*) 4 bordars, and 1 plough and 1 serf. Then worth 10 pounds, now 12, and when the king gave [it to him] 15.

These two entries do not include all the items that are given for some other places; there is no mention, for example, of salt-pans or pasture. But they are representative enough, and they do contain the four recurring standard items that relate to a village as a whole: (1) hides, (2) plough-teams, (3) population, and (4) values. The bearing of these four items of information upon regional variations in prosperity must now be considered. First, however, the omission of any reference to ploughlands must be noted; in this, Essex resembles Norfolk and Suffolk, and also some other counties.[1]

(1) *Hides*

The Essex assessment is stated in terms of hides and acres. Virgates are sometimes mentioned: there was, for example, a holding of 3 hides and 1 virgate at Widdington in Uttlesford (68), but very frequently the unit of 30 acres is entered instead of a virgate. Occasionally, the measurement descends to roods, and at Bendish in Freshwell (34) there was

[1] See p. 107 above. Essex differs from Norfolk and Suffolk, however, in that there is no mention of carucates (*car' terrae*) in the Little Domesday folios that refer to it.

a sokeman holding one acre and one rood (*pertic'*). There is confirmatory evidence that 1 hide equals 4 virgates or 120 acres; thus at Felsted in Hinckford we are given to understand that a hide consists of 3 virgates *plus* 1 virgate (21 b), and at Waltham, it is apparent that 7 hides and half a virgate equals 7 hides 15 acres (15 b), and there are other examples of the same kind of equation.[1]

The system of assessing villages in multiples of 5 hides, so prominent in Cambridgeshire, is not generally apparent in Essex.[2] Even the village of *Fifhida* (now Fyfield) in Ongar is not entered as having 5 hides. Indeed, wrote Round, the 5-hide unit 'has been so obscured in Essex that it might even at first sight be imagined to be non-existent'. But he did find sufficient traces of its original existence 'to warrant the assertion that here also it lay at the root of the system. And this, as might be expected, is best seen in those old intact lordships which were held by the Crown and by the Church'.[3] The following are a few examples of the 5-hide unit: the royal villages of Brightlingsea (6) and Havering-atte-Bower (2 b) were assessed at 10 hides each; the ecclesiastical village of Barking stood at 30 hides (17 b), that of Clacton at 20 hides (11), those of Wrabness (20) and Woodford (16) at 5 hides each. Other villages similarly assessed include Clavering at 15 hides (46 b), and Amberden (73 b), Fobbing (26) and Langdon (42) at 5 hides each. Examples such as these stand out clearly because in each case the village was held by one owner. Taking Essex as a whole, however, the 5-hide unit is a comparatively rare phenomenon.

We cannot say to what extent the incidence of the hidage reflected the agricultural realities of the time. The figures certainly bear no relation to those of plough-teams. The number of hides in Freshwell hundred is less than one-half the number of plough-teams. In Chafford hundred, hides and teams are about equal. In Dengie hundred, the hides outnumber the teams, the ratio being about 3:2. The causes of these divergencies may lie partly in the differing resources of the three hundreds and partly in their previous history; the history of the Essex hidage is very obscure.[4]

[1] For a discussion, see (1) F. W. Maitland, *Domesday Book and Beyond* (Cambridge, 1897), pp. 480–2; (2) *V.C.H. Essex*, I, pp. 334–5.
[2] See p. 274 below.　　　　　　　　[3] *V.C.H. Essex*, I, p. 334.
[4] J. H. Round, *Eng. Hist. Rev.* (1914), XXIX, pp. 477–9. See also George Rickword: (1) 'The Kingdom of the East Saxons and the Tribal Hidage', *Trans. Essex Arch. Soc.* (Colchester, 1911), N.S. vol. XI, pp. 246–65; (2) 'The East Saxon Kingdom', *ibid.* (1913), N.S. vol. XII, pp. 38–50. Stimulated by Round's failure to find much evidence of the 5-hide unit in Essex, Rickword, in the first of these papers, made out 70 groups of approximately 40 hides apiece.

One thing is certain: it would be extremely rash to rely upon the hidage to give us any idea about the relative prosperity of different parts of the county in the eleventh century.

The present count, for the area covered by the modern county, has yielded a total of 2,767 hides, but the hidage for many manors is particularly confusing, and this figure can only be approximate. [1]

(2) Plough-teams

The Essex entries, like those of other counties, usually draw a distinction between the teams held by the lord of a manor in demesne and those held by the peasantry. Occasional entries seem to be defective, e.g. Colne Engaine in Lexden had a recorded population of 18 in 1086, but no plough-teams are entered for it (88b). The present count has yielded a total of 3,864¾ teams in 1086, for the area covered by the modern county. [2] Frequently, there had been changes between 1066 and 1086. Thus on one holding at Rainham (Chafford) there were 'then 2 ploughs on the demesne, and when [the manor was] received 2, now none. Then and afterwards 3 ploughs belonging to the men, now 2' (fo. 24b). There are occasional variations from the normal formula, and additional details are sometimes given. Three examples of enlarged entries are given below, and they show the catastrophic nature of life in the eleventh century:

(1) *Witham* in Witham (1). 'Then the men had 18 ploughs, now 7, and this loss took place (*fuit*) in the time of Suean and of Baignard the sheriffs, and through the death of the beasts.'

(2) *Hatfield Broad Oak* in Harlow (2). 'Then the men had 40 ploughs, now 31½; this loss took place (*fuit*) in the time of all the sheriffs and through the death of the beasts.'

(3) *Higham* in Becontree (78b). 'Then as now 2 ploughs on the demesne, and 4 ploughs belonging to the men.... And when he received this manor, he did not find more than (*praeter*) 1 ox and 1 acre sown (*unam acram seminatam*).'

---

[1] G. Rickword's total, for the Domesday county, came to 2,725 hides (*Trans. Essex Arch. Soc.* N.S. vol. XI, p. 251). F. W. Maitland's total, also for the Domesday county, was 2,650 hides; *op. cit.* p. 400.

[2] G. Rickword's total, for the Domesday county, came to 3,821 teams (*Trans. Essex Arch. Soc.* N.S. vol. XII, p. 40). F. W. Maitland's total, also for the Domesday county, came to 3,920 teams; *op cit.* p. 401.

When the existing teams in 1086 were fewer than those in times past, we are sometimes told that the number could be made good, and a contrast between actual and potential arable is implied. One of the entries for Purleigh in Dengie (53) states: 'Then as now (*semper*) 2 ploughs on the

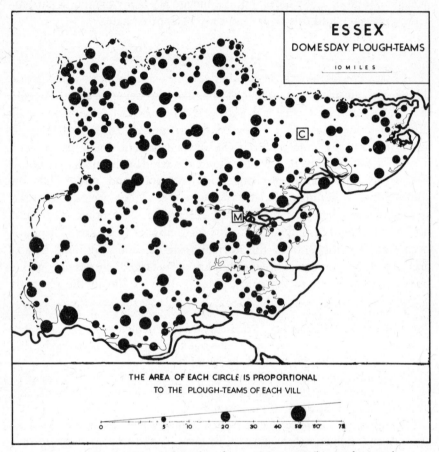

Fig. 57. Essex: Domesday plough-teams in 1086 (by settlements).

Places with burgesses are indicated by initials: C, Colchester; M, Maldon. The boundary of alluvium and peat is shown; see Fig. 54.

demesne. Then 3 ploughs belonging to the men, now 2, and a third could be employed (*et tercia potest fieri*).' Nor was the addition always limited to the restoration of what had once been. At Wakering in Rochford (44) there were 2 ploughs on the demesne in 1086 as in 1066, but we are told that a third might be added (*et tercia posset fieri*). The phrasing of the formula varied. At Clavering (47) the demesne ploughs had increased from 4 to 5 and the men's ploughs had remained at 25, but we are told that yet another plough could be employed (*potest restaurari*). A third,

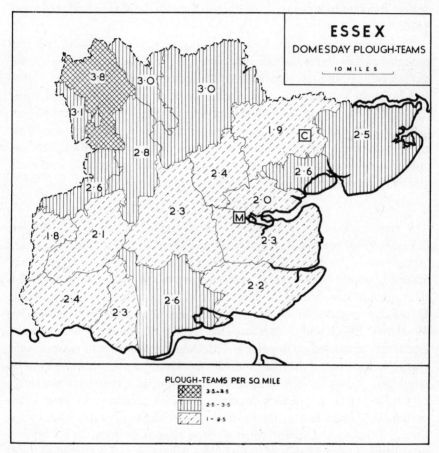

Fig. 58. Essex: Domesday plough-teams in 1086 (by densities).
Places with burgesses are indicated by initials: C, Colchester; M, Maldon.

though less frequent, variation in formula may be illustrated by an entry relating to Thorington in Tendring (25 b) where we are told that another team could be employed (*potest esse*). Sometimes, the potential ploughs did not equal the reduction that had taken place between 1066 and

1086. On one holding at Hallingbury, the demesne ploughs had dropped from 6 to 3, and the men's ploughs from 10½ to 2½, but the ploughs that could be made up (*restaurari*) amounted not to eleven but only to nine (52). Over the county as a whole, there was a decrease of teams in 41 per cent., and an increase in 8 per cent. of the entries with details for both 1066 and 1086.

To sum up: although the Essex folios do not give us information about plough-lands in the sense that it is recorded for some other counties, we can infer this from these details about the increase or decrease in the teams, and from the possibilities of further cultivation that are thus indicated. In this way were the local fortunes of agriculture, varying from place to place, put on record. But it is sometimes difficult to envisage what had really happened; thus at Benfleet in Barstable the number of ploughs on one holding had fallen from 14 to 7, and yet the population had substantially increased (1b).

(3) *Population*

The main bulk of the population was comprised in the five categories of freemen, sokemen, villeins, bordars and serfs. In addition to these main groups were the burgesses, together with a miscellaneous group that included *censores* (rent-payers), *homines*, priests and others. The details of these groups are summarised on p. 225. Two other estimates of the Domesday population of Essex have been published, the old one by Sir Henry Ellis,[1] and a later one by George Rickword.[2] The present estimate is not strictly comparable with these for a variety of reasons, one reason being that it has been made in terms of the modern county boundary. Whatever the differences, one thing is certain; no one who counts Domesday population can claim definitive accuracy. Varying interpretations of many entries are inevitable, especially in the Little Domesday Book. Finally, one point must always be remembered. The figures presumably indicate heads of households. Whatever factor should be used to obtain *actual* population from *recorded* population, the proportions between different categories and between different areas remain unaffected.[3]

The outstanding fact that emerges from the table on p. 225 is the marked contrast between the importance of the free element in Essex on the one

---

[1] Sir Henry Ellis, *A General Introduction to Domesday Book* (London, 1833), II, pp. 441–3. Ellis' total for bordars is 8,002, and seems especially large compared with the present total of 6,969 and Rickword's 6,589.

[2] George Rickword, *Trans. Essex Arch. Soc.* (1913), N.S. vol. XII, p. 40.

[3] See p. 360 below for the position of the serfs.

hand and in Norfolk and Suffolk on the other hand. In Essex, the freemen and sokemen taken together amount merely to about 7 per cent. of the total recorded population. The attempt to distinguish between these two categories is not helped by the Essex entries, and Round, like Maitland,

Recorded Population of Essex in 1086

A. Rural Population

Freemen	432
Sokemen	600
Villeins	4,018
Bordars	6,969
Serfs	1,789
Miscellaneous	100
Total	13,908

Details of Miscellaneous Rural Population

Rent-payers (*censores*)	36
Men (*homines*)	32
Priests	28
Fisherman	1
Forester	1
Hired servant (*mercennarius*) . . .	1
Swineherd	1
Total	100

B. Urban Population

Freemen, villeins, bordars, serfs and the sokeman are also included above.

COLCHESTER   433 *domus*; 16 burgesses; 24 bordars; 2 villeins; 3 serfs.
MALDON   183 *domus*; 6 freemen; 1 sokeman; 9 villeins; 21 bordars; 5 serfs; 18 *mansurae vastatae*.

could only confess himself to be baffled by the difficulties of Domesday terminology.[1] But at any rate, the statistical details of the free peasantry as a whole are not quite as complicated as they are in Norfolk and Suffolk. In the first place, the number (both relative as well as actual) of very minute holdings was much less. There were some, of course; there was, for example, one sokeman in Braxted (Witham) with 4 acres (49),

---

[1] *V.C.H. Essex*, I, pp. 357–9. See p. 114 above.

and a freeman in Pebmarsh (Hinckford) with only 3 acres (102). But, generally speaking, the social order here was very different from that to the north, and the chances of the same person being named more than once were much fewer. In the second place, the Essex entries are without that mysterious phrase, *Alii ibi tenent,* which we have discussed in connection with Norfolk and Suffolk.[1]

On the other hand, in Essex as in Norfolk and Suffolk, occasional uncertainty arises from the fact that the text does not always state categorically whether the numbers of freemen and sokemen refer to 1086 as well as to 1066. The difficulty can be illustrated by the following entry relating to Hedingham in Hinckford (87b):

Hedingham, which was held by 15 freemen in King Edward's time, is held of R[oger] by Garenger as 25 acres. Then as now (*semper*) 5½ ploughs, and 1 villein and 2 serfs. Wood for 70 swine; 11 acres of meadow. It was then worth 40 shillings, now 4 pounds.

What had happened to the 15 freemen? Did they live in the village in 1066, and, if so, were they still there in 1086? We cannot tell. It looks as if the freemen of some villages remained, but with a lowered status; the brief statement for Abberton in Winstree sounds significant: 'Then 1 freeman, now 1 bordar' (46b). The same thing may have happened, for example, at Burnham in Dengie (70):

In the same vill [there were], in King Edward's time, 10 freemen who had 8 hides and 28 acres; and this (*quod*) is [now] held by Robert in demesne. Then 8 bordars, now 16. Then as now (*semper*) 7 serfs and 8 ploughs.

We cannot guess at the fate of two of the ten freemen, but eight of them may have become bordars. At Benfleet in Barstable there was a freeman who by 1086 had become (*effectus est*) one of the villeins (1b). It is, wrote Round, 'one of the most eloquent incidents recorded in the great Survey'.[2] The present analysis has excluded all freemen unless they are specifically stated to be present in 1086. Thus we see that, while some of the perplexities of the other two counties of the Little Domesday Book do not arise in Essex, it is impossible to exclude all doubts.

The outstanding fact about the unfree population is the high proportion of bordars. They were numerous in 1066, but they had increased by 1086 until they amounted to one-half the total recorded population for the

[1] See pp. 115 and 171 above.
[2] J. H. Round, *V.C.H. Essex,* I, p. 357.

county. This notable feature of the Essex folios was emphasised by Maitland:

Let us look, for example, at the changes that take place in some Essex villages during the 20 years that precede the Domesday Inquest. The following table shows them:

		Villani	Bordarii	Servi	Lord's teams	Men's teams
Teidana	T.R.E.	5	3	4	2	4
	T.R.W.	1	17	0	3	3
Waldena	T.R.E.	66	17	16	8	22
	T.R.W.	46	40	20	10	22
Hame	T.R.E.	32	16	3	5	8
	T.R.W.	48	79	3	4	12
Benefelda	T.R.E.	10	2	7	3	7
	T.R.W.	9	11	4	3	4
Wimbeis	T.R.E.	26	18	6	3	21
	T.R.W.	26	55	0	3	15

These are but specimens of the obscure little revolutions that are being accomplished in the Essex villages. In general there has been a marked increase in the number of *bordarii*, at the expense of the villeins on the one part and the serfs on the other, and this, whatever else it may represent, must tell us of a redistribution of tenements, perhaps of a process that substitutes the half-virgate for the virgate as the average holding of an Essex peasant. The jar of conquest has made such revolutions easy.[1]

J. H. Round discussed these changes at length. As he pointed out, the process was not uniform.[2] There were villages where the three classes remained unchanged, or where the numbers of serfs or villeins increased, but 'the one persistent feature is that the bordars either show a marked increase or appear in 1086 in places where there had been none twenty years before'. And, as we have seen, the additional bordars in some villages may have been recruited from the free peasantry. Another general feature is that there was usually an increase in the total number of the three peasant classes between 1066 and 1086. A few entries seem to be defective, and contain either no references, or only a vague reference, to population, but it is impossible to be really certain about the significance of these omissions.[3]

[1] F. W. Maitland, *op. cit.* p. 363; see also p. 35. The entries in Maitland's table are as follows: Theydon (47b), Saffron Walden (62), Ham (64), Bentfield End in Stansted Mountfitchet (65b), and Wimbish (69b). Freemen are recorded in none of these entries except in that relating to Bentfield End where one freeman held the manor in 1066.   [2] *V.C.H. Essex*, I, pp. 359–61.   [3] See p. 214 above.

(4) *Values*

The valuation of estates in Essex seems to have been carried out with
care and in detail. At any rate, that is what the figures suggest. When we

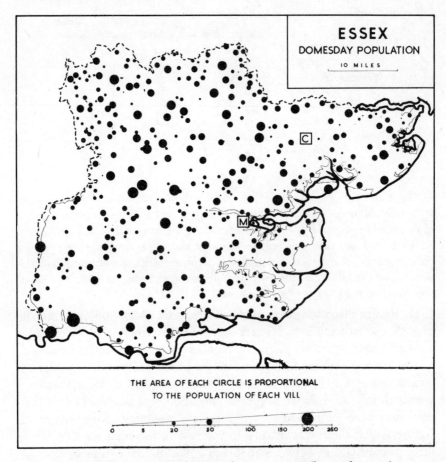

Fig. 59. Essex: Domesday population in 1086 (by settlements).

Places with burgesses are indicated by initials: C, Colchester; M, Maldon. The
boundary of alluvium and peat is indicated; see Fig. 54.

read that Corringham in Barstable was worth £7 in 1066 and £7. 6s. in
1086 (fo. 11b), and that the value of Thundersley in the same hundred
had fallen from 102s. to 100s. (43) we receive the impression of a careful
looking into the facts. Generally speaking, the greater the number of

plough-teams and men on a holding, the higher its value, but it is impossible to discern any consistent relation between resources and value. Thus at Birch in Tendring, the ploughs had decreased from three to two, and all the other stock had disappeared, but the value had risen from £3

Fig. 60. Essex: Domesday population in 1086 (by densities).
Places with burgesses are indicated by initials: C, Colchester; M, Maldon.

to £4. 7s.; it is true that the population had increased from eight to nine, but this hardly seems sufficient to account for the rise (33). At Newenden in Barstable, there was a holding of 40 acres; the only item entered for it was half a plough and even that had disappeared by 1086 (*modo nulla*), but it was still worth 4*s.* (94). Examples of similar inconsistencies could be multiplied.

Occasionally the value of a berewick is included in that of its parent manor; thus Stanway (Lexden) and its two berewicks at Layer and Lexden were not separately valued (4b). The manor of Bocking (Hinckford) had a holding in Mersea (Winstree) on the coast, some 18 miles away, and the value of both was combined in one total (8). Sometimes a series of successive entries were valued together (40). At other times one holding was valued with another; thus the value of a holding in Colne Engaine (Lexden) was 60*s.* but we are told that this was included in that (*in pretio*) of Stansted, across the border in the neighbouring hundred of Hinckford (88b). Generally speaking, these are exceptions, and the inclusion of the value of one holding in that of another does not seem to be frequent, as we have seen it is in Lincolnshire, Norfolk and Suffolk. Normally, each Essex holding is valued separately. An approximate density map of values in Essex could therefore be constructed.

This, however, does not solve the question of what exactly was implied by 'value'. Sometimes, the answer seems to be clear. The manor of Ockendon (Chafford) was worth £16 in 1086; the entry then goes on to give details about 13 sokemen whose possessions were included 'in this rent (*ad hanc firmam*) of £16' (58). There are other entries also which seem to equate 'value' with rent received.[1] But, on the other hand, it is clear that the rent for some holdings exceeded their 'value'. The value of a manor at Coggeshall in Witham (27) had risen from £10 to £14, but it paid £20 (*sed tamen reddit xx libras*). The entry that immediately follows this on fo. 27 refers to a holding at Rivenhall in the same hundred; its value had risen from £9 to £12, but, nevertheless, it paid £20. The value of Amberden in Uttlesford had remained unchanged at £12, but it had paid £18 for 3 years at any rate (74). It is not surprising that there was sometimes disagreement about these values. Barking in Becontree (18) was worth £80 in 1086, but we are told that the French valued (*appretiantur*) it at £100. The value of Waltham was also disputed; some said it was worth £63. 5*s.* 4*d.*, others that it was as much as £100 (15b).

---

[1] Here are three examples: (1) at Thurrock in Chafford (63) there was a holding valued in 1086 at £30, and we are told that in this rent (*in hac firma*) were included some houses in London; (2) at Halstead in Hinckford (103) there was a small holding worth 30*d.* and we are told that the reeve had received these pence (*istos denarios recepit*); (3) at Lawford in Tendring (6b) there was a holding worth 10*s.*, and we are told that hitherto Richard had received that rent (*istum censum*).

It was in the light of these facts that Round summed up the problem of 'value' in Essex: 'It is difficult, if not impossible, to extract from this conflicting evidence a definite conclusion as to the meaning of the word "valet" in Domesday. One may, however, suggest that, as a rule, it represented the rent received, but that in those cases where the rent was notoriously in excess of the value the return made a pointed distinction between the two sums. This may seem but a lame conclusion, and yet no other suggests itself.' [1]

Conclusion

For the purpose of calculating densities, the hundreds themselves have been adopted, and, generally speaking, they form convenient units. In detail, the soils of each hundred are very varied, but taking a broad view they are uniform enough for our rough and ready generalisations (Figs. 54 and 55). There is therefore no necessity for following the precedent of Norfolk and Suffolk, and subdividing some of the hundreds. One modification has, however, been made. The hundred of Colchester has been thrown into that of Lexden and, in doing this, allowance has been made for the area of the town of Colchester itself;[2] the result is nineteen units which form the basis of the density maps.

Of the four standard formulae, those relating to population and plough-teams are most likely to reflect something of the distribution of wealth and prosperity throughout the county. Taken together, they supplement one another; and, when they are compared, certain common features stand out. The most important of these features is a contrast between the north and the south. In the north, the plough-teams average over 3 per square mile; the corresponding figure for the south is about 2 (Fig. 58). The density of population shows a like contrast. In the north, it is between 9 and 13, and in the south between only 6 and 9 (Fig. 60). Comparison with the geological map shows how the soil of the north differs from that of the south. Boulder Clay is dominant in the north, London Clay in the south. The Boulder Clay is relatively easy to work. It is true that in

---

[1] *V.C.H. Essex*, I, p. 364.

[2] In this connection, Round's comments are interesting: 'Lexden, it is important to observe, contains two parishes which are cut off from the rest of the Hundred by the Domesday "Hundred" of Colchester, a district containing between eleven and twelve thousand acres. This arrangement obviously suggests that the district of Colchester had, at some time, been taken out of Lexden Hundred, a suggestion strongly supported by the fact that Lexden parish itself is within the borough boundary.' *V.C.H. Essex*, I, p. 406. (See Fig. 52.)

places it is heavy, but 'there is much chalk, many flints, boulders and coarse sand, and the whole is often underlain by gravel. It differs greatly from London Clay, works more easily, because of its lime content, and is less impervious.'[1] It was, in short, much more inviting for early agriculture. The London Clay of the south, on the other hand, weathers to a heavy, sticky and impervious soil, which is difficult to work in wet weather and which cracks readily in dry weather. It must have been far less inviting to the early farmer. To this generalisation there is one exception. Fig. 54 shows that the London Clay extends north-eastward into the hundred of Tendring, but towards the north-east, its character changes a good deal, and it gives rise to medium, rather than heavy, soils of great fertility (Fig. 55). The modern land utilisation map shows that the northern part of Essex is mainly an arable area, and that the southern part is mainly grassland. We cannot know what the land utilisation of Essex was like in the eleventh century, but one thing is clear—then, as now, the north of Essex, with its attractive soil, was the most arable part of the county.

Figs. 57 and 59 are supplementary to the density maps, but it is necessary to make one reservation about them. As we have seen on p. 212, it is possible that some Domesday names may have covered two or more settlements, e.g. the present-day villages of Chipping Ongar and High Ongar are represented in the Domesday Book by only one name. Only where the Domesday evidence specifically indicates the existence of more than one settlement have they been distinguished on Figs. 57 and 59. A few of the symbols should, therefore, appear as two or more smaller symbols. But the limitation does not affect the general character of the maps.

WOODLAND

Types of entries

As in Norfolk and Suffolk, the extent of woodland on a holding is normally indicated by the number of swine which it could support, and the usual formula is 'wood for *n* swine' (*silva n porcos*). The number ranged from under ten up to over a thousand. The largest amount recorded under a single name was 2,382 for Waltham, made up of two holdings with 2,200 and 182 respectively. The round figures of some of

[1] N. V. Scarfe, *Essex* (London, 1942), p. 412, being Part 82 of *The Land of Britain*, ed. L. Dudley Stamp. See also S. W. Wooldridge and D. J. Smetham, 'The Glacial Drifts of Essex and Hertfordshire, and their Bearing upon the Agricultural and Historical Geography of the Region', *Geog. Journ.* (1931), LXXVIII, pp. 243–69.

the larger entries may indicate that they are estimates rather than precise amounts, but, on the other hand, the very detailed figures of many entries suggest exactness (e.g. 3, 5, 7, 32, 262). It does not necessarily follow that these figures indicate the actual number of swine grazing in a wood; the swine were used merely as units of measurement. Conversely, swine were often entered for places in which there was no wood. Thus there were 15 swine on the demesne at Dunton (Barstable), 20 at Southminster (Dengie) and 30 at Tillingham (Dengie), but no wood was recorded for any of these places.

While swine formed the normal unit of measurement, there are a few exceptional entries that measure wood in other ways—either in hides or acres or by a combination of both. These unusual entries are mainly concentrated in the hundred of Barstable. Thus Vange had half a hide of wood (22b), Langdon 1 hide (42), and Benfleet 30 acres (1b). Sometimes the hidage of wood exceeded the total assessment; there was, for example, a manor in Tilbury assessed at 2 hides but it had 4 hides of wood (42). Frequently, the wood on different holdings in the same place is entered not uniformly, as one might expect, but in terms of all three units—swine, hides and acres. The six wood entries for Wickford provide a good illustration of this mixture:

Fo. 23.	Wood for 30 swine.
Fo. 23.	Wood for 30 swine.
Fo. 23.	1 hide of wood (jointly with Wheatley).
Fo. 42b.	30 acres of wood.
Fo. 42b.	20 acres of wood.
Fo. 43.	'Then 12 hides of wood, now 6 acres'.

The last entry is interesting because the whole holding is assessed at only 10 hides. Altogether, there were six places in Barstable hundred with this mixture of entries, and another six places where hides and acres alone were used. One of the latter was Wheatley which, in addition to its woodland, had half a hide of wasted wood, *silvae vastatae* (43). There were also two other places, besides those already counted, where the wood had been wasted; Fanton had 30 acres of wasted wood (14), and Bowers Gifford had 30 acres on one holding and half a hide and 10 acres on another (86, 98). This makes fourteen places in Barstable where hides and acres are used to measure wood, out of a total of thirty-six places with wood. Outside Barstable, these unusual entries are few. At Hatfield Broad Oak

(Harlow) there were 30 acres of wood in addition to wood for 800 swine
(2). Cold Norton in Dengie (69) was assessed at 8 hides, of which two
were of wood (*ex his hidis sunt ii silvae*). At Wigborough (Winstree)
there was one holding with wood for 100 swine (18) and another holding
(55 b) assessed at 7 hides of land and 1 of wood (*vii hidae terrae et una
silvae*). At Shalford (Hinckford) there was a manor with 100 swine, but
we are told that the manor was short of 30 acres of wood which the
queen had given away (3 b). The exact implications of some of these
entries are extremely obscure. As Round said, they 'would seem to point
to the two methods of reckoning being used indifferently'.[1] To the list
of abnormal entries, three others must be added. At Rayleigh (Rochford),
where there was wood for 40 swine, a park (*parcus*) is also mentioned
(43 b). There was a swineherd (*porcarius*) at Coggeshall in Witham (26 b)
on a holding with wood for 500 swine, but with only 15 swine on the
demesne; and at Writtle (Chelmsford), where there was wood for no
less than 1,300 swine, there was mention of a swineherd who became a
forester (5 b): 'And in Harold's time there was 1 swineherd rendering the
customary due to this manor, and seated (*sedens*) on 1 virgate of land and
15 acres; but Robert Gernon, after the king came [to England], took
(*accepit*) him from the manor and made him forester of the king's wood
(*forestarius de silva regis*).' This is the only reference to the Forest of
Essex in the Domesday Book.

The wood entries for Essex, as for Norfolk and Suffolk, often draw
a contrast between conditions in 1066 and 1086. Thus the entry for
Clavering runs: *Tunc silva dccc porcos modo dc* (47). In some entries, the
time of the clearing is distinguished. At Wethersfield (Hinckford) there
was 'then' wood for 800 swine, but 'afterwards and now' only for 500
(fo. 4); while at Thunderley (Uttlesford) there was 'then and afterwards'
wood for 100 swine, but 'now' only sufficient for 80 (fo. 76 b). The number
of distinct places in Essex where woodland thus decreased was thirty-
eight, including two unspecified localities somewhere in the hundred of
Barstable; the details are summarised in the table on pp. 236–7. To these
we might add an entry for Wickford (Barstable) which speaks of 'Then
12 hides of wood, now 6 acres' (43); it is difficult to be clear about what
precisely it signifies, but it seems, at any rate, to imply reduction. All
these Essex entries are particularly interesting because it was in discussing
them that J. H. Round declared that 'we must assume that this loss of

[1] *V.C.H. Essex*, I, p. 377.

woodland represents that extension of the cultivated area (*terra lucrabilis*) that was always in progress'.[1] Mr Reginald Lennard, however, has shown that the reduction of wood was not accompanied by an extension of the arable.[2] Many of the holdings from which wood had disappeared show not an increased number of plough-teams, as one might expect, but a smaller number in 1086 than in 1066. Thus on one holding at Wethersfield (Hinckford), the number of swine which the wood could support had dropped from 800 to 500, but the number of plough-teams at work showed no corresponding increase; on the contrary, they had decreased from 19 to 13 (fo. 4). Only occasionally was there an increase of plough-teams on a holding where the wood had been reduced. The disappearance of wood must have been due, for the most part, not to assarting but to wasting. And, as we have just seen, there are three entries that specifically tell us that this was so; wasted wood (*silva vastata*) is entered for Wheatley (43), Fanton (14) and Bowers Gifford (86, 98)—all in Barstable hundred. This brings the total number of places in Essex where wood had disappeared up to forty-two.

Distribution of woodland

One of the earliest attempts to map the data of the Domesday Book seems to be J. H. Round's attempt to plot the Essex woodland in 1903. It is true that he did not print a map, but he certainly had one in mind.

The only way in which to gauge the distribution of woodland at the time of King Edward's death is to mark down on a map of the county the amount, reckoned in swine, as given for each parish. The results of this tedious process are of interest if treated with that caution which is always so essential in dealing with Domesday figures. When one finds such estimates as 100, 500, 1,000 frequently made, it is obvious that the estimate can only be accepted as a very rude one. Moreover the number of swine has to be compared with the acreage, a most laborious task. Certain general conclusions are therefore the most that one can hope for. And the first of these to be attained is that the actual woodland was distributed very unevenly, and that we can trace it as most abundant, even at that remote date, in places where its remnants linger down to the present day.[3]

[1] *V.C.H. Essex*, I, p. 378.
[2] Reginald Lennard, 'The Destruction of Woodland in the Eastern Counties under William the Conqueror', *Econ. Hist. Rev.* (1945), XV, pp. 36–40. See p. 126 above.
[3] J. H. Round, *V.C.H. Essex*, I, p. 375. See p. 16 above.

Reduction of Woodland in Essex, 1066–86

The numbers refer to swine for which there was wood in 1066 and 1086 respectively. At the end of the table there are four localities where the reduction of wood is noted in other ways. The folios are those of the Little Domesday Book.

Hundred	Place	1066	1086	Folio
Barstable	Unspecified	100	55	*17b*
,,	Unspecified*	100	50	*59b*
Chelmsford	Writtle	1500	1200	*5b*
Clavering	Clavering	800	600	*47*
,,	Farnham	200	150	*65b*
,,	,,	60	50	*100b*
,,	Ugley	200	160	*76b*
Dunmow	*Alferestuna*	400	350	*61*
,,	Canfield	160	120	*36b*
,,	Dunmow	500	300	*38b*
,,	Easton	200	150	*36*
,,	,,	800	400	*86b*
,,	,,	200	150	*91b*
,,	Lashley	80	60	*101b*
,,	Thaxted	1000	800	*38b*
,,	Yardley	40	30	*81b*
Freshwell	Hersham	40	30	*77*
Harlow	Hallingbury	150	100	*46*
Hinckford	Finchingfield	20	5	*29*
,,	,,	40	30	*101b*
,,	Hedingham	600	500	*83*
,,	,,	200	160	*87b*
,,	Henny	60	30	*84*
,,	,,	30	20	*88*
,,	Maplestead	100	60	*65b*
,,	,,	60	16	*84*
,,	Pooley§	60	40	*37*
,,	Saling	250	200	*84*
,,	Stansted	500	400	*88*
,,	Wethersfield	800	500	*4*
,,	Wickham St Paul's	40	20	*39*
Rochford	Eastwood	50	30	*43b*
Uttlesford	Amberden	250	200	*74*
,,	Birchanger	100	50	*21*
,,	,,	40	30	*62b*
,,	Elsenham†	1300	1000	*94b*
,,	Saffron Walden	1000	800	*62*
,,	,,	50	30	*62b*
,,	Takeley	1000	600	*21*
,,	,,	1000	600	*50*
,,	Thunderley	100	80	*76b*
,,	Wickham Bonhunt	100	60	*93*

* J. H. Round showed that this lay within Tilbury; *V.C.H. Essex*, I, p. 374.

§ Now represented by Hunt's Hall in Pebmarsh.

† The information for Elsenham refers to three dates: 'Then wood for 1,300 swine, and when he received it for 1,100, now for 1,000' (94b).

Hundred	Place	1066	1086	Folio
Uttlesford	Wimbish	500	400	69b
Winstree	Layer	100	60	92b
"	"	40	30	99b
Witham	Coggeshall	600	500	26b
"	Braxted	100	80	55
"	Notley	40	30	46
"	"	330	200	84
"	"	200	100	26b
"	Rivenhall	400	350	27

Other References in Barstable

Wickford	Then 12 hides of wood, now 6 acres (43).
Wheatley	Half a hide of wasted wood (43).
Fanton	30 acres of wasted wood (14).
Bowers Gifford	30 acres of wasted wood (86).
"	Half a hide and 10 acres of wasted wood (98).

But any attempt, along these lines, to calculate densities in terms of the acreages of each parish raises many difficulties. Thus the modern parish of Brentwood, as we have seen, was not mentioned in the Domesday Book, and formed part of the old parish of South Weald.[1] In this, and the many other similar cases, adjustments to the acreages must be made. But it is sometimes impossible to make such adjustments with even the roughest accuracy. In the hundred of Becontree there is a group of five modern parishes not mentioned in the Domesday Book: Dagenham, Romford Rural and Urban, Hornchurch and Noak Hill.[2] Their woods, like their other resources, were possibly entered with those of surrounding parishes,[3] but it is quite impossible to apportion the amounts. The principle upon which Fig. 61 has been constructed avoids such difficulties. While not without many local uncertainties, it gives a better general picture than could any density map. But, even so, Round's analysis must always be interesting as an early experiment in Domesday cartography. It is a pity that the map he had in mind was never published.

Whatever cartographical method be adopted, it is obvious that Essex was a very wooded county.[4] The wood was widely spread over both Boulder and London Clay alike, but the greatest concentration was in

[1] P. H. Reaney, *op. cit.* p. 135. See p. 215 above.

[2] For the earliest mention of the names, see P. H. Reaney, *op. cit.*, under each parish.

[3] But we must bear in mind the possibility that the area 'included a tract of extra-manorial wood that is not recorded in Domesday at all'. R. Lennard, *Eng. Hist. Rev.* (1953), LXVIII, p. 602.

[4] It is interesting to note the frequency of place-name elements in Essex that denote the former presence of wood. See P. H. Reaney, *op. cit.*

the west of the county. Here were many villages with wood for over 1,000 swine, and some with sufficient even for 2,000. The eastern hundreds, on the other hand, were less wooded, and a feature of Fig. 61 is the number of places with but small quantities of wood in Tendring and particularly in Rochford.[1] The map refers to conditions in 1086, but the

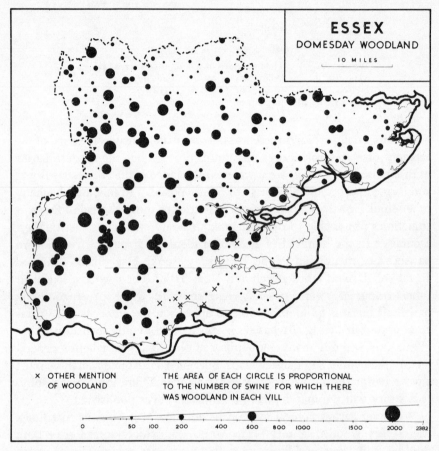

Fig. 61. Essex: Domesday woodland in 1086.

The boundary of alluvium and peat is indicated; see Fig. 54. Where the wood of a village is entered partly in terms of swine and partly in some other way, only the swine are shown.

[1] A different kind of map showing 'the forest area in 1086 A.D.' is that by Rupert Coles in 'The Past History of the Forest of Essex', *Essex Naturalist* (Stratford, Essex, 1935), XXIV, pp. 115–33. This was constructed by (1) converting the hidage figures

cutting that had gone on since 1066 did not affect the general pattern of distribution. A map of woodland in 1066 would present very similar features.

Types of entries

The entries for meadow in Essex are uniform and comparatively straightforward. On holding after holding, the same type of entry repeats itself monotonously—'*n* acres of meadow' (*n acrae prati*). The amount of meadow in each vill varied from 1 acre to over 100 and indeed to over 200. As in the case of other counties, no attempt has been made to translate the Domesday figures into modern acreages. The Domesday acres have been treated merely as conventional units of measurement, and Fig. 62 has been plotted on that assumption.

There are a number of entries that link marsh with meadow. At Canfield in Dunmow (35) there were '48 acres of meadow, counting meadow and marsh (*xlviii acrae prati inter pratum et maresc*)'; at Parndon in Harlow (78b), there were 45 acres of both together (*xlv acrae inter pratum et maresc*); and at Greenstead in Colchester (104), there were likewise 24 acres of both (*xxiiii acrae prati et maresc*). The Essex folios also include two other entries that mention marsh alone. At Tiltey in Dunmow (56b) there were 30 acres of meadow and 20 acres of marsh (*xxx acrae prati, xx acrae de maresc*). Under Peldon in Winstree (94b) a curious entry speaks of '80 acres of arable land and 200 acres of marsh' as being taken away from its 5 hides; this presumably refers to coastal marsh, whereas the other entries refer to marsh along streams.

Distribution of meadowland

The distribution of meadow was far from uniform throughout the county (Fig. 62). It was most frequent in the northern and western half of the county. Substantial amounts were recorded for villages on the streams that flow south-eastward across the Boulder Clay upland—along the Stour, the Colne, the Pant, the Chelmer and their tributaries. In the

into modern acreages on the assumption of 120 statute acres to the hide, and (2) plotting the resulting acreages 'as conventional squares within the parishes'. This area was taken as indicating arable land, the remainder of the county being regarded as marsh, woodland for swine, rough pasture or as 'unaccounted for in 1086'. Both the method and the map raise many doubts, e.g. that associated with the artificial nature of the hide.

south-west, the villages along the Roding and the Lea also carried moderate amounts. The southern and eastern half of the county was very different, and there was relatively little meadow in the coastal hundreds and in the southern half of Chelmsford hundred. It is true that a number

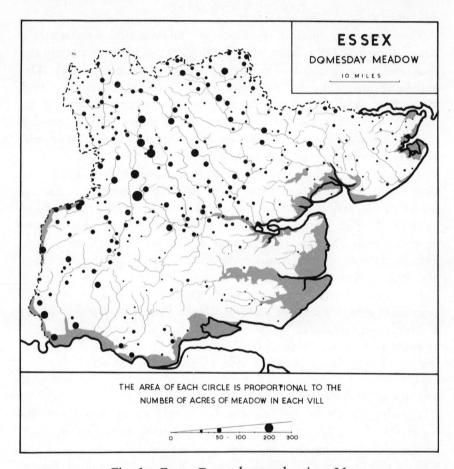

Fig. 62. Essex: Domesday meadow in 1086.

The areas of alluvium and peat are indicated; see Fig. 54. Rivers passing through these areas are not shown. Where the meadow of a village is entered partly in acres and partly in some other way, only the acres are shown.

of villages in this area possessed small amounts of meadow, but nothing to compare with those of the north and west.

PASTURE

Pasture for sheep

One of the peculiarities of the Domesday Survey of Essex is the frequent mention of 'pasture for *n* sheep' (*pastura n oves*). Pasture is recorded for

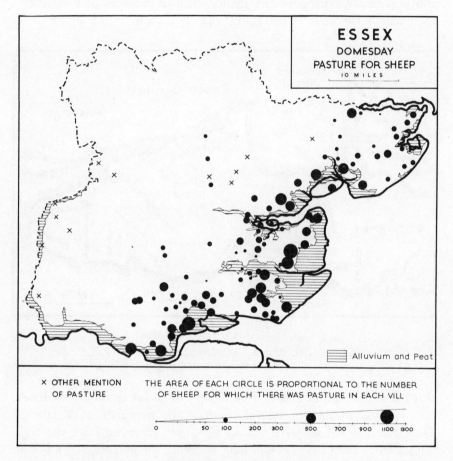

ESSEX
DOMESDAY
PASTURE FOR SHEEP
10 MILES

Alluvium and Peat

× OTHER MENTION OF PASTURE

THE AREA OF EACH CIRCLE IS PROPORTIONAL TO THE NUMBER OF SHEEP FOR WHICH THERE WAS PASTURE IN EACH VILL

0   50   100   200   300   500   700   900   1100   1300

Fig. 63. Essex: Domesday 'pasture for sheep' in 1086.

some other counties, but only rarely do we hear of 'pasture for sheep'. A few examples come from Kent, and one tells us that Higham (on the Thames opposite Tilbury) had 'pasture in Essex for 200 sheep' (vol. 1, fo. 9). The number of sheep varied from under 20 up to 1,300 at Southminster in Dengie (10). A unique entry for Wigborough in Winstree records that

there was 'pasture for 100 sheep, rendering 16 pence' (18). When plotted
on a map, the villages with pasture are seen to lie in a belt parallel with the
coast (Fig. 63), and J. H. Round demonstrated that this Domesday pasture
corresponded with the famous Essex marshes.[1] The large area of coastal
alluvium shown on the modern geological map indicates how extensive
these marshes must have been (Fig. 54). It is clear from later evidence

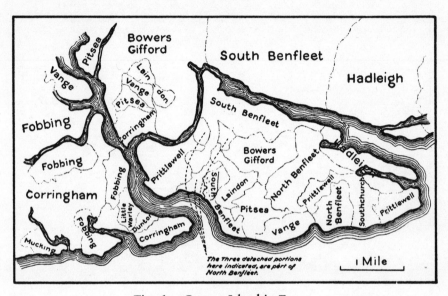

Fig. 64. Canvey Island in Essex.
Reproduced from J. H. Round, 'The Domesday Survey', *V.C.H. Essex*
(London, 1903), I, facing p. 369.

that the production of cheese from sheep's milk was an important Essex
activity, and in the seventeenth century the hundreds of Tendring,
Dengie and Rochford were famous for their 'great and huge cheeses'.
This activity must have been of long standing; the numerous 'wics' that
enter into the names of small places along the coast testify to the primitive
dairies of the marshes, and corroborative evidence is not wanting.[2]

One interesting feature of these pasture entries is that they are not
restricted to those parishes that abut on to the coast. Numerous nearby
inland places are also recorded as having pasture for sheep. 'A glance at

[1] J. H. Round, *V.C.H. Essex*, I, pp. 368–74.
[2] P. H. Reaney, *op. cit.* pp. 569 and 594.

the ordnance map', wrote Round, 'will suggest the explanation of the curious fact that these manors enjoyed feed in the marshes, though themselves inland. Canvey Island affords the clue.'[1] The parish of Canvey was created in 1881, and before then the island was nothing other than a mosaic of detached portions of other parishes situated up to 8 or 10 miles away on the nearby mainland (Fig. 64). The intermixed system of Canvey

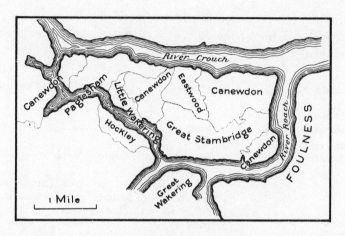

Fig. 65. Wallasea Island in Essex.

Reproduced from J. H. Round, 'The Domesday Survey', *V.C.H. Essex* (London, 1903), I, facing p. 369.

is also to be found elsewhere along the Essex coast. To the north, the island of Foulness, though now a separate parish, was formerly divided among six parishes.[2] The nearby island of Wallasea was likewise divided amongst the five mainland parishes of Canewdon, Great Stambridge, Eastwood, Paglesham and Little Wakering (Fig. 65); the detached portions were bounded by the ditches and drains that separate individual marshes one from another. All these arrangements were relics of a system under which a number of villages had rights in a common pasture. Similar groups of intercommoning villages were encountered in the Fenland and elsewhere. As we have seen, there is mention in the Suffolk folios of a certain pasture common to all the men of the hundred of Colneis (339b),

[1] J. H. Round, *V.C.H. Essex*, I, p. 369.
[2] *Ibid.* p. 371. The six parishes were Rochford, Sutton, Little Wakering, Shopland, Little Stambridge and Eastwood.

close to the Essex border.[1] The Essex folios do not specifically state that this was so in Canvey, Foulness and Wallasea; but the Domesday evidence, taken in conjunction with that of the modern map, shows that something of the older economy can be discerned beneath the changes of later times.

Other pasture

Entries that relate to pasture without specifying sheep are rare in the Essex folios, and they refer only to fourteen places scattered through six hundreds:

BARSTABLE
Wheatley (43)	15 acres of pasture (in addition to pasture for 140 sheep on two other holdings).

BECONTREE
Walthamstow (92)	Pasture worth (de) 8 shillings.

COLCHESTER
Colchester (107)	240 acres of pasture and scrub (inter pasturam et fructetam).
	In the burgesses' common (In commune burgensum) are 80 acres, and 8 perches about (circa) the wall (possibly refers to common pasture).

HARLOW
Hallingbury (52)	Pasture worth (de) 28 pence.
Hatfield Broad Oak (2)	Pasture which renders (reddit) 9 wethers (multones) to (in) the manor and 41 acres of ploughing (de aratura).
Roydon (80)	Pasture worth (de) 2 shillings.

WALTHAM
Nazeing and Epping (80b)	Pasture worth (de) 32 pence.
Waltham (15b)	There is pasture there which is worth 18 shillings (Pastura est ibi que valet xviii solidos).
Waltham (15b)	4 acres of pasture.

WITHAM
Coggeshall (26b)	Pasture worth 10 pence (Tantum pasturae que valet xd.).
Fairstead (72b)	Pasture worth (de) 4 pence.
Notley (84)	Pasture worth (de) 6 pence (as well as pasture for 100 sheep on another holding).
Rivenhall (46)	Pasture worth (de) 4 shillings.
Rivenhall (27)	Pasture from which 3 shillings are received (accipiuntur).
Rivenhall (27)	Pasture worth (de) 6 pence.
Witham (1b)	Pasture which then rendered 6 pence, now 14.

[1] See p. 184 above.

Of these fourteen places, Colchester and Waltham stand out for their large amounts of pasture, and Hatfield Broad Oak for the interest of its entry; it rendered not only 9 wethers but the service of ploughing 41 acres. As in Norfolk and Suffolk, the sum total of these entries cannot represent all the ordinary pasture of the county. Almost every village must have had some, but how much we cannot say.

FISHERIES

Fisheries (*piscinae*) are specifically recorded for 1086 in connection with 27 places.[1] For each of these places, the number of fisheries only is stated and no reference is made to their value as in the case of some other counties. Usually there was but 1 fishery in a village, but more are sometimes recorded, and there were as many as 6 at Chingford (Waltham). Occasional fractions and 'moieties' are also mentioned, but it is impossible to fit them together coherently. At Totham in Thurstable, 1 fisherman (*piscator*) is recorded, but no fishery (11); and at Leigh in Rochford on the banks of the Thames, there were 5 bordars by the water (*super aquam*) who held no land (75b), but whether they were fishermen or not, we cannot tell; Totham appears on Fig. 66, but not Leigh, making a total of 28 places. A distinction is sometimes made between conditions in 1066 and 1086. Thus at Leyton in Becontree there were 9½ fisheries in 1066 but none in 1086 (fos. 78b, 85); at Walthamstow in the same hundred the number had dropped from 6 to 1 (fo. 92); the 2 fisheries at Chadwell in Barstable (23b) had likewise disappeared, but we are told that one of them could be restored (*Tunc i piscina modo nulla sed potest fieri*). More rarely, the reverse seems to have taken place; at Lawling in Dengie, we are told there was 'now 1 fishery' (74b) as if it were a new one.

As Fig. 66 shows, these fisheries lay for the most part along the coast, and particularly along the estuaries of the Thames and Blackwater River. There is nothing to tell us specifically whether or not they were salt-water fisheries, but it seems as if they must have been.[2] Another group of fisheries were those along the River Lea (four places are shown on Fig. 66): 1 at Walthamstow, 6 at Chingford, 5 at Waltham and half a fishery at Nazeing. But there had been more in 1066, 5 more at Walthamstow, 6 at Leyton,

---

[1] For *piscinae*, see p. 367 below.
[2] For a discussion of the salt-water fisheries, see J. H. Round, *V.C.H. Essex*, I, pp. 380 and 424.

and 3½ at Higham. Finally, a few miscellaneous fisheries were recorded elsewhere in the county: at Springfield on the Chelmer, at Bardfield on the Pant, and at Wormingford on the Stour. All these can hardly have been the total number of coastal and river fisheries in eleventh-century Essex, but, at any rate, they provide us with a clue to the activity that went on.

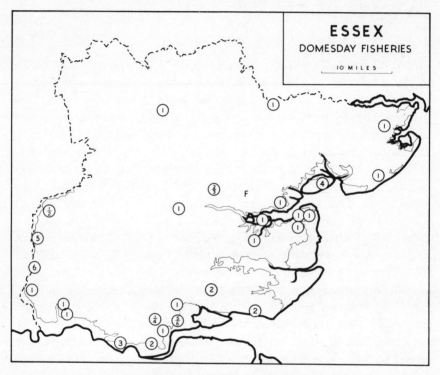

Fig. 66. Essex: Domesday fisheries in 1086.

The figure in each circle indicates the number of fisheries. F indicates a fisherman at Totham in Thurstable. The boundary of alluvium and peat is shown; see Fig. 54.

SALT-PANS

Salt-pans were recorded in 1086 in connection with twenty-two villages in Essex, and, in addition, the king had four pans at an unspecified place in Thurstable hundred (7b). The usual number of pans per village was under 3, but Wigborough had 6, Totham had 7, and what are now the three Tolleshunts had 13 between them. The number of pans only is

stated with no estimate of their value. There had been some changes
between 1066 and 1086; the pans at Totham had increased from 5, those
at the Tolleshunts had decreased from 20. At Goldhanger, the half
salt-pan of 1066 had increased to 1½, but we are given no hint of the
missing fraction. With one exception, the salt-making villages of 1086

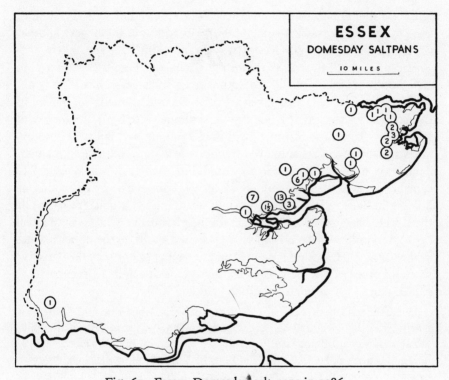

Fig. 67. Essex: Domesday salt-pans in 1086.

The figure in each circle indicates the number of salt-pans. The boundary of alluvium
and peat is shown; see Fig. 54.

were restricted to the three hundreds of Tendring, Winstree and Thurstable; the one exception was the solitary pan at Wanstead (Becontree) in
the south-west corner of the county (Fig. 67). Curiously enough there
was no salt-pan in the Domesday village of Salcott on a creek along the
Blackwater estuary.[1] Were all these the only salt-pans in eleventh-century
Essex? What of the coastal hundreds of Dengie and Rochford to the

[1] For the name see P. H. Reaney, *op. cit.* pp. 322–3.

south, to say nothing of those along the Thames estuary? Minor names suggest that there must have been pans in these districts at one time or another. Whether or not the pans were there in the eleventh century we can only conjecture.

MILLS

Mills are mentioned as existing in 1086 in connection with 151 out of the 440 Domesday settlements in Essex. In addition, there were another sixteen places where mills had existed in 1066, but had, apparently, disappeared by 1086; thus at Woodford in Becontree there was 'then 1 mill, now none' (16). Normally, the number of mills only was stated, but occasionally a value is also given; thus at the unidentified *Hasingham* in Lexden there was '1 mill rendering 15 shillings' (102b). The number of mills in a village varied from a fraction of a mill up to 8 mills. It is sometimes possible to reassemble the fractions in a comprehensible manner. Thus two holdings at Liston in Hinckford each had half a mill, presumably parts of the same mill on the Stour (89b, 95b). Or again, on one holding in Saffron Walden there was a 'third part of a mill' (62b), while there were two-thirds of a mill at the neighbouring village of Manhall (35b); it would seem as if both villages shared a mill on the upper reaches of the Cam. J. H. Round has given an interesting example of the detective work involved in piecing together the fractions of a mill at Rivenhall (27) and Braxted (49) in the hundred of Witham.

Under Rivenhall we read (fo. 27) that there was 'then one mill, (but) now a half'; and that 'Richard de Sachevilla has taken away a moiety of the mill'. What was Richard doing at Rivenhall? We know him only, in Domesday, as holding Aspenden, Herts, under Eudo Dapifer. If we follow the clue thus given us and look for a manor in the neighbourhood held by Eudo, we find that he held Great Braxted, divided only by the stream from Rivenhall, and that his tenant there was 'Richard' (fo. 49). We find, moreover, that on this manor there was 'now half a mill'; and a charter of donation to Eudo's abbey enables us to clinch the matter. For by this charter William 'de Sakevilla' gave a rent of five shillings in Braxted from 'Rivenhall mill'. We thus learn that Eudo's tenant, in 1086, at Braxted, was Richard de Sachevilla, and that he had annexed a moiety of the mill which still stands on the stream between Rivenhall and Braxted. The whole of the mill had belonged to Rivenhall; but thenceforth each of the manors possessed 'half a mill'. A common but obscure Domesday phrase is thus at once explained.[1]

[1] J. H. Round in *V.C.H. Essex*, I, p. 379.

Two-thirds of the villages with mills had only one or a fraction of one mill. The following table cannot be accurate owing to the complications caused by the fractions. Apart from those places with 'under 1 mill', an outstanding fraction of a mill for a village has been counted as a whole mill, and the proportion of villages in each category may be affected. But the general picture given by the table is probably not far wrong, and, in particular, it does show how some villages seem to have had many more than one mill at work.

Domesday Mills in Essex in 1086

Under 1 mill	3 settlements	4 mills	4 settlements
1 „	98 „	6 „	1 settlement
2 mills	35 „	8 „	1 „
3 „	9 „		

The group of 6 mills was at Colne in Lexden, but these mills may have belonged to different villages for there are four parishes of Colne today. The group of 8 was at Ham in Becontree, now represented by East and West Ham; there had been 9 mills there in 1066.

The mills were water-mills, and Fig. 68 shows how they were aligned along the streams. But the general distribution, as opposed to the location of individual mills, is sometimes puzzling. The 9 villages of Clavering hundred had not a single mill between them in 1086; there had been 1 in Clavering village itself in 1066, but apparently it disappeared. Freshwell hundred had only 2 villages with mills out of a total of 12 villages; a third had disappeared from Hadstock since 1066. These two nundreds are among those with the most arable and with the densest population; on the other hand, their streams were small ones. Was the grain of the villages without mills ground by hand, or taken elsewhere? Or is the Domesday record incomplete? These are questions we cannot answer.

CHURCHES

As we have seen, the number of churches mentioned in the Norfolk and Suffolk folios falls far short of the number that must have been in existence. The disparity is far greater in Essex, for, apart from St Peter's in Colchester, churches are specifically mentioned in connection with only sixteen places. 'Domesday only concerned itself with churches', wrote J. H. Round, 'in those cases where their endowments made them sources

of revenue. Any mention of others would only be incidental.'[1] Thus at
Latton in Harlow there was a priest with 'half a hide belonging to one
church' (27); at Stifford in Chafford there was a church with 30 acres
given to it by its neighbours (24b); at Peldon in Winstree there was

Fig. 68. Essex: Domesday mills in 1086.

The areas of alluvium and peat are indicated; see Fig. 54.
Rivers passing through these areas are not shown.

another with 30 acres on which there was half a plough (94b). The value
of a church is occasionally mentioned; the half a church at London,
entered under Barking, used to render 6s. 8d. but 'now does not' (18); at

[1] *V.C.H. Essex*, I, pp. 423-4.

Ramsden in Barstable there was a church with 30 acres 'worth 30 pence' (52b). Priests are only occasionally mentioned in connection with these churches. There are, however, twenty places for which no church is recorded, but for which there is mention of a priest. At Canfield in Dunmow, there were 'then 1 priest and 9 villeins, now 1 priest and 7 villeins' (36b); at Maplestead in Hinckford there were 'then 2 bordars; afterwards 1; now 5 and 1 priest' (84). This makes a total of 37 villages with either a priest or church. Such incidental mention can hardly indicate the part played by the Church in eleventh-century Essex.

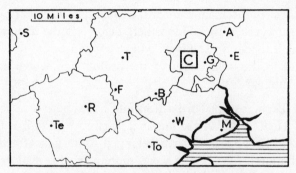

Fig. 69. Places contributory to Colchester.

C indicates Colchester itself. The contributory places are: A, Ardleigh; B, Birch; E, Elmstead; F, Feering; G, Greenstead; M, Mersea; R, Rivenhall; S, Shalford; T, Tey; Te, Terling; To, Tolleshunt; W, Wigborough. Hundred boundaries are shown; see Fig. 52.

URBAN LIFE

Burgesses were recorded for only two places in Essex—Colchester and Maldon. The information about both places is very unsatisfactory, and many details are obscure. They must have possessed markets, for example, yet none is recorded. One interesting urban feature that Essex shares with some other counties is that some urban houses are recorded as belonging to rural manors in the villages around. The implications of this connection between a borough and the surrounding countryside have been much debated and lie outside the theme of this chapter.[1] Here we can

---

[1] For a review of the controversy see (1) C. Petit-Dutaillis, *Studies Supplementary to Stubbs' Constitutional History* (Manchester, 1923), I, pp. 78 *et seq.*; (2) Carl Stephenson, *Borough and Town* (Cambridge, Mass., 1933), pp. 81 *et seq.*

only record the facts.

There were houses belonging to Essex manors not only in Colchester but in some boroughs of other counties—London, Sudbury and possibly Ipswich. London itself had similar connections with rural manors in Middlesex and Surrey, although it is nowhere described in Domesday Book. The Essex connections were three:

(1) Barking (17b). 'In London 28 houses, which render [blank] 13 shillings and 8 pence, and half a church which, in King Edward's time, used to render 6 shillings and 8 pence, and now does not.'

(2) Thurrock (63). 'There are 7 houses in London which belong (*jacent*) to this manor and are [included] in this rent (*firma*).'

(3) Waltham (15b). 'In London there belong to the manor 12 houses which render 20 shillings, and one gate (*porta*) which the king gave to the predecessor of the bishop, and which also renders 20 shillings.'

Sudbury, just across the border in Suffolk, had 15 burgesses belonging to a manor in Hedingham in the hundred of Hinckford (76b). It also had 5 burgesses which appear to have belonged to an unspecified manor in Hinckford hundred (40). There were, moreover, two manors in Henny (also in Hinckford) to which belonged customary dues of 22 pence and 22½ pence from Sudbury (74, 84b). Finally, another Suffolk borough, Ipswich, had a burgess who may have been connected with Moze in Essex (411b).[1]

Colchester

The hundred of Colchester included not only the city (*civitas*) itself, but the two villages of Greenstead and Lexden; for the purposes of this analysis, the latter have been included in the hundred of Lexden. Here we are concerned with the city alone. Its description comes at the end of the Essex folios and is very long (104–107b); there is also a subsidiary entry on fo. 11, relating to a holding of the bishop of London. The lengthy description is extremely difficult and obscure, and it has been discussed in detail by J. H. Round.[2] Its main feature is a long list of holders of houses and plots of land, mostly of only a few acres, but sometimes of 20 or 30 acres. The names of the holders number 295; many are obviously those

---

[1] See p. 193 above.   [2] *V.C.H. Essex*, I, pp. 414–24.

of inhabitants, others are the names of magnates like Count Eustace and the abbot of Westminister; some are names of women. Most of the holders had 1 or 2 houses each, but some held as many as 10 or more houses. The 295 holders had a total of 406 houses and 15 burgesses. [1]

In addition to the main entry, other entries record properties in Colchester. The bishop of London had 14 houses (11). Furthermore a number of houses belonged to neighbouring manors; some are entered in the account of the borough itself and are included in the figure of 406 above; but others are entered under their respective manors. Two manors appear in both groups. Thus under the abbey of Westminster's manor at Feering in Lexden, we are told 'there are 2 houses in Colchester which belong to this manor' (14b), and in the account of the borough we are again told that the abbey held 4 houses 'belonging to Feering' (106b). It is not clear whether the total is six or whether the different figures are due to a scribal error. Belonging to Rivenhall, also in Lexden, there was 'a burgess at Colchester' (27). The full list (Fig. 69) is as follows:

Entered under rural manors		Entered under Colchester	
Birch	2 houses (30)		
Greenstead	2 houses (104)		
Tey	1 house (29b)		
Mersea	1 house (22)		
Wigborough	3 houses (18)		
Rivenhall	1 burgess (27)		
Feering	2 houses (14b)	Feering	4 houses (106b)
Terling	2 houses (72b)	Terling	5 houses (107)
		Ardleigh	2 houses (106b)
		Elmstead	1 house (106b)
		Tolleshunt	1 house (107)
		Shalford	3 houses (106b)

Round showed that, although the Domesday Book does not specifically say so, it is possible that other manors around also held houses in Colchester, e.g. Bromley and Peldon. [2]

The properties entered under rural manors amount to 13 houses and 1 burgess. On the assumption that these were additional to those of the main entry, and including the bishop of London's houses, the total of houses and burgesses is 449. Other categories of people for 1086 comprised 24 bordars, 2 villeins and 3 serfs. The grand total of 478

[1] Including the 2 houses of the church of St Peter enumerated at the end of the main entry.   [2] V.C.H. Essex, I, pp. 385, 412, 418.

implies a total population of well over 2,000. This figure must be an absolute minimum, for we cannot guess at the number of people that escaped mention. The indications of urban life are not many. As we have seen, numerous churches were recorded for Norwich and Ipswich, but at Colchester there is mention only of one, St Peter's. 'It is certain, however,' wrote Round, 'if only from analogy, that Colchester must already have possessed several churches, and indeed seven priests are named in the survey.'[1] One indication of the life of the town is the presence of a mint (*moneta*) for which the burgesses of Colchester and Maldon together rendered £40; there is also reference to the walls of the town, and at least one house lay outside the walls. But these scattered fragments of information hardly give us enough to envisage the activity that sustained the community of burgesses. Of their industry and commerce we know nothing.

Details of the agricultural life of the settlement are likewise few. Altogether, some 5 plough-teams seem to have been at work. There were 85½ acres of meadow, and 240 acres of pasture and scrub (*inter pasturam et fructetam*), but no wood or stock apart from the ploughing beasts. There is also reference to the burgesses' common (*in commune burgensum*) which may refer to common pasture. Three mills and a render of honey complete the list of agrarian resources. Despite the very great interest of the account to students of the English borough, the geographical picture that emerges from it is not a very concrete one.

Maldon

Maldon, reckoned at half a hundred, is described in six entries (4b, 5b, 29, 48, 73 and 75). Taken together, they show clearly the two elements in the life of the settlement—agricultural and urban. There were 11½ ploughs at work in 1086. There was also woodland sufficient to feed 80 swine; there was pasture for 200 sheep; and there were 10 acres of meadow, 1 mill, and a considerable amount of livestock—5 cows, 4 calves, 14 rounceys, 140 animals, 146 swine and as many as 576 sheep. There were, apparently, 6 freemen, 1 sokeman, 9 villeins, 21 bordars, and 5 serfs, making a total of 42 recorded people. The urban portion appears to have belonged wholly to the king. He had '180 houses held by burgesses and 18 messuages (*mansuras*) which are waste; of which [burgesses] 15 hold half a hide and 21 acres, while (*et*) the other men hold no more than their

[1] *V.C.H. Essex*, I, p. 424.

houses in the borough' (5 b).[1] This is a very different state of affairs from that in Colchester where the burgesses had small amounts of land attached to their houses. The king also held another house; and Eudo dapifer held two which may likewise have been additional. On this assumption, the total number of houses and burgesses and other inhabitants amounted to about 225, which implies a population of well over 1,100. These burgesses, we are told, had the duty of finding a horse (*caballum*) for the army and of providing (*faciendam*) a ship (48). But although the general character of eleventh-century Maldon seems fairly clear, it is difficult to get the activities of its inhabitants into clear focus.[2] To what extent were the burgesses farmers as well as townsmen? What were their commercial activities? We cannot say.

LIVESTOCK

The Essex folios, like those of Norfolk and Suffolk, record information about livestock on the demesne land of a village, though only occasionally does the phrase *in dominio* occur to remind us of this. It is inserted, for example, in the account of the settlement of Barstable in the hundred of the same name (22b). The total number in each category of livestock in 1086 is summarised below:[3]

Sheep	46,095	Mares	21
Swine	13,171	Foals	103
Goats	3,576	Cows	160
Animals	3,768	Calves	77
Rounceys	790	Donkeys	26
Horses	3	Mule	1

The figures for 1086 are frequently very different from those for 1066. Thus an entry relating to Theydon in Ongar declares: 'Then as now

---

[1] It is also strange that, although 165 out of 180 burgesses apparently held no land, they all had 'among them' a substantial number of animals—12 rounceys, 140 beasts, 103 swine and 336 sheep; these figures for livestock are included in the statistics given above. It is possible, of course, that these animals belonged only to the 15 burgesses with half a hide and 15 acres.

[2] There is no mention of a mint in the description of Maldon, but that of Colchester says that the burgesses of Colchester and Maldon together rendered £40 for a mint (107b).

[3] There is another count of livestock in M. E. Seebohm's *The Evolution of the English Farm* (London, 1927), p. 156:

Sheep	46,533	Goats	3,405	Cows	166	Horses	34
Swine	12,870	Animals	3,834	Rounceys	783		

2 rounceys. Then 8 animals, now 13. Then 35 swine, now 66. Then 87 sheep, now 100, and 15 goats' (50b). At Eynesworth, in Uttlesford, 'there was no stock when [it was] received (*Tunc nichil recepit*), now [there are] 32 swine, 52 sheep, 2 animals' (38). But we are never given a hint as to the cause of these changes.[1] Occasionally, as in Norfolk and Suffolk, the form of the entry makes it difficult to be absolutely certain whether the amount of stock on a holding in 1066 was still there in 1086 and vice versa.

Horses are fairly frequently mentioned, and there were also a number of foals; but of all the varieties of horse, the one most frequently mentioned is the rouncey (*runcinus*). The demesne of a village usually carried a few, sometimes as many as a dozen or more. Donkeys and mules are only very occasionally mentioned, e.g. there were 5 donkeys (*asini*) at Stansted Mountfitchet in Uttlesford (65) and a mule (*mulus*) at Lawling in Dengie (8).

Goats are recorded on a number of holdings, but much less frequently and in smaller numbers than are sheep. The number of goats on the demesne of a village was very rarely above fifty, and quite often less than ten.

Swine are much more frequently mentioned. The number on the demesne of a holding was rarely the same as the number its woodland could support. Usually it was less, but occasionally it was more, and swine are sometimes recorded for holdings without any wood. There were 30 swine on the demesne at Tillingham (Dengie) in 1086, but there is no mention of wood in the village (13).

Animals presumably included all the non-ploughing beasts. Cows are mentioned more frequently than in Norfolk and Suffolk; even so they are far from being numerous, yet they must have been kept in large numbers for breeding the all important ploughing oxen. They may often have been included under the general heading of *animalia*. Calves (*vituli*) are occasionally specified, e.g. at Bowers Gifford in Barstable (71b). These 'animals' are recorded for a large number of villages, usually less than thirty in each, but sometimes more.

The distribution of each of these major groups of livestock was fairly widespread, and presents no special features of interest. There is, however, one group that merits more detailed treatment. Sheep are recorded in large numbers, and their distribution must be examined more closely, especially in view of the additional statement about 'pasture for sheep' that is found in many entries.

[1] See p. 221 above for the death of oxen.

Sheep

Fig. 70, of course, is a map only of sheep on the demesne lands; but, although thus limited, it may give some hint about the general distribution of sheep throughout the county. The demesne sheep were most numerous

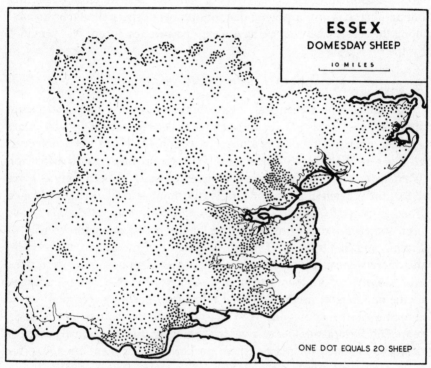

Fig. 70. Essex: Domesday sheep on the demesne in 1086.
The boundary of alluvium and peat is shown; see Fig. 54.

along the coastal marshes, and flocks of 300–400, and even more, are entered for many villages in the hundreds of Winstree, Thurstable, Dengie and Rochford. The number of sheep frequently varied between the years 1066 and 1086. At Childerditch in Chafford they had decreased from 50 to 12 (92b); at Berden in Clavering they had increased from 25 to 122 (fo. 47); at Hanningfield in Chelmsford they had increased from 117 to as much as 810 (fo. 25). But the reason for such changes lies beyond our reach.

DDG

17

In view of their incomplete nature, it is not surprising that the statistics for sheep cannot be related to the information about 'pasture for sheep'. There were 42 sheep on the demesne at Langdon in Barstable, but there was enough pasture attached to the village for 100 sheep (42). Conversely there were 500 sheep at Corringham but pasture sufficient for only 400 (fo. 12). But although the two sets of statistics bear no close relation to one another, it is not surprising that the number of sheep should be greatest along the coast, where, as we have seen, 'pasture for sheep' was provided by the marshes.

MISCELLANEOUS INFORMATION

Beehives

Associated with statistics about stock, there is occasionally a statement about hives of bees (*vasa apum*). The number recorded is usually under a dozen, and sometimes it is a mere two or three. There were, however, 20 hives at Waltham in Chelmsford (58) and as many as 30 at Saffron Walden (62b). Their numbers fluctuated; there had been only 4 hives at Saffron Walden in 1066; conversely, the number at Clavering had fallen from 12 to 5 (fo. 46b). The fluctuation, Round suggested, 'may have been sometimes due to mere shifting of the hives, as where we read of Frating and St Osyth [in Tendring], which had the same under-tenant, that there were six hives at Frating where there had been none, and none at St Osyth's where there had been six (fo. 75b)'.[1] No value is attached to the numbers of hives. The total number of beehives recorded on the demesne of the county in 1086 is 599.[2] All the entries can scarcely represent the total number of hives in the county, and occasionally a render of honey is stated for places where no beehives are mentioned, e.g. for Colchester itself (107).

Vineyards

There are nine entries relating to vineyards (*vineae*) in the Essex folios, and, with one exception, the vineyards are measured in terms of arpents (*arpenni*), a French unit of measurement.[3] Round argued that the Normans reintroduced the culture of the vine into England.[4] 'The evidence for this proposition,' he wrote, 'is largely drawn from Essex. Domesday proves that the vineyards existing at the time of the great Survey had

[1] *V.C.H. Essex*, I, p. 383.
[2] M. E. Seebohm, *op. cit.* p. 156, gives the number as 612.
[3] See p. 203 above.   [4] *V.C.H. Essex*, I, p. 382.

been often planted since the days of the Confessor; that they had not, in some cases, yet begun to bear; that they were almost universally reckoned by "arpents", a foreign measure; and that they are normally found on manors held in the lord's hand and probably containing a lord's residence. By "lord" I here mean a "baron" or tenant-in-chief.' In view of the interest of these entries, they are all set out below:

(1) *Rayleigh* in Rochford (43b). '6 arpents of vineyard, and [it] renders 20 muids (*modios*) of wine if it does well (*si bene procedit*)'.

(2) *Hedingham* in Hinckford (76b). 'Now 6 arpents of vineyard.'

(3) *Belchamp* in Hinckford (77). 'Now 11 arpents of vineyard, [of which] 1 is in bearing (*portat*).'

(4) *Waltham* in Chelmsford (58). 'Now 10 arpents of vineyard.'

(5) *Stebbing* in Hinckford (74). 'Now 2½ arpents of vineyard, and only the half is in bearing (*portat*).'

(6) *Debden* in Uttlesford (73b). 'Now 2 arpents of vineyard in bearing (*portantes*), and 2 not in bearing (*non portantes*).'

(7) *Mundon* in Dengie (49b). '2 arpents of vineyard'.

(8) *Stambourne and Toppesfield* in Hinckford (55b). '1 arpent of vineyard.'

(9) *Ashdon* in Freshwell (71). '1 acre of vineyard (*i acra vineae*).'

Other references

The entry for Rayleigh in Rochford (43b) mentions both a park (*i parcus*) and a castle. The reference to the latter reads: 'In this manor Suen built his castle' (*In hoc manerio Suenus fecit suum castellum*).

REGIONAL SUMMARY

Essex has been variously subdivided from time to time,[1] but for our purpose it will be sufficient to draw what amounts to a broad distinction between the north and south of the county, and then to consider the Tendring-Colchester Loam area which lies in the north-east of the county (Fig. 71).

[1] For a subdivision based on present land-use, see N. V. Scarfe, *Essex* (London, 1942), p. 435, being Part 82 of *The Land of Britain*, ed. L. Dudley Stamp. This also contains maps indicating the divisions made by Charles Vancouver (1795) and Arthur Young (1807). See also: (1) S. W. Wooldridge, 'The physiographic evolution of the London Basin', *Geography* (1932), XVII, pp. 99–116; (2) S. W. Wooldridge and D. J. Smetham, 'The glacial drifts of Essex and Hertfordshire', *Geog. Journ.* (1931), LXXVIII, pp. 243–69; (3) Annie R. Hatley, 'Notes on the regional geography of Essex', *Geography* (1928), XIV, pp. 309–14.

(1) *The Boulder Clay Plateau*

This north-western portion of Essex lies for the most part over 200 ft. above sea-level; much of it is over 300 ft., and, in places, it rises to over

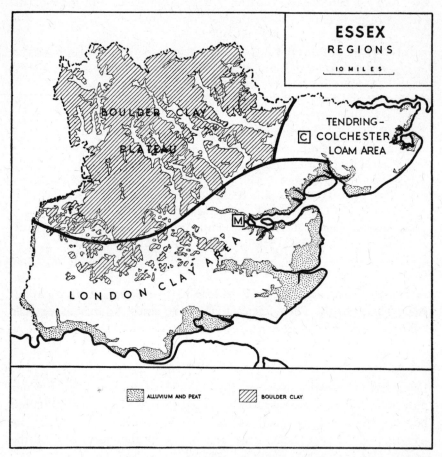

Fig. 71. Essex: Regional subdivisions.
Places with burgesses are indicated by initials: C, Colchester; M, Maldon.

400 ft. The general slope of the plateau is from the north-west towards the south-east. This sloping surface is broken in the west by the valleys of the Cam and the Stort, and to the east by those of the Colne, the Pant and the Chelmer that flow south-eastwards into the Essex estuaries. The

important fact about the soils of the area is the presence of chalky Boulder Clay. This varies a great deal from place to place, but it gives rise to loams rather than clays, and it contains interstratified beds of sand and gravel. Further variety is provided (1) by strips of underlying gravel and London Clay exposed in the valleys of the streams that cross the plateau, and (2) by an expanse of chalk in the north-west. In the valleys lie numerous villages, most of which had a fair amount of meadow. The general prosperity of the region, as indicated by plough-teams and population, resembled that of 'High Suffolk' to the north. The region was originally wooded, and it still had a very considerable amount of wood in 1086. Sheep, or at any rate, demesne sheep, were fairly widely distributed.

(2) *The London Clay Area*

The London Clay area, to the south of the Boulder Clay plateau, is lower, and rarely rises to over 300 ft. above sea-level. The surface is far from being continuous, and the summits of the hills often have a capping of Bagshot Sands. In the north, there are numerous patches of Boulder Clay. Further variety is given to the region by the gravel terraces of the Thames estuary, by the patch of loam in the neighbourhood of Southend, by the spread of glacial sand and gravel near Chelmsford, and by the coastal alluvium that extends inland along the river estuaries. But despite this variety, it is London Clay that forms the dominating feature of the soils of the region. As we have seen, these are in general heavier than the Boulder Clay soils, and were less attractive to the early farmer. It is not surprising, therefore, that the Domesday prosperity of the area, as indicated by plough-teams and population, was below that of the Boulder Clay lands to the north. The streams that traverse the London Clay surface are without wide alluvial belts and most of the villages here had little or no meadowland. There was, on the other hand, much wood in the region, although it was not as great as might be expected in relation to that of the Boulder Clay area. It is not possible, for the eleventh century at any rate, to draw a contrast between heavily wooded London Clay and relatively lighter wooded Boulder Clay. The wood thinned towards the south-east coast, and the villages of Rochford hundred, in particular, had only small quantities of wood returned for them.

The coastlands, with their marsh, gave a distinctive character to the region. Large areas of 'pasture for sheep' formed an important element in the economy of many villages; entries for demesne sheep were frequent. Salt-making was important around the Blackwater and Colne estuaries, but was strangely absent to the south, that is if we may believe the Domesday entries. Fisheries were to be found around the Blackwater estuary and also along the north bank of the Thames, and along the Lea valley.

(3) *The Tendring and Colchester Loam Area*

This is a low-lying country set between the estuaries of the Stour and the Colne. Its soil is largely glacial loam in the west and London Clay in the east. This London Clay, however, is very different from the cold wet clay of southern Essex, and it yields fertile medium soils. The density of its plough-teams in 1086 approximated to that of the Boulder Clay country. Woodland was moderately abundant, but there was relatively little meadow. There was a fair amount of 'pasture for sheep', but not as much as in the hundreds of Dengie, Rochford and Barstable to the south. Salt-making was obviously an important activity. Finally, there were a few fisheries, but not as many as might be expected.

BIBLIOGRAPHICAL NOTE

(1) An older translation of the Domesday text relating to Essex is T. C. Chisenhale-Marsh's *Domesday Book relating to Essex* (Chelmsford, 1864). Even J. H. Round described it as being 'of remarkable excellence for its date' (*V.C.H. Essex*, I, p. 426).

A more modern translation that pays great attention to place-name identification was made by J. H. Round himself in *V.C.H. Essex* (London, 1903), I, pp. 427–578. This is accompanied by an introduction (pp. 333–425) which is a remarkably fine achievement of far more than local interest. It discusses not only the feudal and economic content of the survey, but also many points of geographical interest. Round was peculiarly well equipped to write it, not only by virtue of his Domesday scholarship but also because Essex was his native county.

(2) The following deal with various aspects:

RUPERT COLES, 'Past History of the Forest of Essex', *Essex Naturalist* (Stratford, Essex, 1935), XXIV, pp. 115–33.

H. C. DARBY, 'Domesday Woodland in East Anglia', *Antiquity* (Gloucester, 1934), XIV, pp. 211–14.

R. WELLDON FINN, 'The Essex Entries in the *Inquisitio Eliensis*', *Trans. Essex Arch. Soc.* (Colchester, 1964), 3rd Ser. vol. 1, pp. 190–5.

R. WELLDON FINN, *Domesday Studies: The Eastern Counties* (London, 1967).

GEORGE RICKWORD, 'The Kingdom of the East Saxons and the Tribal Hidage', *Trans. Essex Arch. Soc.* (Colchester, 1911), N.S. vol. XI, pp. 246–65.

GEORGE RICKWORD, 'The East Saxon Kingdom', *ibid.* (1913), N.S. vol. XII, pp. 38–50.

J. H. ROUND, 'Essex Vineyards in Domesday', *ibid.* (1900), N.S. vol. VII, pp. 249–51.

S. W. WOOLDRIDGE and D. J. SMETHAM, 'The glacial drifts of Essex and Hertfordshire, and their bearing upon the agricultural and historical geography of the region', *Geog. Journ.* (1931), LXXVIII, pp. 243–69.

(3) The method and contents of the Little Domesday Book and of the *Inquisitio Eliensis* are discussed in many of the general works dealing with the Domesday Book (see pp. 3 *et seq.* and pp. 7 *et seq.* above, and p. 264 below).

(4) A valuable aid to the Domesday study of the county is P. H. Reaney's *The Place-Names of Essex* (Cambridge, 1935).

CHAPTER VI

CAMBRIDGESHIRE

The Cambridgeshire folios are of supreme interest to any student of the Domesday Book because there exist for portions of the county two other versions of the original returns. One of these is the *Inquisitio Eliensis* which gives an account of the estates held or claimed by the abbey of Ely in the counties of Cambridge, Hertford, Essex, Norfolk, Suffolk and Huntingdon. The other, and even more important, version is the *Inquisitio Comitatus Cantabrigiensis* which surveys the greater part of thirteen out of the sixteen Domesday hundreds of the county. From the body of the manuscript there is missing a leaf which must have described holdings at a number of places in the hundreds of Longstow and Papworth. The manuscript, too, breaks off abruptly in the middle of describing North-stow hundred and the lost portion must have described the hundred of Chesterton and the two hundreds of Ely. In spite of these defects, what remains surveys the greater part of the upland of southern Cambridgeshire. It was J. H. Round's work on this document that laid the foundations of the modern study of the Domesday Book, and he opened his masterly account, first published in 1895, by saying: 'The true key to the Domesday Survey, and to the system of land assessment it records, is found in the *Inquisitio Comitatus Cantabrigiensis.*'[1]

The existence of these two subsidiary documents means that for a great part of the county there is a parallel Domesday account, and for many of the widespread Ely estates even a third account. By careful collation, Round was led to the conclusion that the three accounts were independent of one another, and that both the *Inquisitiones* were 'copies of the actual returns made by the Domesday jurors'.[2] Later scholarship has qualified Round's views, but the two documents still remain of the greatest interest in the study of the Domesday Book.[3]

Whereas Domesday Book arranges the holdings in terms of fiefs, the *I.C.C.* arranges them on the geographical basis of whole vills and their hundreds. Both the *I.C.C.* and the *I.E.* show that the original information must have been more detailed than that which we now have in the

[1] J. H. Round, *Feudal England* (London, 1895), p. 3.
[2] *Ibid.* p. 8.
[3] For a revaluation see V. H. Galbraith, *The Making of Domesday Book* (Oxford, 1961), pp. 123–45. For the statistics of the *I.E.*, see pp. 99–101 above.

Domesday Book, for they both contain, for example, information about the livestock on the demesne lands. The extracts relating to the village of Hauxton, on pp. 278–9, show how the three versions compare with one another.

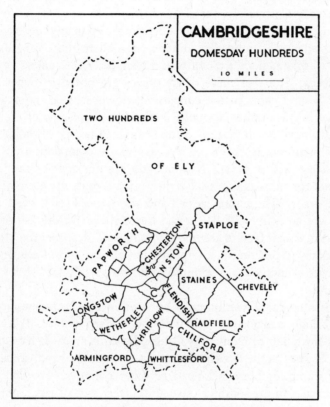

Fig. 72. Cambridgeshire: Domesday hundreds.

C indicates the Domesday borough of Cambridge which 'was assessed at one hundred'. The southern tip of the county was included in Domesday Essex.

The existence of three versions at once raises the question of which is the most accurate. 'There are cases', wrote Round, 'in which the *I.C.C.* corrects *D.B.*, cases in which *D.B.* corrects the *I.C.C.*, and cases in which the *I.C.C.* corrects itself. There are also several cases of discrepancy between the two, in which we cannot positively pronounce which, if either, is right.'[1] The *I.E.* agrees sometimes with the *I.C.C.* and sometimes with the Domesday Book; and in the account of a holding at Shelford, Round showed that it corrects both.[2] The Domesday Book omits some small estates which are included in the *I.C.C.*; one of these, for example, is the holding of Guy de Raimbercurt at Haslingfield (p. 73). Conversely, the *I.C.C.* for some mysterious reason, leaves out some of the royal estates.[3] There are also many divergencies in phrasing and many numerical differences. Where the Domesday Book records 16 sokemen, or 2 ploughs or 7 men, the *I.C.C.* enters 15, 1 and 6 respectively. Some of these discrepancies are noted in the pages that follow. Round came to the conclusion, however, that 'comparing the omissions and errors, as a whole, in these two versions of the original returns, it may be said that the comparison is in favour of the Domesday Book text, although, from the process of its compilation, it was far the most exposed to error. No one who has not analysed and collated such texts for himself can realise the extreme difficulty of avoiding occasional error. The abbreviations and the *formulæ* employed in these surveys are so many pitfalls for the transcriber, and the use of Roman numerals is almost fatal to accuracy.'[4] While it is clear that the Domesday text is not without errors, the evidence of these subsidiary documents only serves to increase our admiration for the clerkly skill that went into its making.

One further consideration must be mentioned. The Domesday county of Cambridge was not identical with the modern county. Thus Exning, which formed part of Domesday Cambridgeshire, seems to have passed to Suffolk as early as the twelfth century. On the other hand, some villages now in Cambridgeshire belonged to other counties. Heydon and the two Chishalls, in the south of the county, were part of Essex until as late as 1895, and therefore they appear in the Little Domesday Book.[5] On the western side of the county, a part of Papworth St Agnes was until recently included in Huntingdonshire, and there is one entry relating to it among the Huntingdonshire folios (206b). And, as we shall see,

---

[1] J. H. Round, *op. cit.* pp. 17–18.

[2] *Ibid.* p. 18. But for the statistics of the *I.E.*, see pp. 99–101 above.

[3] L. F. Salzman in *V.C.H. Cambridge* (Oxford, 1938), I, pp. 336–7. But for a possible explanation of the omission, see V. H. Galbraith, *Eng. Hist. Rev.* LVII, pp. 174–5.

[4] J. H. Round, *op. cit.* p. 20.

[5] The references are: Great and Little Chishall (33b, 38, 52b, 62b, 100b, 103b); Heydon (19b, 97).

Stanground is still shared with Huntingdonshire, and Outwell and Upwell with Norfolk. Boundaries in the Fenland must have been uncertain; we know that even as late as the thirteenth century there were doubts about them.[1] Finally, as we have seen above, there were a few holdings in Cambridgeshire that belonged to manors in Essex and so are referred to in both sets of folios. Holdings in Babraham (190) and Hinxton (189b) belonged to Chesterford, and another in Shelford belonged to Newport (190).[2]

SETTLEMENTS AND THEIR DISTRIBUTION

The total number of separate places mentioned for Cambridgeshire seems to be approximately 142, including the town of Cambridge itself. This figure, however, may not be quite accurate because, today, there are a number of instances of two adjoining villages bearing the same surname, and it is not always clear whether both units existed in the eleventh century. Only when there is specific mention of a second village in the Domesday Book itself, has it been included in the total of 142. Thus the existence of Guilden Morden and Steeple Morden in the eleventh century is indicated by the mention of *Mordune* and *Alia Mordune*, and of the two Lintons (Great and Little) by *Lintone* and *Alia Lintone*, although Little Linton is today included in Linton parish.[3] There is, on the other hand, no indication that, say, the Papworth St Agnes and Papworth Everard of today existed as separate villages; the Domesday information about them is entered under one name only, and their distinctive appellations are derived from two twelfth-century people, *Agnes de Papewurda* and *Evrard de Beche*.[4] In the same way, explicit record of the distinction between Great and Little Abington does not appear until the thirteenth century, and the same applies to the two Eversdens, the two Shelfords and the two Camps. We are sometimes given a hint of the stages by which two such settlements obtained separate names. The Domesday Book makes no distinction

[1] H. C. Darby, *The Medieval Fenland* (Cambridge, 1940), p. 75.
[2] See *V.C.H. Cambridge*, I, pp. 361, 362, 385, and *V.C.H. Essex*, I, p. 338. See p. 211 above.
[3] The two adjacent villages of Hatley St George and East Hatley are not separately distinguished in the Domesday Book. They both appear under the name *Hatelai*, but they lie in separate hundreds and are rubricated accordingly, so that separate settlements are presumably implied. There is a third Hatley across the border in Bedfordshire, Cockayne Hatley. The three parishes must have formed a single area at one time.
[4] For the history of this, and of all other names mentioned in this chapter, see P. H. Reaney, *The Place-Names of Cambridgeshire and the Isle of Ely* (Cambridge, 1943).

between Great and Little Wilbraham; the *I.C.C.* likewise makes no distinction but it does speak of 'two Wilbrahams (*ii Wilburgeham*)'; the earliest record of the names *Magna* and *Parva* does not appear, however, until

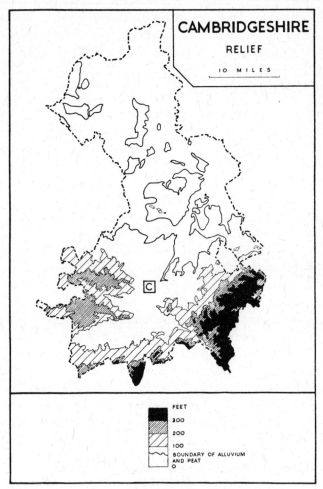

Fig. 73. Cambridgeshire: Relief.
C indicates the Domesday borough of Cambridge.

the thirteenth century. In the same way, the Domesday Book does not differentiate between Swaffham Prior and Swaffham Bulbeck; but one of the documents appended to the *I.E.* mentions *Suuafham* and *Altera*

Suuafham (p. 192); the distinctive names also seem to go back to the eleventh century, being derived from the Prior of Ely and from Hugo de Bolebec mentioned in both the *I.C.C.* and the *I.E.* (pp. 12 and 102). In each of these cases, it seems that one vill had become two vills by what Maitland called 'some process of colonization or subdivision'.[1] But we are only rarely able to say whether the change had already taken place by Domesday times, and even then it seems that some time had to elapse before the clumsy term 'other' was replaced by a more distinctive designation.

Not all the 142 Domesday names appear as the names of villages on the present-day map of Cambridgeshire. Some are represented by hamlets, by individual houses or by the names of topographical features. Thus Stuntney is now a hamlet in the parish of Ely Trinity, and not far away the Domesday island of *Haneia* appears as Henny Hill and Henny Farm in the parish of Soham.[2] On the island of Ely itself, *Helle* is now the hamlet of Hill Row in Haddenham, and *Lindone* appears as Linden End in the same parish. In the south of the county, *Sextone* is now represented by the hamlet of Saxon Street and by Saxton Hall, both in Woodditton; *Witeuulle* is Whitwell Farm in Barton;[3] *Bellingeham* is the hamlet of Badlingham in Chippenham; *Bercheham* is Barham Hall in Linton which, as we have seen, also contains the hamlet of Little Linton. The Domesday *Cloptune* has entirely disappeared and only a few mounds remain to mark its site; the territory of the former village has been amalgamated into the modern parish of Croydon cum Clopton.[4] The Domesday *Werateuuorde* has even more completely disappeared; the name as well as the village has gone, and its territory is now included partly in Orwell and partly in Wimpole.

On the other hand, there are a number of villages on the modern map that are not mentioned in the Domesday Book. Some of their names appear in pre-Domesday documents. Others are not recorded until the twelfth, thirteenth or even fourteenth century. On the upland, the

---

[1] F. W. Maitland, *Domesday Book and Beyond* (Cambridge, 1897), p. 14.

[2] The entry is: *Haneia est i insula in qua est terrae dimidia hida. Hoc geldum non dat nec unquam dedit T.R.E.* (192). One manuscript of the *I.E.* has: *nota de henney quod est parcella villae de Ely* (p. 119).

[3] A stage in the decline of Whitwell is indicated by a reference in 1316 to *Villa de Bertone cum Wytewell; Feudal Aids* (London, 1899), I, p. 153.

[4] See W. M. Palmer, 'A History of Clopton, Cambridgeshire', *Proc. Camb. Antiq. Soc.* (1933), XXXIII, pp. 3–60.

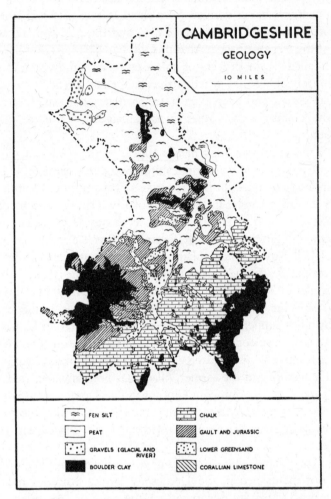

Fig. 74. Cambridgeshire: Surface geology.

Based on Geological Survey Quarter-Inch Sheets 12 and 16 together with the special Quarter-Inch 'Geological Map of the Country around Cambridge' produced by the Geological Survey on the occasion of the visit of the British Association to Cambridge in 1938. The boundary between Fen silt and peat is taken from the map accompanying S. B. J. Skertchly's *The Geology of the Fenland* (London, 1877). This boundary is 'very obscure, for the peat thins out insensibly...' (*op. cit.* p. 129).

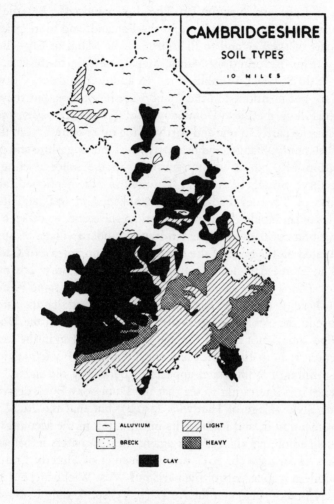

Fig. 75. Cambridgeshire: Soil types.

Redrawn from the map in *An Economic Survey of Agriculture in the Eastern Counties of England*, p. viii (Heffer, Cambridge, 1932). This is Report No. 19 of the Farm Economics Branch of the Department of Agriculture in the University of Cambridge.

names are scattered: Bartlow, Brinkley, Coton, Fen Ditton, Kneesworth, Landwade, Lode and Newton (in Thriplow hundred). But the greater number, as might be expected, are in the Fenland, and more particularly in that part of the Fenland to the north of the island of Ely—Benwick, Coveney, Elm, Leverington, Manea, Mepal, Newton-in-the-Isle, Parson Drove, Tydd St Giles, Wimblington. In addition to these, Outwell and Upwell are not mentioned in the Cambridgeshire folios, but they appear under Norfolk in the Little Domesday Book (*Wella, Utwella*), and today the parishes lie partly in one and partly in the other county. On the other side of the county, Stanground lies partly in Cambridgeshire and partly in Huntingdonshire, but it is only surveyed in the folios relating to the latter county. Strangely enough, Thorney is not mentioned, although the House of Thorney had been re-established in 972, and its abbot appears as a landholder both in Cambridgeshire and in other counties. An interesting curiosity is presented by the modern village of Stow cum Quy, situated on the edge of the Fenland to the north-east of Cambridge town. The Domesday Book makes no reference to Stow but mentions only Quy (*Coeia*); the *I.C.C.*, however, presents the same information under the heading *Choeie et Stoua* (p. 15), thus showing that the name Stow was in use in the eleventh century although not named in the Domesday Book. The same is not true of Carlton cum Willingham in the south-east of the county; both the *I.C.C.* and the Domesday Book mention only Carlton, although Willingham appears to be a very old name. On the other hand, it is interesting to see that the Domesday Book describes the Abbot of Ely's village of Hardwick (191b), but that the *I.C.C.* (p. 87) does not mention it, and includes its information in the account of Toft, which is an adjoining village.[1] Or again, the *I.E.* enters information for *Wicheham et Stratleie* (p. 103), and the hamlet of Streetly End appears on the modern map as part of the parish of West Wickham; but both the Domesday Book (191a) and the *I.C.C.* (p. 33) speak only of *Wicheham*.[2] Curiosities like this help to explain how names came to be omitted from the Survey.

The distribution of Domesday names was naturally very uneven in a county with such marked physical contrasts as Cambridgeshire (Fig. 76). The fen peat provided no stable foundations on which to build, and, consequently, the only villages here were those on the islands: Littleport,

---

[1] The *I.E.* (p. 110), however, mentions Hardwick.
[2] The *I.E.* summary on p. 168 mentions only *Stratleie*.

Whittlesey, Chatteris, March and Doddington, and, more especially, the large island of Ely.[1] The silt area of the northern Fenland, however, offered better opportunities for continuous settlement. It is true that, in Domesday times, Wisbech alone stood here, but in modern times the

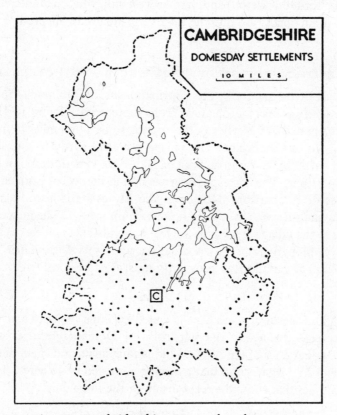

CAMBRIDGESHIRE
DOMESDAY SETTLEMENTS
10 MILES

Fig. 76. Cambridgeshire: Domesday place-names.

C indicates the Domesday borough of Cambridge. The
boundary of alluvium and peat is shown; see Fig. 74.

silt area bears a number of additional villages. On the upland in the south of the county, villages were fairly widespread, but there were some empty areas. The upper portions of the western clay plateau (above 200 ft.) were

[1] For the factors affecting the sites of villages, see John Jones: (1) *A Human Geography of Cambridgeshire* (London, 1924); (2) 'The Villages of Cambridgeshire', in *The Cambridge Region*, ed. H. C. Darby (Cambridge, 1938).

almost villageless. A noticeable empty area was the belt of chalk in the south-east of the county. Villages were to be found, however, in the south-westerly portion of the chalk belt, where it is crossed by the Cam and the Granta (e.g. the line of villages from Stapleford to Bartlow and from Shelford to Ickleton) and, farther west still, where a number of small streams drain northward into the Rhee (e.g. Meldreth, Shepreth, Foxton).

THE DISTRIBUTION OF PROSPERITY AND POPULATION

Some idea of the nature of the information in the Domesday folios for Cambridgeshire may be obtained from the entries relating to Hauxton which is situated in the valley of the Granta, some 3 or 4 miles to the south of the town of Cambridge. The village was held partly by the abbot of Ely and partly by Harduin de Scalers, and so the description of it appears in two portions. The corresponding version in the *I.C.C.* is given for the purposes of comparison. Moreover, the Ely estate is also described in the *I.E.*, and this version, too, is set out on pp. 278–9. The general items relating to the village as a whole are five in number: (1) hides, (2) plough-lands, (3) plough-teams, (4) population, and (5) values. Their bearing upon regional variations in prosperity must now be considered.

(1) *Hides*

The Cambridgeshire assessment is stated in terms of hides and virgates and, occasionally, acres. A comparison of Domesday entries with the corresponding ones of the *I.C.C.* demonstrates again and again that a hide consisted of 4 virgates and that a virgate consisted of 30 acres. Here are two examples that show the relationship of the three units:

	Domesday Book	I.C.C.
Comberton (Wetherley)	¼ hide minus 20 acres (202b)	1 virgate and 10 acres (p. 69)
East Hatley (Armingford)	1 hide and 3 virgates (194)	1½ hides and 1 virgate (p. 56)

The acres are, of course, not units of area, but geld acres, i.e. units of assessment.

It was while working on the Cambridgeshire returns that Round was led to the conclusion that the assessment of much of England was based upon a conventional unit of 5 hides. The importance of the 5-hide unit is apparent at once in the *I.C.C.* which, as we can see on p. 278, states the total assessment for each vill before recording the details of its constituent holdings; the assessment of vill after vill is entered either as 5 hides or a multiple of 5. In the Domesday Book itself, this feature is obvious only when a village consisted of 1 holding; thus Borough Green (Radfield) was held by Count Alan for 5 hides (195b) and Bottisham by Count Eustace for 10 hides (196a). The same feature can be seen, however, when the various holdings in some villages are assembled together from the different folios. Here, for example, are the 7 holdings in the village of Croydon in Armingford hundred:

	Hides	Virgates
(1) Earl Roger (193a)	—	3
(2) Count Alan (194a)	—	2½
(3) Count Alan (194a)	—	1
(4) Eudo (197b)	2	—
(5) Harduin de Scalers (198a)	3	1
(6) Picot of Cambridge (200b)	2 (less ½ virgate)	
(7) Picot of Cambridge (200b)	1	1
Total	10	0

We are able to see the 5-hide system so clearly in Cambridgeshire because the Domesday Book and the *I.C.C.* frequently supplement and correct each other. Thus the *I.C.C.* states that the village of Barrington (Wetherley) is assessed at 10 hides, but the total of its holdings, as entered in the Domesday Book, comes to 10 hides 1 virgate; this is because one Domesday holding is said to be 7 hides 2½ virgates (196b), whereas the *I.C.C.* enters it correctly as 7 hides 1½ virgates (p. 74). Or again, Haslingfield (also in Wetherley) is assessed in the *I.C.C.* at 20 hides (p. 72), but, in the Domesday Book, the sum of the holdings within the vill falls short of this amount by 1 hide 3 virgates and 3 acres because the Domesday scribe omitted to enter Guy de Raimbercurt's holding of this amount. Conversely, the Domesday Book supplies information about the royal estates which the *I.C.C.* omits. In the case of Haslingfield, for example, the *I.C.C.* does not mention the king's holding of 7 hides 1 virgate. It is the collation of the two accounts, in the Domesday Book and the *I.C.C.* respectively, that shows how the 20 hides of Haslingfield are made up. It is not surprising that in other counties without the counterpart of the *I.C.C.*, the presence of the 5-hide unit cannot be demonstrated with the same clarity as in Cambridgeshire. Even here, the holdings of some vills, both in the *I.C.C.* and in the Domesday Book, do not add up to the exact amount of the assessment. Thus for Litlington in Armingford there is 1 virgate too much (p. 59), and for Kingston in Longstow a quarter of a virgate too little (pp. 85–6).

There are, however, some Cambridgeshire villages that are assessed neither at 5 hides nor at some multiple of 5 hides. But Round carried his argument further, and demonstrated that the apparently irregular villages of some hundreds could be grouped into blocks which showed that the same principle of assessment was at work. Here are the assessments of the hundred of Wetherley, together with Round's comment:

Hidage of Hundred of Wetherley

Comberton	6	
Barton	7	20
Grantchester	7	
Haslingfield		20[1]
Harlton	5	
Barrington	10	20
Shepreth	5	
Orwell	4	
Wratworth	4	
Whitwell	4	20
Wimpole	4	
Arrington	4	

It is important to observe that, though the grouping is my own, the *order* of the Vills is exactly that which is given in the *Inq. Com. Cant.*, and by that order the grouping is confirmed. Note also how, without such grouping, we should have but a chaos of Vills, whereas, by its aid, from this chaos is evolved perfect symmetry. Lastly, glance at the four 'quarters' and see how variously they are subdivided.[2]

Similar arrangements can be demonstrated for other hundreds.

Here are the indications of what Round described as 'a vast system of artificial hidation'.[3] To each county was assigned a certain number of hides. A county then distributed its quota among its hundreds. Each

[1] This total is completed from the Domesday Book; see p. 275 above.
[2] J. H. Round, *op. cit.* pp. 47–8.
[3] *Ibid.* p. 49.

hundred in turn divided its responsibility among its vills on the basis of the 5-hide unit. Finally, the hides were allotted to the holdings within each vill. The origins of this system of taxation are obscure and wrapped in controversy, but its implications for an analysis of the Domesday Book are clear enough. The assessment was artificial and bore little or no relation to agricultural realities in 1086. We cannot say whether considerations of area and value had ever entered, in a very rough-and-ready way, into any of the various subdivisions of responsibility, but we can be sure enough that the Domesday statistics bear the unmistakable stamp of artificiality. Take, for instance, the hundred of Staines:

Hundred of Staines

Vill	Hides	Plough-lands
Bottisham	10	20
Swaffham Bulbeck	10	16
Swaffham Prior	10	$13\frac{1}{4}$
Wilbraham	10	25
Stow cum Quy	10	12
Totals	50	$86\frac{1}{4}$

The details for Swaffham have been divided between the two modern villages in the light of their post-Domesday history.[1] The vills are all assessed alike, yet they vary from 12 to 25 plough-lands. The same feature is seen when the hundred totals are compared. In the hundred of Chilford the ratio of plough-lands to hides is roughly 2:1, in Cheveley it is $1\frac{1}{2}$:1, in Whittlesford it is 1:1, in Northstow it is as low as $\frac{3}{4}$:1.

The present count, for the area covered by the modern county, has yielded a total of 1,308 hides for 1066.[2] In view of the discrepancies and inaccuracies of the text it is only rarely that the totals for the hundreds come to round figures. But quite apart from such discrepancies there is a big complication. The assessments of certain hundreds were reduced between 1066 and 1086. This reduction is recorded in the Domesday Book only where a vill was in the hands of a single tenant. Where a vill comprised a number of holdings, the reduction is apparent only in the *I.C.C.* The

---

[1] W. Farrer, *Feudal Cambridgeshire* (Cambridge, 1920), pp. 127–8.

[2] For the Domesday county, Corbett's figure was 1,317 and Maitland's was 1,233 plus another 100 for the borough—W. J. Corbett, 'The Tribal Hidage', *Trans. Roy. Hist. Soc.* (London, 1900), N.S. vol. XIV, p. 218; F. W. Maitland, *op. cit.* pp. 400 and 409.

HAUXTON

(in Thriplow Hundred)

A. *Domesday Book*

(1) *Abbot of Ely* (191). The manor of Hauxton is assessed at 8½ hides (*pro viii hidis et dimidia se defendit*). There is land for 12 ploughs. [There are] 5 hides in demesne, and there are 4 ploughs, and 16 villeins and 4 bordars with 8 ploughs. There [are] 3 serfs, and 2 mills worth (*de*) 50 shillings. Meadow for 4 ploughs. Pasture for the cattle of the vill. In all, it is and was worth £13. *T.R.E.* [it was worth] £14. This manor pertains (*iacet*) and always pertained (*iacuit*) to the demesne of the church of Ely.

(2) *Harduin de Scalers* (198). In Hauxton Harduin holds (*tenet*) 1½ hides. There is land for 2 ploughs, and they are there with 4 bordars. There are 1½ hides in demesne, and 1 mill worth 20 shillings. Meadow for 2 ploughs; pasture for the cattle of the vill. It is and was worth 60 shillings. *T.R.E.* [it was worth] £4. Bund held 3 virgates of this land from the abbot of Ely, and could sell (*vendere potuit*), but the soke remained to the abbot, and another sokeman of Earl Algar held 3 virgates and could depart with his land (*cum terra sua recedere potuit*).

B. *Inquisitio Comitatus Cantabrigiensis*

P. 47. In this hundred Hauxton was assessed at 10 hides (*pro x hidis se defendit*) *T.R.E.*, and [the same] now. Of these 10 hides the abbot of Ely holds 8½ hides. There is land for 12 ploughs, [and there are] 4 ploughs and 5 hides in demesne and 8 ploughs [belonging to] the villeins. [There are] 16 villeins, 2 bordars, 3 serfs; 2 mills worth 50 shillings. Meadow for 4 ploughs. Pasture for the cattle of the vill. [There are] 2 non-ploughing animals (*animalia ociosa*); 100 sheep; 38 pigs. In all it is worth £13, and when received, £13. *T.R.E.* [it was worth] £14. This manor pertains and always pertained to the demesne of the church of St Etheldreda of Ely. And of these 10 hides Harduin de Scalers holds 1½ hides from the King. There is land for 2 ploughs, and the ploughs are there, and 1½ hides in demesne. And there are 4 bordars, and 1 mill worth 20 shillings. Meadow for 2 ploughs; pasture for the cattle of the vill. [There are] 18 non-ploughing animals, 200 sheep less 4, 19 swine and 4 foals. In all it is worth 60 shillings, and when received, 60 shillings. *T.R.E.* [it was worth] £4. Bund held 3 virgates of this land from the abbot of Ely, [and] could depart (*potuit recedere*) to whom he would, and sell his land without the soke. And another sokeman held 3 virgates from Count Alan, [and] could give and sell [his land] to whom he would.

C. *Inquisitio Eliensis*

P. 106. In Hauxton the abbot of Ely holds 8½ hides. There is land for 12 ploughs, [and there are] 4 ploughs and 5 hides in demesne, and 8 ploughs [belonging to] the men. [There are] 16 villeins, 4 bordars, 3 serfs; 2 mills worth 50 shillings; meadow for 4 ploughs; pasture for the cattle of the vill; 2 non-ploughing animals, 100 sheep, 38 swine. In all it is worth £13; when received, £13. *T.R.E.* [it was worth] £14. This manor pertains and always pertained to the demesne of the church of St Etheldreda. In this vill Harduin holds 3 virgates. It is the land of a certain sokeman named Bund, which he held from the abbot of Ely *T.R.E.* [and] he was able to depart without permission [but] without the soke, and it is worth 40 shillings.

---

hundreds affected were Armingford, Longstow, Papworth, Northstow, Staploe and Cheveley. It is difficult to see why these particular hundreds should have been so treated. In Armingford, for example, a reduction of 20 per cent. was applied uniformly to all vills, so that a 5-hide vill was assessed at 4 hides in 1086. These complications only serve to emphasise once more the importance of the hundred in the assessment of the geld.[1]

(2) *Plough-lands*

The normal formula runs: 'there is land for n plough-teams' (*terra est n carucis*), and it then goes on to say how many teams were held in demesne and how many were held by the peasantry. The total number of plough-lands for the area covered by the modern county amounts to 1,693, as compared with 1,494⅛ plough-teams,[2] but the relation between the two figures varies a great deal in individual entries. Where the number of teams on a holding is less than that of the plough-lands, there is usually a statement to the effect that additional teams 'might be' or 'could be employed', either on the demesne or on the lands of the peasantry or on both. It says, in effect, that the land could carry more teams than were at work, and it indicates therefore the possibility of further cultivation. Here are some sample entries that illustrate the variety of phrasing:

(1) Duxford (Whittlesford). *Terra est v carucis. In dominio est i caruca et ii plus possunt esse, et iiii villani cum v bordarii habent ii carucas* (196b).

---

[1] For a discussion of the reduction, see L. F. Salzman, *V.C.H. Cambridge*, I, p. 342.
[2] We have assumed that plough-lands equalled teams (and potential teams) where a figure for the former is not given, e.g. for the vills in Domesday Essex. F. W. Maitland's figures for the Domesday county were 1,676 plough-lands and 1,443 plough-teams; *op. cit.* p. 401.

(2) Bassingbourn (Armingford). *Terra est iii carucis. In dominio i hida et ibi est i caruca. Ibi unus villanus et iiii bordarii cum i caruca et altera potest fieri* (190).

(3) Bourn (Longstow). *Terra est v carucis et dimidia. In dominio est i caruca et adhuc dimidia potest fieri. Ibi ix villani cum xiii bordarii habent iii carucas et iiiita [quarta] potest fieri* (195).

One of the entries for Fulbourn seems to emphasise the deficiency (191): there was land for 6 teams; the peasantry had 3, and the demesne could have carried another 3, but we are definitely told that the abbot of Ely had none (*ubi possunt esse iii carucae, sed nulla ibi habetur*).[1] The *potest fieri* formula, or one of its variants, is to be found in Domesday entries relating to about one-half of the 141 settlements of Cambridgeshire.[2] Even so, it is clear that the Domesday scribe occasionally omitted what he ought to have put in. Thus on an Ely manor at Cottenham there were 8 plough-lands and only 7 teams, but no reference is made to the possible addition of another team (191b). The *I.E.* version of the same entry (p. 114), however, supplies the missing information, and says that 'another could be employed (*aliaque potest fieri*)'.[3] The *I.C.C.* likewise supplies supplements to the Domesday accounts of holdings at Fulbourn (201b, p. 25) and Kirtling (202, p. 11).

There are entries in which the Domesday Book records the lack of plough-teams in another way. One of the holdings at Comberton had land for one plough, but the entry goes on to say that the team itself was not there, *Terra est i caruca sed non est ibi caruca* (201b); the *I.C.C.* version varies the phrasing by saying *Et caruca abest* (p. 69). Plough-lands in other villages were in a like plight, e.g. at Teversham (193b) and at about half a dozen other places as well. Quite often, however, especially on the smaller holdings, the Domesday text leaves us to assume the absence of teams. It merely says, as for Swavesey (197), 'There is land for one plough', and it omits any mention of teams that 'were not there' or that 'could be employed'. For most of these laconic entries, the *I.C.C.* and the *I.E.* versions (where available) agree with the Domesday text. But

[1] The *I.C.C.* says *iii carucae possunt fieri* (p. 26); and the *I.E.*, *non est caruca in dominio sed iii possunt fieri* (p. 102). It is interesting to note that another Fulbourn entry emphasises the presence of ploughs: *Terra est ibi vi carucae et ibi sunt* (190).

[2] It is interesting to note that where the Domesday Book and the *I.C.C.* enter *potest fieri* for Snailwell (199, p. 3), the *I.E.* enters *potest restaurari* (p. 101) which is reminiscent of some of the formulae of the Little Domesday Book.

[3] No account of Cottenham is available in the *I.C.C.*

not always. For one holding at Wendy, the Domesday text merely says: 'there is land for 3 oxen' (198); but the *I.C.C.* (p. 59) adds 'the oxen are there (*sunt boves*)'. And for another holding at Wratworth, where the Domesday merely records land for half a plough (194b), the *I.C.C.* adds 'and it is (*et est*)', presumably, there (p. 80). In these two instances, the Domesday text is apparently defective, and the number of teams has been omitted by accident not design;[1] but the omission is too frequent for us to suppose that it is generally the result of carelessness. We can only assume that most of these entries mean what they say, and that they indicate understocked holdings.

It is possible that the plough-land entry refers to conditions in 1066 and that the discrepancy between plough-lands and plough-teams indicates incomplete recovery after lean years when the land had been wasted or had gone out of cultivation. In most of these entries, the value shows a reduction between 1066 and 1086 which would support this contention. But, on the other hand, on some holdings the ploughs were fewer than the plough-lands, and yet the values had risen—which seems unlikely if the plough-land is taken as a measure of the arable of 1066. That was the situation on some holdings in the three villages of Abington, Bassingbourn and Balsham:

	Plough-lands	Plough-teams	Values		
			1066	Inter-mediate	1086
Abington (199b)	8	6	£6	£8	£8
Bassingbourn (194)	18	16	£26	£26	£30
Balsham (190b)	19	17	£12	£10	£17

This is not conclusive evidence because even when plough-lands and plough-teams are the same, the value fluctuates, being sometimes greater and sometimes less than in 1066. Whether the plough-land entry refers to conditions in 1066 or not, the fact of understocking remains. An estate deficient in teams was not being tilled up to capacity; the arable of 1086 was capable of extension.

On some estates, however, the reverse was true. There were more plough-teams than plough-lands. On one holding at Longstanton, for example, there were 5 plough-lands but as many as 8 teams, 2 on the

---

[1] The reverse is seen in an entry for Fulbourn. The Domesday Book says that there was land for 3 ploughs and that there were 3 ploughs (197); the *I.C.C.* merely says that there was land for 3 ploughs (p. 26).

demesne and 6 with the peasants (195). There was also an excess of teams at Barton (201b) and at Wilbraham (199b). The point is emphasised only occasionally, and the total number of teams is explicitly stated. This is so in the *I.C.C.* version of an entry relating to East Hatley in Armingford:[1]

Domesday Book (194). There is land for 3 ploughs. There is 1 plough on the demesne, and 2 villeins and 5 bordars with 3 ploughs. There [are] 3 serfs.

I.C.C. (p. 56). There is land for 3 ploughs, and 4 ploughs are there, 1 plough on the demesne [and] 3 ploughs with the villeins. 2 villeins, 6 bordars, 3 serfs.

In one of the entries for Shelford, likewise with excess teams, the Domesday text (198), as well as that of the *I.C.C.* (p. 48), states explicitly what the total number of teams was.

Sometimes it is the total of the actual and potential teams that is in excess of the plough-lands. The Domesday entry for Snailwell is incomplete (199), but the *I.C.C.* version says that there was land for 10 teams, that there were 2 teams in demesne and 8 with the peasants, and that yet another team could be added on the demesne (p. 3). Snailwell was an Ely manor and its description in the *I.E.* also mentions the extra team (p. 101).[2] The totals of actual and potential teams on holdings at Oakington (202b) and Wilbraham (189b) are likewise in excess of their respective plough-lands. Some of these figures, of course, may be scribal errors. How easy it would be to read 'vi' instead of 'iii' for Longstanton (195), or 'vii' instead of 'iiii' for Wilbraham (199b)! Indeed, there are entries where the *I.C.C.* corrects, or seems to correct, the Domesday figures. A Domesday entry for Toft says that there was land for 4 teams, and that there was 1 on the demesne and 4 with the peasants (194b); but the *I.C.C.* attributes only 3 teams to the peasants, which would make the sum correct (p. 87). Or again, at Woodditton, the Domesday Book says that there was land for 16 teams, and that there were 2 on the demesne and 3 with the peasantry, and that 13 others could be added (189b); but the *I.C.C.* correctly reads 11 instead of 13 (p. 10). The statistics for the Ely manor of

---

[1] As can be seen, the statistics for population in these two entries do not agree.

[2] There are slight differences in terminology between the three accounts. The Domesday Book says *iiicia potest fieri*; the *I.C.C.* says *tercia fieri potest*; while the *I.E.* says *adhuc potest una restaurari*, which is reminiscent of the East Anglian formula (see p. 165 above).

Horningsea are likewise confused; the three versions that are available do not agree with one another:

	Plough-lands	Demesne teams	Other teams	Total teams
Domesday Book (191)	17	8½	9	17½
I.C.C. (p. 28)	17	8	9	17
I.E. (p. 103)	17½	8½	9	17½

In one of the entries for another Ely holding at West Wickham, the Domesday Book and the *I.C.C.* agree, but the *I.E.* differs:

	Plough-lands	Demesne teams	Other teams	Total teams
Domesday Book (191)	4	2½	2	4½
I.C.C. (p. 33)	4	2½	2	4½
I.E. (p. 103)	4	2	2	4

Finally, an excess half-team appears in the *I.C.C.* account of a holding at Longstanton, but not in the Domesday version:

Domesday Book (201). There is land for 4 ploughs. There are 2 on the demesne, and 6 bordars with 5 cottars could have (*possunt habere*) 2 ploughs.

I.C.C. (p. 94). There is land for 4 ploughs. [There are] 2 ploughs on the demesne. And there could be (*possunt fieri*) 2 ploughs with the villeins. [There is] half a plough with the villeins. 6 bordars. 5 cottars.

The Domesday arithmetic is the neater. How the half-plough came to be entered in the *I.C.C.* we cannot say;[1] it may indicate that recovery had begun.

Thus of the Domesday entries that show excess teams, it is possible that some may be errors. In addition, there is the mysterious *I.C.C.* entry for Longstanton. Whatever be the explanation of this occasional over-stocking, the Cambridgeshire folios throw no more light on it than do those of Lincolnshire.[2] Over the county as a whole, there was a deficiency of teams in 29 per cent., and an excess in 2 per cent. of the entries which record both plough-lands and teams.

---

[1] There is also another instance of excess oxen in the *I.C.C.* account of Horseheath, but it seems to be an error. The Domesday version reads: *Terra est vi bobus. Ibi ii bordarii* (193b). But the *I.C.C.* version adds something: *vi bobus ibi est terra duo bordarii de ii carucis* (p. 30). Mr L. F. Salzman, in the *V.C.H. Cambridge*, I, p. 408, suggests that 'car" may be a mistake for 'acr/is'.   [2] See p. 41 above.

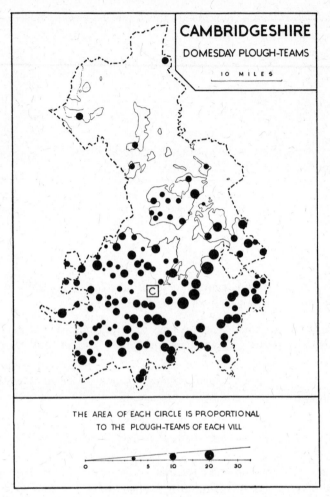

Fig. 77. Cambridgeshire: Domesday plough-teams
in 1086 (by settlements).

C indicates the Domesday borough of Cambridge. The
boundary of alluvium and peat is shown; see Fig. 74.

(3) *Plough-teams*

The Cambridgeshire entries for plough-teams, like those of other
counties, usually draw a distinction between the teams held on the
demesne and those held by the peasantry. The Domesday text describes

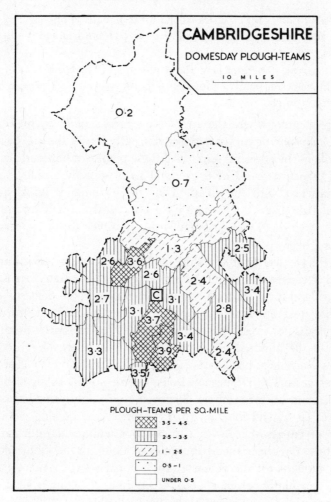

Fig. 78. Cambridgeshire: Domesday plough-teams
in 1086 (by densities).

C indicates the Domesday borough of Cambridge.

the latter as being held by so many villeins and bordars or cottars, but
the *I.C.C.* enters them as being 'with the villeins' irrespective of whether
the holding contained villeins or not. The contrast between the two
formulae may be seen, for example, in the account of Shingay.

Domesday Book (193). There is land for 6 ploughs. [There are] 3 hides in demesne and there are 2 ploughs. There [are] 11 bordars and 7 cottars with 4 ploughs.

I.C.C. (p. 59). There is land for 6 ploughs. [There are] 2 ploughs and 3 hides in demesne [and] 4 ploughs with the villeins (*iiii carucae villanis*). 11 bordars. 7 cottars.

Quite frequently, where the *I.C.C.* says *carucae villanis*, the *I.E.* says *carucae hominibus* or *carucae ad homines*. Obviously the *I.C.C.* uses the word 'villein' in a general sense. All these plough-teams were, as Round showed, standard teams of 8 oxen.[1] This is seen by a collation of the Domesday text with the *I.C.C.* Thus the Domesday Book speaks of 4 oxen at Babraham (202) where the *I.C.C.* speaks of half a plough-team (p. 37). And the Domesday half-team at Over (201) appears in the *I.C.C.* as 4 oxen (p. 92).

As we have seen in discussing plough-lands, there are a number of Domesday entries that seem to be defective or inaccurate. At Knapwell there was land for 8 teams; there were 2 teams on the demesne, but the Domesday text enters none for the peasants (192b). Unfortunately, Knapwell was not an Ely manor and there is a leaf missing from the *I.C.C.* account of the hundred in which it occurs; no alternative versions are therefore available to provide a check upon this omission which seems due to carelessness. The Domesday Book likewise omits to enter the teams of the peasants at, for example, Snailwell (199), but in this instance both the *I.C.C.* (p. 3) and the *I.E.* (p. 101) supply the missing details. In a number of entries the *I.C.C.* supplies not additional information but corrections. On one of the Ely holdings at Meldreth the Domesday Book enters 3 ploughs for the peasants (191), but the *I.C.C.* enters 5 ploughs which is apparently correct (p. 66); at any rate this figure is what the *I.E.* also gives (p. 108), and it makes the teams equal to the plough-lands. The *I.C.C.* likewise corrects the Domesday Book over the teams of Carlton (196, p. 21) and of a few other places. On occasion, the *I.C.C.* version only increases the confusion as may be seen from a comparison of the two versions for a holding at Harston. There were 9 plough-lands but the Domesday text accounts only for 8 teams, and the *I.C.C.* only for 6½:

Domesday Book (200). There is land for 9 ploughs. On the demesne 3 hides and there are 2 ploughs, and there might be (*potest fieri*) a third. Six villeins and 15 cottars have 4 ploughs and there could be a fifth.

[1] J. H. Round, *op. cit.* p. 35. See p. 44 above for a discussion of the equation.

I.C.C. (p. 45). There is land for 9 ploughs. [There are] 2 ploughs on the demesne and there could be (*potest fieri*) a third. And [there are] 3 hides on the demesne. And 3½ ploughs with the villeins, and 6 villeins and 15 cottars with their gardens (*de suis hortis*).

On other occasions, it is the Domesday Book that supplements or corrects the *I.C.C.*, e.g. at Isleham where the *I.C.C.* omits the demesne plough (199, p. 8), at Silverley where the *I.C.C.* omits the peasant ploughs (199b, p. 9), and elsewhere.

These omissions and mistakes illustrate the margin of error that must always be remembered when dealing with Domesday statistics. While the errors are important for individual localities, they amount to a small fraction of the 1,494⅛ teams recorded for the area covered by the modern county. Taken as a whole, the record of teams provides a reasonable index of the arable land of Cambridgeshire in the eleventh century.

(4) *Population*

The main bulk of the population was comprised in the five categories of villeins, bordars, cottars, serfs and sokemen. In addition to these main groups were the burgesses, together with a miscellaneous group that included fishermen and others. No freemen were recorded. The details of the groups are summarised on p. 292. Both the estimates of Sir Henry Ellis[1] and of the Rev. Bryan Walker[2] were made in terms of the Domesday county (not the modern one), and no strict comparison with the present count is therefore possible. In any case, one thing is certain; no one who counts Domesday population can claim definitive accuracy. Finally, one point must always be remembered. The figures presumably indicate heads of households. Whatever factor should be used to obtain the *actual* population from the *recorded* population, the proportions between different categories and between different areas remain unaffected.[3]

Half-villeins are entered for seven places, but in none of the entries is any clue given about the other half.[4] One of these places is Tadlow where

[1] Sir Henry Ellis, *A General Introduction to Domesday Book* (London, 1933), II, p. 428.

[2] Bryan Walker, 'On the Measurements and Valuations of the Domesday of Cambridgeshire', *Comm. Camb. Antiq. Soc.* (1886), v, p. 125.

[3] See p. 360 below for the position of the serfs.

[4] Half-villeins 'might mean a man holding half a villein tenement, or one whose land and services were shared between two estates' (*V.C.H. Cambridge*, I, p. 347). Half-villeins were recorded at Burwell (192b), Carlton (196a), Croydon (197b), Grantchester (196), Horseheath (199b), Tadlow (202), and Whaddon (194b).

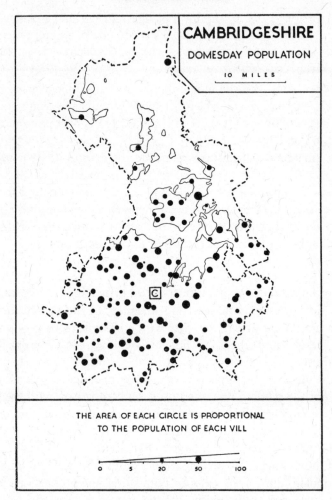

Fig. 79. Cambridgeshire: Domesday population
in 1086 (by settlements).

C indicates the Domesday borough of Cambridge. The
boundary of alluvium and peat is shown; see Fig. 74.

half a villein with 7 bordars had 1½ ploughs (202).[1] It is interesting to
note that for another of the three holdings at Tadlow, the Domesday text
simply speaks of villeins (200) where the *I.C.C.* reads '2½ villeins' (p. 52),

---

[1] The *I.C.C.* reads 1½ villeins and 6 bordars (p. 53).

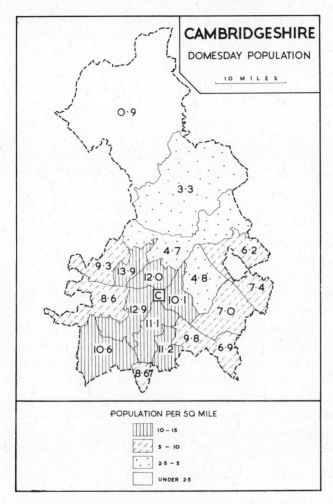

Fig. 80. Cambridgeshire: Domesday population
in 1086 (by densities).

C indicates the Domesday borough of Cambridge.

thus bringing the *I.C.C.* total of villeins in the village up to a whole
number. Another discrepancy can be seen in one of the entries for
Duxford; the Domesday text records '2 villeins, 6 bordars' (196), but the
I.C.C. version reads '2½ villeins and 5 bordars' (p. 41). Both bordars and
cottars are entered for some estates, but the distinction between them is

obscure.[1] Like the serfs they present no special features of interest for our purpose. For these four groups of people, the Domesday Book gives particulars relating only to 1086. The sokemen, however, are treated differently. In addition to the normal statement of their number in 1086, there is also another statement saying how many there had been in 1066. The contrast between the total sokemen in the county at these two dates is very striking. It is not possible, however, to be precise about the number of sokemen in 1066 because we cannot always be sure whether a sokeman recorded at a place in 1086 had also been there 20 years earlier. Occasionally, too, the details for 1066 are not clear.[2] But despite these doubts, it is obvious that there must have been between 800 and 900 sokemen in the county in 1066. Twenty years later, this figure had been reduced to only 176.[3] Thus on a manor at Meldreth there were 15 bordars, 3 cottars and 1 serf, but we are also told that there had been 16 sokemen there in 1066; these had disappeared, and were presumably represented among the bordars and cottars of 1086 (199b).[4] Or again, at Hinxton there were 20 villeins and 12 bordars in 1086, and there had been 20 sokemen in 1066 (200). It would be unsafe to assume, however, that the 20 sokemen had become the 20 villeins, for that would imply that there had been no villeins on the estate in 1066; but taking the sokemen as a class, it is clear that here too they had been displaced. In Maitland's words, 'Displacements such as this we may see in village after village. No one can read the survey of Cambridgeshire without seeing that the freer sorts of the peasantry have been thrust out, or rather thrust down'.[5]

[1] At Soham the Domesday text (190b) reads '10 bordars' where the *I.E.* reads '10 cottars' (p. 101); and at Whaddon the Domesday text reads '15 cottars' (191) where the *I.E.* reads '15 bordars' (p. 107). Or again where the Domesday Book (194b) enters 2 bordars at Barrington, the *I.C.C.* enters 3 cottars (p. 75).

For a discussion of the differences between bordars and cottars, see F. W. Maitland, *Domesday Book and Beyond*, pp. 38 et seq., and P. Vinogradoff, *English Society in the Eleventh Century*, pp. 456 et seq.

[2] Thus the *I.C.C.* says that 22 sokemen had been at Bourn in 1066 (p. 89), but this is not clear at first sight from the Domesday text itself (200b). At Comberton, on the other hand, the Domesday text specifically tells us of a sokeman who had not been there in 1066 (189b).

[3] Sir Henry Ellis estimated the sokemen of 1086 at 213, but Maitland thought that he had 'exaggerated' the number; *Domesday Book and Beyond*, p. 62. Mr L. F. Salzman made the total 169; *V.C.H. Cambridge*, I, p. 347.

[4] The Domesday text says 16 sokemen, but it is clear from what follows that 15 is meant; the *I.C.C.* says 15 (p. 65). See p. 291 below.

[5] F. W. Maitland, *Domesday Book and Beyond*, p. 63. See also L. F. Salzman in *V.C.H. Cambridge*, I, p. 347.

A few entries seem to be defective and contain no reference, or else only a vague reference, to population. There was, for example, one holding at Fordham where the sokemen had 3 ploughs (195 b), but we are not told how many sokemen there were; unfortunately no alternative version is available for this entry, either in the *I.C.C.* or the *I.E.* Or again at Ashley we are merely told that the villeins had 2 teams (199 b), and the *I.C.C.* version is equally vague (p. 10). In the same way both the Domesday (197) and the *I.C.C.* (p. 26) accounts of a holding at Fulbourn omit any reference to population despite the fact that there were three teams on the holding.[1] It looks as if the omissions must have been in the original returns. Sometimes, however, as we have seen in the case of Tadlow (200), the *I.C.C.* (p. 52) provides the missing information.[2] In this case, the Domesday scribe seems to have been conscious of the incomplete nature of his information because in the margin of the Domesday manuscript he wrote a note to remind him to look into the matter: *rq qot vill*, i.e. *require quot villani*. The *I.C.C.* version of this particular holding at Tadlow, although fuller, contains one error, for it speaks of 7 sokemen where the Domesday Book more correctly reads only 3; we can tell that the latter is the correct figure from other information in the entry. Conversely, in an entry relating to Meldreth the Domesday text speaks of 16 sokemen (199 b) where the *I.C.C.* more correctly reads 15 (p. 65). Minor differences of this kind are not unusual.[3] Finally, there are a number of small Domesday holdings that omit all reference to population in the same way that, as we have seen, they omit any mention of plough-teams.[4] It is impossible to be certain about the significance of all these omissions; but, taken as a whole, the population statistics of Cambridgeshire seem fairly straightforward, certainly more so than those of the Little Domesday Book. The various discrepancies that appear when they are collated with the *I.C.C.* and the *I.E.* are minor in character.

---

[1] The teams are mentioned only in the Domesday Book; see p. 281, n. 1 above.

[2] See p. 288 above.

[3] Thus there are two discrepancies in the entries for Kennett. The Domesday entry (196b) reads 7 villeins, 5 bordars, 12 serfs, for which the *I.C.C.* (p. 1) records 6 villeins, 1 priest, 12 serfs. The Domesday text appears to group the priest with the villeins while the *I.C.C.* omits the bordars. The priest in our count was at Chesterton (189b).

[4] At Pampisford there were five holdings ranging from 5 acres to 3 virgates, all without recorded population (197b, 198, 199, 200, 202). The three-virgate holding had 1 plough-land with 1 team together with 2 acres of meadow, and it was worth 10s. in 1086 as in 1066 (200).

Recorded Population of Cambridgeshire in 1086

A. Rural Population

Sokemen	177
Villeins	1,929
Bordars	1,400
Cottars	770
Serfs	539
Miscellaneous	34
Total	4,849

Details of Miscellaneous Rural Population

Fishermen	28
Milites francigenae	3
Francigenae	2
Priest	1
Total	34

B. Urban Population

CAMBRIDGE   324 *masurae* (? including 29 burgesses, 3 *francigenae*, 1 priest); 49 *masurae vastae*; 27 *domus destructae*.

(5) Values

The usual three sets of values are almost invariably entered for each holding. The values of the greater number of holdings had fallen between 1066 and 1086, but some had remained constant, and a number of holdings had even increased in value. Generally speaking, the more plough-lands and ploughs on an estate, the greater its value, but any attempt at detailed correlation breaks down; moreover, the value of an estate sometimes increased even when the number of ploughs fell below the number of plough-lands. It is possible, of course, that the variation in the arable land of a holding may not reflect the variation in its total resources. In any case, we are without a clue to the vicissitudes that lay behind these changes in value, and it is clear that the Cambridgeshire evidence does not throw light upon the exact significance attached to the Domesday 'value' of an estate.

Conditions in the following five villages indicate the kind of variation that is encountered:

Village	Plough-lands	Plough-teams	Values 1066	Values Inter-mediate	Values 1086
Bassingbourn					
i (190)	3	2	£3	£2	£3
ii (194)	18	16	£26	£26	£30
iii (198b)	1	1	£2	£1. 10s.	£1. 10s.
Woodditton					
i (189b)	16	5	£15	£15	£12
ii (195)	10	10	£7	£14	£10
Shingay (193)	6	6	£14	£7	£7
Eltisley (196)	9	9	£13	£13	£13
Cherry Hinton (193b)	13	13	£12	£18	£18

There are seven manors of the ancient demesne of King Edward for which further details are given.[1] Each of these in 1086 paid a sum varying from £10 to £25 together with a sum of £13. 8s. 4d. which represented the commuting of earlier renders in corn, honey and malt and other customary dues. The addition of these two sums gives each manor a very great 'value' in relation to its arable capacity.[2]

But if the Cambridgeshire values raise many problems, they are in one respect relatively straightforward. Almost every holding has a value attached to it. There are, it is true, some exceptions. Among the holdings at Histon, two were valued with adjoining villages, one (191b) with Impington (*est appreciata cum*), and the other (193) in Girton (*appreciata est in*). There were also 40 acres in Balsham which were valued 'with other land' (195b). Or again, there was a holding at Childerley valued in the neighbouring village of Lolworth (201b); and at Hinxton there was another which, we are told, was 'valued in Essex' (189b).[3] In Abington Pigotts there was land which 'lay in' or 'pertained to' (*iacet*) the adjoining village of Litlington and which was also valued there (190). But this was unusual, for we are normally given the value of a holding even if it 'pertained' elsewhere, e.g. on the same folio another holding is entered as pertaining to Litlington but it is separately valued. One of the entries for Conington is more explicit; we are told its soke pertained (*iacuit*) to Longstanton, but its value, too, is separately entered (197).

[1] Soham, Fordham, Isleham, Cheveley, Wilbraham, Haslingfield and Chesterton, all on fo. 189b.

[2] For a discussion of these payments see L. F. Salzman in *V.C.H. Cambridge*, I, p. 346.   [3] See p. 267 above.

The value of berewicks is likewise separately given, e.g. that of Hill which was a berewick of Linden (192). But although, in this respect, the 'values' of the Cambridgeshire holdings are more straightforward than those of Lincolnshire and also than many of those of Norfolk and Suffolk, the fact remains that the value entry for Cambridgeshire, as for other counties, is cloaked in much obscurity.

Conclusion

The sixteen hundreds of the county have been adopted as the main basis for constructing the density maps, but a number of modifications have been made. Along the edge of the Fenland many parishes stretch from the upland down to the fen, and portions of four hundreds have therefore been detached to form a fen margin zone, intermediate between upland and fenland. Even so, this still leaves a considerable stretch of fen within the 'upland' hundred of Staines, where the long narrow parishes make it difficult to divide the hundred. One of the fen margin hundreds is Chesterton, the rest of which has been amalgamated with Northstow, and the joint area has been divided into eastern and western portions. The two Domesday hundreds of Ely are intermixed, and their parishes have therefore been regrouped into northern and southern portions. In the south of the county, the hundred of Chilford has been divided into two; and, finally, the southern tip of the county, formerly in Essex, has been treated as a separate unit. The result of these modifications is nineteen units which form a rough-and-ready basis for distinguishing variations over the face of the county. This does not enable us to arrive at as perfect a regional division as a geographer would like, but we must be content with its limitations. The parishes of Radfield hundred, for example, stretch from the Boulder Clay in the south-east on to the chalk. But difficulties like this are inherent in plotting any statistical information upon a parish basis.

Of the five standard formulae, those relating to plough-teams and population are the most likely to reflect something of the distribution of wealth and prosperity throughout the county in 1086. Taken together, they supplement one another; and, when they are compared, certain common features stand out. The most prominent of these features is the contrast between the Fenland and the upland. In the northern fens, the densities of both teams and population are very low as might be expected (Figs. 78 and 80). As we have seen, many village names in this area do

not appear until post-Domesday times.[1] The figures for the southern
Fenland are relatively large because so much of the area is occupied by the
island of Ely, which stood out as a well-cultivated area amidst the undrained marsh. The figures for the fen margin zone are higher still. To the
south lies the mainland with the highest densities in the county. The
differences between fenland and upland are greater for plough-lands and
plough-teams than for population, and we may hazard a guess that the
non-agricultural occupations of the Fenland may account for its relatively
higher density of population. The following table compares the densities
per square mile for the three fenland units and for three representative
upland units:

	Plough-lands	Plough-teams	Population
Wisbech	0·15	0·15	0·89
Ely	0·73	0·69	3·3
Fen margin	1·4	1·3	4·7
Thriplow	4·0	3·7	11·1
Longstow	3·3	2·7	8·6
Wetherley	3·4	3·1	12·9

The plough-team densities of the upland (about 3 or 4 per square
mile) form a continuous belt with those of Suffolk on the east and with
those of Huntingdonshire on the west. The population densities of upland Cambridgeshire, however, are somewhat lower than those of the
adjoining parts of Suffolk. Both plough-team and population maps show
the superiority of the main valley of the Cam and its tributaries in the
middle portion of the upland. On either side there is a less prosperous
area that extends on to the Boulder Clay areas along the eastern and
western sides of the county. The densities for the hundred of Staines are
below those for the other upland hundreds because it includes a considerable stretch of fen.

Figs. 77 and 79 are supplementary to the density maps; but, as we have
seen, a few of the symbols should appear as two or more smaller symbols
because some Domesday names may have covered two or more separate
settlements, e.g. Great and Little Abington.[2] Fig. 81, showing the distribution of plough-lands, confirms in a general way the other two. Comparison of the plough-land and plough-team map shows that the land of
some hundreds was not being tilled up to capacity.

[1] See pp. 271–2 above.
[2] See p. 267 above.

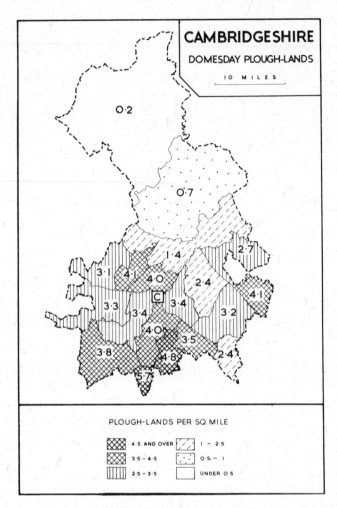

Fig. 81. Cambridgeshire: Domesday plough-
lands (by densities).

C indicates the Domesday borough of Cambridge.

WOODLAND

Types of entries

The wood entries in the Cambridgeshire folios are of two kinds. In the first place, the woodland of many villages was measured in terms of the swine for which it afforded pasture. The usual formula is the same as that in the Little Domesday Book, 'wood for *n* swine' (*silva n porcis* or *silva ad n porcos*), and the number recorded for each village varied from 4 swine at March up to 450 at Woodditton and 511 at Camps. The round figures of many entries suggest that they were estimates rather than precise amounts, but, on the other hand, there are detailed figures that suggest exactness (e.g. 4, 5, 11 and 12). The other type of wood entry merely indicates the presence of sufficient wood for 'making fences' or 'for the houses' or, in one entry, for fuel. The phrasing varies as the following examples show:

Childerley (190b)	*Nemus ad sepes.*
Clopton (197b)	*Nemus ad sepes reficiendas.*
Graveley (192b)	*Nemus ad sepes et domos.*
Bourn (195)	*Nemus ad domos et sepes.*
Elsworth (192b)	*Nemus ad domos curie.*
Croydon (200b)	*Nemus ad sepes reficiendas tantum.*
Orwell (198b)	*Nemus ad sepes claudendas.*
Toft (202b)	*Nemus ad sepes et ad focum.*
Wimpole (197b)	*Silva ad sepes.*
Stapleford (191)	*Silva ad sepes reficiendas.*

The *I.C.C.* sometimes enters *silva* where the Domesday Book enters *nemus*, e.g. at Wendy (194, p. 58), Arrington (193b, p. 77) and elsewhere. There are also other variants; thus in one entry for Orwell, the Domesday text reads *nemus ad sepes claudendas* (198b) where the *I.C.C.* reads *silva ad sepes reficiendas* (p. 78). Only occasionally the *I.C.C.* supplies what the Domesday Book leaves out. The *I.C.C.* version of a holding in Harlton speaks of *silva ad sepes reficiendas* (p. 74), but the corresponding Domesday entry makes no reference to wood (196a); the same addition also occurs in one of the *I.C.C.* entries for Tadlow (200, p. 52). With one exception, these 'fence and house' entries are never recorded for a village where there was wood for swine; the exception is Gamlingay where there was wood (*silva*) for 10 swine (197b) and also wood (*nemus*) for the fences (202).

In addition to these two main types, there are some miscellaneous entries. At Snailwell (199b), there was wood for fencing with 2 carts from the king's wood at Cheveley (*Silva ad clausuram cum duobus curribus de silva regis de chavelai*).[1] At Gransden (191b), there was wood for 60 swine as well as 2s. in customary dues from the wood (*et de consuetudine silvae ii solidi*). While both at Borough Green (195b) and at Kirtling (202) there was a park for wild beasts (*parcus bestiarum silvaticarum*).[2] Finally, the entries for Chishall and Heydon in the Essex folios are in terms of swine like those of Cambridgeshire except that 24 acres of wood are mentioned in the Heydon entry as belonging to the manor of Littlebury (vol. II, 19b).

Distribution of woodland

When plotted on a map, the two types of entry are seen to be characteristic of different areas (Fig. 82). Nearly all the upland villages with wood for swine are situated in the south-east of the county where there is a stretch of Boulder Clay lying at over 200 ft. above sea-level. This wooded area in Cambridgeshire formed an extension of the more densely wooded claylands of Suffolk and Essex. The villages with the 'fence and house' entries, on the other hand, lie on the western claylands of the county, also for the most part over 200 ft. above sea-level. The difference in the method of recording was certainly not due to the absence of swine in the west, for the stock entries of the *I.C.C.* record many swine in the hundreds of Longstow, Armingford and Wetherley. But, apparently, the woodland of this area was not dense enough to provide pasture for them, although it was sufficient for the miscellaneous needs of the inhabitants. There were, however, a few of these western villages with small amounts of wood for swine—Eltisley (20 swine), Gamlingay (10 swine) and Gransden (60 swine). All this lightly wooded western area adjoined the fairly light woodlands of south Huntingdonshire, where, however, the method of recording was different.[3] Between the eastern and western woodlands lay the great sweep of open chalk country. This was entirely without wood except for the solitary village of Stapleford where there was wood for repairing the fences.

---

[1] The corresponding *I.C.C.* entry runs: *silva est ad clausuram de duobus curribus. De dominica silva regis de cheveleie* (p. 3).

[2] The corresponding entries in the *I.C.C.* both for Borough Green (p. 20) and for Kirtling (p. 11) read *ferarum* for *bestiarum*.   [3] See p. 338 below.

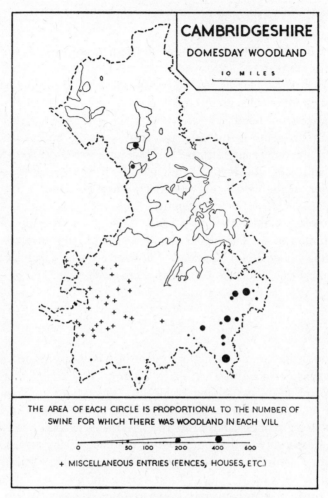

Fig. 82. Cambridgeshire: Domesday
woodland in 1086.

The boundary of alluvium and peat is shown; see Fig. 74.
Where the wood of a village is entered partly in terms of swine
and partly in some other way, only the swine are shown.

In the north of the county there was but little woodland in spite of the
fact that the fen islands are composed largely of clay (Gault or Boulder
Clay). Six villages alone had 'wood for swine'. Three of these stood on
the island of Ely: Downham with 100 swine, Wentworth with 20, and

Sutton with 5. On the other islands, Chatteris had wood for 120 swine, Doddington for 250 and March for 4.

These stretches of woodland—moderately heavy in the south-east, light in the south-west, and scattered on the fen islands—were relics of much wider areas. Dr P. H. Reaney's study of the place-names of Cambridgeshire enables us to compare the Domesday distribution with that of place-names and field-names that show the former presence of wood.[1] In the south-east, in the parishes along the Suffolk and Essex borders, there are many names incorporating *leah*, *(ge)haeg*, *ryding*, *stocking* and *holt*; the form of the villages here also seem to reflect colonisation of the woodland.[2] On the western clayland, too, there are similar place-name elements, together with many examples of *weald* (e.g. Croydon Wilds, Hatley Wilds). Finally, 'woodland terms are more common in the Isle of Ely than one would have suspected'. But most of this woodland on the island of Ely and elsewhere had disappeared by the time King William's Commissioners made their survey.

MEADOW

Types of entries

The Domesday meadow of Cambridgeshire is measured for the most part in terms of plough-teams, i.e. by stating the number of teams of 8 oxen the meadow was capable of feeding. The usual formula is *pratum n carucis* or *pratum n bobus*. The amount is always equal to or less than the number of plough-lands; there is never any excess. Occasionally, and more especially in the south-east of the county, the acre is used as the unit of measurement, *n acrae prati*. There are villages with meadow measured in both ways; thus at West Wickham there were 4½ acres of meadow (191, 198) and also meadow for 3 plough-teams (193b, 196b).[3]

---

[1] P. H. Reaney, *The Place-Names of Cambridgeshire and the Isle of Ely*, p. xxvi.

[2] Cyril Fox, *The Archaeology of the Cambridge Region* (Cambridge, 1923), p. 311.

[3] The meadow of the following places is entered in acres alone: Ashley (1 acre), Balsham (12), Borough Green (4), Silverley (1), Chishall (28), Heydon (8); the last two places are surveyed in the Essex folios and their meadow is therefore naturally recorded in terms of acres. The meadow of the following places is entered in both plough-teams and acres: Carlton (2 acres), Cottenham (5), Horseheath (4), Guilden Morden (1), Pampisford (2½), Papworth (10), Westley Waterless (2), Weston Colville (4), West Wickham (4½), West Wratting (8½). One of the holdings in Papworth is surveyed in the Huntingdonshire folios, and its meadow is therefore naturally recorded in terms of acres.

There was a very unusual entry for one of the holdings at Stetchworth, where the abbot of Ely had 'half a hide of meadow in demesne' (190b). Finally, profits were returned for two places. At Abington Pigotts (190) there was meadow for 5 ploughs and 2s.; and at Shingay (193) there was meadow for 6 ploughs, 'and 2 shillings from the rent of the meadow (*et de reddita prati ii solidi*)'.

It would greatly help our mapping if we could convert the plough-team measurements into acres, and so bring the Cambridgeshire meadow into line with that of the other eastern counties. At first sight it does seem as if this is possible, for there are three holdings in Radfield hundred where the meadow is measured differently in the Domesday Book and in the *I.C.C.*, and for one of them there is further confirmation in the *I.E.*

	Domesday Book	I.C.C.	I.E.
Westley Waterless (i)	2 oxen (190b)	2 acres (p. 19)	2 acres (p. 104)
" " (ii)	2 acres (202)	2 oxen (p. 19)	—
Borough Green	4 acres (195b)	4 oxen (p. 20)	—

Unfortunately this equation of 1 ox = 1 acre breaks down in an entry relating to Carlton; the Domesday text says 2 acres (202), but the *I.C.C.* says 1 plough (p. 20). As this only allows ¼ acre for an ox, Mr L. F. Salzman suggests that it is probably a mistake.[1] It is also possible that the substitution of 'acres' for 'oxen' in the other entries may have been due to slips of the pen. Nor does the duplicate entry relating to Shelford in the Domesday Book (190) and the Little Domesday Book (vol. 11, 7) help, for the other figures in these two entries also disagree.[2] On the basis of later evidence G. H. Fowler suggested that 3 acres of meadow provided sufficient meadow for 1 ox,[3] but this is not conclusive, and in view of these difficulties, no attempt has been made to convert the acres into teams on Fig. 83. Where the meadow of a village is entered partly in teams and partly in acres, the acres have been disregarded; but this cannot appreciably affect the map as the amounts involved are very small.[4]

[1] *V.C.H. Cambridge*, 1, p. 344.
[2] The Domesday entry is meadow for 4 ploughs; that of the Little Domesday Book is 15 acres of meadow. See *V.C.H. Essex*, 1, p. 338, and *V.C.H. Cambridge*, 1, p. 362.
[3] G. H. Fowler, *Bedfordshire in 1086* (Beds. Hist. Record Soc. 1922), pp. 61–2 and 106–7.
[4] See p. 300, n. 3 above.

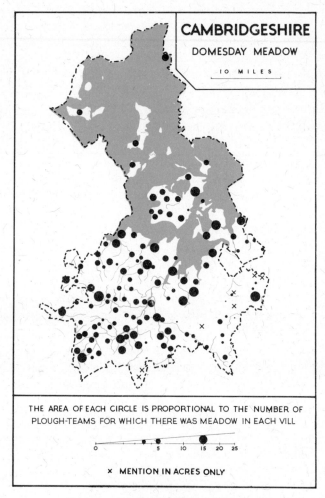

CAMBRIDGESHIRE

DOMESDAY MEADOW

10 MILES

THE AREA OF EACH CIRCLE IS PROPORTIONAL TO THE NUMBER OF
PLOUGH-TEAMS FOR WHICH THERE WAS MEADOW IN EACH VILL

0   5   10   15   20   25

× MENTION IN ACRES ONLY

Fig. 83. Cambridgeshire: Domesday
meadow in 1086.

The areas of alluvium and peat are indicated; see Fig. 74.
Rivers passing through these areas are not shown. Where the
meadow of a village is entered partly in terms of plough-teams
and partly in some other way, only the plough-teams are
shown.

Distribution of meadowland

The smallest amount of meadowland was to be found in two areas:
(1) in the south-east, on the dry chalk belt and in the densely wooded
area; (2) in the northern Fenland where there was most marsh. The
villages of the southern Fenland had substantial amounts of meadow,
which must have been located in the fens around the island of Ely.
Appreciable quantities, too, were to be found in some of the fen-margin
villages. But the greatest amount lay in the western part of the upland
along the Bourn Brook, along the River Cam or Rhee, and along the
small streams that flowed into the fens to the north-west of Cambridge.
To the south of Cambridge, the River Cam or Granta was also bordered
by substantial amounts; but the meadows of the Granta itself, in its
passage through places like Linton, Hildersham and Abington, seem to
have been relatively small.

PASTURE

Pasture is recorded for 74 out of the 142 Domesday settlements of
Cambridgeshire; this stands in contrast to the meadow entries which
occur for almost every settlement in the county. The usual formula is
the bare statement that there was 'pasture for the cattle of the vill
(*pastura ad pecuniam villae*).' There are, however, a number of variants
which are set out below:

(1) Abington (199b)   From the pasture 6 ploughshares (*soci*).[1]
(2) Balsham (190b)   From the pasture 32 pence.
(3) Camps (199b)   From the pasturage of the vill (*De herbagia villae*)
                            8 shillings.
(4) Cherry Hinton (193b)   Pasture for the cattle of the vill and 4 ploughshares.
(5) Croxton (202)   Pasture for the cattle, and from the pasturage
                            (*de herbagio*) 16 pence.
(6) Duxford (198)   From the pasture 1 ploughshare.
(7) Fowlmere (196b)   Pasture for the cattle of the vill and 10 pence.
(8) Trumpington (196b)   Pasture for the cattle of the vill and 4 ploughshares.
(9) Woodditton (189b)   Pasture for the cattle of the vill. Wood for
                            300 pigs. From the pasturage (*De herbagia*)
                            of the vill 6s. and 6d.

[1] The Domesday version is: *De pastura vi soc.*; that of the *I.C.C.* is: *Pastura reddit
v sochos* (p. 31). Another example of discrepancy between the two versions.

There is a curious entry for Hill, on the island of Ely, which says:
'Pasture for the cattle of the vill and from the port (*de portu*) 3 ploughshares' (192); but it is possible that *portu* is a misspelling for *pastura* or
herbagia. Finally, there is a reference to the common pasture (*communem
pasturam*) which Picot the Sheriff had taken from the burgesses at Cambridge (189). There are occasional discrepancies between the Domesday
text and the *I.C.C.*; thus one of the Domesday entries for Duxford
(196b) makes no reference to pasture, but the corresponding entry in the
I.C.C. says: 'From the pasture 1 ploughshare' (42).

The distribution of villages with pasture is fairly general and presents
no special features. One question that naturally arises is what of the
villages with no record of pasture. Did the fallow field together with the
hay from the meadow suffice for their stock.[1] It is impossible to say, but
it does seem unlikely that nearly one-half of the villages of the county
were without pasture. Mr L. F. Salzman's suggestion may well represent
the facts: 'Apparently there was rarely more pasture than was required
for the stock; it was therefore not a source of income and it is more likely
that it was omitted in many entries for that reason than that these estates
were carrying stock with no permanent pasture for their support.'[2]

FISHERIES AND MARSH

One of the outstanding characteristics of the Domesday folios for
Cambridgeshire is the frequent mention of fisheries (Fig. 84). They
reflect the wide extent of the undrained Fenland where fish were present
not only in great quantity but also in great variety.[3] The Domesday
entries, however, only distinguish eels which may have constituted the
most abundant species. Renders of eels are repeated again and again.
Sometimes they are described as being 'from the marsh (*de marescho*)',
more often 'from the fisheries (*de piscariis*)'. The render of 500 eels from
the marsh of Croxton (202) is specifically stated to be yearly (*per annum*).
A number of the renders were accompanied by money payments or
'presents'. Thus from one holding in the marsh at Cottenham (192b)

---

[1] Villages elsewhere with no pasture except upon the fallow field are recorded in
the early thirteenth century (1222) document known as the 'Domesday of St Paul's';
F. W. Maitland, *Domesday Book and Beyond*, pp. 399 n., 446.

[2] *V.C.H. Cambridge*, I, p. 344.

[3] Their variety as well as its quantity is clear from the Anglo-Norman compilation
known as the *Liber Eliensis* edited by E. O. Blake (London, 1962), pp. 180–1.

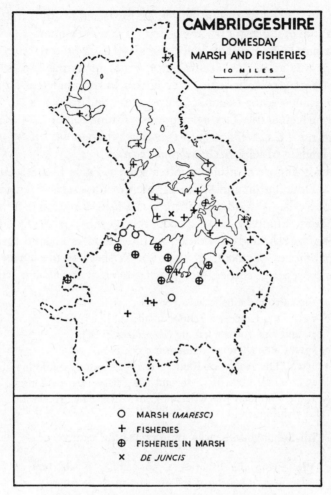

Fig. 84. Cambridgeshire: Domesday marsh
and fisheries in 1086.

The boundary of alluvium and peat is marked; see Fig. 74. For
the reference *de juncis* at Wilburton, see p. 307.

there came not only 500 eels but also a payment of 12*d*. (*et de presentatione
xii denarii*). From the marsh at Bottisham came not only 400 eels but
3 ploughshares (*soci*) as well (196); and in this connection it is interesting
to note that the Domesday account of one holding at Swaffham returns
6*d*. from the marsh (190b), whereas the *I.C.C.* version is 3 ploughshares

or 6d. (p. 13). The fisheries of Sutton, off the island of Ely, rendered not eels but a sum of money (44s.) alone (192). There are a number of variants in the formula. Occasionally, eels are entered as the return from a weir; thus there was a weir at Trumpington (200) rendering 450 eels (ccccl *anguillae de gurgite*). Or again, they appear as the render of a mill; the mill at Horningsea, for example, returned 10s. and 1000 eels (191). One of the Swaffham entries (190b) mentions a fishing toll of 6s. (*de theloneo retis*), and the *I.C.C.* version (p. 13) declares this amount of 6s. to come from the landing of ships (*de appulatione navium*).

The most important fishing centres seem to have been at Littleport, Stuntney, Doddington and Wisbech; each of these places returned well over 10,000 eels. At Littleport there was a fishery returning 17,000 eels (191b); from Stuntney came 24,000 eels (191b); from Doddington, 27,150 eels (191b); and in addition to these renders in kind there were substantial money payments as well. For Wisbech in the northern fens, there are six separate entries, each making reference to fishing activity:

(1) *Fo.* 192. From the fisheries 1,500 eels.
(2) *Fo.* 192. Two fishermen render to the Abbot [of Ely] 14,000 eels, and 13s. and 14d. for the tribute (*de presentatione*).
(3) *Fo.* 192. One fisherman rendering 5,000 eels.
(4) *Fo.* 192b. The Abbot of Ramsey has 8 fishermen rendering 5,260 eels.
(5) *Fo.* 193. The Abbot of Crowland has 3 fishermen rendering 4,000 eels.
(6) *Fo.* 196b. William [de Warenne] has 6 fishermen rendering 3,500 eels and 5 shillings.

Soham, with Soham Mere, was another fishing centre:

(1) *Fo.* 189. From the fisheries 3,500 eels.... There [are] 7 fishermen rendering to the king a tribute of fish three times yearly according to their ability (*quod possunt*).
(2) *Fo.* 190b. A boat which fishes in the mere by custom (*una navis quae piscatur in mara per consuetudinem*).
(3) *Fo.* 192. There is 1 fisherman having 1 net (*sagenam*) in the mere (*lacu*) of that vill.
(4) *Fo.* 195b. 1,500 eels and 1 net (*sagena*) in Soham Mere by custom.
(5) *Fo.* 195b. By custom 3 nets in Soham Mere (in entry for Wicken).

There were also fisheries at Ely itself (vol. I, 192; vol. II, 392), and, it would seem, a fishing boat (*navis ad piscandum*) which appears in a Lakenheath entry in the Suffolk folios (392).

Amongst the other fishing centres in the Fenland, mention must be made of Whittlesey; the entries are only two in number:

(1) *Fo.* 191 b. 2 shillings from the weir.
(2) *Fo.* 192 b. 4 shillings from the weir, and also (*praeter hoc*) 20 shillings from fish.

But this is explained by the fact that Whittlesey Mere itself was in the county of Huntingdon.[1] On the upland the render of 5,500 eels at Kirtling (202), in the east of the county, is surprisingly large for the upper reaches of the River Kennett are but small streams. On the western upland, the 500 eels annually from Croxton (202) are also a little unexpected, because the tributaries of the Huntingdonshire Ouse are likewise but small streams.

Not only fish, but many other resources—rushes, wildfowl and turf—must have formed, judging from later medieval documents, important items in the economy of the Fenland during the eleventh century.[2] But the only mention of these other products in the Domesday folios is the entry of '16 pence from the rushes (*de juncis xvi denarii*)' at Wilburton on the island of Ely (192). There are, however, three *de maresco* entries which make no mention of eels but merely return a money payment—25*d.* from the marsh at Cherry Hinton (193 b), 6*s.* 4*d.* from that at Over (192 b), and 6*s.* from that at Willingham (191 b). But whether these, or any of the other money payments, referred to anything other than eels we cannot say.

MILLS

Mills are mentioned as existing in 1086 in connection with 52 out of the 142 Domesday settlements in Cambridgeshire. Their annual value is normally stated, and this ranges from a mill yielding 12*d.* at Whaddon (194 b) to 2 mills yielding 100*s.* between them, apparently at Grantchester; they had been worth as much as £8 (194 b).[3] Many mills are valued at some multiple of 16*d.* which was the Danish *ora*; two of the mills at Steeple Morden are specifically stated to yield 2 *orae* (198).[4] In addition to money, a few mills rendered eels from the mill-pond as well; thus three of

[1] See p. 342 below.
[2] See H. C. Darby, *The Medieval Fenland*, p. 21.
[3] We cannot be certain that these were at Grantchester. The entry which mentions them starts off by saying *In hoc eodem hundredo*; the preceding entry, however, relates to Grantchester. There is no *I.C.C.* or *I.E.* version to provide a check.
[4] The frequency of this unit of 16*d.* is pointed out by Mr L. F. Salzman in *V.C.H. Cambridge*, I, p. 345.

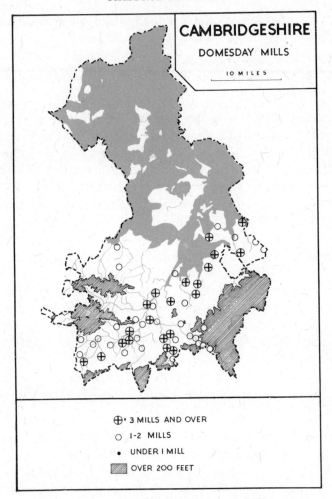

Fig. 85. Cambridgeshire: Domesday mills in 1086.

The areas of alluvium and peat are indicated; see Fig. 74.
Rivers passing through these areas are not shown.

the mills at Swaffham provided 29s. 8d. and 300 eels (196). At Shelford, two mills rendered 45s. and 2 pigs (191), which the *I.C.C.* (p. 48) explains by saying that '2 pigs are fattened from the mills (*ii porci impinguantur de molinis*)'.[1] In Cambridgeshire, unlike East Anglia, there is no mention of sites where mills had formerly existed, but both at Kennett (196b) and at

[1] The *I.E.* version is *et ii porcos pascere* (p. 107).

Lolworth (201) there was a mill worth nothing (*nil reddit*). At Duxford (196) there was a mill which was broken but which could be repaired (*modo confractum sed potest restaurari*).[1] A few mills were held jointly by a number of owners. The two landholders at Foxton, for example, each held half a mill worth 10s. 8d. (193, 197); or, again, at Isleham, the king held 3½ mills (189b) and the bishop of Rochester held another half-mill (190b). Sometimes, neighbouring villages seem to have shared a mill; thus there was half a mill at Harlton (196) which may have formed part of the 2½ mills at Barrington (193, 196b). On the other hand, there were 1½ mills at Melbourn (200),[2] and four mills and 'the sixth part of a mill' in the adjoining village of Shepreth (194b); but there is no clue to the missing fractions. These are rare examples; fractions of mills in Cambridgeshire do not present the problem they do in East Anglia. Most of the villages with mills had only one or two apiece, but there were some with three or four, and with even larger numbers, as the following table shows:

Domesday Mills in Cambridgeshire in 1086

Under 1 mill	1 settlement	4 mills	10 settlements
1 ,,	19 settlements	5 ,,	4 ,,
2 mills	11 ,,	8 ,,	1 settlement
3 ,,	6 ,,		

The group of eight was at Meldreth on the upper waters of the River Cam or Rhee. The groups of five were at Steeple Morden, Shepreth, Swaffham and at Cambridge town itself.

Fig. 85 shows the alignment of the mills along the upland streams of the Cam and the Granta. A number also lay along some of the smaller streams that flow into the Fenland to the east of Cambridge. The Fenland itself had no mills, and they were also absent from some of the upland hundreds. Thus the hundreds of Longstow and Cheveley had no mills, and Papworth and Radfield had only one mill apiece. Was the grain of their villages ground elsewhere, or by hand? Or is the Domesday record incomplete? These are questions we cannot answer.

[1] The *I.C.C.* version is *sed molendinum potest reedificari* (p. 42).
[2] The Domesday Book (200) assigns the half-mill to Meldreth, but the *I.C.C.* (p. 66) puts it under Melbourn where it obviously belongs.

CHURCHES

Churches are recorded for only three villages in Cambridgeshire—at Meldreth (198b), Shelford (191) and Teversham (201b). Each of the first two is entered as *monasterium*, but both the *I.C.C.* (p. 66) and the *I.E.* account (p. 109) of Meldreth use the word *ecclesia*. All three were on holdings formerly in the possession of the abbot of Ely. No values are associated with any of them. These can only be a very small fraction of the total number of churches in Domesday Cambridgeshire. Priests are very occasionally mentioned as landholders; there was a priest holding half a virgate at Pampisford (202) and another holding 15 acres at Oakington (191b), but there is no mention of a church in either of these places.

URBAN LIFE

The Domesday description of the county begins with an account of the borough (*burgum*) of Cambridge (189), which is the only place in the county for which burgesses are mentioned.[1] It was situated on the banks of the Cam where the fenland met the upland, and where there was a convenient ford that had been used by the Via Devana. It was assessed as a hundred, and it was divided into ten wards (*custodiae*); but the first ward had been reckoned as two in 1066—that was before 27 houses had been destroyed to make room for the castle. The list of wards omits the sixth, and the total number of messuages (*masurae*) in the rest amounted to 373 in 1066; this figure, apparently, does not include those on the site of the castle. Of the 373 messuages, 49 were waste (*wastae*) in 1086. The remainder (324) imply a population of at least 1,600 or so, probably more. The actual number of people mentioned in various contexts amounts only to 29 burgesses, 3 *francigenae* and 1 priest; no sokemen, villeins, bordars cottars or serfs are enumerated. The only hint of the town as a centre of jurisdiction is an incidental reference to 'lawmen (*lagemanni*)'. There is no mention of a market or a mint, nor is there any other indication of commercial activity.[2] The *I.E.* (p. 121) alone mentions a church.

But whatever the administrative and commercial functions of eleventh-century Cambridge, it clearly contained a large rural element. In 1066,

[1] For a full discussion of the problems raised by the Domesday entries for Cambridge town, see H. M. Cam, 'The Origin of the Borough of Cambridge', *Proc. Camb. Antiq. Soc.* (1935), XXXV, pp. 33–53.

[2] A mint had been established in Cambridge in pre-Conquest times; see A. Ballard, *Domesday Boroughs*, p. 118.

the burgesses used to lend the sheriff their plough-teams (*carucas*) three times a year; in 1086 these were demanded (*exiguntur*) nine times, but we are not told how many teams were involved. The sheriff, too, had deprived the burgesses of their common pasture, and he had also built 3 mills 'by which the pasture is taken up and many houses destroyed'. There were two other mills, and all five apparently yielded £9 a year. That is all we have to go on. But it does tell us something. As Mr L. F. Salzman has written, 'everything points to Cambridge being an agricultural community, as primitive as any county borough well could be'.[1]

LIVESTOCK

Both the *I.C.C.* and the *I.E.* record livestock on the demesne. The first entry in the *I.C.C.* relates to Kennett, and it specifically states 'livestock on the demesne (*pecunia in dominio*)'. The categories of livestock are those of the Little Domesday Book: non-ploughing cattle (*animalia ociosa*), sheep, swine, rounceys (*runcini*) and occasionally mares (*equae*) and foals (*pulli*). Other miscellaneous items include 24 unbroken mares (*equas silvaticas*) at Doddington (p. 116), and one lame mare (*una equa clauda*) at Wilburton (p. 117). Donkeys (*asini*) are occasionally mentioned; there were four, for example, at Eversden (p. 84). There was a mule (*unus mulus*) at Ickleton (p. 41), and at Clopton (p. 55) there was a *hercerarius*, which seems to have been an animal for harrowing. Goats are recorded for a few places in Chilford hundred, and also for Woodditton in Cheveley where there were 40 goats (p. 10). It is interesting to see that one reference to livestock has crept into the Domesday folios. At Abington, Aubrey de Vere had stolen, amongst other things, some 380 sheep, and he still retained them (190, repeated on 199b).

The following table summarises the stock on the demesne lands of the hundred of Whittlesford as recorded in the *I.C.C.* (pp. 38–43). No wood was recorded for the hundred, and no pasture except at Duxford:

	Animalia ociosa	Sheep	Swine	Rounceys	Etc.
Duxford	—	429	79	1	—
Hinxton	—	268	69	1	—
Ickleton	2	40	15	—	2 mares 1 mule
Sawston	13	178	61	1	—
Whittlesford	—	109	35	1	—

[1] *V.C.H. Cambridge*, I, p. 357.

No map of demesne livestock is feasible because, as we have seen, the *I.C.C.* does not cover the whole county, and it omits some of the royal estates even from the area it does cover.[1] The holding of Count Eustace in Duxford has no livestock entered for its demesne (pp. 41–2), but whether by design or accident we cannot say. Still, the figures for this sample hundred indicate the order of magnitude involved.

MISCELLANEOUS INFORMATION

Both at Borough Green (195b) and at Kirtling (202) there was a park for wild beasts (*parcus bestiarum silvaticarum*). Hives of bees, so numerous in the Little Domesday Book, do not appear, but at Histon (190b) there was a man of the abbot of Ely who rendered yearly a sester of honey (*in anno sextarium mellis*). At Ely itself (192) there were 3 arpents of vineyard (*ibi iii arpendi vineae*).[2] The Domesday account of Clopton (200b) mentions a close or garden (*ortus*). The word occurs again in the account of Cottenham (201b). The *I.C.C.*, however, very frequently mentions it in connection with cottars. Where, for example, the Domesday account of a holding at Harlton merely records 15 cottars (200), the *I.C.C.* (pp. 45–6) records '15 cottars with their gardens' (*de suis hortis*). There was a castle at Cambridge (189).

REGIONAL SUMMARY

The main regional contrast in Cambridgeshire is between fenland and upland (Fig. 74). The Fenland consists largely of peat, but there is a broad band of silt in the extreme north. The peat surface is relieved by clay islands, particularly by the island of Ely which rises to over 100 ft. above sea-level and which is large enough to support many villages. As might be expected, the general density of plough-teams and of population was very low throughout all the Fenland, and it was especially low in the extreme north where there were very few villages. Medieval colonisation had yet to change the character of the silt-lands. In the southern Fenland, the presence of cultivated and populated islands increased these densities very considerably. The clay surface of the islands carried a little wood, but, as place-name evidence shows, only a vestige of what had once existed. The villages of the fen islands and of the fen margins had some meadow, but their distinctive feature was the frequent presence of fisheries and

---

[1] See pp. 263 and 265 above.
[2] See p. 258 above.

fishermen. We are, however, left to guess at the other products of the Fenland, apart from the solitary mention of rushes at Wilburton, a village on the southern shore of the island of Ely.

The upland consists of two clay areas in east and west, separated by a belt of chalk country with lighter soils; and it is across this belt that the streams of the Cam-Granta system flow. The two clay areas coincide with the higher ground, and lie for the most part over 200 ft. above sea-level; much of the eastern area is over 300 ft. and in some isolated spots even over 400 ft. Villages were fairly frequently distributed over all the upland, but there were, and still are, villageless tracts along the chalk belt. The densities of teams and of population were very considerably higher than those of the Fenland, and they showed a tendency to be highest in the valley of the Cam-Granta system, and lowest on the clay-lands on either side. These two clay areas still carried relics of their former wood-cover; the wood of the western plateau was apparently light; that of the east was more abundant, and formed an outlier of the great Essex-Suffolk woodlands. Another feature of the eastern villages was the paucity of meadow compared with the other upland villages. The streams of the Cam-Granta system were marked by frequent mills, and also, in their lower reaches, by some fisheries.

BIBLIOGRAPHICAL NOTE

(1) An older edition of the Domesday text relating to Cambridgeshire is that produced by C. H. and H. G. Evelyn-White, *The Cambridgeshire portion of the Great Survey of England* (London, 1910). This first appeared in instalments in the *East Anglian* (Norwich, 1905–8), XI and XII. It consists of an introduction, an extended text and a translation; the last was the work of the Rev. William Bawdwen, made in the middle of the nineteenth century and presented to the British Museum (Additional MS. 27,769). It is not altogether reliable.

This has been superseded by the translation made by Miss Jocelyn Otway-Ruthven in *V.C.H. Cambridge* (Oxford, 1938), I, pp. 359–99. It is accompanied by a valuable introduction (pp. 335–57) by Mr L. F. Salzman.

(2) The following deal with various aspects:

B. WALKER, 'On the Measurements and Valuations of the Domesday of Cambridgeshire', *Comm. Camb. Antiq. Soc.* (Cambridge, 1886), v, pp. 93–129; this has a supplement containing a detailed tabular analysis, village by village, of the Cambridgeshire Domesday; see p. 13 above.

O. C. PELL, 'Upon Libere Tenentes, Virgatae and Carucae in Domesday...',
    Comm. Camb. Antiq. Soc. (1891), VI, pp. 17–40.

O. C. PELL, 'On the Domesday Geldable Hide...', *Comm. Camb. Antiq. Soc.*
    (1891), VI, pp. 65–176.

The strange ideas of Pell received the severest criticism, e.g. in J. H. Round's
Feudal England, p. 64.

H. M. CAM, 'The Origin of the Borough of Cambridge', *Proc. Camb. Antiq.*
    Soc. (1935), XXXV, pp. 33–53.

H. C. DARBY, 'The Domesday Geography of Cambridgeshire', *Proc. Camb.*
    Antiq. Soc. (1936), XXXVI, pp. 35–57.

H. C. DARBY, 'Domesday Cambridgeshire', *V.C.H. Cambridge* (Oxford, 1948),
    II, pp. 49–58.

E. MILLER, *The Abbey and Archbishopric of Ely* (Cambridge, 1951).

R. WELLDON FINN, 'Some Reflections on the Cambridgeshire Domesday',
    Proc. Camb. Antiq. Soc. (1960), LIII, pp. 29–38.

(3) *I.C.C.* was printed by N. E. S. A. Hamilton, *Inquisitio Comitatus Cantabrigiensis* (London, 1876), pp. 1–96. It was discussed in B. Walker's 'On the
Inquisitio Comitatus Cantabrigiensis', *Comm. Camb. Antiq. Soc.* (1891), VI,
pp. 45–64. But it was J. H. Round, in *Feudal England* (London, 1895), who
demonstrated its bearing upon Domesday interpretation; see p. 264 above.
It is discussed in many of the general works dealing with the Domesday Book
(see p. 22 above). There is a translation by Miss Jocelyn Otway-Ruthven in
V.C.H. Cambridge (Oxford, 1938), I, pp. 400–27.

(4) The *I.E.* was printed by Sir Henry Ellis in vol. IV of the *Libri Censualis
vocati Domesday Book* (London, 1816), pp. 497–528; see p. 22 above. It was
reprinted by N. E. S. A. Hamilton in *Inquisitio Comitatus Cantabrigiensis*, pp. 97–
195 and discussed by J. H. Round in *Feudal England*. It is also discussed in
many of the general works dealing with the Domesday Book (see p. 22 above),
but it still needs critical study.

See also R. WELLDON FINN, 'The Inquisitio Eliensis Re-considered', *Eng. Hist.*
    Rev. (1960), LXXV, pp. 385–409.

(5) A valuable aid to the Domesday study of the county is P. H. Reaney's
The Place-Names of Cambridgeshire (Cambridge, 1943).

CHAPTER VII

HUNTINGDONSHIRE

The Huntingdonshire folios raise few points that are of unusual interest in a geographical analysis of the Domesday Book. The county is a small one, and the entries, as Domesday entries go, seem relatively straightforward. It is true that a special feature of the Domesday description of the county is the presence of what amounts to an appendix dealing with matters in dispute. This is of great concern to students of law and administration, and has been discussed by Sir Frank Stenton,[1] but it adds nothing to a picture of the Huntingdonshire countryside in the eleventh century. Parts of the county were held by the abbey of Ely, and these holdings accordingly appear in the *Inquisitio Eliensis* (pp. 166–7) in a somewhat more detailed form than in the Domesday Book itself.[2] The holdings comprised the four manors of Bluntisham, Colne, Somersham and Spaldwick, together with the berewicks of Stow, Easton, Barham and Little Catworth belonging to Spaldwick. This limited material does not provide opportunity for extensive comparison, but it does provide some extremely interesting information that is discussed in the relevant sections below.

There is one complication, however, that must be mentioned. The modern county of Huntingdon does not correspond exactly with the area described in the Huntingdonshire folios. The Northamptonshire villages of Hargrave, Lutton, Luddington and Thurning are described partly under Northamptonshire and partly under Huntingdonshire; the last three still straddled the county boundary in the nineteenth century.[3] There was a similar intermixture along the Bedfordshire border. The Bedfordshire village of Keysoe is described partly under Bedfordshire (212b, 216b)

[1] F. M. Stenton in *V.C.H. Huntingdon* (London, 1926), I, p. 315.

[2] J. H. Round refused to express an opinion about the source of the Huntingdon section of the *I.E.*—whether or not it was derived from the original returns (*Feudal England*, p. 135). But Professor Galbraith suggests that it was 'derived from an intermediate or pre-Domesday return, analogous to Exon Domesday or to that for East Anglia of which Little Domesday is the fair copy', *Eng. Hist. Rev.* LVII, p. 168. The draft of the *I.E.* may have been revised in 1093—see pp. 99–101 above.

[3] *V.C.H. Huntingdon*, II, p. 104. The Domesday folios for the holdings in both counties are as follows: Hargrave, 204, 206, 226; Lutton, 204b, 221b, 222; Luddington, 206, 221b; Thurning, 204, 206, 221.

and partly under Huntingdonshire (205b, 207b), and the second of the Huntingdon entries says that a holding of one virgate 'lies in (*jacet in*) Bedfordshire, but gives geld in Huntingdonshire'. Pertenhall is wholly described under Huntingdonshire, but we are told that 'this land is

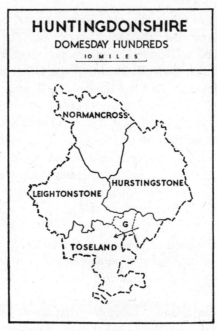

Fig. 86. Huntingdonshire: Domesday hundreds.

G indicates Godmanchester which according to the Domesday Book belonged to Leightonstone hundred (203b). It more naturally belongs to Toseland where subsequent documents place it. Its inclusion in Domesday Leightonstone may simply have been an error.

   The soke of a manor in Gidding is said to lie 'in the hundred of Cresseuelle'. This mysterious hundred was apparently obsolete by 1086 and is not mentioned again. The Domesday Book also mentions a number of places in a hundred of Kimbolton. It likewise never appears again, and all the places are included in Leightonstone; see F. M. Stenton in *V.C.H. Huntingdon*, i, pp. 318–19.

situated in (*Haec terra sita est in*) Bedfordshire, but renders geld and service in Huntingdonshire' (203b, 208); Swineshead was transferred from Huntingdonshire to Bedfordshire in 1888, and so is described in the Huntingdon folios (205b, 206); Everton was rather different in character in that it straddled the county boundary and so was naturally named in both counties (207, 217b). Along the eastern boundary, one holding in the Cambridge village of Papworth is described in the Huntingdon folios (206b).[1] There are also some examples of the reverse, of holdings in Huntingdonshire villages entered among folios relating to other counties. Thus one holding in Catworth (222) and another in Stibbington (229) and two each in Elton (221, 222) and Winwick (221b, 228) are described in the Northamptonshire folios.[2] Tilbrook is entirely surveyed in the Bedford folios (211b), for it was transferred to Huntingdonshire as late as 1888. Finally, one-sixth of a hide belonging to Easton, a berewick of Spaldwick, is said to pay geld in Bedfordshire (288). Thus we see that, while some of these anomalies are due to nothing other than subsequent modifications in the county boundaries, there are some which reflect ancient tenurial or fiscal arrangements.[3]

SETTLEMENTS AND THEIR DISTRIBUTION

The total number of separate places mentioned for Huntingdonshire seems to be approximately 83. This figure, however, may not be quite accurate because, today, there are some instances of two or more adjoining villages bearing the same surname, and it is not always clear whether more than one existed in the eleventh century. Only where there is specific mention of a second village in the Domesday Book itself has it been included in the total of 83. Thus the separate existence of Hemingford Abbots and Hemingford Grey in the eleventh century is indicated by the mention of *Emingeforde* and *Alia Emingeforde*, and of Catworth and Little Catworth by the mention of *Cateuuorde* and *Parva* or *Alia Cateuuorde*. There is, on the other hand, no indication that, say, the Orton Longueville and Orton Waterville of today existed as separate villages; the Domesday information about them is entered under one name only, though there may well have been separate settlements in the eleventh century.

Not all the 83 Domesday names appear as the names of villages on the present-day map of Huntingdonshire. Thus Dillington is a hamlet in Great Staughton; Botolph Bridge is another in Orton Longueville. Boughton is a third, partly in Southoe and partly in Diddington;[4] Perry is yet

---

[1] The Cambridge folios are 195, 196b, 197b, 199, 199b, 201.

[2] *V.C.H. Northampton* (London, 1902), I, pp. 313, 316, 318, 350, 356. It is interesting to note that eight little detached portions of Northamptonshire are marked on older maps as being in the parish of Catworth; *V.C.H. Huntingdon*, III, p. 29.

[3] *V.C.H. Huntingdon*, I, p. 322.   [4] *Ibid.* II, pp. 347, 351.

another, partly in Grafham and partly in Great Staughton (East and West Perry),[1] and Little Catworth is now another hamlet in the parish of Catworth itself.[2] The modern parish of Sibson cum Stibbington illustrates a stage in these amalgamations; the two names are entered separately in the Domesday Book, but the villages seem to have become amalgamated at an early date.[3] One Domesday settlement, that of *Cotes*, has ceased to be even a hamlet, and has been identified with land in Eynesbury and St Neots.[4]

On the other hand, there are a number of villages on the modern map that are not mentioned in the Domesday Book, and whose names do not appear until later in the Middle Ages. Their territories must have been surveyed with those of neighbouring villages. Thus the earliest record of Hilton comes from 1196, and it seems to have been part of Fenstanton until it was made into a separate parish as late as 1873.[5] The names of the modern parish of Pidley cum Fenton are likewise not mentioned, and do not appear until 1228 and 1236 respectively; previous to these dates they seem to have been part of Somersham.[6] King's Ripton was described in 1279 as 'a hamlet belonging to Hartford', and it must have been included in the Domesday description of Hartford.[7] Earith, first mentioned in 1244, must likewise have been included with Bluntisham.[8] Or again, the names of Old Hurst and Wood Hurst do not appear until after Domesday times, and they must have formed part of the 20-hide manor of St Ives.[9] The information about churches seems to suggest that some Domesday names may have covered more than one settlement.[10]

An interesting example of Domesday silence is to be seen in the entry relating to Paxton (207). This large manor was assessed at 25 hides and included land for as many as 41 plough-teams. Interlined above the name is the phrase *cum Berewitis iii,* but we are not told the names of these three berewicks whose resources were thus reckoned with those of Paxton itself. Later evidence, however, indicates that two of the berewicks were the villages of Toseland and Little Paxton. The third is uncertain, and it may have been either the village of Abbotsley or of Buckworth or the hamlet of Agden (in Great Staughton).[11] Perhaps an even more interesting

[1] *V.C.H. Huntingdon,* II, p. 356; III, p. 60.   [2] *Ibid.* III, p. 28.   [3] *Ibid.* III, p.217.
[4] *Ibid.* II, p. 276. But for an identification with Cotton Farm in Offord Darcy, see A. Mawer and F. M. Stenton, *The Place-Names of Bedfordshire and Huntingdonshire* (Cambridge, 1926), p. 263.   [5] *Ibid.* II, p. 315.   [6] *Ibid.* II, p. 185.   [7] *Ibid.* II, p. 207.   [8] *Ibid.* II, p. 153.   [9] *Ibid.* II, pp. 181, 250.   [10] See p. 346, n. 2 below.
[11] *Ibid.* II, p. 328.

example of the silence of the Domesday Book is provided by the entry relating to Spaldwick, a manor assessed at 15 hides and including land for 15 plough-teams (204). Fortunately, Spaldwick belonged to the monastery

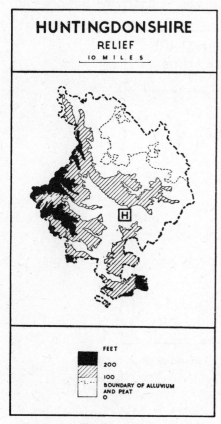

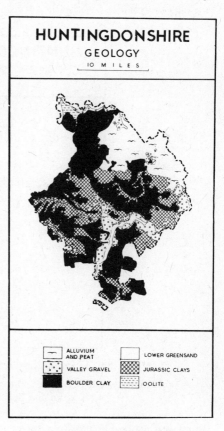

Fig. 87. Huntingdonshire: Relief.
H indicates the Domesday borough
of Huntingdon.

Fig. 88. Huntingdonshire:
Surface geology.

Based on Geological Survey Quarter-Inch
Sheets 12 and 16, and One-Inch (New
Series) Sheets 171, 186 and 187.

of Ely, and the corresponding entry in the *I.E.* mentions the fact that the totals for Spaldwick include the three berewicks of Stow, Barham and Easton (p. 166). All three are now separate parishes, but none of them is mentioned in the main body of the Domesday text; Easton alone is

mentioned in the appendix on disputed claims (208).[1] Then, again, there
are yet other modern villages which we know existed in the eleventh
century although they are not mentioned in the Domesday Book. Thus
we can search the Domesday folios in vain to find Little Raveley and

Fig. 89. Huntingdonshire: Domesday place-names.

H indicates the Domesday borough of Huntingdon. The boundary
of alluvium and peat is shown; see Fig. 88.

Bury, but a pre-Domesday charter of 974 speaks of *Wicstoue cum Roflea,
et Byrig, berewicis suis*.[2] The details for Little Raveley and Bury are
presumably entered in the Domesday totals for Wistow. Another

---

[1] Some confusion has arisen about Easton (*Estone*). There are a number of entries
relating to an *Estone* in the Bedfordshire folios, and Round suggested that these referred
to the Huntingdonshire village; *V.C.H. Bedford*, I, p. 215; see also *V.C.H. Huntingdon*,
I, p. 322. But 'there is no doubt that "Estone", Beds, was Little Staughton' in that
county; *V.C.H. Huntingdon*, III, p. 42. The Easton of the appendix and of the *I.E.*
belonged to the abbey of Ely's manor of Spaldwick, and refers to the Huntingdonshire
village.

[2] *Cartularium Monasterii de Rameseia* (ed. W. H. Hart and P. A. Lyons, Rolls
Series, 1886), II, p. 56. See also *V.C.H. Huntingdon*, II, pp. 164, 201, 247.

village that finds no mention in the Domesday Book is Great Raveley, but the same charter of 974 speaks of *rus illud Upwode nominatur, cum Rorflea berewico suo*;[1] the Domesday survey of Upwood thus seems to include more than the present village of that name. These various examples of concealed villages in the Domesday Book suggest village colonisation; the outlying hamlets had not achieved the dignity of separate units by 1086.[2] There is one other omission that must be mentioned—Ramsey itself. The abbey had been founded in 969, and its abbot appears as the landholder of many Domesday estates, yet there is no mention of the monks and their agricultural activities, nor indeed any mention of a settlement at Ramsey. It may have formed part of Wistow or of Bury, or it may have been omitted because of special rights exercised by the abbot.[3]

There are no special features about the general distribution of Domesday names in Huntingdonshire beyond the contrast between upland and fenland (Fig. 89). Villages are fairly frequent on the former, but the peat fen of the latter is devoid of names, and in this respect resembles the adjoining Fenland of Cambridgeshire.

THE DISTRIBUTION OF PROSPERITY AND POPULATION

Some idea of the nature of the information conveyed by the Huntingdonshire folios may be obtained from the entry relating to Buckden in the hundred of Toseland (203 b). As it was held entirely by the bishop of Lincoln, it is covered by a single entry:

In Buckden the bishop of Lincoln had 20 hides [assessed] to the geld (*xx hidas ad geldum*). Land for 20 ploughs. There [are] now 5 ploughs on the demesne, and 37 villeins and 20 bordars having (*habentes*) 14 ploughs. There [is] a church and a priest and one mill [rendering] 30s., and 84 acres of meadow. Wood for pannage one league in length and one in breadth. T.R.E. it was worth 20 *li.*, now 16 *li.* and 10s.

The general items relating to the village as a whole are five in number: (1) hides, (2) plough-lands, (3) plough-teams, (4) population, and (5) values. Their bearing upon regional variations in prosperity must now

---

[1] *Cartularium Mon. de Ram.* II, p. 55. See also *V.C.H. Huntingdon*, II, pp. 198, 238.
[2] For a discussion of this point see Cyril Fox, *Archaeology of the Cambridge Region*, (Cambridge, 1923), p. 310.
[3] *V.C.H. Huntingdon*, II, pp. 188 and 193.

be considered. Reference must also be made to the measurements given for the few villages that appear in the *I.E.*

(1) *Hides*

In Huntingdonshire as in Cambridgeshire there is strong evidence of the artificial character of the assessment and of the 5-hide unit. Seventeen villages in the modern county were rated at 5 hides, nine at 10 hides, five at 15 hides, and six at 20 or more hides.[1] This means that nearly one-half the villages in the county were assessed either at 5 hides or at some multiple of 5; there were, moreover, a few villages at 2½ hides each, and the town of Huntingdon at 50 hides. Frequently, the 5-hide unit is at once apparent because a number of villages each consisted of one holding only; thus the first village described in the Huntingdon folios was the royal manor of Hartford assessed at 15 hides. But where a village was divided amongst a number of lords, the same feature is often apparent when the entries are assembled, as the following two examples will show:

	STILTON			WARESLEY	
	Hides	Virgates		Hides	Virgates
(i) King (203b)		3	(i) Suain (205b)	7	0
(ii) Bishop of Lincoln (203b)	2	0	(ii) Eustace (206b)		2
(iii) Eustace (206)	2	1	(iii) William (207)	2	2
	5	0		10	0

In the light of the artificial nature of this imposition, it is obvious that the hidage can in no way reflect the agrarian realities of a district. 'It is, indeed, probable enough', writes Sir Frank Stenton, 'that when the assessment of a county was first established, the attempt was made to adjust the assessment of each village to its arable capacity, to provide that a village which contained land for ten eight-ox plough-teams should pay twice as much geld as a village which contained land for only five. But it is quite certain that only the roughest of correspondences between assessment and arable capacity was ever attempted, and it is also clear that by the date of Domesday any correspondence which may originally have been established had become seriously distorted by the growth of some villages and the decay of others.'[2]

---

[1] The figures for the Domesday county are different, but they bear out the same general point; see *V.C.H. Huntingdon*, I, p. 316.

[2] *V.C.H. Huntingdon*, I, p. 316.

The hidage totals for the area covered by the modern county are summarised in the table on p. 325. As is explained in the underline to the table, these totals are not exactly the same as those of the Domesday county, but the differences are not great, and the hidage of each hundred seems to be round about 200. Sir Frank Stenton has pointed out that these figures raise a 'strong presumption' that the Domesday county was assessed at 800 hides, divided equally between the four hundreds.[1] This presumption is supported by the fact that we are definitely told that the borough of Huntingdon once paid geld 'for 50 hides as the fourth part of Hurstingstone hundred' (203). The fact that some hundreds are more and others less than 200 hides may be the result of arrangements that are completely lost to us, e.g. a village in one hundred may, for some local reason, have paid geld in another. It may be interesting to note in this connection that, for example, Spaldwick (Leightonstone) is entered under Hurstingstone (204), which strongly suggests an error on the part of the scribe.

The picture of the Huntingdonshire assessment must be completed by reference to a curious entry for Sawtry in Normancross (207b); no hides are mentioned, but we are told that Aluuine had half a carucate assessed to the geld (*dim' car' ad gld*), and, incidentally, had land for 6 oxen. The other holdings in Sawtry are assessed normally in terms of hides.

(2) *Plough-lands*

With plough-lands we seem to be on firmer ground. The normal formula runs: 'land for *n* plough-teams' (*terra n carucis*), but the corresponding entry in the short Huntingdon section of the *I.E.* has variants of this phrase. For Spaldwick the phrase is *xv carucae possunt arare terram istam* (p. 166), and for some other places the variant is *ad arandum x carucae* (p. 167). It is difficult to say whether in Huntingdonshire, as in Lincolnshire, an artificial element enters into these estimates of plough-lands.[2] Roughly speaking, in one out of every five entries for Huntingdonshire, the number of plough-lands is the same as the number of hides, but it may well be that this correspondence represents no more than the ordinary chances of agreement between the two figures. There is apparently no

---

[1] *V.C.H. Huntingdon*, 1, p. 320.
[2] See p. 42 above. For the suggestion that the Huntingdonshire plough-lands represent an earlier assessment, see Cyril Hart, 'The hidation of Huntingdonshire', *Proc. Camb. Antiq. Soc.* (1968), LXI, pp. 55–66.

reason to believe that the number of plough-lands does not measure the cultivable land on each holding. One peculiarity about the relation of plough-lands to hides must be noted. At the end of the account of the borough of Huntingdon there is a statement to the effect that 'in Hursting-stone Hundred, demesne plough-lands are exempt from the king's geld' (203). Almost all the entries for the hundred bear this out; thus the manor of Upwood was assessed at 10 hides and there was land for 16 ploughs there but, we are told, the abbey of Ramsey had 'land for 3 ploughs in demesne apart from the aforesaid hides' (204). The reason for this exemption must remain a matter for conjecture. There are occasional exemptions of a similar character in other hundreds, e.g. at Elton in Normancross (204b), but this large-scale series of exemptions in Hurstingstone 'remains a striking fact, and is in sharp contrast to the occasional character of similar exemptions recorded elsewhere in Domesday'.[1]

Generally speaking, the number of plough-teams on an estate corresponded very roughly with the number of plough-lands. Sometimes it was the same, more often it was somewhat smaller, and occasionally it was considerably smaller. At Haddon in Normancross, there was land for 12 ploughs, and there were 8 at work there (205), while at Godman-chester there was land for as many as 57 ploughs, but there were only 26 there (203b).[2] The arable land of these and similar estates was, presumably, not being tilled up to full capacity. It is impossible to say whether the number of plough-lands represents conditions in 1066, and the number of ploughs those in 1086. Changes in the values of estates do not throw any light on the problem. On those estates with fewer ploughs than plough-lands, it is true that the values sometimes fell, but quite often they remained the same, or occasionally increased, as the following examples show:

	Plough-lands	Plough-teams	Values	
			1066	1086
Old Weston (204b)	13	9	£10	£10
Coppingford (205b)	5	4	£4	£4
Glatton (205)	24	16	£10	£10
Diddington (207)	3¾	2	£2	£3

[1] F. M. Stenton in *V.C.H. Huntingdon*, I, p. 323. See also J. H. Round, 'Danegeld and the Finance of Domesday', in *Domesday Studies*, ed. P. E. Dove (London, 1888), I, pp. 96–7, 107–8.
[2] This is a curious entry: 14 hides, 57 plough-lands, 26 plough-teams, worth £40 in both 1066 and 1086. Very possibly it is a scribal error.

This is not conclusive evidence because other considerations apart from amount of arable land entered into the value of an estate, and even when ploughs and plough-lands were equal, the value sometimes fluctuated.

Hides, Plough-lands, Plough-teams and Population
in Huntingdonshire

	Hides	Plough-lands	Teams	Population
Normancross	188	285	228	526
Hurstingstone	187	238	192	599
Leightonstone	203	278	313	744
Toseland	227	380	290	667
Total	805	1,181	1,023	2,536

Note

(1) The figures are given to the nearest whole number.

(2) In this table Godmanchester is included in Toseland as on the density maps (Figs. 91, 93 and 94). The figures for Godmanchester are: 14 hides; 57 ploughlands; 26 plough-teams; 97 people (203 b).

(3) The modern county boundary has been adopted as the basis of the table, e.g. the village of Tilbrook has been transferred from Bedfordshire to Leightonstone, and certain places in Domesday Huntingdonshire have been excluded (see pp. 315–17). This means that the figures are not exactly the same as for the Domesday county. Sir Frank Stenton's totals, based on the Domesday county, are as follows (the 14 hides of Godmanchester are included in Leightonstone):

Normancross	188 hides	Leightonstone	220½ hides
Hurstingstone	137¼ ,,	Toseland	214 ,,

The total for the Domesday county amounts therefore to 759¾ hides plus the 50 hides laid on the borough of Huntingdon as part of Hurstingstone hundred; see *V.C.H. Huntingdon*, I, pp. 319–20. Corbett's total for the Domesday county was 817¼ hides, and that of Maitland was 797—W. J. Corbett, 'The Tribal Hidage', *Trans. Roy. Hist. Soc.* (1900), N.S. vol. xiv, p. 218; F. W. Maitland, *op. cit.* pp. 400 and 409.

(4) F. W. Maitland (*op. cit.* p. 400–1) counted 1,120 plough-lands and 967 plough-teams for the Domesday county. Maitland's count, like the present one, was on the basis of 8 oxen to a team—see p. 44 above.

Sometimes, the number of ploughs on an estate exceeded the number of its plough-lands. Denton (Normancross) was assessed at 5 hides, and had land for 2 ploughs, but there were 6 ploughs at work, 1 on the demesne and 5 held by the peasantry (203 b). Or again, at Molesworth in Leightonstone there were 6 ploughs on an estate that contained arable land for only 4 (fo. 206 b). The phrasing of one of the entries relating to Elton, in the Northamptonshire folios, is interesting, and it may indicate that excess of oxen did not pass unnoticed by the Domesday scribe: 'There is land for half a plough. Nevertheless (*Tamen*) 2 villeins have one plough there' (222). Examples of excess ploughs could be multiplied, but the Huntingdonshire evidence throws no more light on this problem of surplus teams than does that of Cambridgeshire and Lincolnshire. The total number of plough-lands is considerably greater than that of teams, as the table on p. 325 shows. Every now and then there are what appear to be defective entries that mention ploughs but make no reference to plough-lands, e.g. at Hamerton (205 b) and Gidding (207), both in Leightonstone. In these cases, the number of plough-lands has been assumed to be equal to the number of ploughs. Over the county as a whole, there was a deficiency of teams in 63 per cent. of the entries, and an excess in 20 per cent. of the entries which record both plough-lands and teams.

(3) *Plough-teams*

The entries for plough-teams and oxen seem fairly straightforward, and, like those of other counties, a distinction is usually drawn between the teams held on the demesne of an estate and those held by the peasantry. There are a few minor departures from the normal formula, and some of these are mentioned below:

(1) At *Grafham* in Leightonstone (206) a certain Oilard the larderer held land of Eustace the Sheriff, and he 'ploughs there (*arat ibi*) with 6 oxen'. No plough-lands are mentioned in this entry.

(2) At *Orton* in Normancross (206), one man held '3 oxen in a plough (*iii boves in caruca*)', and another held 5 oxen similarly.

(3) At *Stilton* in Normancross (206) one man held '6 oxen ploughing (*vi boves arantes*)'.

A few entries seem to be incomplete, and do not mention plough-teams. In the account of Stanground in Normancross, for example, there is a short blank in the manuscript, and we are not told how many teams were worked by the 16 villeins and 6 bordars of the estate (205). Or again, there was land for one plough on a holding at Woolley, but no plough-

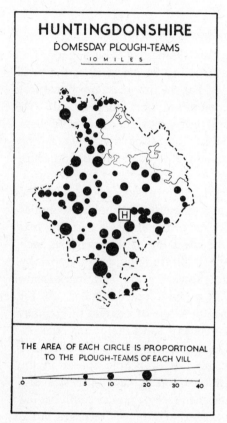

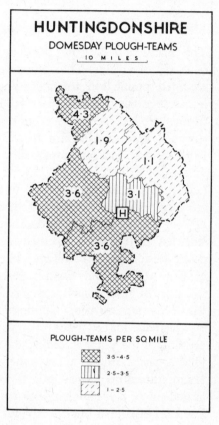

Fig. 90. Huntingdonshire: Domesday plough-teams in 1086 (by settlements).

H indicates the Domesday borough of Huntingdon. The boundary of alluvium and peat is shown; see Fig. 88.

Fig..91. Huntingdonshire: Domesday plough-teams in 1086 (by densities).

H indicates the Domesday borough of Huntingdon.

teams or men are recorded as being there (206); there may, of course, have been no ploughs there, but this seems strange because some other holdings without teams are described as being waste.[1] But despite these

---

[1] See p. 344 below.

perplexities, the evidence afforded by the plough-team statistics seems to provide a reasonable index of the agricultural resources of the Huntingdonshire villages in the eleventh century.

(4) *Population*

The main bulk of the population of Domesday Huntingdonshire consisted of villeins. They amounted to nearly 80 per cent. of the total recorded population for the county. Far below these in numerical importance came the bordars who comprised only 16 per cent. No freemen are recorded for the county, and only 52 sokemen; but 33 of these sokemen are recorded not in the Huntingdonshire folios but in the Bedfordshire and Northamptonshire folios relating to the Huntingdonshire villages of Tilbrook (211 b), Catworth (222), Elton (221) and Winwick (221 b). There is nothing for Huntingdonshire to correspond with the information about sokemen in 1066 that is given for the adjoining counties of Bedfordshire and Cambridgeshire. One of the entries for Orton, it is true, has an interlined statement to the effect that 7 sokemen had been there, presumably in 1066 (206), but that is all. Judging from the analogy of Bedfordshire and Cambridgeshire, however, the Huntingdonshire sokemen of 1086 constituted a relic of a much larger number. As Sir Frank Stenton has said, 'Huntingdonshire is one of a group of counties in which the higher grades of peasant society had suffered material depression in the years preceding the Domesday inquiry'.[1] In addition to villeins and bordars, a few other categories of people appear in the Huntingdonshire folios—priests mentioned on p. 346, burgesses discussed on p. 347, together with 5 fishermen (see p. 342), 1 smith having five acres of land at Buckworth (205 b), 1 serf at Winwick recorded in the Northamptonshire folios (228), and 8 men at Catworth (206b).[2] A few entries contain no reference to population, e.g. at Woolley (206); but it is impossible to be certain about the significance of these omissions.

The details of these groups are summarised on p. 329. Tenants-in-chief and under-tenants have been omitted for the reasons stated on pp. 51–4. Partly for this reason, and partly because it has been made in terms of the modern county boundary, this estimate is not strictly comparable with

---

[1]　*V.C.H. Huntingdon*, I, p. 324.

[2]　The text runs: *ibi sunt viii homines et sub eis vii bordarii*. It is interesting to note that there had been 8 thegns here in 1066.

Recorded Population of Huntingdonshire in 1086

A. Rural Population

Sokemen	52
Villeins	1,938
Bordars	483
Serf	1
Miscellaneous	62
Total	2,536

Details of Miscellaneous Rural Population

Priests . . .	48	Fishermen . .	5	
Men (*homines*) . .	8	Smith . . .	1	
		Total . .	62	

B. Urban Population

Bordars and fishermen are also included above.

HUNTINGDON   256 burgesses; 100 bordars; 3 fishermen; 21 *mansiones quae modo abest*; 112 *mansiones wastae*.

those of Sir Henry Ellis[1] and Sir Frank Stenton.[2] Finally, one point must always be remembered. The figures presumably indicate heads of households. Whatever factor should be used to obtain the *actual* population from the recorded population, the proportions between different categories and between different areas remain unaffected.[3]

One very interesting feature emerges when the Domesday population is compared with that of the *I.E.* The latter gives information for the time of Abbot Thurstan(1066) as well as for that of Abbot Symeon(1086 or after),[4] and, as we have seen, it covers the manors of Bluntisham, Colne, Somersham and Spaldwick. The later figures agree with those of the Domesday Book with the exception of those relating to Somersham, but it is only

[1] Sir Henry Ellis, *A General Introduction to Domesday Book* (London, 1833), II, p. 458; Ellis' grand total for the county came to 2,914; this figure included 22 sokemen, 1,933 villeins and 490 bordars. The figure for bordars presumably included the 100 in Huntingdon, unlike Sir Frank Stenton's estimate; see next note.

[2] Sir Frank Stenton says that 'the Huntingdonshire Domesday records 21 sokemen, 1,929 villeins and 384 *bordarii*'; *V.C.H. Huntingdon*, I, p. 324.

[3] See p. 360 below for the position of the serfs.   [4] See pp. 99–101 above.

fair to say that the Somersham entry as a whole appears to be confused. These facts, however, do not exhaust the interest of the *I.E.* as far as the population of Huntingdonshire is concerned. The main text of the *I.E.*

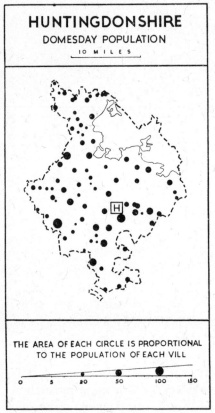

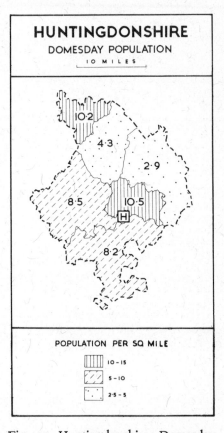

Fig. 92. Huntingdonshire: Domesday population in 1086 (by settlements).

H indicates the Domesday borough of Huntingdon. The boundary of alluvium and peat is shown; see Fig. 88.

Fig. 93. Huntingdonshire: Domesday population in 1086 (by densities).

H indicates the Domesday borough of Huntingdon.

is followed by a series of documents that includes an abstract setting out the teams and population of many of the Ely estates. The figures for the Huntingdonshire villages likewise agree with those of the Domesday Book, again with the exception of Somersham. But, surprisingly enough, they also record the existence of serfs in these villages as in those of other eastern counties (p. 169). The details are set out in the table below. Although they were omitted from the main text of the *I.E.* as from the Domesday Book itself, the mention of these serfs raises the question whether, after all, Huntingdonshire may have had serfs just as its neighbours Cambridgeshire and Northamptonshire had. And, if this is so, can we be sure that there were not some serfs even in the 'free' county of Lincolnshire, where, again, the Domesday Book mentions none? Taking the last column of the table, there are 16 serfs out of a total recorded population of 148, which is just under 11 per cent. It is perhaps not fair to regard this as a random sample, but we can at any rate note that the percentage is approximately the same as those for Cambridgeshire (11·4 per cent.) and Northamptonshire (10·1 per cent.).

Huntingdonshire: Domesday Book and I.E. population figures

| | *I.E.* Main version | | Domesday | |
	1066	1086 or after	Book	*I.E.* Summary
Colne	19 villeins	13 villeins	13 villeins	13 villeins
	5 bordars	5 bordars	5 bordars	5 bordars
				3 serfs
Bluntisham	20 villeins	10 villeins	10 villeins	10 villeins
	5 bordars	3 bordars	3 bordars	3 bordars
				3 serfs
Somersham	28 villeins*	Omitted	32 villeins	28 villeins
	9 bordars	13 bordars	9 bordars	13 bordars
				4 serfs
Spaldwick	42 villeins	50 villeins	50 villeins	50 villeins
	8 bordars	10 bordars	10 bordars	10 bordars
				6 serfs
Catworth†	8 villeins	7 villeins‡	7 villeins	Omitted

* Another MS. has 29 villeins.
† Catworth was a berewick of Spaldwick.
‡ Another MS. has 8 villeins.

(5) *Values*

The value of a Domesday holding is usually given both for 1066 and 1086, but not for an intermediate date as in some counties. On very many holdings, the value in 1086 is the same as in 1066. Occasionally, the value in 1086 only is entered, and we are left to conjecture whether this was also the value in 1066, e.g. in a few entries on fo. 205 b. The values of most holdings had fallen since 1066; some had remained the same, and only on a few had there been an increase. The difficulty that arises over the values of the Lincolnshire sokelands does not seem to be acute here. In Huntingdonshire, a parcel of sokeland normally has a separate value entered for it. It is true that there are occasional obscurities. On fo. 205 b, for example, the manor of Kimbolton had sokeland in four other places; three of these have values attached to them, but one is without any statement about value. Why this should be so we cannot say. Nor can we be sure whether or not the three values that are stated have been included in the total value for the manor of Kimbolton. If the Domesday Book were only a little less telegraphic in form, many of these difficulties would disappear. Thus an Ely estate in Little Catworth is said to be a berewick of Spaldwick (204). No value is entered for it, but we can assume that this is included in the total value for Spaldwick. That this assumption is correct is shown by the additional information provided by the *I.E.*: *hoc est appretiata in spalduuic* (p. 167).

The Huntingdonshire 'values' share the general difficulties raised by all Domesday values. Generally speaking, the more plough-lands and ploughs on an estate, the greater its value, but any attempt at detailed correlation breaks down. Moreover, as we have seen, the value of an estate sometimes increased even when the number of ploughs was below that of plough-lands.[1]

(6) *Measurements*

As we have seen, one of the peculiarities of the Norfolk and Suffolk folios is the systematic appearance of a general statement giving the linear measurements of a holding.[2] Only occasionally are similar measurements given for isolated holdings in other counties, e.g. in Lincolnshire.[3] Such a feature does not appear either regularly or sporadically for Huntingdonshire. That the information may have been generally included in the original returns seems, however, to be indicated by the fact that it is entered for the four Huntingdonshire manors of the *I.E.* (pp. 166–7):

(1) Spaldwick	*Totum iii leugae longo et ii leugae lato.*	
(2) Colne	*Totum ii leugae longitudinis et i leuga latitudinis.*	
(3) Bluntisham	*Totum ii leugae longo et i lato.*	
(4) Somersham	*Totum iii leugae longo et i leuga lato.*	

[1] See table on p. 324 above.
See pp. 119 and 175 above.　　　　　　[3] See pp. 46–7 above.

The wood in Spaldwick was recorded in terms of acres; that of the other three places by means of linear dimensions. Colne also had marsh measured in the same way, so that its linear measurements were as follows: total 2 × 1 league; wood 1 × ½ league; marsh 1 × ¼ league. The rest of the holding must therefore have amounted to 1 × 1 league, but it is difficult to envisage what any of these figures mean. Even had the measurements been available for all the manors of Huntingdonshire, they would have given us no more help than did the corresponding ones for Norfolk and Suffolk.

Conclusion

The four hundreds of the county have been adopted as the main basis for constructing the density maps, but a few modifications have been made. In the first place, the two hundreds of Normancross and Hursting-stone have each been divided into two, an upland and a fenland portion. In the second place, the large parish of Godmanchester has been trans-ferred from Leightonstone to Toseland with which it more conveniently falls by geographical position. The result of these modifications is six units which form convenient entities for the purpose of calculation.

Of the five recurring standard formulae, the two that seem most faith-fully to reflect geographical realities are those relating to plough-teams and population. Neither is without some of the uncertainties common to all Domesday statistics; but when the information is plotted, the two maps confirm each other in a general way (Figs. 91 and 93). The territory of the fen-line villages stands out as an area of low densities; the densities of the fen portion of Normancross are higher than those of the Hursting-stone fenland because the parishes of the former unit include so much upland. The adjoining upland shows no great regional variations because the county is so small and the general character of its upland so uniform. Toseland and Leightonstone, each with an average of 3·6 teams per square mile, stand below the upland portion of Normancross with 4·1 teams; so does upland Hurstingstone with 3·2 teams. The real interest of the two maps is, perhaps, the comparison they afford with the corresponding maps of other counties. The heavy Huntingdonshire claylands carried as much arable land as the adjoining upland of Cambridgeshire, and as much as a great part of East Anglia. The population map, likewise, shows similar densities to those of the neighbouring parts of Cambridgeshire.

Figs. 90 and 92 are supplementary to the density maps; but, as we have seen, a few of the symbols should appear as two or more smaller symbols, because some separate settlements were grouped together for the purposes of the survey. The map showing the distribution of plough-lands (Fig. 94) confirms in a general way the other two. Comparison of the plough-land and plough-team map shows that there was still arable land to be occupied in many parts of the county.

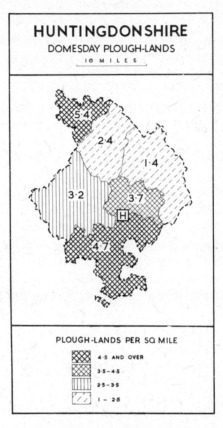

Fig. 94. Huntingdonshire: Domesday plough-lands (by densities).

H indicates the Domesday borough of Huntingdon.

WOODLAND

Types of entries

The amount of woodland on a holding in Huntingdonshire is usually measured in terms of linear dimensions. The entry for Bluntisham is characteristic (204): 'Wood for pannage, 1 league in length and 4 furlongs in breadth (*Silva pastilis i leuga longa et iiii quarentenis lata*).' The length of a Domesday league (*leuca*, *leuga* or *leuua*) has been a matter for much discussion. The twelfth-century Register of Battle Abbey in Sussex stated that a league comprised 12 *quarentenae* or furlongs, that a *quarentena* comprised 40 perches. Comparison of the Suffolk Domesday with the *I.E.* seems also to indicate a league of 12 furlongs.[1] This would make a league equivalent to 1½ miles, but it must be remembered that the number of feet in a perch is obscure, and that the whole subject is complicated by local usage and by the existence of local or 'customary', as distinct from standard, units.[2] Furthermore, in his study of Worcestershire, J. H. Round thought that a league might well have comprised only 4 furlongs (i.e. about half a mile) because he never found a figure higher than 3 furlongs below the league.[3] Our knowledge of the measures characterising different districts is far too slight to allow us to speak with confidence on these matters. All we can do for each county is to regard the figures as indicating conventional units by which relative density may be gauged.

Quite apart from the problem of the size of the units, there are other difficulties; the exact significance of this type of entry is not clear.[4] Is it giving extreme diameters of irregularly shaped woods, or is it making rough estimates of mean diameters, or is it attempting to convey some other notion? We cannot tell, but we certainly cannot assume that a definite geometrical figure was in the minds of the Commissioners. We cannot hope to convert these linear measurements into acres by any process of simple arithmetic; and it would be rash to make any assumptions about the superficial extent of woodland measured in this way. All we can safely do is to regard the dimensions as conventional units and to plot

[1] See p. 176 above.

[2] F. W. Maitland, *Domesday Book and Beyond*, pp. 371 and 432. For earlier discussions, see (1) Henry Ellis, *op. cit.* I, pp. 157–60; (2) R. W. Eyton, *A Key to Domesday ...the Dorset Survey* (London, 1878), pp. 24–8.

[3] J. H. Round in *V.C.H. Worcester* (London, 1901), I, pp. 271–2. See also Round's discussions in *V.C.H. Northampton*, I, pp. 279–81.

[4] See (1) F. W. Maitland, *op. cit.* pp. 371, 432; (2) P. Vinogradoff, *English Society in the Eleventh Century* (Oxford, 1908), pp. 302–3. See also p. 56 above.

them diagrammatically as intersecting straight lines. This objective method will, at any rate, give us some idea of its relative distribution over the face of a county. The obscurity is not helped by the entry for Keyston (Leightonstone) where there was wood 5 furlongs by 1½ (203 b); these dimensions are preceded by the words *silve pastilis per loca*, which seem to imply a scattered distribution. The phrase *per loca* is also found occasionally in connection with the Lincolnshire woodland, but that is measured in acres.[1] Whatever notions the Commissioners had in mind, it is clear that they were trying to be accurate. At any rate, a number of entries suggest precision. At Wood Walton in Normancross (205 b), for example, there was wood 16 furlongs long by 6 furlongs and 2 roods (*virgae*) broad, while at Folksworth in the same hundred (205 b) there was other wood 6 furlongs long by 2 furlongs and 6 perches (*perticae*) broad. There is a curiously complicated entry for Paxton (207): 'Wood for pannage half a league in length and half a league and one furlong in breadth, and other wood (*alia silva*) half a league in length and 3 furlongs in breadth.' Is this duality the result of some peculiarity in the lay-out of the wood? Or does it arise from the fact that three berewicks were included in the Paxton totals, though other places with berewicks do not show this feature? Or, yet again, does the 'other wood' refer to underwood which appears in some entries (see p. 337)? The last possibility seems likely, but it may well be that the duality is merely the result of some scribal idiosyncrasy.

The wood of some places was recorded not in terms of dimensions but in terms of acres. The number of acres varied from 16 at Offord to 70 at Hail Weston, both in Toseland. There was a smaller amount entered for Botolph Bridge (Normancross) but this falls into a special category, for the entry says that there were '12 acres of wood for pannage in Northamptonshire' (203 b). The wood of Sawtry, also in Normancross, was measured differently on different holdings:

  (i) *Fo.* 204 b. 2 furlongs by 1 furlong.
  (ii) *Fo.* 206. 30 acres.
  (iii) *Fo.* 206 b. 18 furlongs by 4 furlongs.
  (iv) *Fo.* 207 b. Nil.

If we could only equate acres with dimensions, how much easier our mapping would be.

[1] See p. 56 above.

Underwood (*silva minuta*) was mentioned on a number of holdings. With one exception, the amount was always recorded in terms of acres, and the figures ranged from 1 acre to 100 acres. The exception was at

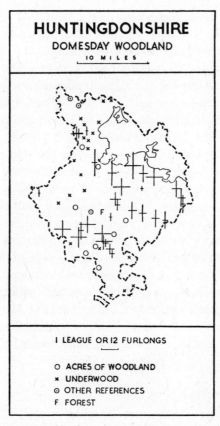

Fig. 95. Huntingdonshire: Domesday woodland in 1086.
The boundary of alluvium and peat is shown; see Fig. 88.

Gidding in Leightonstone (204b) where there were 2 furlongs of underwood (*silvae minutae ii quarentenae*). It is strange to find extent described in terms of one linear dimension, and the entry may owe its present form to a scribal error.[1] Some villages contained both wood and underwood. At Glatton (Normancross) there were '2 acres of wood for pannage, and

[1] But for 'areal leagues', see R. W. Eyton, *A Key to Domesday...the Dorset Survey* (London, 1878), pp. 31–5.

20 acres of underwood' (205), and one of the entries for Southoe (Tose-land) also reads: '10 acres of wood for pannage and 5 acres of underwood' (207). As we have seen, the curious entry for Paxton (207) may also fall into this category.

In addition to these, there are a few exceptional entries. At Water Newton (Normancross) there was 'one custom (*consuetudo*) [rendering] 2 shillings in the wood of the abbot of Peterborough' (205); and in the neighbouring village of Chesterton there were two similar customs (205, 206). Each of these implied the right to take timber to the value of 2s., but there is no wood recorded for either village, nor did any of the four holdings of Peterborough Abbey in Huntingdonshire carry wood. Another curiosity occurs in the account of Ellington in Leightonstone (204b). It was assessed at 10 hides, but we are told that one of these 10 hides was waste (*wasta*) because of the king's wood (*per silvam regis*). In later times this was assessed with the Forest of Weybridge in the adjoining village of Alconbury.[1] Another indication of the royal forest in this part of Huntingdonshire is given by an entry in the appendix dealing with disputes: 'They say that 36 hides of land in Brampton which Richard Inganie claims to belong to the forest (*foresta*) were of the king's demesne farm, and did not belong to the forest' (208). Brampton, which adjoins Ellington and Alconbury, was a royal manor with wood only half a league by 2 furlongs entered for it in the text (203b). Here, apparently, in Ellington, Alconbury and Brampton was a stretch of royal forest before Henry II put the whole of Huntingdonshire under forest law upon his accession.[2]

Distribution of woodland

As might be expected from its heavy clay soil, a great part of the upland of Huntingdonshire was well covered with wood in the eleventh century. The woods of Hurstingstone hundred stand out on Fig. 95, and it is interesting to note the numerous wood elements in the place-names of this area (Old and Wood Hurst, Upwood, Wood Walton, Warboys). The hundred itself seems to owe its name to the *Hyrstingas* or woodland

[1] *Cartularium Monasterii de Rameseia*, III, p. 305: 'Et decima hida est in nemore Walberg [Weybridge] per praeceptum Henrici Regis.' See also *V.C.H. Huntingdon*, III, p. 44.

[2] *V.C.H. Huntingdon*, III, p. 16: 'These 36 hides probably included the Forests of Weybridge and Harthay and must have been distributed among the king's demesnes in Brampton, Alconbury and apparently the waste hide in Ellington.'

dwellers.[1] There is another concentration of wood in the south of the county, to the west of the Ouse valley. The higher land in the west of the county seems to have carried but little wood, at any rate there was nothing much there beyond underwood.

MEADOW

Types of entries

The entries for meadow in Huntingdonshire are uniform and straight-forward. The same type of entry repeats itself monotonously—'*n* acres of meadow' (*n acrae prati*), except in the entry for Tilbrook which follows the pattern of the Bedfordshire entries, and records meadow for 5 plough-teams (211b). The amount in each vill varied from 3 acres to 170, but amounts over 100 were comparatively rare. The only indication of the value of this meadow occurs in the account of Godmanchester where there were 160 acres of meadow; a little later in the entry comes the statement: *De pratis lxx solidi.* There is an interesting reference to meadow in an entry relating to Botolph Bridge in Normancross (203b): 'In this manor of the king and in other manors the weir (*exclusa*) of the abbot of Thorney is doing harm to 300 acres of meadow.' Presumably this referred to some interference along the Nene, and there were several villages in the Nene valley held by the abbey of Thorney. As in the case of other of the eastern counties, no attempt has been made to translate the Domesday figures into modern acreages. The Domesday acres have been treated merely as conventional units of measurement, and Fig. 96 has been plotted on that assumption.

Distribution of meadowland

In the south of the county, the line of the Ouse stands out, and along it there were a number of villages with substantial amounts of meadow: Fenstanton (80 acres), St Ives (60), Hemingford Abbots (150), Houghton (60), Godmanchester (160), Brampton (100), Buckden (84), Offord (60), Paxton (80), Eynesbury (133½) and *Cotes* (60). In the north of the county there is another line of places, each with over 60 acres, along the Nene which forms the county boundary for some distance: Botolph Bridge (63), Orton (99), Water Newton (60), and Elton (184). Considering that the western part of the county is without large streams, it carried

[1] A. Mawer and F. M. Stenton, *The Place-Names of Bedfordshire and Huntingdonshire* (Cambridge, 1926), p. 203.

a fairly heavy amount of meadow. The line of Keyston (86), Bythorn (30), Molesworth (60), Brington (40), Spaldwick with its berewicks (160) and Ellington (60) follows the upper reaches of a tributary of the Ouse which

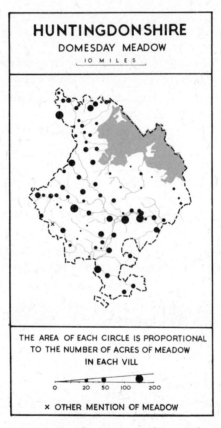

Fig. 96. Huntingdonshire: Domesday meadow in 1086.

The areas of alluvium and peat are indicated; see Fig. 88.
Rivers passing through these areas are not shown.

is not named on the One Inch Ordnance Survey Map. The line of Gidding (110), Hamerton (60), Upton (50), Buckworth (80) and Alconbury (40) follows another tributary of the Ouse (Alconbury Brook). In the south of the county, Covington (48) and Kimbolton (70) are along yet another tributary (the Kym).

The greater part of Hurstingstone hundred was deficient in meadow despite the fact that so much of it was fenland; a few places had as much as 20 acres each, but Upwood had only 6 acres and Warboys only 3 acres. The fen-line villages of Normancross seem to have been better served; Sawtry had 68 acres and Glatton had 60 acres, while Conington and Stilton had 40 and 32 acres respectively.

PASTURE

Pasture is mentioned in connection with only two places in Huntingdonshire, both of them royal manors (fo. 203b):

(i) Gransden (Toseland)   *De pastura v solidi et iiii denarii exeunt.*

(ii) Godmanchester (Leightonstone)   *De pastura xx solidi.*

There is also a vague reference to pasture for pigs in an account of Whittlesey Mere, but this cannot be assigned to a definite locality.[1] These cannot represent all the pasture in the county, but the entries may imply that some grazing in each of the two places was not subject to free common right, but had to be paid for.[2]

MARSH

Marsh is mentioned in connection with only three places, all in Hurstingstone hundred:

(i) Colne (204)   *Silva pastilis i leuga longa et dimidia lata et maresc tantundem.*

(ii) Holywell (204)   *Maresc i leuga longa et i lata.*

(iii) Warboys (204b)   *Maresc i leuga longa et dimidia leuga lata.*

The amounts for Colne and Holywell are large when viewed in the light of the present-day parish boundaries of these two villages, but it is possible that conditions may have been different in the eleventh century. No value is assigned to the marsh, which makes its mention for only these three villages all the more mysterious. We cannot say whether there

---

[1] See p. 342 below.

[2] For a discussion of the pasture entries in the neighbouring county of Bedford, see G. H. Fowler, *Bedfordshire in 1086* (The Bedfordshire Historical Record Society, 1922), p. 63.

were local arrangements peculiar to these villages, or whether these marsh entries are due to an idiosyncrasy of the Domesday scribe. The considerable stretch of marsh in north-eastern Huntingdonshire went unrecorded, but it must have played a part in the economy of the fen-line villages. Some indication of the Fenland, however, is given by a reference to the meres it contained (see below.)

FISHERIES

Fisheries or fishermen are mentioned in connection with six places in Huntingdonshire, and, in addition to these, there is a fairly long account of the fishing activity on Whittlesey Mere (Fig. 97). The simplest plan is to make a list of the places. The first four lay along the Ouse, the fifth was on the Nene, while Somersham lay on the edge of the Fenland.[1]

(i)	Eynesbury (207)	1 *piscaria* which is valued with the manor.
(ii)	Southoe (206b)	1 *piscaria* [rendering] a thousand eels, and 3 gifts (*presentationes*) annually worth 49 pence.
(iii)	Huntingdon (203)	3 fishermen rendering (*reddentes*) 3 shillings.
(iv)	Hemingford (207)	A *piscina* [rendering] 6 shillings.
(v)	Alwalton (205)	1 *piscaria* [rendering] 500 eels [worth?] 5 shillings.
(vi)	Somersham (204)	3 *piscinae* [rendering] 8 shillings.

One would have expected many more fisheries to be recorded along the Ouse and the Nene, and also in association with the fen-line villages. The account of Whittlesey Mere, however, gives a picture of the activity in the northern part of the Huntingdonshire Fenland (205):

In Whittlesey Mere (*Witelesmare*) the abbot of Ramsey has one boat (*navis*), and the abbot of Peterborough one boat, and the abbot of Thorney two boats. One of these two boats, and two fisheries and two fishermen and one virgate of land, the abbot of Peterborough holds of the abbot of Thorney, and for these he gives pasture sufficient for 120 swine, and if pasture fails, he feeds and fattens 60 pigs with corn. Moreover, he finds timber for one house of 60 ft., and rods for the enclosure (*curia*) around the house. He also

---

[1] *Piscariae* and *piscinae* imply the same thing—see p. 367 below.

repairs the house and enclosure if they are in decay. This agreement was made between them in King Edward's time.

The fisheries and meres (*marae*) of the abbot of Ramsey in Huntingdonshire are valued at 10 *li.*, those of the abbot of Thorney, at 60*s.*, those of the abbot of Peterborough at 4 *li.*

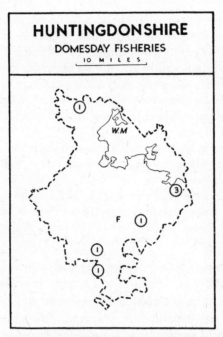

Fig. 97. Huntingdonshire: Domesday fisheries in 1086.

The figure in each circle indicates the number of fisheries. F indicates the three fishermen at Huntingdon. *W.M.* indicates the site of Whittlesey Mere. The boundary of alluvium and peat is shown; see Fig. 88.

In the light of this account, we might ask what about the activity in the Fenland to the south, and what about Ramsey Mere which was well known for its fish later in the Middle Ages.[1] But the Domesday Book is silent.

[1] *Chronicon Abbatiae Ramesiensis*, ed. by W. D. Macray (Rolls Series, 1886), p. 8. The mere may not have been mentioned because it was in the *banlieue* of Ramsey Abbey; see p. 321 above.

WASTE

Apart from the waste messuages in the borough of Huntingdon, holdings described as being waste (*wasta*) are recorded in connection with four places in Huntingdonshire:

(i) *Waresley* in Toseland (206b). 'In Waresley Summerled had half a hide [assessed] to the geld. There is land for half a plough. It is waste. Roger holds it of Eustace [the Sheriff]. *T.R.E.* it was worth 10s., now [it is worth] 2s.' But we are told nothing of the resources that made it still worth as much as 2 shillings in 1086.

(ii) *Stukeley* in Hurstingstone (206). 'In Stukeley Eustace [the Sheriff] has 1 virgate of land [assessed] to the geld. It is waste. Herbert holds it of him.'

(iii) *Hemingford* in Toseland (207). 'Aluuin blach had 1 hide [assessed] to the geld. There is land for 1 plough. It is waste. Ralf the son of Osmund has it.'

(iv) *Ellington* in Leightonstone (204b): 'In Ellington the abbot of Ramsey had 10 hides [assessed] to the geld. There is land for 16 ploughs. One of these 10 hides is waste because of the king's wood (*per silvam regis*).'

The Domesday term 'waste' presumably indicates a lapse from former land utilisation. Only at Ellington is a reason given for the waste. The waste in the other villages presumably reflected the local vicissitudes of agriculture that are beyond our knowing. Ellington, moreover, was clearly only partially waste, but so were the other places because each had holdings under cultivation.

MILLS

Mills are mentioned in connection with 23 out of the 83 Domesday settlements in Huntingdonshire. Their annual value is stated in every case, and this ranges from mills worth only two or three shillings up to the two mills at Hemingford Abbots in Toseland which were worth £6 a year between them (207). Fractions of mills do not present the problem they do in East Anglia; they were only entered for the one village of Sibson (Normancross) where Thorney Abbey and Count Eustace had half a mill each (205). There is no mention of sites where mills had formerly existed. One-half the Huntingdonshire villages with mills had only one each as the following table indicates:

Domesday Mills in Huntingdonshire in 1086

1 mill   13 settlements
2 mills   6   „
3   „   4   „

There were no large groups as in some other counties.

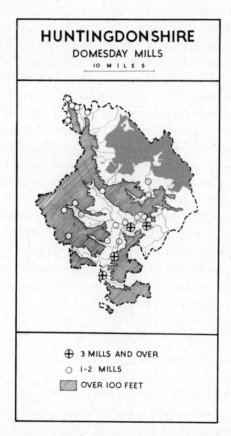

Fig. 98. Huntingdonshire: Domesday mills in 1086.
The areas of alluvium and peat are indicated; see Fig. 88.
Rivers passing through these areas are not shown.

The distribution of the mills raises no special points (Fig. 98). Many were situated along the Ouse, and these included the four villages with three mills each, Hemingford, Godmanchester, Paxton and Eynesbury;

some of the Paxton mills may have been located in one of its berewicks;[1] the Hemingford mills seem also, from other documents, to have been shared between the two adjacent villages of that name. The remaining mills of the county were along the tributaries of the Ouse or along the Nene in the north.

CHURCHES

Churches are mentioned in connection with 52 villages and, in addition, Huntingdon itself had 2 churches. The usual form of the entry runs 'there is a church and a priest', but a number of entries omit any reference to a priest, and in the entry for Houghton (Hurstingstone) we are specifically told: 'There is a church [but] not a priest' (204b). There were three places in Hurstingstone with 2 churches each, that is apart from Huntingdon; St Ives (204) and Stukeley (204, 206b) had 2 priests each as well, but Hartford had only 1 priest despite its 2 churches (203b).[2] At Sawtry, in Normancross, there were 3 churches but only 2 priests (204b, 206, 206b). Altogether 48 priests are mentioned. The entries do not involve some of the obscurities that are encountered, for example, in Norfolk and Suffolk. No value or holding is entered for any of the churches, and there is no complicated fractioning; the only village where fractions occur is Sibson (Normancross) where Thorney Abbey and Count Eustace had half a church each (205). But despite the comparative simplicity of the entries, many things are far from clear, and we can never know to what extent the Domesday churches represent all the churches there were in the county in the eleventh century.

URBAN LIFE

The Domesday description of the county begins with an account of the borough (*burgus*) of Huntingdon (203) which is the only place in the county for which burgesses are recorded. It was situated where Ermine Street crosses the Ouse, and its bridge was probably the lowest on the river until the bridge at St Ives was built in the twelfth century. Its strategic position was therefore an important one, and it featured in the Danish campaigns of the tenth century. We cannot be surprised therefore

[1] See p. 318 above.
[2] One of the churches under St Ives may have been at Old Hurst or Wood Hurst; the churches at Stukeley may have been at Great and Little Stukeley respectively; one of the churches under Hartford may have been at King's Ripton; see p. 318 above.

that the borough was very much larger in 1086 than its later history might lead us to suppose.[1] It was divided into four quarters (*ferlingi*) or wards, and, in 1086 as in 1066, it had 256 burgesses.[2] The other people mentioned as being there in 1086 comprise 100 bordars and 3 fishermen. To what extent this was a complete record of the population of the borough in 1086 we cannot say. The bordars, for example, are mentioned in connection with only two of the wards; we might expect to find others in the other two wards, but it is not so. The total recorded population of 359 implies an actual population of upwards of 2,000; and we may hazard a guess that it was more rather than less. Of the 256 burgesses, 140 are said to have 80 *hagae* which we have not counted as additional. Groups amounting to a total of 104 burgesses, 16 *domus*, 2 *mansurae* and 1 toft are also mentioned, and it is is not clear whether any or all of these were additional. We have assumed that they were not.

It is strange that the number of burgesses should have remained the same in 1086 as in 1066 because on the site of the castle there had been 21 messuages (*mansiones*) that had disappeared by 1086; and there were also another 8 waste messuages (*mansiones wastae*) formerly occupied in 1066. Furthermore, there had already been 104 messuages waste in 1066 and these remained waste in 1086, although we are told that they 'gave and give their customs'. We are not told, however, why they were waste, and the implications of the statement are obscure, but it seems to imply that the borough was impoverished. There were 3 moneyers rendering 40s. at Huntingdon in 1066, but they had gone by the time of the survey.

The other information about the borough does not amount to a great deal. Two churches are mentioned, one of which, we learn from the appendix on disputes was named after St Mary (208). There was also a mill which rendered as much as 60s. No hint is given about the commerce of the borough, nor, strange to say, is there any mention of a market. But whatever the commercial activities of the borough, it is clear from the following statement that there was also an agricultural element:

---

[1] For a topographical discussion of the Domesday account of Huntingdon, see S. Inskip Ladds, 'The Borough of Huntingdon and Domesday Book', *Trans. Cambs. and Hunts. Arch. Soc.* (Ely, 1937), V, pp. 105–12.

[2] Made up as follows: (a) Two quarters with 116 burgesses; (b) Two quarters with 140 burgesses less half a house (*cxl burgesses dimidia domus minus*). We have disregarded the 'half house' in our calculation.

To this borough there belong (*jacent*) 2 carucates[1] and 40 acres of land and 10 acres of meadow, of which the king, with two parts, and the earl, with the third part, divide the rent. The burgesses cultivate (*colunt*) this land and take it on lease (*locant*) through the servants of the king and the earl.

All this is very far from being as informative as we should like it to be. What it really amounts to is that here was a town of not less than about 2,000 people who presumably maintained themselves by a mixture of commerce and agriculture.

MISCELLANEOUS INFORMATION

The miscellaneous information recorded in the Huntingdonshire folios is not very much. There are, for example, no markets or vineyards. In one of the entries for Eynesbury (Toseland) there is, however, one very unexpected item. It reads: 'In the same vill there is a certain sheepfold (*ovile*) for 662 sheep' (206b). Sheepfolds must have existed in most, if not all, villages, but why this solitary and exceptional reference should be made to the fold at Eynesbury it is quite impossible to say. It is just one of the tantalising curiosities of the Domesday Book. No stock, of course, is recorded for any of the Huntingdonshire villages, but the *I.E.* (pp. 166–7) enters that for the demesne of the four Ely manors in Huntingdonshire. Finally, there was a castle at Huntingdon (203).

REGIONAL SUMMARY

The small size of Huntingdonshire does not give much scope for regional division. The main contrasts are between fenland and upland (Fig. 88). The Fenland was devoid of villages, and the low density of plough-teams and of population in the fen-line parishes continue the same features of northern Cambridgeshire to the east. The Domesday description of Whittlesey Mere shows what much of the fen surface must have been like. The clay upland not only supported a substantial amount of arable land, but also a moderate amount of wood. Its surface was relieved by the valleys of the Ouse and its tributaries and by the Nene along the northern boundary of the county. These valleys had quite appreciable amounts of meadow, and their streams were marked by mills and by occasional fisheries.

---

[1] *Hidae* was originally written in the text, but *carrucat'* is interlined above it.

BIBLIOGRAPHICAL NOTE

(1) An older translation of the Domesday text relating to Huntingdonshire is the *Translation of Domesday Book or the Great Survey of England of William the Conqueror, A.D. mlxxxvi, with notes and explanations, so far as relates to Huntingdonshire* (Robert Edis, Huntingdon, 1864). The name of the editor is not given, but it was the Rev. George Johnstone of Broughton Rectory, and the introduction was written from the rectory.

This has been superseded by the translation made by F. M. Stenton in *V.C.H. Huntingdonshire* (London, 1926), I, pp. 337–55, accompanied by a valuable introduction (pp. 315–36).

(2) The following deal with various aspects:

S. INSKIP LADDS, 'The Borough of Huntingdon and Domesday Book', *Trans. Cambs. and Hunts. Arch. Soc.* (Ely, 1937), V, pp. 105–12.

H. C. DARBY, 'Domesday Woodland in Huntingdonshire', *ibid.* (Ely, 1937), V, pp. 269–73.

CYRIL HART, 'The Hidation of Huntingdonshire', *Proc. Camb. Antiq. Soc.* (1968), LXI, pp. 55–66.

(3) The method and contents of the *Inquisitio Eliensis* are discussed in many of the general works dealing with the Domesday Book; see pp. 22 and 314 above.

(4) A valuable aid to the Domesday study of the county is A. Mawer and F. M. Stenton, *The Place-Names of Bedfordshire and Huntingdonshire* (Cambridge, 1926).

CHAPTER VIII

THE EASTERN COUNTIES

The Domesday information for a county gains greatly in interest when set against that of neighbouring counties. There are many differences in phraseology between individual counties and between groups of counties. Some of these differences arose from varying economic and social conditions. Others may reflect nothing more than the ideas and language of different sets of Commissioners. One of the most obvious differences lies in the method of assessment. Some counties were assessed in terms of hides and virgates or of hides and acres; others in terms of carucates and bovates; others in yet different ways. Nor are the differences between county and county confined to the method of assessment. The statement about plough-lands appears on the surface to be solid and satisfactory, but the significance of the information may not always be the same; the form of the entry varies, and, besides, there seems to be a strong conventional element about some of the statistics. Where the number of plough-lands exceeds that of plough-teams, the entries for some counties draw attention to the fact, and state that so many teams could be added or restored; but such explicit declaration is far from general. For a number of counties there is even no statement about plough-lands, and we are left to infer their number from the information given about the teams themselves. The information about population is equally varied. In some counties there were many freemen and sokemen; in others, they were rare or completely absent. The unfree population, too, varied greatly. In some counties, villeins formed the largest group; in others, it was the bordar class that was important. Or again, serfs are mentioned for some counties, but not for others. The statement about values likewise differs greatly. There are counties for which values are given for 1066 and 1086, while the description of other counties also includes the value of an estate at some intermediate date between the Conquest and the Survey.

Furthermore, the miscellaneous resources of each county are often measured differently, and the entries for wood, meadow and the like show great diversity. Pasture is very frequently recorded for the villages of some counties, seldom to never for those of other counties. Moreover, in recording fisheries, salt-pans and mills, the entries for some counties give numbers only, while those for other counties also state the value, as well as the number, of each of these items. Or again, churches are fairly regularly recorded for some counties; yet in other counties, the mention of a church is a very rare feature. Finally, livestock is entered only for the demense of the villages described in the *I.C.C.* and the Little Domesday Book, and for that of the Ely holdings described in the *I.E.*

Many of these differences are assembled in tabular form on pp. 374–9. These tables do not provide a complete statement of every variation in language and content between the six eastern counties. They are intended only as a general guide to the salient features that have already been discussed in the preceding chapters. The first paragraph of this volume stated that the survey was carried out 'with a high degree of uniformity'; the tables now indicate the limitations of this statement. The general framework of the survey was the same for all counties, but the detailed recording of the information was far from uniform. The full implication of all the differences cannot be explored until similar tables are available for all the counties of the survey.

The assembly of information, county by county, is interesting not only from the viewpoints of the language and the content of the Domesday Book, but also because of the light it sheds upon geographical variations in eleventh-century England. Composite maps have been made not for all the items of the survey, but only for those most relevant to an understanding of landscape and economic geography—for settlements, ploughteams, population, woodland, meadow, fisheries, salt-pans and vineyards. These maps must now be discussed separately.

SETTLEMENTS

Two reservations must be borne in mind when looking at a map of Domesday names. The first is the fact that some Domesday names may have covered more than one settlement; the evidence of documents both before and after the date of the Domesday Book shows that some names certainly did; others we cannot be sure about. The second reservation arises from the fact that some Domesday names remain unidentified and so cannot be marked on the map. Generally speaking, this is not a serious omission, and it is always possible that subsequent place-name investigation may clear up even these recalcitrant names. Despite these reservations, a map of Domesday names probably gives a fair general picture of the intensity of settlement over most areas.

One outstanding feature of a map showing the distribution of Domesday names in the eastern counties is the relatively empty expanse of the Fen-land (Fig. 99). But the Fenland was not uniformly devoid of Domesday names, for there was a great contrast between the southern peat-lands and the northern silt-lands. Settlement was prohibited on the peat area of the southern Fenland because the soil provided no stable foundations upon which to build; what villages existed in this area were upon the islands, and particularly upon the large island of Ely. To the north, the silt area bordering the Wash is composed of a substance more solid than fen peat, and it offered better opportunities for continuous settlement in early times. Later medieval colonisation was to do much to people this area, but, even in the eleventh century, it formed a belt of occupied territory connecting the uplands of Lincolnshire and Norfolk. On Fig. 99 the present-day coastline is marked, but the eleventh-century coastline of the Wash probably lay not far beyond the line of villages.

Outside the Fenland, the first impression of Fig. 99 is one of surprising uniformity. Names lie thick almost everywhere on the map. But closer inspection shows some areas of relative sparsity. The most prominent of these is the Breckland along the eastern margin of the Fenland. This infertile tract of hungry sands rivalled the Fenland in its emptiness. Another empty area was the Isle of Axholme which formed a small replica of the Fenland; it contained no villages except those on the island itself. Other smaller patches of emptiness stand out here and there— the chalklands of south-east Cambridgeshire, the limestone uplands to the north and south of Lincoln, and occasional alluvial districts along the coast which must have been marshy in Domesday times. There are yet other areas where the spread of names is thin—on the light soils of northern Lindsey and north-western Norfolk, and on the very heavy clays of south-west Essex, where the fragments of Epping Forest testify to the former nature of the countryside.

In view of the unsystematic and incomplete nature of the statistics for the Domesday boroughs, it is impossible to discuss their relative size and importance; but it does seem as if Norwich and Lincoln stood above the rest in 1086. The economic activities of all the eighteen boroughs in the eastern counties are wrapped in much obscurity, and it is difficult to arrive at any clear idea of the relative importance of the agrarian and commercial elements in each. From the few hints that the Domesday Book provides, it is clear that the burgesses must have had some means

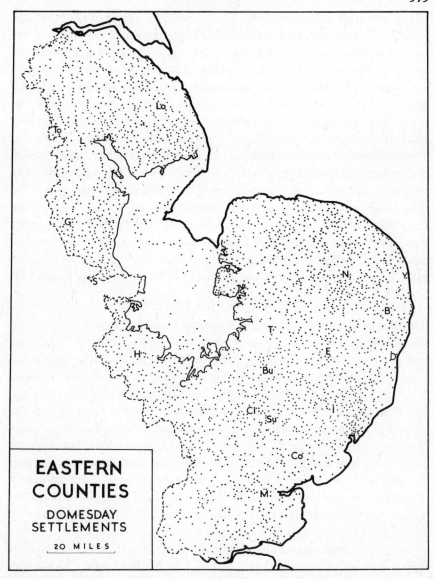

Fig. 99. Eastern Counties: Domesday place-names.

The boundary of the Fenland is shown. Places with burgesses are indicated by initials: B, Beccles; Bu, Bury St Edmunds; C, Cambridge; Cl, Clare; Co, Colchester; D, Dunwich; E, Eye; G, Grantham; H, Huntingdon; I, Ipswich; L, Lincoln; Lo, Louth; M, Maldon; N, Norwich; S, Stamford; Su, Sudbury; T, Thetford; To, Torksey; Y, Yarmouth.

of support other than agriculture. Thus at Maldon, 15 out of 180 burgesses
held 'half a hide and 21 acres' in 1086, while the remaining 165 had 'no
more than their houses in the borough'. Or again at Ipswich in 1066 there
were 538 burgesses with only 40 acres of land between them. Markets
are recorded for only five of the boroughs, Beccles, Clare, Eye, Louth
and Sudbury. Fourteen other places also had markets, but none of these
places was a borough. It is interesting to note that of the total of nineteen
markets recorded for the eastern counties, none is entered for Essex,
Cambridgeshire or Huntingdonshire. Some information about mints
and churches helps to fill in the details given for some towns, but only too
frequently the urban element is obscured by rural matters—the wood, the
farm-stock, the plough-teams and, maybe, the vineyard. Only in the
description of one place does the Domesday Book give any substantial
detail about the economic life of the community; this is in the account of
Bury St Edmunds, which is described not as a borough but merely as a
villa. We can only wish that the information for other places was as full.

PLOUGH-TEAMS AND POPULATION

The distribution of prosperity, as measured by plough-teams and population, shows much variation over the face of the eastern counties. Figs. 100
and 101 complete the general impression given by the map showing the
distribution of Domesday names. The Fenland stands out on both as an
area of great poverty. The plough-team map shows also the relatively
low densities of western Norfolk and the Breckland portion of Suffolk,
of southern Essex, and of much of the Lincolnshire uplands. The population map agrees with the plough-team map in a general way, but there are
some areas on it that have relatively more people than teams, e.g. western
Norfolk and much of Lincolnshire; while other areas have relatively
fewer people, e.g. the Huntingdonshire upland. Taking both maps together, the main fact about the area outside the Fenland is the superiority
of much of Norfolk and Suffolk.

It must be remembered that the densities on Fig. 101 refer not to total
population but to recorded population. As Maitland said, 'Domesday
Book never enables us to count heads. It states the number of the tenants
of various classes, *sochemanni*, *villani*, *bordarii*, and the like, and leaves us
to suppose that each of these persons is, or may be, the head of a house-
hold'.[1] Whether this be so or not, the fact remains that in order to obtain

---

[1] F. W. Maitland, *Domesday Book and Beyond*, p. 17.

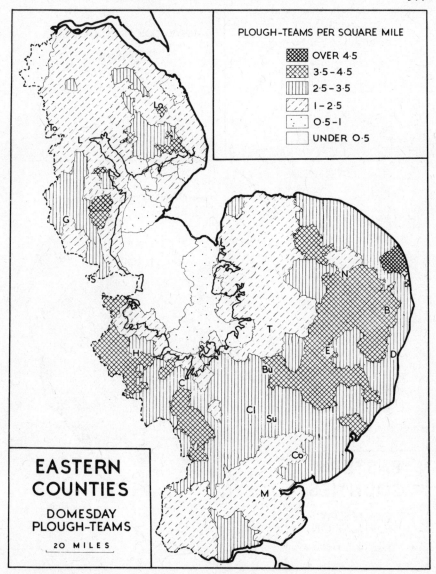

Fig. 100. Eastern Counties: Domesday plough-teams in 1086.

The boundary of the Fenland is shown. Places with burgesses are indicated by initials: B, Beccles; Bu, Bury St Edmunds; C, Cambridge; Cl, Clare; Co, Colchester; D, Dunwich; E, Eye; G, Grantham; H, Huntingdon; I, Ipswich; L, Lincoln; Lo, Louth; M, Maldon; N, Norwich; S, Stamford; Su, Sudbury; T, Thetford; To, Torksey; Y, Yarmouth.

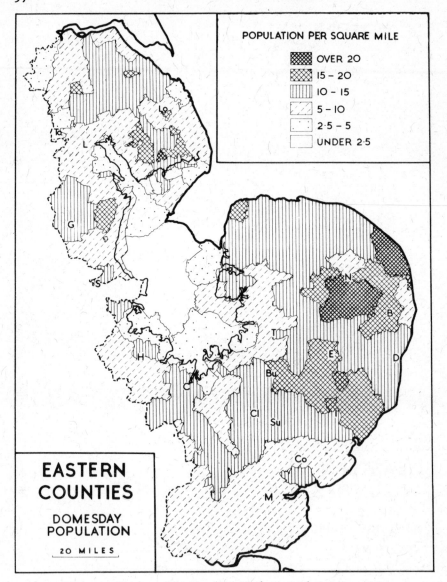

Fig. 101. Eastern Counties: Domesday population in 1086.

The boundary of the Fenland is shown. Places with burgesses are indicated by initials:
B, Beccles; Bu, Bury St Edmunds; C, Cambridge; Cl, Clare; Co, Colchester; D,
Dunwich; E, Eye; G, Grantham; H, Huntingdon; I, Ipswich; L, Lincoln; Lo, Louth;
M, Maldon; N, Norwich; S, Stamford; Su, Sudbury; T, Thetford; To, Torksey;
Y, Yarmouth.

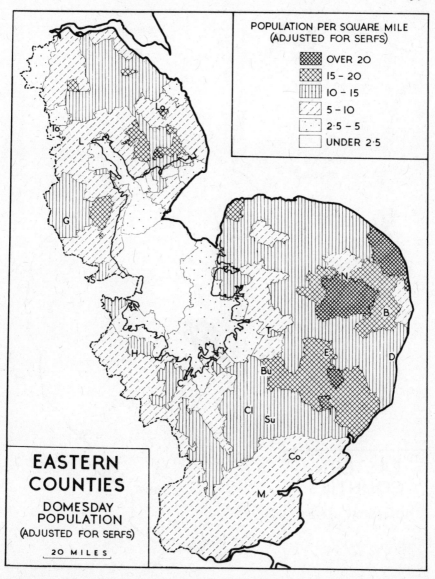

POPULATION PER SQUARE MILE
(ADJUSTED FOR SERFS)

OVER 20
15 – 20
10 – 15
5 – 10
2·5 – 5
UNDER 2·5

EASTERN
COUNTIES
DOMESDAY
POPULATION
(ADJUSTED FOR SERFS)

20 MILES

Fig. 102. Eastern Counties: Domesday population in 1086 (adjusted for serfs).

On this map, the serfs have been regarded as individuals and not as heads of households. Their numbers have been divided by the arbitrary figure of four before calculating densities of population.

The boundary of the Fenland is shown. Places with burgesses are indicated by initials: B, Beccles; Bu, Bury St Edmunds; C, Cambridge; Cl, Clare; Co, Colchester; D, Dunwich; E, Eye; G, Grantham; H, Huntingdon; I, Ipswich; L, Lincoln; Lo, Louth; M, Maldon; N, Norwich; S, Stamford; Su, Sudbury; T, Thetford; To, Torksey; Y, Yarmouth.

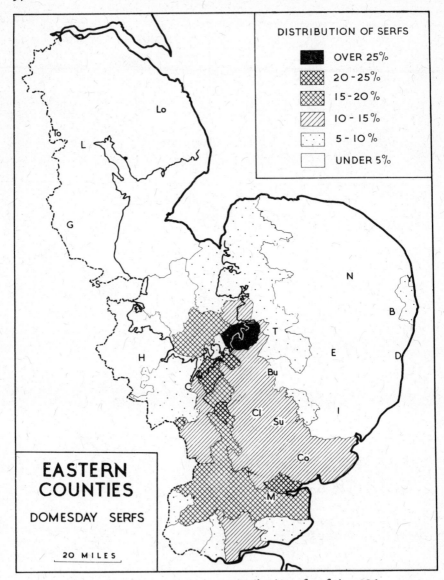

DISTRIBUTION OF SERFS

- OVER 25%
- 20-25%
- 15-20%
- 10-15%
- 5-10%
- UNDER 5%

EASTERN
COUNTIES

DOMESDAY SERFS

20 MILES

Fig. 103. Eastern Counties: Distribution of serfs in 1086.

The boundary of the Fenland is shown. Places with burgesses are indicated by initials:
B, Beccles; Bu, Bury St Edmunds; C, Cambridge; Cl, Clare; Co, Colchester; D, Dun-
wich; E, Eye; G, Grantham; H, Huntingdon; I, Ipswich; L, Lincoln; Lo, Louth;
M, Maldon; N, Norwich; S. Stamford; Su, Sudbury; T, Thetford; To, Torksey;
Y, Yarmouth. See p. 331 for possible serfs in Huntingdonshire.

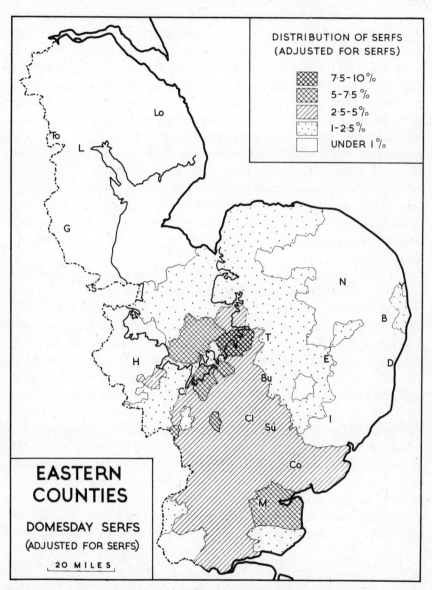

Fig. 104. Eastern Counties: Distribution of serfs in 1086 (adjusted for serfs).

On this map, the serfs have been regarded as individuals and not as heads of households. Their numbers have been divided by the arbitrary figure of four before calculating percentages.

The boundary of the Fenland is shown. Places with burgesses are indicated by
initials: B, Beccles; Bu, Bury St Edmunds; C, Cambridge; Cl, Clare; Co, Colchester;
D, Dunwich; E, Eye; G, Grantham; H, Huntingdon; I, Ipswich; L, Lincoln; Lo, Louth;
M, Maldon; N, Norwich; S, Stamford; Su, Sudbury; T, Thetford; To, Torksey;
Y, Yarmouth.

the actual population from the recorded population, we must multiply the latter by some factor, say four, or perhaps five, according to our ideas about the medieval family.[1] This, of course, does not affect the value of the statistics for estimating relative densities between one area and another. There are, however, a number of other considerations that have to be borne in mind in interpreting the population map. And in the light of these, it seems as if the distribution of plough-teams provides a more certain index of the relative distribution of prosperity.

One reservation arises from the fact that the greater detail of the Little Domesday Book, and the possible duplication of people in the entries for Norfolk and Suffolk, may enter into the relatively high densities for parts of East Anglia. But it is only fair to say that East Anglia was famed for its fertility during the Middle Ages. Moreover, the two counties had escaped the worst evils of trampling armies in the years following the Conquest.

A second reservation arises from the fact that serfs may stand in a different position from other categories of population. They may have been recorded as individuals, and not as heads of households or representatives of tenements in the village fields. Villages with many serfs may therefore appear to be more populous than they really were. Maitland put the problem, but gave no answer: 'Whether we ought to suppose that only the heads of servile households are reckoned, or whether we ought to think of the *servi* as having no households but as living within the lord's gates and being enumerated, men, women and able-bodied children, by the head—this is a difficult question.'[2] Vinogradoff also considered the problem and, as he said, hesitated to construe the numbers of serfs as indicating individuals.[3] Whatever the answer, the incidence of serfs as between one hundred and another, and between one county and the next, is uneven, so that the problem (if it be one) becomes increasingly acute as the county maps are assembled together. Fig. 102 has been constructed in an attempt to meet this difficulty. The

---

[1] F. W. Maitland suggested 5 'for the sake of argument' (*op. cit.* p. 437). Russell has more recently suggested 3·5; J. C. Russell, *British Medieval Population* (University of New Mexico Press, Albuquerque, U.S.A., 1948), pp. 38, 52.

[2] F. W. Maitland, *op. cit.* p. 17.

[3] P. Vinogradoff, *English Society in the Eleventh Century* (Oxford, 1908), pp. 463–4, 'I think the serfs entered in the record are those who held *ministeria*, definite offices connected with the estates or farms; both the members of their families and stray personal attendants must have been omitted'.

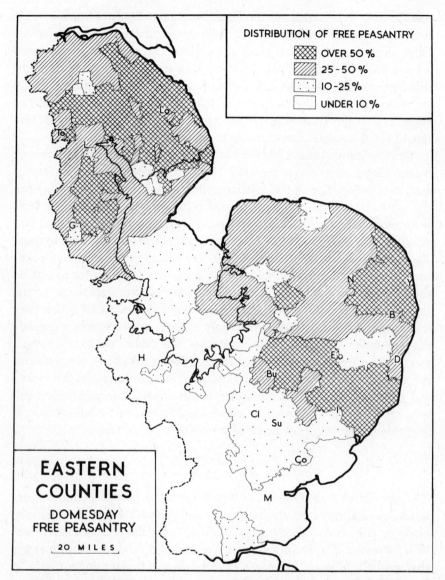

Fig. 105. Eastern Counties: Distribution of free peasantry in 1086.

The free peasantry includes freemen and sokemen. The boundary of the Fenland is shown. Places with burgesses are indicated by initials: B, Beccles; Bu, Bury St Edmunds; C, Cambridge; Cl, Clare; Co, Colchester; D, Dunwich; E, Eye; G, Grantham; H, Huntingdon; I, Ipswich; L, Lincoln; Lo, Louth; M, Maldon; N, Norwich; S, Stamford; Su, Sudbury; T, Thetford; To, Torksey; Y, Yarmouth.

serfs have been regarded as individuals and not as heads of houses. Their numbers have been divided by the arbitrary figure of four before calculating densities of population per square mile. To what extent this gives a more accurate picture, we cannot say; but its general pattern does not differ very widely from that of Fig. 101. Even if this adjustment brings us nearer the truth, the fact remains that the Huntingdonshire evidence suggests that the Domesday record may be incomplete for some at any rate of those counties for which serfs are not entered.[1]

Three other maps have been drawn to show the relative distribution of certain elements in the population. Fig. 103 shows the distribution of serfs as a percentage of the total recorded population, and on Fig. 104 the same information has been plotted on the assumption that the serfs were recorded as individuals. The percentages on this second map are very much lower, but the same general pattern of distribution appears. Fig. 105 shows the distribution of the free peasantry, freemen and sokemen being reckoned together for this purpose. If this information be re-calculated with adjustment for serfs, many of the percentages of the free peasantry show some increase, but the differences are such that they hardly modify Fig. 105 at all, certainly not enough to justify a separate map. Supplementary to these maps are the tables on p. 379 which summarise the relative importance of the different categories of population in each county as a whole. Any discussion of the significance of these maps and tables lies far beyond the scope of this study. Moreover, their full implication cannot begin to be appreciated until similar information is available for the whole of England.[2]

WOODLAND

The distribution of Domesday woodland in the eastern counties illustrates in a clear way both the limitations and the advantages of Domesday mapping (Fig. 106). For Norfolk, Suffolk, Essex and eastern Cambridgeshire, woodland is recorded mainly in terms of the number of swine that could feed upon its acorns or beechmast. In Huntingdonshire, it is recorded in terms of its length and breadth. In Lincolnshire, it is recorded in terms of acres, both of wood and of underwood. There are also

---

[1] See p. 331 above.

[2] For a preliminary view on a county basis see the maps (based on the figures of Ellis) in F. Seebohm, *The English Village Community* (London, 1883; reprinted at Cambridge, 1926), p. 85.

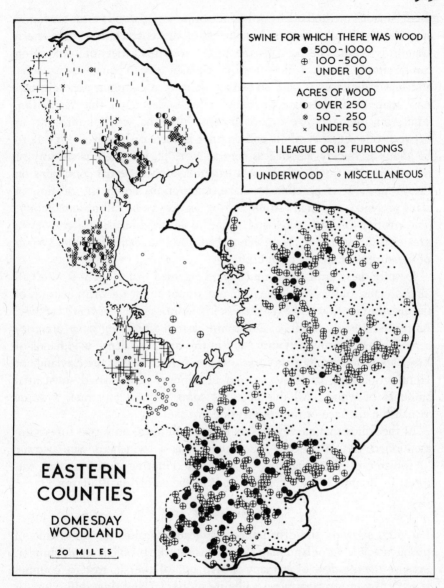

Fig. 106. Eastern Counties: Domesday woodland in 1086.
The boundary of the Fenland is shown.

miscellaneous methods of recording the presence of wood; these are found sporadically in all counties, but are especially characteristic of western Cambridgeshire. The difficulty that arises from this variety of information can be simply stated. It is impossible satisfactorily to equate swine, acres and linear dimensions, and so reduce them to a common denominator. Any map of Domesday woodland must suffer from this restriction. Thus, on Fig. 106, we cannot be sure that the visual impression as between one set of symbols and another is correct; Kesteven appears to be about as thickly wooded as central Norfolk, but there is no way of being sure that this similarity is a true reflection of actual conditions on the ground. It is possible to make assumptions about the relation of acres to swine, but such assumptions must always be full of uncertainty. The relation of both acres and swine to linear dimensions raises even greater difficulties, for, as we have seen, the implications of this system of measurement are far from clear.

Despite these limitations, much can be gained from Fig. 106. With all its problems, it does not leave us in any doubt about the main features of the distribution of wood over the eastern counties in the eleventh century. As far as Norfolk, Suffolk, Essex and eastern Cambridgeshire are concerned, there is no uncertainty; and in this area, the dense woodlands of Essex stand out prominently. Elsewhere, it is clear that the claylands of Huntingdonshire, of Kesteven and of Lindsey also carried substantial amounts of wood. All this takes us some way, at any rate, towards visualising the face of the countryside in 1086.

In the folios that survey the six eastern counties, only two forests are mentioned. At Writtle in Essex there was a swineherd who became 'a forester of the king's wood'; and in Huntingdonshire there was forest in Brampton and 'king's wood' in the adjoining Ellington.

MEADOW

Fig. 107, showing the distribution of meadow, raises the same kind of problem as the woodland map. At first sight, the problem seems simpler, because the meadow of as many as five out of the six eastern counties is recorded in terms of acres. The meadow of Cambridgeshire alone is measured by the number of teams of oxen which it could support. It is true that we cannot convert these plough-teams into acres with any certainty but, for the other five counties at any rate, the picture conveyed by Fig. 107 should be satisfactory.

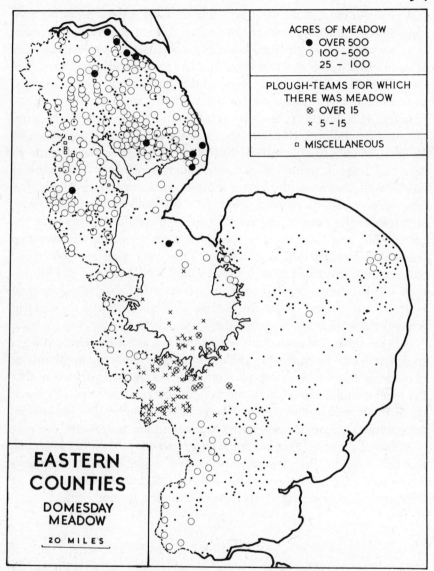

ACRES OF MEADOW
● OVER 500
○ 100 – 500
25 – 100

PLOUGH-TEAMS FOR WHICH
THERE WAS MEADOW
⊗ OVER 15
× 5 – 15

□ MISCELLANEOUS

EASTERN
COUNTIES

DOMESDAY
MEADOW

20 MILES

Fig. 107. Eastern Counties: Domesday meadow in 1086.
The boundary of the Fenland is shown. For the great difficulties raised by the
interpretation of this map, see p. 366.

A glance at the map shows at once that there is a great contrast between conditions in Lincolnshire and those in East Anglia. A very large number of villages in Lincolnshire (and especially in Lindsey) have over 100 acres of meadow each; the amounts range up to 500 acres, and even above. The villages of Norfolk and Suffolk, on the other hand, rarely have as much as 50 acres each; the amounts are for the most part small quantities of 20–30 acres. It is difficult to see why there should be this contrast between Lincolnshire and, say, Norfolk. As far as the geographical conditions of the two counties are concerned, Norfolk is as likely as Lincolnshire to have had large quantities of meadow. Many Norfolk villages were at least as well placed for meadow as those of the Lincolnshire Wolds, and there seems to be no physical reason why it should not have been there. Might an explanation of the contrast lie in the differing nature of the Lincolnshire and East Anglian 'acre'? Was one a measure of superficial area and the other a geld or fiscal acre? Or if they were both superficial measures, did they differ considerably in size? Or did the men of Lincolnshire use the term meadow in a more extensive sense than those of Norfolk? Or do the Domesday figures after all represent the facts in a straightforward way? We cannot say.[1]

It is interesting to note that the meadow entries of the Essex villages are intermediate in character; villages with over 50 acres are almost as frequent as those with under 50 acres. It does not seem therefore that the small quantities in Norfolk and Suffolk represent some peculiarity of the Little Domesday Book. The villages of Huntingdonshire likewise fall into an intermediate category between Lincolnshire and Norfolk.

This account of Fig. 107 has raised more questions than it has answered. But one thing is clear: the meadow map of a single county may give a true picture of conditions within that county, but the implications of a meadow map covering all six eastern counties are not clear.

FISHERIES

Fisheries are recorded in a variety of ways. For some counties, the usual practice was merely to state the number of fisheries on a holding; for other counties, the yield of the fisheries in terms of eels or of money was also given. And there is also occasional mention of the fishermen them-

---

[1] F. W. Maitland's comments on the varying area of the 'acre' and on the fiscal acre are interesting – *op. cit.* pp. 373–86 and 475–90.

selves and of their activities. A fishery is usually called *piscaria*, but *piscina* occasionally appears; this latter is often translated as a fishpond, but the *Inquisitio Eliensis* frequently uses *piscina* where the Domesday text speaks of *piscaria*. It would seem that they are but variant forms and they have been so treated in this volume.[1] When the Essex folios extend *pisc'* it is always to *piscina*. On Fig. 108 all these references have been consolidated into one category, and each place with some fishing activity recorded for 1086 has been indicated. The clustering of fisheries near the eastern margin of the Fenland, and along the streams that drained into the Fenland from Norfolk, Suffolk and Cambridgeshire, is very noticeable. There were also some fisheries along the Witham, although relatively few were recorded for the northern Fenland as a whole. It is difficult to believe that there were not more in the fen-line villages of Kesteven, for example, or in the villages at the foot of the Wolds along the northern margins of the Fenland. Huntingdonshire, too, must have had many more fisheries.

Few of these references tell us anything of the actual operations involved in fishing. There is, it is true, a very interesting description of Whittlesey Mere with its fisheries and fishermen and their boats; there are also references to boats and nets in Soham Mere. An entry for Swaffham in Cambridgeshire mentions a fishing toll which the *I.C.C.* declares to come from the landing of boats; there was also a fishing boat (*navis ad piscandum*) at Ely. Other entries mention fish in connection with weirs. But the Domesday Book as a whole is silent about the gear of the fishermen and about their methods of catching fish. There is likewise no mention of any species apart from eels and herrings; the Cambridgeshire folios are particularly full of references to eels caught in and around the Fenland. We know, however, that fish were present not only in great quantity but also in great variety from the twelfth-century Anglo-Norman compilation called the *Liber Eliensis*. The Domesday evidence relating to the fisheries of the Fenland is therefore very incomplete, but it is enough to show the important part played by the fisherman in the economy of the region.

Beyond the Fenland, fisheries appear in connection with the marshes of the Isle of Axholme and also in connection with some of the Essex rivers, more particularly the Thames and the Lea. Occasional references also appear for villages along the streams of other counties. But there are

[1] See R. Lennard, *Rural England, 1086–1135* (Oxford, 1959), p. 248.

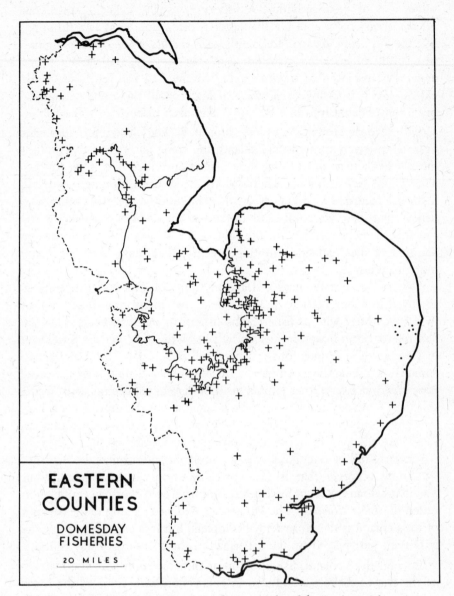

Fig. 108. Eastern Counties: Domesday fisheries in 1086.

The boundary of the Fenland is shown. The herring renders of Suffolk are
indicated by small dots; see Fig. 47.

some surprising gaps. No fisheries are mentioned for any of the Broadland villages where there surely must have been some. Were they left out because they did not contribute to the profits of their respective villages? Or because of some idiosyncrasy of the local jurors? We cannot say.

The fisheries we have hitherto been considering were those of marsh and stream. The Domesday Book very rarely records a fishery for a coastal village, and even when it does, there is no means of knowing whether this refers to maritime activity or not. Among the six eastern counties, however, the Suffolk folios form an exception. Herring rents are entered for a number of villages on or near the Suffolk coast. There is also reference to a sea-weir at Southwold, which may be connected with fishing activity; there were also 24 fishermen at Yarmouth. Other east-coast villages must have had activities similar to those that these Suffolk entries indicate, but the Domesday Book does not tell us anything about them.

SALT-PANS

Salt-pans, like fisheries, are recorded in a variety of ways. For some counties, the usual practice was merely to state the number of pans on a holding; for other counties, the render of the pans in terms of money was also given. On Fig. 109 all these references have been consolidated on a uniform plan, and each place with salt-making activity in 1086 has been indicated. A striking feature of the map is the great cluster of salt-pans in north-western Norfolk. Some of these pans could not possibly have been located in the villages responsible for their profits, and they must have been physically situated in the Fenland or along the nearby coast of the Wash. Salt-pans are also recorded for many of the villages of the Lincolnshire Fenland, and it is clear that salt-making must have been an important activity all around the shores of the Wash. Later documents also contain frequent reference to the salt industry of this area.

Beyond the Fenland, the salt-pans of the eastern counties were disposed almost entirely in three areas. One group lay along the eastern coast of Lincolnshire; some of the villages for which these pans were entered were situated some distance inland, and the pans themselves must have lain on or near the shores of the North Sea. A second group of pans comprised those of the Norfolk Broadland; here was a conspicuous cluster of 23 salt-making villages, some of them with very large numbers of pans; there

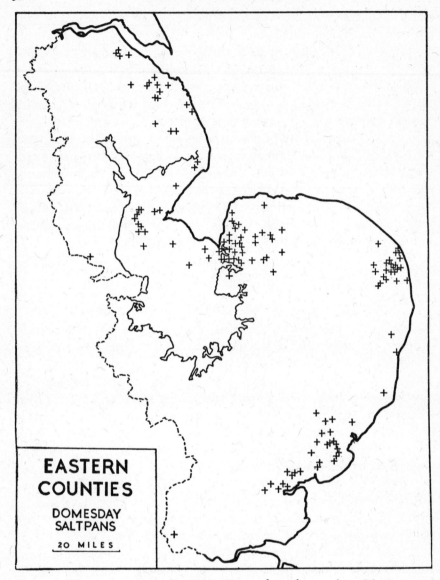

EASTERN
COUNTIES

DOMESDAY
SALTPANS

20 MILES

Fig. 109. Eastern Counties: Domesday salt-pans in 1086.

The boundary of the Fenland is shown. For a caution about the location of some of these pans, see p. 369.

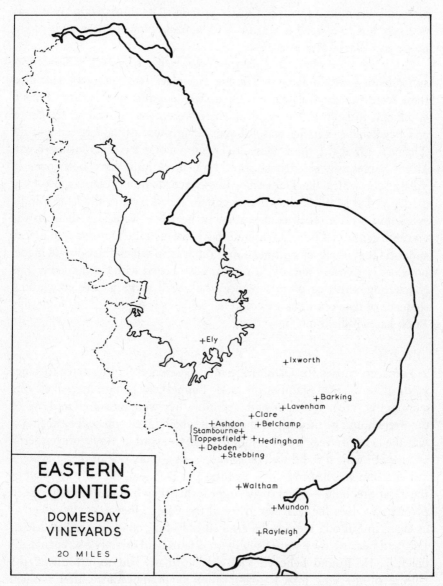

Fig. 110. Eastern Counties: Domesday vineyards in 1086.

The boundary of the Fenland is shown. Stambourne and Toppesfield had one arpent of vineyard between them.

were, for example, 45 pans at Caister in 1086. The third group lay mainly in Essex but to a small extent in Suffolk, and comprised the pans of the Stour and Blackwater estuaries.

While very revealing, this picture of eleventh-century salt-making does suffer from some limitations. In the first place, we cannot be sure that these were the only salt-pans in the eastern counties at this time. Thus it is difficult to believe that in Essex there were pans only along the Stour and Blackwater estuaries and not also along those of the Crouch and the Thames. Or again, there were surely more along the Lincolnshire coast. Minor names suggest that at some time there must have been pans in villages for which the Domesday Book records none; there is also clear evidence that some of the villages certainly had pans in the later Middle Ages, but we can only conjecture whether they were also there in the eleventh century. The other limitation from which the Domesday evidence suffers is that it tells us nothing about the way in which the salt was made, nor does it give any hint of the customs associated with the industry. The concluding sentence of this section may well serve as the concluding sentence of the volume as a whole. In giving us something, the Domesday Book has withheld much.

VINEYARDS

Fourteen entries for Cambridgeshire, Essex and Suffolk refer to vine-yards at 15 places, Stambourne and Toppesfield being entered as one manor (Fig. 110). With but one exception they were measured in terms of the French unit of the arpent, the size of which is uncertain; the exception was the acre of vineyard at Ashdon. The vineyard at Rayleigh rendered 20 *modii* of wine if it did well (*si bene procedit*). Only one of the 11 arpents at Belchamp was bearing, only 2 of the 4 at Debden, and only one half of the 2½ at Stebbing—which may suggest that they had only recently been planted. So does the fact that many of the Essex vineyards, and also that at Clare in Suffolk, seem to be entered only for 1086 (*modo*). Because of this, and because they were usually on estates held directly by tenants-in-chief, J. H. Round believed that the Normans had re-introduced the culture of the vine into England since its disappearance after Roman times. But we hear of vineyards in England in the eighth, ninth and tenth centuries,[1] and it seems therefore not that the Normans re-introduced it but that they extended its cultivation.

[1] George Ordish, *Wine Growing in England* (London, 1953), pp. 20–1.

APPENDIX I

SUMMARY OF DOMESDAY BOOK FOR THE EASTERN COUNTIES

County	Assessment	Plough-lands	Plough-teams
LINCOLN	Carucates and bovates *ad geldum* Many traces of duo-decimal system	Usually *Terra ad n carucas* or *Terra n carucis* Often agrees with assessment; indication of artificiality	Deficiency in 42% of entries; excess in 42%
NORFOLK	Geld of 20*s.* levied on a hundred, and divided among vills Dimensions in leagues and furlongs Carucates and acres also given	None Frequent mention of teams that could be added	Usually for 3 dates Decrease (1066–86) in 34% of entries; increase in 6%
SUFFOLK	As for Norfolk	As for Norfolk	Usually for 3 dates Decrease (1066–86) in 48% of entries; increase in 4%
ESSEX	Hides and acres (occasional virgates) *Pro n hidis* frequent Few traces of 5-hide unit	As for Norfolk	Usually for 3 dates Decrease (1066–86) in 41% of entries; increase in 8%
CAMBRIDGE	Hides and virgates (occasional acres) *Se defendit pro n hidis* frequent 5-hide unit frequent Reduction in some hundreds	*Terra est n carucis* Frequent mention of teams that could be added	Deficiency in 29% of entries; excess in 2%
HUNTINGDON	Hides and virgates *ad geldum* 5-hide unit frequent Hurstingstone demesne exempted	*Terra n carucis*	Deficiency in 63% of entries; excess in 20%

		No. of Place-names
Population	Values	
Main groups: sokemen, villeins, bordars High percentage of sokemen (51%) No freemen or serfs mentioned	Data for 1066 and 1086 only Value of parcels of sokeland usually included in that of chief manor	754
Main groups: bordars, sokemen, freemen, villeins, serfs High percentages of freemen (20%) and sokemen (21%); their holdings are separately distinguished, and are often very small Data for 3 dates frequently given	Data for 3 dates frequently given A number of places are valued in with other places	731
Main groups: freemen, bordars, villeins, serfs, sokemen Very high percentage of freemen (40%) but low percentage of sokemen (5%) note contrast with Norfolk sokemen. Holdings of freemen and sokemen separately distinguished, and often very small Data for 3 dates frequently given	As for Norfolk	640
Main groups: bordars, villeins, serfs, sokemen, freemen Freemen and sokemen together amount only to 7% of total; note contrast with free element of Norfolk and Suffolk. Holdings of freemen and sokemen separately distinguished and often very small Data for 3 dates frequently given	As for Norfolk except that only very few places are valued in with other places	440
Main groups: villeins, bordars, cottars, serfs, sokemen No freemen mentioned. Number of sokemen often given for 1066 as well as 1086, and shows a great decline	Data for 3 dates almost always given	142
Main groups: villeins, bordars, sokemen No freemen or serfs are mentioned, but note mention of serfs in *I.E.* Villeins amounted to as much as 76% of total	Data for 1066 and 1086 only	83

County	Wood	Meadow	Pasture	Marsh
LINCOLN	Normally in acres, occasionally in linear dimensions Underwood frequently mentioned	Usually in acres, sometimes in linear dimensions Large amounts, sometimes over 500 acres	Mentioned only three times, in acres and in linear dimensions	Rare (15 places); either in acres or linear dimensions
NORFOLK	Normally in swine, very rarely in acres Contrast between 1066 and 1086 sometimes made	Entirely in acres Small amounts, rarely over 50 acres	Mentioned for 11 places in a variety of ways —sheep, acres, dimensions, etc.	Very rare (3 places)
SUFFOLK	As for Norfolk	As for Norfolk	Very rare (2 places) Also common pasture in Colneis hundred	None
ESSEX	Normally in swine, very rarely in acres or hides Contrast between 1066 and 1086 sometimes made	As for Norfolk, except that amounts above 50 acres are more frequent	'Pasture for sheep' frequent Otherwise rare (14 places) Possibly common pasture at Colchester	Very rare, only in 2 places; and in 3 other places linking meadow and marsh
CAMBRIDGE	Partly in swine, and partly in miscellaneous ways, such as fences, houses	Almost invariably in terms of plough-teams	Frequent (74 places). The usual entry is *pastura ad pecuniam villae*, Common pasture at Cambridge	Occasional mention in connection with fisheries Reference to rushes at Wilburton
HUNTINGDON	*Silva pastilis*, usually in linear dimensions, rarely in acres Underwood sometimes mentioned	Entirely in acres Amounts above 50 acres frequent	Very rare (2 places); money renders	Very rare (3 places); in linear dimensions Note also description of Whittlesey Mere

Fisheries	Salt-pans	Waste	Mills	Churches
In 43 places Number stated, and render in money or eels usually given; there were also 2 villages with sites of fisheries	In 34 places Number of pans stated, and render in money sometimes given	In 52 places Also houses at Lincoln, Stamford, Torksey; and an occasional salt-pan	In 255 places Number stated, and render usually given in money Frequent fractions	In 248 places Frequent fractions
In 61 places Number only stated; no renders Frequent fractions	In 62 places Number of pans only stated Occasional fractions	In one place Also houses at Norwich and Thetford	In 302 places Number only stated; no render given Frequent fractions	In 220 places Holding and value usually given Occasional fractions
In 19 places Number only stated; no renders Frequent fractions Herring renders along coast	In 10 places As for Norfolk	In 2 places Also houses at Ipswich	In 178 places Number only stated; no render given Occasional fractions Five places with winter mills	In 352 places Holding and value usually given Numerous fractions
In 28 places Number only stated; no renders Occasional fractions	In 22 places As for Norfolk	None But houses at Maldon; and wood for 3 places	In 151 places Number only usually stated, but occasional renders in money given Occasional fractions	In 17 places only Holding and value occasionally given
Frequent mention of eels *de piscariis* or *de marescho* or *de gurgite* Occasional money renders	None	None But houses at Cambridge	In 52 places Number stated, and render in money or eels usually given Few fractions	In 3 places
In 6 places Renders in eels or money Also activity in Whittlesey Mere	None	In 4 places Also houses at Huntingdon	In 23 places Number stated, and render in money given Fractions very rare	In 53 places

County	Miscellaneous	Boroughs
LINCOLN	Large number of great 'sokes' covering ten or more villages Occasional groups of as many as 5 villages entered together Appendix on disputes (*Clamores*) at end Evidence of Danish *ora* in valuation of fisheries, salt-pans, mills Seven places with markets; six with ferries; three with iron-works Castles for Lincoln, Stamford	Lincoln Stamford Torksey Grantham Louth
NORFOLK	Demesne livestock and beehives entered for 3 dates Frequent reference to fold-soke Three places with markets Many entries duplicated in *I.E.* Castle for Norwich	Norwich Thetford Yarmouth
SUFFOLK	Demesne livestock and beehives entered for 3 dates Frequent reference to fold-soke Nine places with markets; one with a fair Four places with vineyards Very many entries duplicated in *I.E.* Castle for Eye	Ipswich Dunwich Eye Beccles Clare Sudbury (?Bury St Edmunds)
ESSEX	Demesne livestock and beehives entered for 3 dates Ten places with vineyards A few entries duplicated in *I.E.* Forester mentioned on fo. 56 Castle for Rayleigh	Colchester Maldon
CAMBRIDGE	Evidence of Danish *ora* in valuation of mills One place with a vineyard Very many entries duplicated in *I.E.* *I.C.C.* version for 13 out of 16 hundreds Castle for Cambridge	Cambridge
HUNTINGDON	A few entries duplicated in *I.E.* Folio dealing with disputes at end Forest indicated in fos. 204b and 208 Castle for Huntingdon	Huntingdon

EASTERN COUNTIES

Summary of Rural Population in 1086

This summary includes the apparently rural element in the boroughs—see the respective county summaries.

A. Total Figures

	Freemen	Sokemen	Villeins	Bordars	Cottars	Serfs	Others	Total
LINCOLN	—	10,882	7,029	3,379	—	—	172	21,462
NORFOLK	5,250	5,410	4,617	9,910	—	977	206	26,370
SUFFOLK	7,730	859	3,130	6,460	—	910	34	19,123
ESSEX	432	600	4,018	6,969	—	1,789	100	13,908
CAMBRIDGE	—	177	1,929	1,400	770	539	34	4,849
HUNTINGDON	—	52	1,938	483	—	1	62	2,536
Total	13,412	17,980	22,661	28,601	770	4,216	608	88,248

B. Percentages

	Freemen	Sokemen	Villeins	Bordars	Cottars	Serfs	Others
LINCOLN	—	50·7	32·7	15·8	—	—	0·8
NORFOLK	19·9	20·5	17·5	37·6	—	3·7	0·8
SUFFOLK	40·4	4·5	16·4	33·8	—	4·7	0·2
ESSEX	3·1	4·3	28·9	50·1	—	12·9	0·7
CAMBRIDGE	—	3·7	39·8	28·9	15·8	11·1	0·7
HUNTINGDON	—	2·1	76·4	19·0	—	0	2·5
Total	15·2	20·4	25·7	32·4	0·9	4·8	0·6

EASTERN COUNTIES

General Summary

For the various doubts associated with individual figures, see the text. The assessment, plough-lands, plough-teams and rural population of the boroughs are included in these totals, but it must be noted that the information given for the boroughs is often very fragmentary.

	Settlements	Assessment	Plough-lands	Plough-teams	Rural pop.	Boroughs
LINCOLN	754	4,205c	5,028	4,810	21,462	5
NORFOLK	731	2,428c	—	5,034	26,370	3
SUFFOLK	640	2,404c	—	4,502	19,123	6
ESSEX	440	2,767h	—	3,865	13,908	2
CAMBRIDGE	142	1,308h	1,693	1,495	4,849	1
HUNTINGDON	83	805h	1,180	1,023	2,536	1
Total	2,790	—	—	20,729	88,248	18

c — Carucates.   h — Hides.

APPENDIX II

EXTENSION AND TRANSLATION OF FRONTISPIECE

(Part of folio 190 of Domesday Book)

EXTENSION

In Basingborne tenet isdem episcopus i hidam et ii virgatas et dimidiam. Terra est iii carucis. In dominio i hida, et ibi est i caruca. Ibi unus villanus et iiii bordarii cum i caruca et altera potest fieri. Ibi ii molini de xx solidis. Pratum i carucae. Valet lx solidos. Quando recepit xl solidos. Tempore Regis Edwardi lx solidos. Haec terra iacuit et iacet in ecclesia Sancti Petri Wintoniensis, et ibi fuit i sochemmanus homo Stigandi archiepiscopi dimidiam virgatam tenuit et dare et vendere potuit.

iii. TERRA EPISCOPI LINCOLNIENSIS

In Witelesford hundredo. Episcopus Lincolniensis tenet in histetone ii hidas et Robertus de eo. Terra est ii carucis. Una est ibi et alia potest fieri. Ibi ii villani et ii bordarii. Pratum ii carucis et i molinum de viii solidis. Valet xl solidos. Quando recepit xx solidos. Tempore Regis Edwardi iiii libras. Hanc terram tenuit Siuuardus de comite Heraldo, et potuit dare cui voluit.

In Norestou hundredo. In Madinglei tenet Picot de episcopo Remigio i virgatam terrae et dimidiam. Valet et valuit v solidos. Tempore Regis Edwardi x solidos. Hanc terram tenuit Blacuin homo regis Edwardi et recedere potuit, sed soca Wluuio episcopo remansit.

In Cestretone hundredo. Manerium Histone pro xxvi hidis et dimidia se defendit. Hoc manerium est unum de duodecim maneriis dominicis episcopatus Lincolniensis. Ibi tenet Remigius episcopus xvii hidas i virgatam minus. Terra est xiii carucis. In dominio viii hidae et ibi sunt ii carucae et tercia potest fieri. Ibi xviii villani et xviii bordarii cum ix carucis.

TRANSLATION

In Bassingbourn the same Bishop holds 1 hide and 2½ virgates. There is land for 3 ploughs. In demesne 1 hide, and 1 plough is there. There, one villein and 4 bordars with 1 plough and there could be another. There, 2 mills yielding 20 shillings. Meadow for 1 plough. It is worth 60 shillings. When he received [it], 40 shillings. In the time of King Edward, 60 shillings. This land pertained and pertains to the church of St Peter of Winchester, and there was 1 sokeman, the man of Archbishop Stigand, who held half a virgate and he could give and sell [it].

III. THE LAND OF THE BISHOP OF LINCOLN

In Whittlesford hundred. The Bishop of Lincoln holds 2 hides in Hinxton, and Robert [holds] from him. There is land for 2 ploughs. One is there and there could be another. There, 2 villeins and 2 bordars. Meadow for 2 ploughs and 1 mill yielding 8 shillings. It is worth 40 shillings. When he received [it], 20 shillings. In the time of King Edward, 4 pounds. Siward held this land from Earl Harold, and he could give [it] to whom he would.

In Northstow hundred. In Madingley Picot holds 1½ virgates of land from Bishop Remigius. It is and was worth 5 shillings. In the time of King Edward, 10 shillings. Blacuin, the man of King Edward, held this land, and could depart, but the soke remained with Bishop Wlwius.

In Chesterton hundred. The manor of Histon is assessed at 26½ hides. This manor is one of the 12 demesne manors of the bishopric of Lincoln. There, Bishop Remigius holds 17 hides less 1 virgate. There is land for 13 ploughs. In demesne 8 hides and 2 ploughs are there and there could be a third. There, 18 villeins and 18 bordars with 9 ploughs.

INDEX

LIBRARY
OF
MOUNT ST. MARY'S
COLLEGE
EMMITSBURG, MARYLAND

LIBRARY OF MOUNT ST. MARY'S COLLEGE EMMITSBURG, MARYLAND

98960

JUL 1 0 1972